The Sagebrush Ocean

*Remember that the yield of a hard country
is a love deeper than a fat and easy
land inspires, that throughout the arid
West the Americans have found a secret
treasure . . . a stern and desolate country,
a high bare country, a country brimming
with a beauty not to be found elsewhere.*

> —Bernard DeVoto,
> *The Year of Decision: 1846,* 1942

*Thus is the earth at once a desert and a
paradise.*

> —Antoine de Saint Exupéry,
> *Wind, Sand and Stars,* 1940

Books by Stephen Trimble

Natural History

The Bright Edge: A Guide to the National Parks of the Colorado Plateau (1979)

Longs Peak: A Rocky Mountain Chronicle (1984)

Canyon Country (with photographs by Dewitt Jones; 1986)

The Sagebrush Ocean: A Natural History of the Great Basin (1989)

Native Americans

Our Voices, Our Land (editor; 1986)

Talking with the Clay: The Art of Pueblo Pottery (1987)

The People: Indians of the American Southwest (1993)

Essays

Words from the Land: Encounters with Natural History Writing (editor; 1988; expanded edition, 1995)

The Geography of Childhood: Why Children Need Wild Places (with Gary Paul Nabhan; 1994)

Testimony: Writers of the West Speak on Behalf of Utah Wilderness (co-compiled with Terry Tempest Williams; 1996)

Photography

Blessed By Light: Visions of the Colorado Plateau (editor; 1986)

Earth Fire: A Hopi Legend of the Sunset Crater Eruption (with text by Ekkehart Malotki with Michael Lomatuway'ma; 1987)

Navajo Pottery: Traditions and Innovations (with text by Russell Hartman; 1987)

The Nepal Trekker's Handbook (with text by Amy R. Kaplan; 1989)

Earthtones: A Nevada Album (with text by Ann Ronald; 1995)

Mud Matters: Stories from a Mud Lover (with text by Jennifer Owings Dewey; 1998)

For Children

The Village of Blue Stone (1990)

The Sagebrush Ocean

A Natural History
of the Great Basin

Text and

Photographs by

Stephen Trimble

Foreword by

Barry Lopez

Illustrations by

Jennifer Dewey

▲▲ University of Nevada Press Reno and Las Vegas

For this hard country
and for Jennifer

Max C. Fleischmann Series in Great Basin Natural History

University of Nevada Press, Reno, Nevada 89557 USA

Copyright © 1989 by University of Nevada Press

New preface © 1999 by University of Nevada Press

Manufactured in the United States of America

Designed by Richard Hendel

Library of Congress Cataloging-in-Publication Data

Trimble, Stephen, 1950–

The sagebrush ocean : a natural history of the Great
Basin / text and photographs by Stephen Trimble ; foreword
by Barry Lopez ; illustrations by Jennifer Dewey. —10th
anniversary ed.

p. cm.

Originally published: 1989, in series: Max C.
Fleischmann series in Great Basin natural history. With new
preface.

Includes bibliographical references (p.   ) and index.

ISBN 0-87417-343-4 (alk. paper)

1. Natural history—Great Basin. I. Title.

QH104.5.G68T75   1999   99-23164

508.79—dc21   CIP

Tenth Anniversary Edition, 1999

First Printing

08 07 06 05 04 03 02 01 00 99   5 4 3 2 1

Contents

Foreword

A vast and subtle stretch of North America lies east of the Sierra Nevada, south of the Snake River, west of the Wasatch Range, and north of the Mojave Desert. Parts of this Great Basin country are known well enough to be named: the Black Rock Desert, the Humboldt River, Great Salt Lake, the Deep Creek Range, and Ruby Mountains. Much of it, however, is virtually unknown to most Americans. Only cattlemen and miners are intimate with some of these latter places; and their industries and desires, and government programs and laws enacted on their behalf, have changed these retreats, as the passage of time changes other landscapes.

This huge and lonely country the author has made his own, from four-thousand-year-old bristlecone pines entrenched on high mountain ridges to iodine bush growing along the edges of sun-baked playas. Chapter by chapter, as he discusses climate, paleoecology, and the biology of various Great Basin species, Stephen Trimble opens this landscape up for our enjoyment and edification. The role of the Pinyon Jay and Clark's Nutcracker in shaping the Great Basin forests, the stunning changes in species makeup that have taken place in the Great Basin grasslands, and the remarkable Holocene history of water here are all part of his elucidations.

Twenty years ago I rolled a sleeping bag out in this land for the first time and I've not grown jaded in the face of its charm. It seems important to offer this thought, for on first glance the country appears hopelessly bleak and unattractive. One wonders if there is anything at all here to hold the imagination. There is, of course, but with this part of the continent it is either love

at first sight or else many miles of driving and hiking before its dimensions are revealed as complicated, formidable, and spectacular. Either way, more time is then required, the time it takes any relationship to mature, the years in which you see its countenance change, its character strengthen. Its charm endures, I think, because its simplicity is so deceiving. It never says all it has to say in the first encounter.

In these pages Mr. Trimble tries to save us some of the time it takes to know a place by making what is vague, esoteric, or elusive more obvious. He means his words to be an outline of the experience of being there, but not a substitute for it. In his extensive bibliography (the foundation from which he draws the summaries in his chapters) and in his personal observations, he is directing us toward a place he loves. He urges us to do what we should do in any country new to us—step out, breathe deeply, listen, take a careful look, put our hands to the various surfaces.

The Great Basin is one of the least novelized, least painted, least eulogized of American landscapes. Stephen Trimble has opened it up with the perception of a frontier scout, but for a different set of people this time: people more eager to know than to possess, more eager to understand than to utilize. In making it come alive he serves the reader well; but, just as important, he conveys his respect for the myriad individual landscapes in which he has tried to corroborate all that he tells us. This reciprocity, offering homage in exchange for understanding, earns our trust, and lets us know this is a worthy guide to a part of the Great Unknown.

Barry Lopez

Preface

Alistair Cooke sent one of the film crews for his television series "America" to the stretch of U.S. Highway 50 that winds across the central Great Basin mountains and deserts. He asked them to shoot whatever looked interesting—particularly ghost towns—between Ely and Sparks, Nevada. Their report: "Everything looks like East St. Louis."

The remarkable stories of this land are not obvious. Even in the truck stops that make up most of the Great Basin's "towns" one can never be certain of things. In Utah the waitress looks askance if you make the mistake of ordering a beer with your hamburger; in Nevada she may look askance if you do not.

My original assignment from the University of Nevada Press was to write the life zone volume in the Great Basin Natural History Series. But Great Basin life zones are not always neat and tidy and easily described; my focus widened to ecological communities and biogeography.

The latter word seems the best summary of what I include in this book. A 1983 textbook on biogeography (by James Brown and Arthur Gibson) sums up the fundamental question of the science: "How do the number and kinds of species vary, from region to region, over the surface of the earth, and how can we account for this variation?"

Traditional, descriptive biogeographers map this geographical variation. But to address the latter part of the question above—to "account for" the variety—takes us into ecology, evolutionary biology, paleontology, and natural and human history. In trying to understand the delicate and complex relationships that determine where organisms live, we think, in turn, as paleoecologists, phytogeographers, zoogeographers, population geneticists, and systematists. I adopt this broad view of life zones and hope that by doing so I succeed in presenting a general introduction to the natural history of the Great Basin.

One note about scientific names: I avoid using them in the text. All animals and plants mentioned appear in an appendix in a species list that provides Latin binomials. But in the text I use the scientific name only when it is necessary for identification. Thus, I refer to Coville's phlox without appending the Latin (*Phlox covillei*); the English is precise enough. I make exceptions to this rule when a plant or animal is central to the story and its genus or species name is important information—for example, the species and subspecies of sagebrush in this ocean of sagebrush.

Many people helped me learn enough about the Great Basin to write this book. I thank the following scientists, who were generous with their knowledge and their time: James Brown, Wayne Burckhardt, Richard Eckert, Raymond Evans, Steven Jenkins, Donald Klebenow, Harold Klieforth, Ronald Lanner, E. Durant McArthur, James MacMahon, Hugh Mozingo, Fred Ryser, Howard Stutz, Robert Thompson, Donald Trimble, Paul Tueller, Neil West, Al Winward, Jim Yoakum, and James Young.

Friends who read parts of the text and gave me useful critical comments include Laura Bremner, David Johnson, Rebecca Staples, and Donald Trimble. Jennifer Dewey read the manuscript as I wrote it, and her keen perceptions of what constitutes good writing kept me on track when I needed encouragement.

Dwight Billings, James MacMahon, Hugh Mozingo, Fred Ryser, Neil West, and James Young formally reviewed the manuscript and caught me in many missteps away from clarity. I thank them all. Any remaining errors are my own.

Librarians in five states helped me with research. In particular, Dorothy Good at the University of Nevada Life Science Library in Reno and Dottie House at the Museum of Northern Arizona in Flagstaff allowed extended loans of basic references.

I did nearly all of the fieldwork with only my dog Carlos as partner, and though he is loyal and enthusiastic I greatly appreciated having additional company on several trips; Rick and Chris Stetter, Jennifer Dewey, David Johnson, and Joanne Slotnik put up with flat tires, driving into ditches, and long waits for photographs, but they also shared dinners on the Black Rock Desert, golden aspen on Mount Jefferson, and bottles of wine cooled in Wheeler Peak streams. Roger and Amy Scholl divulged some of the Basin's secret places to me. And the people behind the front desks at the Bureau of Land Management, Forest Service, National Wildlife Refuge, and National Monument offices across five states were unfailingly helpful.

The staff (former and present) at the University of Nevada Press in Reno was my family while I was on the road. Their enthusiasm meant a great deal. I thank them all—Bob Laxalt, Nick Cady, Cam Sutherland, Sue Dely, and Katie Gude, in particular.

Mary Hill and Kate Harrie did impeccable jobs of copyediting. My friend Ed Purcell gave me exactly what I needed in editorial criticism on the next-to-last draft; only a crackerjack editor can do that in one reading. Jennifer Dewey drew the delightful animals; Deborah Reade made the crisply drawn maps; and Linda Montoya made the black-and-white prints of my photographs with the same care she would give her own. I thank Richard Hendel for his good taste; I am thrilled that he designed my book.

I am honored that Barry Lopez took the time to contribute the foreword.

And lastly I thank Rick Stetter. His patience and trust through the six-year odyssey of this book were more than I deserved sometimes, but they were a true measure of his friendship. He taught me a lot along the way, and this book is for him.

Jaconita, New Mexico
September 1987

Preface to the Tenth Anniversary Edition

I came to the Great Basin in 1981—nearly eighteen years ago now. When the University of Nevada Press asked me to work on its new Great Basin Natural History Series, I had been writing and photographing in the hot deserts, the Colorado Plateau, and the Rocky Mountains for twelve of my thirty years. But I did not know the Great Basin.

The three other North American deserts conform to an art director's expectation that they look picturesque. Saguaro and cholla cacti prick the skies of the Sonoran Desert, Joshua trees spread a latticework of tentacled arms over the Mojave, and the canyons of the Rio Grande gash and cleave the Chihuahuan Desert. The Great Basin, instead, has sagebrush and shadscale and silence. Nowhere else in the West is there such a sweep of undeveloped country filled with such silence—a soothing bowl of wild basins and ranges sufficient, I have learned, for a lifetime of exploring.

Even the most casual Great Basin explorers come to grips with the distinctiveness of this desert. On the Colorado Plateau, when travelers journey into the canyons, they enter the earth. In the Rocky Mountains or Sierra Nevada, people are dwarfed or enclosed. Here in the Great Basin, each of us stands above basin floors or on the ridges of bald mountains, tall among the stands of saltbush or greasewood or bunchgrass, piercing space and time, creating a scene, a drama.

In the 1980s, I traveled across this odd and wonderful Great Basin Desert, completing fieldwork for *The Sagebrush Ocean*. I spent some seven months, on trips scattered through six years, hiking, backpacking, photograph-ing, and living out of my truck in the Basin. Along the way, I scrawled in my journals, read the basic sources, and talked with the experts. I spun off gumbo-slick roads sixty miles from the nearest tow truck, mangled my tripod and cameras in falls from rickety tufa columns, often drove one hundred miles without meeting another vehicle, and grew used to the finest, most pungently choking alkaline dust I have ever encountered. I had a glorious time.

After each trip, I went home (a place that migrated during those years from Flagstaff, Arizona, to the Pojoaque Valley, New Mexico, to Salt Lake City, within the Great Basin, where I live today) to vacuum out my cameras and my truck, to work through the technical literature, edit slides, pore over black-and-white contact sheets, and to write and write and rewrite.

I have worked on many other books along the way, but creating this book about the Great Basin became the pivotal act in my journey to professional maturity.

I did not come to the desert to generate new data or to test theories. I am a naturalist, not a scientist. I enter a new landscape for the pure joy of learning and experiencing—and for the challenge and exhilaration of striving to translate my observations into strong photographs and readable prose for lay people. In writing the words, I grow to understand the land far better. The stories we tell are rooted just as absolutely in language as they are in the landscape itself. We find the land in the words as surely as we find it with our senses when we're out in wild country.

One of my favorite quotes comes from Mary Austin, whose desert soul was largely shaped by the Great Basin, her *Land of Little Rain*. In

1920, she articulated what happens when a person listens to this place. In that moment, what matters is neither the land alone nor a totally inward epiphany, but "a third thing . . . the sum of what passed between me and the Land which has not, perhaps never could, come into being with anyone else." What matters is relationship, and the stark stage of the Great Basin highlights relationship.

I initiate that relationship by photographing. I learn the lay of the land, drive the roads, hike the trails, look at the work of other photographers, quiz the local authorities for leads on their secret and favorite places. I make lists: an agenda of landscapes, mountain ranges, and vegetation zones to shoot. Then I spend as much time as I can out there—staying tuned to the light, creating opportunities for "luck."

It's an active form of patience. I plot my days, noticing where the light defines morning places and afternoon places; I plan my position for moonrises and moonsets. I choose camps with vistas. I go looking for rainbows after thunderstorms. This is easier to do for a single national park, of course, than it is for a major landscape of the continent. But the approach is the same; it involves persistence and a willingness to react quickly to changing possibilities more than anything else.

Photography is in many ways more direct than writing. The natural history writers I spoke with when I edited *Words from the Land: Encounters with Natural History Writing* talked about "circling" in their thinking. Gary Nabhan talks about imagining a written piece as a puzzle, filling in the images as you would fit pieces into a mosaic. None of us ever knows quite what story the landscape has to tell until we go out and wander around in it and listen—and then try to articulate what we hear.

I mull over images and ideas as I walk, or as I sit with my enameled steel cup of scotch in camp at the end of the day. Then I pull out my journal and start writing. I begin by describing what I see before me—the colors, the smells, any outrageous metaphors the scotch

(or my imagination) has engendered. I note the telling details: cottonwood fluff caught in a spider web, bits of dried scurfpea rhizomes blown into cupped tracks pressed softly into the surface of dunes by coyotes. And then I dream, confessing my fantasies about the inner voices of bristlecone pines, my visions of mountain lions appearing on ridgetops. These seed the journal, enliven the finished piece of writing—and they often are the things that can't be photographed.

I returned with my family to the Basin in the 1990s for a new project, *Earthtones: A Nevada Album*, pairing my photographs with Ann Ronald's essays. I discovered that the book you hold in your hands, originally published in 1989, had become an historic document. The resurgence in gold mining that began in the mid-1980s had brought improved roads to mountain range after mountain range. New mining roads not on my maps crossed the old roads at unlikely angles. Backcountry faith— "this dirt track feels right and will go where I think it will"—no longer sufficed. Lonely two-tracks were now graded, graveled, and sometimes even gated.

The boom has already peaked. The "world's largest mining machine" now clanks and blinks not out on some lonely range but in the lobby of the Silver Legacy Hotel in Reno. No sustainability here.

What will happen next? Can the Great Basin fill in—in the way so much of the West is filling in? In some places, yes; Nevada is doubling in population every ten years. Subdivisions may yet reach continuously from Elko to Wells. Most of Nevada, however, remains a place where it's prudent to gas up at every town, lest you run dry a few miles short of Gerlach or Jarbidge or Warm Springs. This is a land with limited water, limited resources, and limited amounts of what those attuned to the greens of Ireland, Bavaria, or Kentucky define as beauty. Such starkness is the salvation of the Great Basin as open space.

This is also, of course, its misfortune. Too many people see the Great Basin as a dumping ground, a place for nuclear waste repositories, bombing ranges, and missile test ranges (and at Groom Lake, military uses so secret we aren't even supposed to know the base exists). After all, the politicians innocently assure us, there's nothing out there but empty, barren, useless, godforsaken desert.

Today, controversy surrounds large-format photo books of "pristine" wild country. They are dismissed as boring or nostalgic, or even destructive, for conservationists worry that more books of beautiful landscape photography will make the public complacent. Westerners constantly battle the old myth of the frontier, and it may be that these photos of the West as we dream it to be perpetuate the myth of unbounded, untouched resources just waiting to be developed by enterprising sagebrush rebels.

Yet we know that wild country still exists. We have seen it. We retreat to it. Some of us live in it. But should we photograph it?

We have moved from a time when photos could save a place by alerting the world to its existence and its magic, to a time when we worry if publishing photos will alert so many hikers and off-road vehicle enthusiasts to the existence of a place that in short order its wild spirit will disappear, inundated by visitors.

One reviewer of *The Sagebrush Ocean* even suggests (only partly tongue-in-cheek) that books like this one "should be banned." He goes on: "Why? Just basic selfishness. . . . What I do not understand is why someone who clearly cares about the Basin as much as I do could produce something that is sure to attract the L.L. Bean crowd. I much prefer those accounts that give the usual cursory view of the Basin as an 'abomination of desolation'. . . . Now, unfortunately, we have Great Basin National Park and books like Trimble's. If we keep this up the Basin will be just like California."

It's a danger, surely. But the Great Basin is big enough to have empty places, even after those crowds arrive. And the L.L. Beaners write letters to congresspeople. (Some of them *are* congresspeople!) If those legislators have

never heard of the Great Basin, as my reviewer hopes, then when it comes time to ratify the next M-X missile system or nuclear waste repository proposed for Nevada or Utah, we can guess how they will vote. After all, there's nothing out here, is there?

Several recent events suggest that these attitudes are changing. Conservationists have discovered the Great Basin. Over the past twenty years, on the fringes of the Basin in Bend, Oregon, Donald Kerr created The High Desert Museum—the premier institution for public interpretation of the Great Basin and Columbia Plateau. The Oregon Natural Desert Association, watchdog for the High Desert and sponsor of the annual Desert Conference each spring at Malheur Refuge, also works out of Bend. The Friends of Nevada Wilderness keep track of comparable issues from their twin bases in Reno and Las Vegas. The Friends of the Great Salt Lake formed in Salt Lake City in 1994, and the Great Basin Bird Observatory began work from Reno in 1997. And in 1998, the Utah Wilderness Coalition greatly expanded its proposal to designate wilderness in Utah by acknowledging enormous acreages of overlooked wild country in the West Desert.

In 1989, the United States Congress designated 733,000 acres in Nevada as wilderness, protecting fourteen outstanding mountain islands. In 1990, the Lahontan Valley Wetlands Coalition negotiated a landmark settlement transferring water rights from agriculture to wildlife, guaranteeing water delivery to Pyramid and Carson Lakes and to the Stillwater National Wildlife Refuge. In 1994, a landmark California State Water Board decision in favor of the Mono Lake Committee decreed that Mono Lake must be maintained at levels sufficient for its wildlife to flourish—though the details of restoring the lake are complicated and ongoing.

The most easily perceived layers of the Great Basin continue to seem harsh at first look. Much remains to be done. Walker Lake is threatened. The Great Salt Lake remains largely a mystery to the million and a half humans who live along Utah's Wasatch Front—

while salt imbalances, chlorine contamination, and encroaching development threaten the fragile lacework of factors that leads from its wetlands to its millions of birds.

Peel the outer skin, and surprises lurk beneath first impressions. The landscape reveals itself. Nevada sand dunes turn out to harbor ten unique beetles. Great Basin fish remain so poorly known that brand-new species may still exist, undescribed. The Great Basin reminds us to take nothing for granted.

Beginning in the summer of 1994, my six-year-old daughter, Dory, joined me on many of my trips westward from our home in Salt Lake City. Each time we let go of the civilized rim of the Great Basin and risked the plunge into its great spaces, we found ourselves engaged with the remoteness of the place. The approach was always a shock—the crossing of the Great Salt Lake Desert, its salt pan protecting the central Nevada mountains like a barrier reef. Mirages and glare hovered over the hard white crystalline surface, an unequivocal sign that we were entering new territory.

We reveled in the scent of sagebrush, pungent after a summer thunderstorm in Monitor Valley. We wandered in search of abandoned ranches and old mines; we camped alone at the end of the unmarked ruts that lead into Pete Hanson Canyon in the Roberts Mountains. We drove back roads for twenty-four hours without meeting another vehicle.

After that twenty-four hours ended, we crossed Interstate 80 near Elko on our way from nowhere to nowhere, from the ghost towns of the Cortez Mountains north toward Tuscarora. We happened on the Carlin interchange when shifts changed at the Goldstrike Mine. We waited for a gap in the stream of mud-spattered pickups headed back to Elko, then crossed the pavement quickly, turning off onto our next dirt road, and, within half an hour, were lost again in a filigree of gated ranch tracks.

The congestion of the mine traffic seemed like a dream. It's so easy to become confused here.

I love the fact that my daughter will take such experiences for granted, a matter-of-fact part of her childhood. Her younger brother, Jake, soon grew eager to join her. At three, with a wistful look, he asked, "Dad, when I'm four, will I be old enough to go to Nevada?" Now seven, he too has let go of the rim and explored with me in the Great Basin.

The paradoxes of this place traveled with us everywhere. Space and silence and a spare landscape left no doubt that we had entered the realm so consistently dismissed. We also found ourselves in a place of rich complexity, with animal companions wherever we went.

Wild horses grazed through our campsite in the ghost town of Hamilton, high in a basin in the White Pine Range. When we came to rest in a small canyon above the Black Rock Desert, a desert horned lizard clambered away from our truck through contorted branches of sagebrush—the leaves redolent from bruising by our tires. A nesting pair of long-eared owls perched in an isolated aspen grove in the Hot Creek Valley. A buck mule deer in Denay Valley suddenly bounded away from his doe and fawn, arcing against golden grass.

The buck brought to life the huge, still valley. Tracing a line of bounce and rhythm across the valley, springing upward and then jolting back to earth, planting his hooves in Great Basin alkali over and over, he ran out of sight while his family remained still, farther and farther behind. The sound of his hooves meeting earth came to us with a clumppp, softer and softer, until the buck was too far across the valley for us to hear.

We were left with the silence that so many writers settle on as the defining descriptor of this place.

I'm not sure my children notice this silence, but I savor this precious quiet in a noisy world. I listen next for what fills the silence—the sounds of coyote, kestrel, cicada, and raucous bands of piñon jays. Aspen leaves, spears of wildrye, brushes of juniper needles, and sprays of Indian ricegrass—all speak in the wind.

The poet Gary Snyder writes of a "ghost wilderness" that hovers around the edges of such landscapes. All the missing native bunchgrasses, the legions of exterminated predators, and the herds of native grazers exist in our dreams, on the wind, as a background chorus. These ghosts, too, hum in the Great Basin silence.

Even "emptiness" and "wildness" are deceiving here. The Great Basin feels "undeveloped," certainly, but everywhere we go, Paiute, Washoe, and Shoshone hunters and seed gatherers, geologists, miners, cattle ranchers, and Bureau of Land Management range managers have been there before us (and their effects on the place deserve a separate book). Introduced species of plants, livestock grazing, range manipulation, and water development projects have all transformed this land—"shattered" the native ecosystems, in ecologist James Young's words. This is a dynamic landscape, adapting constantly to changing climate, changing land-use patterns, a landscape managed to produce revenue—a wilderness, with cows.

How has our understanding of Great Basin ecology changed in the last ten years? For one thing, the mountain islands are not quite so isolated as we thought. Conifers, for instance, turn out to be more widely distributed than we knew: white fir on seven more mountain ranges, for example, and western juniper on forty-three additional ranges. Butterflies have their share of ecological specialists and isolated populations, but most montane and alpine species have not become distinct endemics. The classic isolation of James H. Brown's "mammals on mountaintops" may be in part an artifact of our ignorance. When paleogeographers Donald Grayson and Stephanie Livingston visited the Roberts Mountains in central Nevada in 1991, they doubled the known montane mammal population of the range from four to eight in just a few days—without setting a single trap.

Donald Grayson went on to fill a niche my book does not attempt to fill. His 1993 book, *The Desert's Past: A Natural Prehistory of the Great Basin,* is a wonderful companion volume to *The Sagebrush Ocean.* Grayson, an archaeologist and paleontologist, extends the story to people, with a definitive summary of Great Basin prehistory and archaeology.

Two other books deserve special mention: Ella Sorenson's *Seductive Beauty of Great Salt Lake: Images of a Lake Unknown* and Michael Cohen's *A Garden of Bristlecones: Tales of Change in the Great Basin,* both first-rate interdisciplinary essays with careful, accurate science.

Such added detail—rather than great changes in fundamental understanding—characterize the decade's research. The invasion of nonnative plant species begun by cheatgrass and halogeton continues, with "exotics" dominating so many western landscapes that ecologist David Dobkin worries about "potential ecological catastrophes" resulting from such wholesale replacement of natives.

The shift in emphasis in the science of ecology toward "conservation biology" and "restoration ecology" reinforces the theme of *The Sagebrush Ocean*—the dynamic nature of the desert. In a landscape where more than 99 percent of sagebrush-grass communities have been negatively affected by livestock, as noted by Peter Brussard and his coauthors in the review article cited below, restoration is indeed a key to the future.

Every attentive look at this "barren" desert verifies that it is not barren at all. An ecologist working here never uses the word. Neither would a sage grouse or a Great Basin spadefoot toad.

My goal is to understand this Great Basin experience, to understand the character of the place so clearly that I have a visceral awareness of its boundaries when I cross them. My desire to share this with readers grows from my belief that only through experience and knowledge do we grow to care about this place, or any place. Only our passion will protect the landscapes of Earth from those solely intent on exploitation.

I hope these words and photographs give you a feel for the spirit of this major North American landscape and answer some of the questions that you puzzled over out there. I hope these stories about the desert make you want to return. I hope they help in making the Great Basin a part of your spiritual home.

Notes

The Mary Austin quote comes from a 1920 letter to her guide and confidant, Professor Daniel Tremblay MacDougal, as she prepared to explore the Sonoran Desert. The letter is archived in Special Collections, University of Arizona Library, and quoted in Larry Evers's introduction to Austin's *The Land of Journey's Ending* (1924; reprint, Tucson: University of Arizona Press, 1983).

References to my other books include *Words from the Land: Encounters with Natural History Writing*, Stephen Trimble, ed.; 2d ed. (Reno: University of Nevada Press, 1995); and *Earthtones: A Nevada Album*, Ann Ronald, essays; Stephen Trimble, photographs (Reno: University of Nevada Press, 1995).

David B. Madsen's review of *The Sagebrush Ocean* appeared in the *Utah Historical Quarterly* (winter 1990). Gary Snyder's comments come from *The Practice of the Wild* (San Francisco: North Point Press, 1990), 15.

I highly recommend Donald K. Grayson, *The Desert's Past: A Natural Prehistory of the Great Basin* (Washington, D.C.: Smithsonian Institution Press, 1993); Ella Sorenson, *Seductive Beauty of Great Salt Lake:*

Images of a Lake Unknown, with photographs by John P. George (Layton, Utah: Gibbs Smith, 1997); and Michael P. Cohen, *A Garden of Bristlecones: Tales of Change in the Great Basin* (Reno: University of Nevada Press, 1998). Peter F. Brussard, David A. Charlet, and David S. Dobkin summarize our current understanding and provide a terrific bibliography of recent research papers in "Great Basin-Mojave Desert Region," in *Status and Trends of the Nation's Biological Resources*, eds. M. J. Mack, P. A. Opler, C. E. Puckett Hacker, and P. D. Doran, 1–39 (Washington, D.C.: U.S. Department of the Interior, U.S. Geological Survey, in press).

Lastly, I have based portions of this preface on three of my previously published essays:

Stephen Trimble, "The Sagebrush Ocean: A Naturalist's Vision of the Great Basin," *The Chiles Award Papers*, 8 pp. (Bend, Ore.: The High Desert Museum, 1990).
———, "Reinventing the West," *Buzzworm Magazine* (Nov./Dec. 1991), 46–54.
———, "Letting Go of the Rim." In *Reclaiming the Native Home of Hope: Community, Ecology, and the American West*, edited by Robert B. Keiter (Salt Lake City: University of Utah Press, 1998), 136–43.

I

The Setting
The Great Basin Desert

The Four Great Basins

1

Three or four little puddles, an interminable string of crazy, warped, arid mountains with broad valleys swung between them; a few waterholes, a few springs . . . a few little valleys where irrigation is possible and where the alfalfa looks incredibly green as you break down out of the pass . . . that about sums up the Great Basin. Its rivers run nowhere but into the ground; its lakes are probably salty or brackish; its rainfall is negligible and its scenery depressing to all but the few who have lived in it long enough to acquire a new set of values about scenery. Its snake population is large and its human population small. Its climate shows extremes of temperature that would tire out anything but a very strong thermometer. It is a dead land, though a very rich one.

—Wallace Stegner,
Mormon Country, 1942

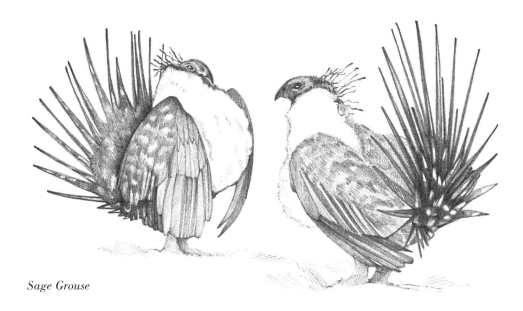

Sage Grouse

The great dry lake bed of the Black Rock Desert, largest playa in the Great Basin.

You've been up to Gerlach. I'd know that dust anywhere—I can tell by its color and I can tell by its smell."

I was cleaning finely sifted alkali from my truck at a car wash in Reno, and the manager strolled by, sniffing at the dusty clouds billowing past the tailgate. "You'll never get the smell out."

He was wrong about the smell. But he knew where I had been.

The little town of Gerlach, Nevada, sits at the south end of the Black Rock Desert, the biggest playa in the Great Basin. Traveling up from Reno past Pyramid Lake to Gerlach and out onto the playa is a journey into an ever more unearthly landscape. Y-shaped, the great dry lake bed nestles around the central spit of the Black Rock Range. Smoke Creek Desert, reaching Gerlach from the southwest, almost connects with the Black Rock Desert, making for a nearly continuous hundred miles of absolutely barren clay.

Such breadth of landscape characterizes this place, the Great Basin Desert. This is no single parcel of land easily swallowed, but a giant sweep of the West, sparsely populated and largely unknown, covering most of Nevada, the West Desert of Utah, the southeastern corners of Oregon and Idaho, and California east of the Sierra.

On the huge playa, I camped miles from "shore." What seemed awesome became comprehensible through simplicity. The size of the playa made me feel small, yet no visible living thing separated me from mountains forty miles away, a realization that created intimacy. The playa disoriented because nothing gave it scale—no plants, no birds, no lizards, not even rocks. Mosquitoes, a wasp, a dragonfly nearby made little difference. I was alone.

But not lonely. Lesley Hazleton speaks of this in her fine book on the Sinai and Negev deserts, *Where Mountains Roar:*

> One can only be lonely in relation to people. And being alone in the desert is to be alone *with* this expanse of wildness and wilderness, of rock and sky, stone and thorn. In loneliness, I feel closed

in on myself, cut off. But in the desert, alone, it is as if I were expanding to join this vastness. Instead of being cut off, I was becoming part of it.

Night brings a similar feeling of expansion. The Great Basin—even the immense Black Rock Desert—feels linear by day, long valley after long, thin mountain range always stretching perceptions north-south, to left and right into the invisible distance of map awareness. Such straight lines recede with the dusk. At night this linear world appears circular.

Sleeping in canyons and mountain valleys you see a narrow strip of stars—the universe from the side. But on the playa the sky is a bowl; you look up into its center. Once again, the immensity of the desert landscape becomes intimate. You are the center of the universe.

In 1844, John Charles Frémont passed through the Black Rock Desert on his way across the dry country from Oregon to the foot of the Wasatch Range in Utah. In several months of travel he saw not a single river headed for the sea. Frémont named this enormous landscape "between the Rocky Mountains and the next range, containing many lakes, with their own system of rivers and creeks (of which the Great Salt Lake is the principal), and which have no connection with the ocean or the great rivers which flow into it," the "Great Basin."

We can conclusively outline on a map the piece of the West that drains inward, and this remains the most explicit definition of the Great Basin. It forms a huge triangle between the crest of the Sierra Nevada on the west, the Rocky Mountains and Colorado River drainage on the east, and the Snake River country on the north. It reaches into Wyoming at the edge of the Green River drainage and north into Oregon as far as the forty-fourth parallel. The southern point of its triangle pierces the rugged and arid Salton Trough of northern Baja California near the thirty-second parallel. Along its greatest length it measures more than eight hundred miles.

This is one Great Basin, the hydrographic one defined by inland drainage of surface

*The hydrographic
Great Basin—the
most explicitly
defined Great
Basin—embraces
all the land in the
West that drains
inward, without
an outlet to the
sea.*

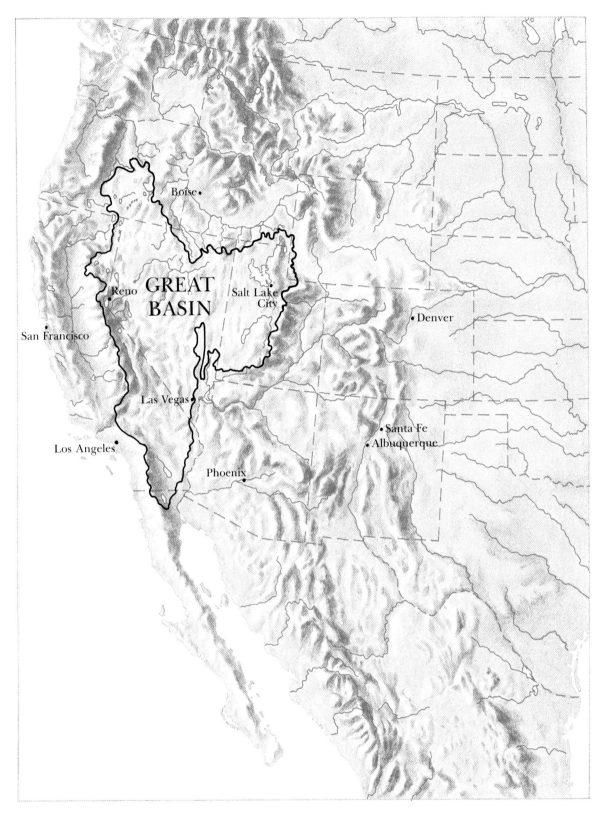

waters. It is not really singular, but contains
dozens of separate drainage areas, each with
no outlet, ranging from small valleys to the
enormous Bonneville basin surrounding the
Great Salt Lake.

The hydrographic fact of interior drainage

gives the basins their character. Most descend
to flat playas rimmed with shimmers of alkali.
Basin is a better word than *valley* for these
between-mountain lowlands. The word valley
brings to mind a gentle green pathway to the
sea. What few river valleys exist here always

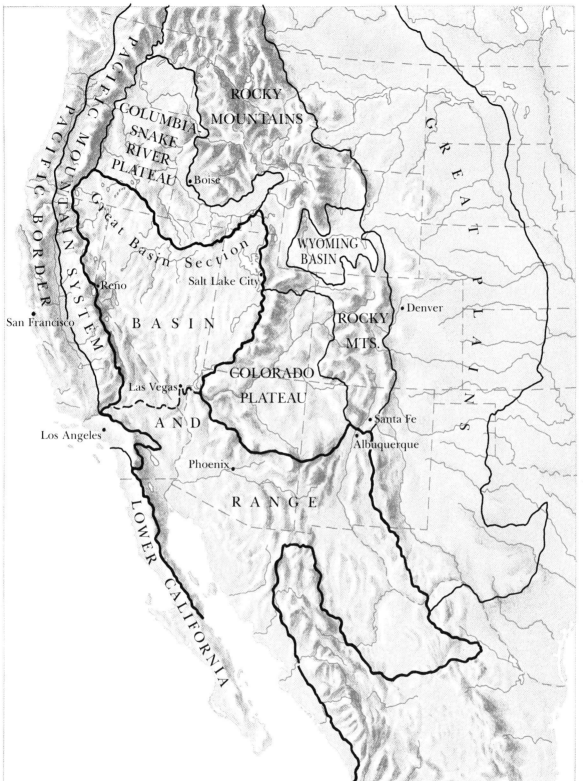

The physiographic
Great Basin is
one section of
the enormous
Basin and Range
Province, defined
by distinctive
landforms and
geologic structure.
(Based on Hunt,
1974)

7

*The Four
Great Basins*

lead to a closed basin with a central sump, a dead heart.

The second Great Basin is physiographic. In dividing the continent into natural regions with distinctive landforms and structure, geologists incorporate the hydrographic Great Basin in an even larger Basin and Range province that sweeps from Oregon to California, across southern Arizona and New Mexico to west Texas, and southward to central Mexico. To further confuse matters, they identify a Great Basin section of the Basin and Range province—

a landform-defined Great Basin that includes the northern three-fourths of the hydrographic Great Basin and about half of the entire Basin and Range province.

Throughout the physiographer's Great Basin section, mountain ranges alternate with desert basins in lilting rhythm. Their magnitudes are equal. One to one, basin to range. *Taut* is the word that fits this country. The elasticity of the earth's crust seems palpable, the surface pulled tight until it gives way in the parallel fault blocks that create the bowls of basins and the ridges of ranges.

The distance between what we now call the Sierra and Wasatch has increased some fifty miles in the twenty-five million years or so since the continental forces began their work. The land continues to stretch, faults continue to slip. Range after range moves up while basins move down; erosion meanwhile whittles at ranges and fills basins. Eventually the tectonic forces tugging at North America will open a rift through the Great Basin—no matter how we define it—and turn it into an ocean.

The third Great Basin saw its pivotal times in the mid-1800s, when the Humboldt River corridor formed what historian Dale Morgan called the "highroad of the West," the yellow brick road to California. The people of the immigrant trains defined a historic Great Basin. Their vision took in only what they could see from the long march along the California Trail. This historic Great Basin cut a decisive swath through the desert from the Bear River in Idaho to the Carson and Truckee river meadows at the eastern base of the Sierra. The Hastings and Lassen cut-offs added the Great Salt Lake and Black Rock deserts.

The main stem of the trail passed through the northern hydrographic Great Basin along its only real river, the Humboldt. Peter Skene Ogden of the Hudson's Bay Company had discovered the river in 1828 and the next year followed it to where it disappeared in a marshy sink near present-day Lovelock, Nevada. Before him, in 1827, Jedediah Smith had made the first documented crossing of the Sierra and then headed directly east across the nastiest

stretch of the Great Basin, south of Walker Lake. But no one would want to repeat his nearly waterless route.

It fell to another mountain man, Joseph Walker, to put together a route usable by the immigrants bound for Oregon and California. First to ride the length of the Humboldt, he pushed on across the Forty-Mile Desert to the Carson River, then up and over the Sierra. He managed this from the east in 1833, retraced the route in reverse from California the next year, and ten years later was guiding wagon trains over the same trail. Zenas Leonard, Walker's clerk for the 1833 explorations, said that Joe Walker "could find water quicker than any man I ever met."

Maps available to immigrants in the 1840s showed the more than five hundred miles between Great Salt Lake and the Sierra spotted with apocryphal rivers and nonexistent lakes. Each wagon party's struggle with arid reality proved the maps to be myths. The Humboldt turned out to be undependable in flow and bitter in taste until it petered out completely. Frustrated travelers renamed it the "Humbug."

Just beyond lay the Carson Desert, one of those peculiarly Great Basin places, a playa (dry lake bed) that was sometimes waterless and sometimes a vast marsh, its already sparse vegetation made sparser by the overland immigration. It became a primary terror for the overlanders. Imagine being the last in line in 1849, when 22,500 people with their 60,000 hungry draft animals passed over the trail to California.

Survivors didn't much care about the details of the Great Basin Desert. Once in California, the dry land behind the Sierra maintained its mythic quality, the hell they had beaten and never wished to see again. Most of us still imagine Nevada as a network of highways traversing a void surrounding the pulsing neon of Reno and Las Vegas—to which all these highways lead.

This book is about the void beyond these strips of asphalt, the fourth Great Basin, the biologically defined Great Basin Desert.

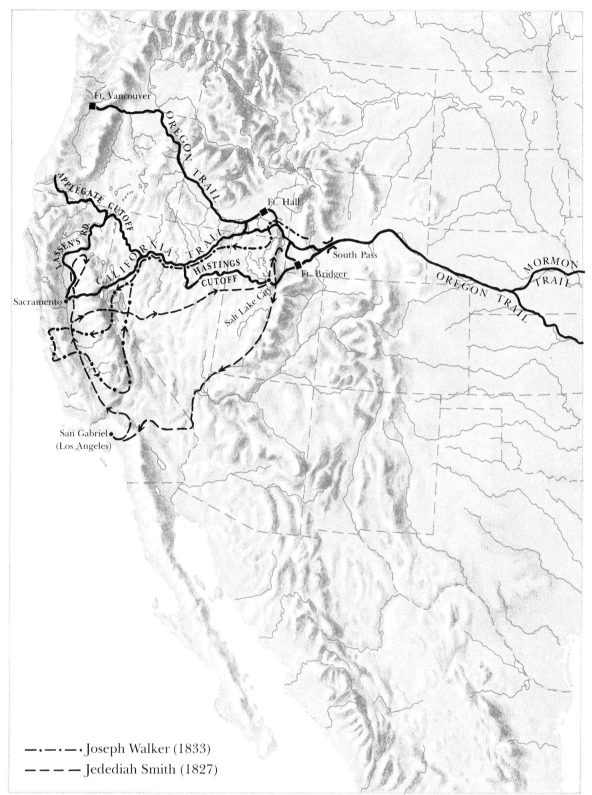

—·—·— Joseph Walker (1833)

— — — — Jedediah Smith (1827)

The lucky hydrographer outlining the Great Basin simply determines the divide separating inward and seaward drainage. Ecologists attempting to draw boundaries for the North American deserts must make more subjective decisions, looking at the ranges of hundreds of plants and animals characteristic of specific ecological communities.

Life pulses out there in even more dramatic fashion than the rhythm of the Reno casinos. The plants and animals of the desert "void" form living communities whose patterns are

The Forty Mile Desert of the Carson Sink, last obstacle of the historic Great Basin before the overlanders and their wagon trains grappled with the Sierra Nevada.

10

———

The Setting

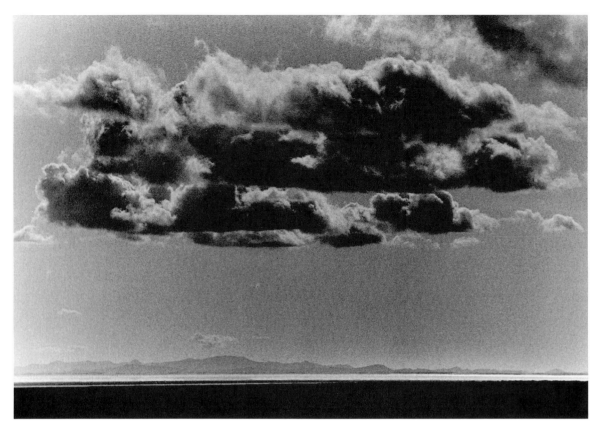

visible, remarkably dynamic, and complex in their interrelationships. These patterns constitute the biological geography of the land, the geographical biography of its resident plants and animals—in short, its biogeography: what lives where, and why.

Biogeographers agree on the key features of the Great Basin: a temperate desert, with cold snowy winters and hot dry summers, dominated in valleys by sagebrush and shadscale and centered in the northern hydrographic Great Basin, spanning the corrugation of isolated island ranges in the rain shadow of the Pacific mountain system—the Sierra and Cascades. Yet each author who tackles the challenge of putting Great Basin Desert boundaries on a map adds to a long list of variations on this theme.

The dean of desert biogeographers, Forrest Shreve, first mapped the four North American deserts—the Great Basin, Mojave, Sonoran, and Chihuahuan—in 1942, without reference to desert animals. In his widely used 1957 book *The North American Deserts*, Edmund C. Jaeger modified Shreve's boundaries here and there, most notably adding a fifth major desert. From Shreve's Great Basin Desert, Jaeger lopped off a major portion of the Colorado Plateau in Four Corners country, added a bit to it, and called it the Painted Desert.

Many desert ecologists separate the Colorado Plateau even more decisively. They exclude it from the North American deserts (largely because it lacks many typical Great Basin animals), bestowing on it semidesert status.

In 1979, ecologist James MacMahon reviewed these desert boundaries once again, for the first time considering animal distribution. His deserts incorporate current knowledge, along with a good balance between conservative and liberal biogeographic politics. My own boundaries for the Great Basin Desert most closely follow MacMahon's.

Every ecologist places the Great Basin Desert between the cordilleras: on the west the Sierra Nevada and on the east the line of highlands in central Utah formed by the Wasatch Range (one range within the greater Rocky Mountains) and the High Plateaus section of the Colorado Plateau. Mountains make just as powerful biological boundaries as they do structural landmarks.

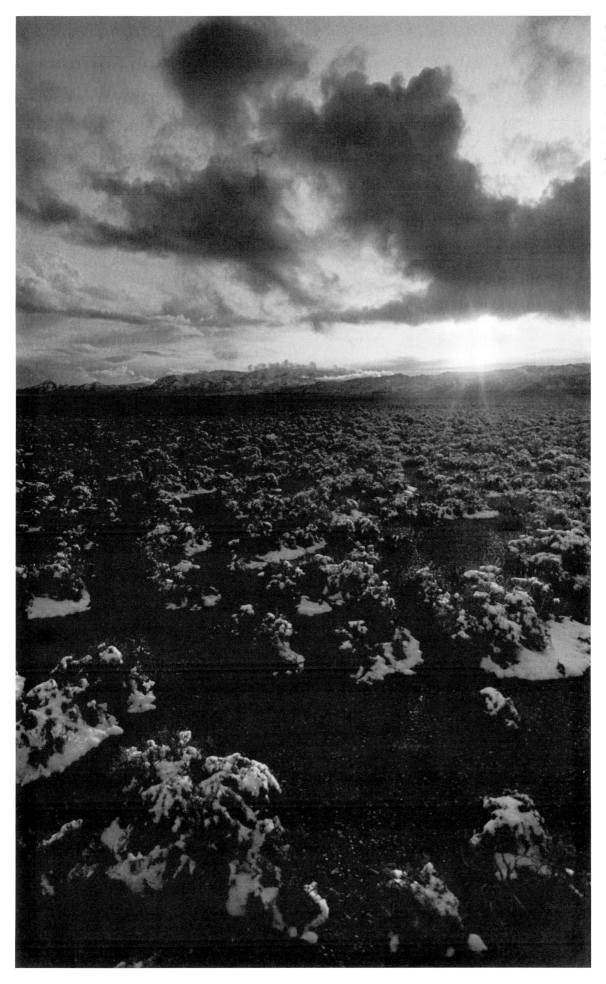

A sagebrush ocean, an embayment of the closed inland sea of desert with its archipelagoes of mountains, fills the Monitor Valley below Mount Jefferson, central Nevada.

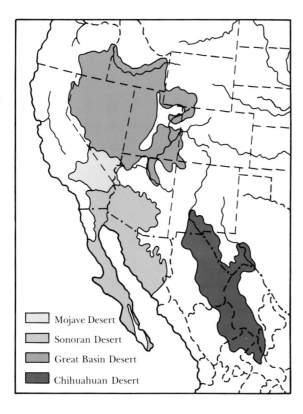

Mojave Desert

Sonoran Desert

Great Basin Desert

Chihuahuan Desert

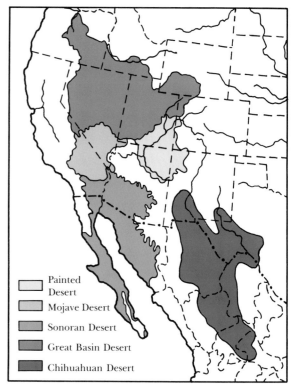

Painted Desert

Mojave Desert

Sonoran Desert

Great Basin Desert

Chihuahuan Desert

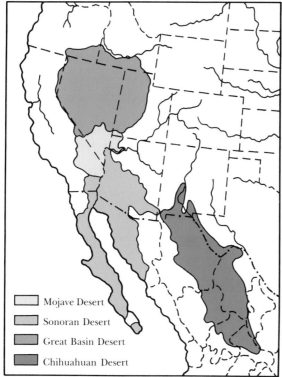

Mojave Desert

Sonoran Desert

Great Basin Desert

Chihuahuan Desert

South of the Great Basin lies the Mojave Desert with its creosote bush flats and Joshua trees. The Mojave is drier and hotter than the Great Basin Desert. The southern boundary of the Great Basin Desert is easily fixed by the northern frontier of creosote. In basins, continuous creosote bush (Mojave Desert) gives way to continuous shadscale and then to sagebrush (both Great Basin Desert). Sagebrush is not a single species but a complex of related plants, and in a later chapter I will describe sagebrush ecology in detail. Joshua trees overlay this basic pattern; they range a bit farther northward into sagebrush than creosote and make it clear that even this relatively crisp boundary is a transition, not a precise line.

Some maps extend the Great Basin Desert far to the northeast into Wyoming. To do this requires including the full-blown Rocky Mountain forests of the Uintas and Wasatch within the desert boundary. Alternately, the desert border can be angled around the north end of these Rocky Mountain ranges, connecting the Wyoming and Uinta basins to the hydrographic Great Basin with a narrow corridor of sagebrush. This seems forced. Southwestern Wyoming and the Uinta Basin resemble the central

Great Basin in vegetation but lack many typical Great Basin animals.

Trickier is my decision to exclude the Snake River Plain. Biologically, the high desert of southeast Oregon's Great Basin grades evenly into the Owyhee Desert along the Idaho border and eastward on across the volcanic plains to Pocatello. Hydrographically and physiographically, however, the Snake River Plain clearly does not belong in the Great Basin. Though sagebrush country in the Wyoming and Uinta basins and Snake River Plain is not officially part of the Great Basin Desert, most of the natural history in this book still applies.

The mountain ranges along this northeastern edge of the Great Basin, from the Jarbidge Mountains in Nevada east to the Bannock Range above Pocatello, sit on the physiographic/hydrographic Great Basin boundary. Ecologically, however, these are the northernmost Great Basin ranges, no matter which way their waters drain.

Such fine points of biogeographic dissent seem distantly removed from the land. But to truly know the Great Basin requires making sense out of complicated topography and esoteric science as well as reveling in the smell of sage crushed between your fingertips or absorbing sixty miles of the Big Smoky Valley in a single eye-filling view. The more we know the more we see. Attentiveness counts for everything. Once the Great Basin boundaries are fixed in your mind, each time you cross them they grow more dramatic.

Red Rock Pass: at the north end of Cache Valley in southern Idaho, the Great Basin pinches out between low pink crags where Lake Bonneville overflowed its highest level about fifteen thousand years ago in a flood of incomprehensible power. Pine Valley: travel north from St. George, Utah, and climb through orange and white stone in Snow Canyon, up and over the meadows and forests of the Pine Valley Mountains, and enter the Basin at the piñon-juniper woods and sage flats surrounding Enterprise. The character of the air and light changes from the clarity and heat of the Colorado Plateau, stained with the colors of red sandstone, to the cooler, hazier light of Great Basin sagebrush country, softened by alkali dust. Jarbidge: head north out of Nevada's Jarbidge Mountains and the rhythm of basin and range is broken. It is a long way to the next mountain range, all the way across the irrigated greens and rough lava channels of the Snake River Plain.

Each conception of the Great Basin—hydrographic, physiographic, historic, and ecologic—contributes to understanding its reality.

Physiographic structure stamps topography with the alternation of range with closed basin, strung out for hundreds of miles in a continuous barricade of north-south walls. John McPhee, in *Basin and Range*, marks the cadence of this landscape:

> Basin. Fault. Range. Basin. Fault. Range. A mile of relief between basin and range. Stillwater Range. Pleasant Valley. Tobin Range. Jersey Valley. Sonoma Range. Pumpernickel Valley. Shoshone Range. Reese River Valley. Pequop Mountains. Steptoe Valley. Ondographic rhythms of the Basin and Range.

The historic vision of the Great Basin has changed little from the original outraged reaction of people trudging along the California Trail. That vision started even earlier, in the early 1800s, when explorers Zebulon Pike and Stephen Long christened what they saw of the West the "Great American Desert." It mattered little just what part of the West Pike and Long had in mind. Ever since, Americans with the shining, stubborn gleam of Manifest Destiny in their eyes have tried to prove them wrong.

Immigrant wagon trains and homesteaders struggled with drought from the hundredth meridian in Kansas west to California and Oregon. Ever since then, land promoters and overenthusiastic chambers of commerce have tried to convince us that rain really does follow the plow.

Europeans were discovering, or rediscovering, deserts in other places at the same time.

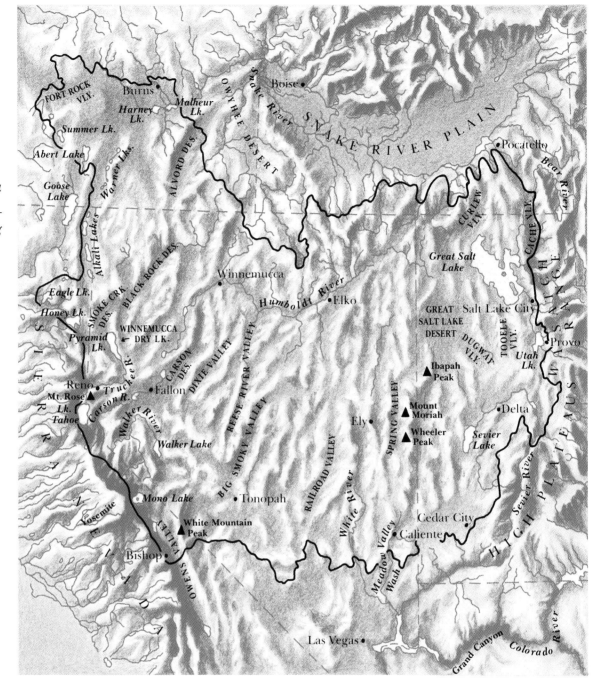

Though deserts spawned many of the great cultures, religions, and philosophers, African and Asian peoples had their deserts to themselves after classical Roman times. Not until 1826 did Scotsman Gordon Laing become the first modern European to reach the legendary Saharan city of Timbuktu. In the next year Jed Smith ventured into the Great Basin.

In the West, mountains and deserts remain entangled—by geography and biology and by law, in water compacts. At the heart of the West, between the cordilleras, the Great Basin embodies such complications. It is a desert full of mountains. Its summers are parched, its winters frigid. Even its definition is fourfold.

Only a vague notion as a public place, in reality it is absolutely distinct from other places. The Great Basin's meager resources—except for mining districts here and there—have saved it from massive development. Too dry to farm, too cold to retire to, too harsh for most seekers

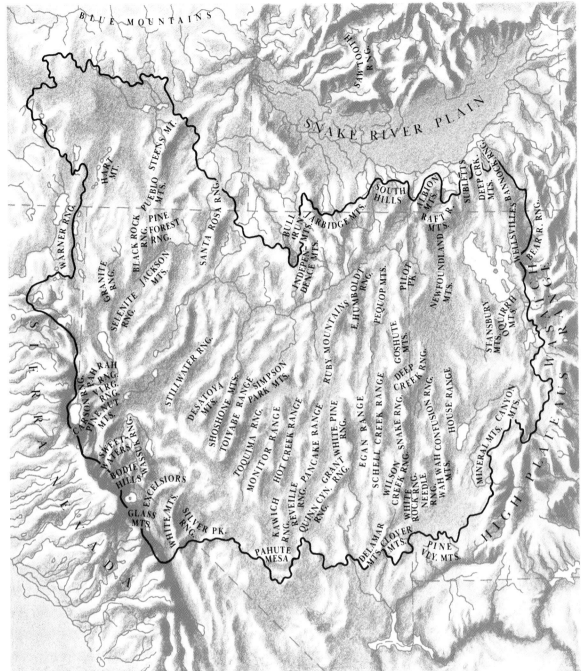

The map contains the following labels:

BLUE MOUNTAINS
SAWTOOTH RNG.
SNAKE RIVER PLAIN
HART MT.
STEENS MT.
PUEBLO MTS.
PINE FOREST RNG.
BLACK ROCK RNG.
WARNER RNG.
GRANITE RNG.
SELENITE RNG.
JACKSON MTS.
SANTA ROSA RNG.
BULL RUN MTS.
JARBIDGE MTS.
INDEPENDENCE MTS.
SOUTH HILLS
ALBION MTS.
RAFT RIVER MTS.
SUBLETTS
DEEP CRK. MTS.
GOOSE CR. RNG.
WELLSVILLE RNG.
BANNOCK RNG.
BEAR R. RNG.
E. HUMBOLDT
PEQUOP MTS.
PILOT PK.
NEWFOUNDLAND MTS.
RUBY MOUNTAINS
GOSHUTE MTS.
STANSBURY MTS.
OQUIRRH MTS.
WASATCH RANGE
CARSON RNG.
PAH RAH RNG.
VIRG. RNG.
PINENUT MTS.
SWEETWATERS RNG.
WASSUK RNG.
BODIE HILLS
STILLWATER RNG.
DESATOYA MTS.
SHOSHONE MTS.
TOIYABE RANGE
SIMPSON PARK MTS.
MONITOR RANGE
TOQUIMA RNG.
HOT CREEK RANGE
PANCAKE RANGE
WHITE PINE RNG.
GRANT RNG.
EGAN RANGE
SCHELL CREEK RANGE
DEEP CREEK RNG.
SNAKE RNG.
WILSON CREEK RNG.
WHITE ROCK RNG.
NEEDLE RNG.
WAH WAH MTS.
CONFUSION RNG.
HOUSE RANGE
MINERAL MTS.
CANYON MTS.
HIGH PLATEAUS
EXCELSIORS
GLASS MTS.
WHITE MTS.
SILVER PK. RNG.
KAWICH RNG.
REVEILLE RNG.
QUINN CYN. RNG.
PAHUTE MESA
DELAMAR MTS.
CLOVER MTS.
PINE VLY. MTS.
SIERRA NEVADA

The Great Basin Desert as defined in this book—in the rain shadow of the Sierra Nevada; west of the Wasatch Range of the Rocky Mountains; south of the Snake River Plain; and north of the creosote bushes and Joshua trees of the Mojave Desert.

of beauty, even today the Great Basin remains sparse in population—a blank spot on vacation maps. Just as in the 1850s, nearly all the people of the Basin reside on its far perimeter at the foot of the Wasatch and the Sierra. The western edge sees tourists at California's White Mountains, the highest range in the Basin, and in the Lake Tahoe and Carson Range area above Reno. But of all Great Basin mountains, eastern Nevada's Snake Range is arguably the best known.

Wheeler Peak is the reason. Studded with bristlecone pines, with a paved road nearly to tree line, it is the only Great Basin peak outside the White Mountains that rises above thirteen thousand feet. Limestone caverns penetrate the base of the mountain, and for many years Lehman Caves National Monument protected them—the only national park or monument in the Great Basin Desert. Conservationists repeatedly proposed expanding the monument to embrace much of the Snake

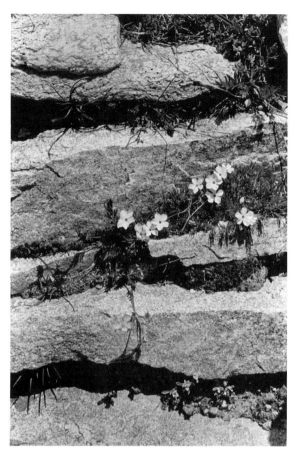

Great Basin mountains rise to over 14,000 feet, and several harbor alpine tundra. This rock garden lies along the crest of the Ruby Mountains at Liberty Pass.

16

——

The Setting

Range, perhaps even the wild country around Mount Moriah to the north, across U.S. Highway 50 and Sacramento Pass, in a Great Basin National Park. Meanwhile, the Forest Service designated a twenty-eight-thousand-acre scenic area from Wheeler Peak south. Finally, in October 1986, a Great Basin National Park became reality, its seventy-seven thousand acres incorporating the old national monument and the Forest Service scenic area to include most of the high country of the southern Snake Range.

Drive down Interstate 80 from the mountains to the Basin at Donner Pass on the west or through the Wasatch on the east. Both descents reveal transformations within a few miles: from forest to desert, from mountain massif to basin and range, from bubbling streams to lakes that exist most often in mirages.

You have entered all four Great Basins at once. You have reached a closed inland sea of desert with archipelagoes of mountains in the middle of the ecological mosaic of North America. The deserts are poisoned with salt and the mountains are drifted with snow. Beyond the sagebrush horizon the pale ranges go on and on, in rhythms that give the silent land its music. This is the Great Basin Desert.

The Making of a Desert

2

I find most interesting the conspiracy of life in the desert to circumvent the death rays of the all-conquering sun. The beaten earth appears defeated and dead, but it only appears so. A vast and inventive organization of living matter survives by seeming to have lost. The gray and dusty sage wears oily armor to protect its inward small moistness. . . . those animals which must drink moisture get it at second hand—a rabbit from a leaf, a coyote from the blood of a rabbit.

. . . the desert, the dry and sun-lashed desert, is a good school in which to observe the cleverness and the infinite variety of techniques of survival under pitiless opposition. Life could not change the sun or water the desert, so it changed itself. . . . The desert has mothered magic things.

—John Steinbeck
Travels with Charley, 1962

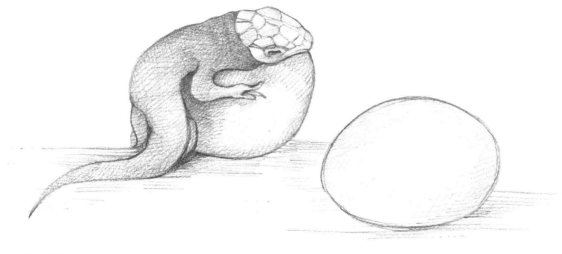

*Hatchling
sagebrush lizard*

The Great Basin is a cold desert, and winter in the Reese River Valley below the Toiyabe Range proves it.

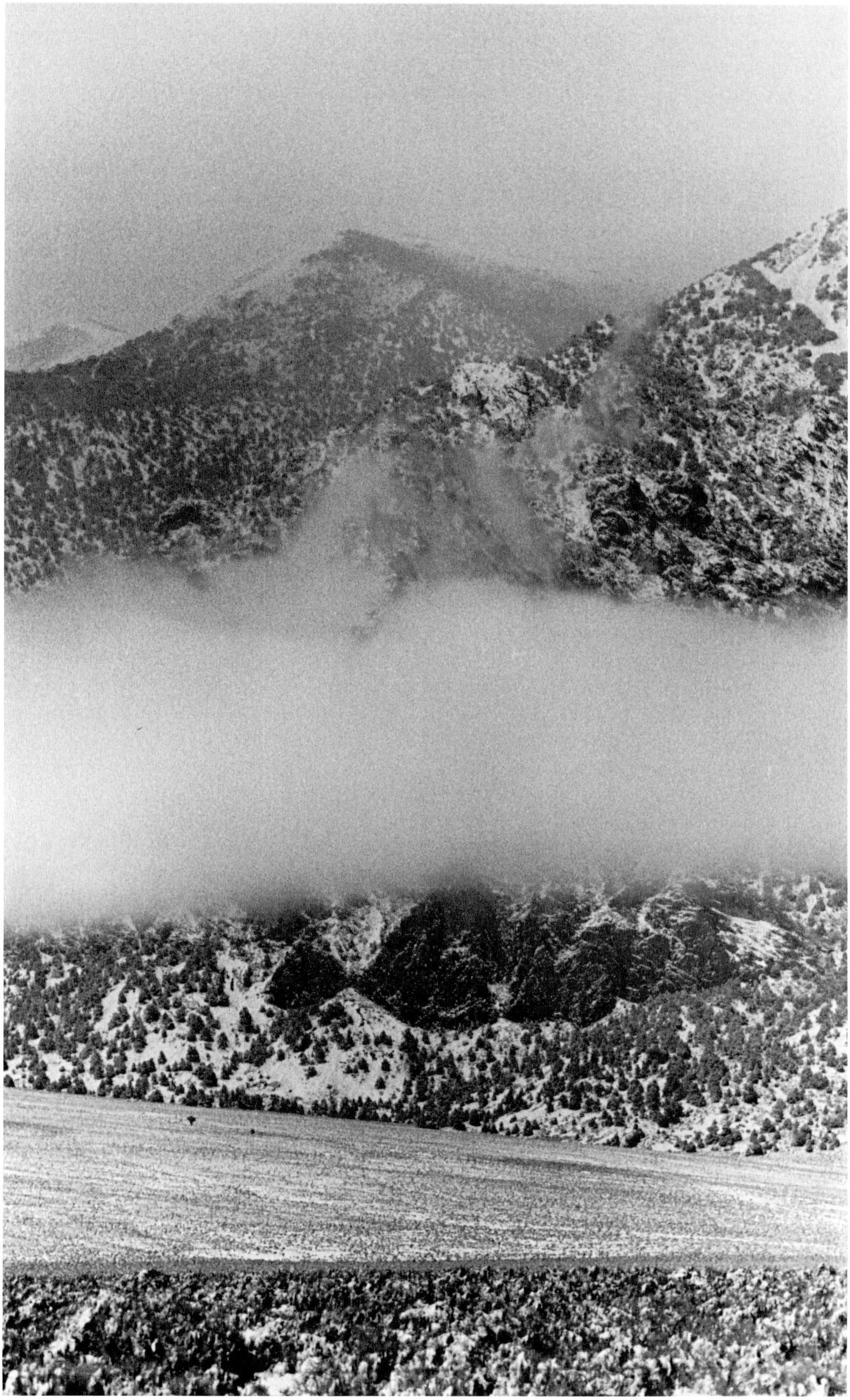

Nevada has the lowest average annual rainfall of the fifty states: nine inches. In Julys of different years, Winnemucca has recorded 105-degree temperatures and traces of snow. Elko, with an average annual precipitation of ten inches, saw almost four of those inches fall in a single hour one August. Andrews, Oregon, has recorded temperatures ranging through 140 degrees; Elko can claim a 150-degree range, from −43 degrees to 107 degrees Fahrenheit. Some 60 percent of the Great Basin's precipitation comes as snow, when plants are dormant; much of the moisture that comes in the summer growing season runs off too quickly in flash floods for plants to absorb the water.

Reno receives 80 percent of the sunshine possible at its latitude; Miami, Florida, enjoys just 66 percent of its potential total; Seattle manages only 45 percent; and Los Angeles receives the same as Ely, 73 percent. At Pyramid Lake, Nevada, evaporation exceeds precipitation by eight times.

These facts say that the Great Basin is dry. Its climate is unpredictable and subject to huge fluctuations. Much of its moisture comes at times or in ways useless to plants. And it receives enough solar radiation to evaporate more of its soil water than precipitation can replenish. The climatic extremes embedded within these generalizations render the Great Basin a desert.

Everyone uses the word *desert* in a slightly different way. The dictionary definition doesn't help: "a dry, barren region, largely treeless and sandy." Most deserts are not sandy, and most are far from barren of life.

Ecologists and climatologists attempt to define deserts more precisely: areas with fewer than ten inches of rainfall or where potential evaporation exceeds precipitation. Even these efforts at clarity break down, for the concept of a desert is not simply climatological but individualized by every animal and plant. As Forrest Shreve summarized the problem, "An adequate definition of desert . . . must be based on the degree to which a scanty and irregular water supply becomes an item of first moment in the life of plants and animals."

The most barren wastes of the Sahara or the nearly rainless Atacama Desert in Chile form one extreme in the scale of desert aridity. Oceans of desert shrubs in the Great Basin fall close to the other end of the scale—a desert to North American ecologists, but to one Egyptian desert scientist conditioned by the Sahara "not a desert, but a veritable botanical garden."

No matter whether the Great Basin achieves the climatic category arid, semiarid, or subhumid, no matter whether it receives nine, twelve, or fifteen inches of yearly rainfall, to a kangaroo rat in the Winnemucca dunes in July, to a Black-throated Sparrow in the Mono Basin searching for seeds in iron-hard caliche, to a greasewood plant on the alkaline edge of the Great Salt Lake this is a desert.

Brittle curls of shrunken clay crunch under my feet. I step between tufts of saltgrass almost as brittle as the dried mud, the papery leaves as sharp as the salt crystals the grass tolerates.

Here on the dried mud flat at the edge of southeast Oregon's Alvord Desert, kangaroo rat burrows lace the bases of greasewood clumps. Jackrabbits leap from underfoot and bounce off over the next rise. In this treeless world they seem huge—as big as antelope.

One jackrabbit does not go far but keeps nibbling on juicy, salty greasewood leaves. I creep closer and closer, eye to camera viewfinder, eye to eye with the hare. It regards me sidelong, with one great round brown eye, and when I come too close, it moves through saltgrass to the other side of a greasewood and keeps feeding.

The jackrabbit lives its life in this place where I am a visitor. Most of the year, moist plants quench its thirst. Living where it cannot hide, it relies on speed and an erratic dash for cover in a "forest" of low shrubs to escape hungry coyotes and eagles, reaching forty miles per hour at full lope.

Great Basin Indians relied on jackrabbits for food and clothing. For life. Though I do not hunt, I feel an old connection between humans and game when I look the jackrabbit in the eye. Though not the only connection we can feel with animals, this is a powerful and ancient one.

We come to the desert in part to share in this flow of lives other than our own. Cities obscure the flow by banishing most animals except humans. A sensitive observer like Loren Eiseley could find the magic—the "mystery of being and becoming"—in an orb-weaving spider in suburbia, in pigeons in Manhattan. In the Great Basin Desert one need not be Loren Eiseley, or a mystic, to feel it.

Every naturalist writes about sensing this power of Life. Aldo Leopold called it "a vast pulsing harmony." Annie Dillard found it in silence, "the blended note of the ten thousand things."

This silence makes for clear thinking about how one fits into the world. The jackrabbit snaps me into place in the scheme of life. This single hare nibbling a greasewood clump in the Alvord Desert connects me—the mystery of all wild beings pooled in brown jackrabbit eyes.

When I stand to leave, I feel drained and exhilarated. And it matters that the jackrabbit is wild. Making eye contact with my dog, who is curled up and waiting on the dried mud of the playa, I do not have the same experience; I know him too well. There is no sense of entering another world.

The jackrabbit needs no acknowledgment. It lives in a world sufficient unto itself, a wilderness of animals. I may participate, but life flows on with vigor regardless of my presence. And its vigor shows life not merely surviving but *at home* in this desert.

What makes this place a desert is the Pacific mountain system, the great green wall of the Sierra Nevada and the Cascades, thrust up fourteen thousand feet above the ocean and claiming the moisture of incoming storms for itself.

The general weather pattern in the West is remarkably straightforward. Westerly winds dominate these temperate mid-latitudes. In winter, the westerlies sweep cold fronts inland from a storm-generating oceanic low-pressure zone centered over the Aleutian Islands. In summer, the huge subtropical Pacific high-pressure zone shifts north, shoving the westerlies into Canada, blocking out the storms, and bringing clear, dry days through autumn.

The Sierra Nevada shields the interior basin from storm-bearing Pacific winds. Forced upward to hurdle the Sierra-Cascades, the moisture-laden maritime air rises, condenses, and drops most of its rain and snow on the mountains, leaving the Great Basin in a rain shadow, as a desert.

In essence, these few facts explain the aridity of the Great Basin. Some details need to be added, however.

Rising air cools at a constant rate as the mass of air enters lower pressure at higher elevations and expands. As it cools, it condenses and releases its moisture. When condensation occurs, the cooling rate slows down, because as water molecules condense, they release heat into the clouds. Once past the summit of a mountain range, the air begins to descend, clouds quickly evaporate, and the air warms at the faster rate associated with dry air.

This simple physical difference in the rate of temperature change of rising condensing air and falling dry air means that air warms more coming down a mountain than it cooled going up. It means that air at a given temperature and elevation on the windward side of a mountain will be warmer once it reaches the same elevation on the leeward side. And drier.

In summer, continental subtropical air dominates the entire Basin, producing clear, hot days followed by cool nights as the earth radiates its heat into the cold, starry sky. Only summer thundershowers modify this calm, with passing tempests of thunder, lightning, and sometimes heavy rain.

In Sand Spring Valley I watched a summer storm move across the playa, Troy Peak in the Grant Range standing high and dry behind the thunderhead. A great self-contained cloud with streamers of rain turned gold by the setting sun—sunlight all around it, shadow around

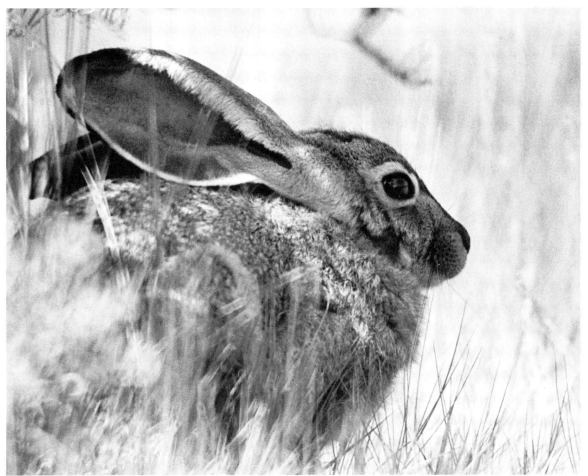

me—advanced with dignity from the Quinn Canyon Range to Worthington Peak. Lightning playing in the cloud looked like streaks in a great glass-enclosed experimental chamber.

Two factors combine to create such thundershowers. As the desert heats during the day, it warms the air above it, which rises. If the rising column of air encounters moisture aloft, billows of cumulus begin to form, and with enough moisture, cumulus become cumulonimbus, thunderheads that produce rain to nourish the parched desert.

The key is moisture: even at eighteen thousand feet, normal Great Basin summer skies remain as dry as its land. The Pacific sends little moist air inland because the cold California current keeps water temperatures low; cool, stable air unlikely to rise and move inland blankets the ocean surface. Only when moist air penetrates the continent from the Gulfs of Mexico or California can thunderclouds form to shower the desert.

Southeast winds associated with the sub-

tropical high regularly bring such gulf maritime air to Arizona and the Rocky Mountain states in July and August. The central and eastern Basin garner considerable precipitation from such summer thundershowers. In Nevada, only White Pine County (with its high ranges, the Snakes, Schell Creeks, and White Pines) gets a month's worth (on the average) of what southwesterners call the "monsoons." Western Nevada receives only half as many thunderstorms. Rarely do these moist air masses penetrate as far as northwest Nevada and southeast Oregon.

The huge subtropical Great Basin high persists into the fall, bringing stable fair weather. Finally, it begins to retreat southward, and storm tracks once again begin to trail Pacific fronts across the northern Great Basin. As winter proceeds, these Pacific storms become more frequent, bringing with them sharp temperature drops—and most of the annual precipitation for California, Oregon, and western Nevada.

Centered on the Nevada-Idaho border, a

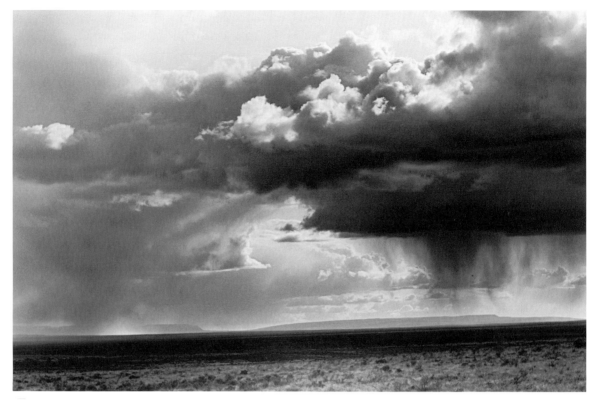

high-pressure center (the winter version of the Great Basin high) can keep stagnant cold air sitting on the surface for long spells of clear weather between storms. When these highs dominate, they block Nevada from the path of winter storms and make for fair, dry, very cold winters.

A second type of winter storm rakes the Great Basin, most commonly from April to June. Low-pressure centers that develop in the lee of the Sierra (and that may derive some of their moisture from snowmelt as well as from the Pacific) move east from the southwest Basin across eastern Nevada into Utah. Their origin gives them their name: Great Basin, or Tonopah, lows. Their power brings central and eastern Nevada and northwestern Utah maximum precipitation—and highest winds—in spring and makes the Great Basin the most frequent generator of continental storms in North America.

At the far eastern edge of the Great Basin, the Rocky Mountains and the nearby Utah and Great Salt lakes modify the general Basin weather pattern. Cities along the Wasatch front endure (or enjoy) twice as much precipitation

(more than sixteen inches) as other locations at similar elevations in western Utah. Dreaded Wasatch winds sweeping down on these cities from the east have peaked at more than one hundred miles per hour in Bountiful, Utah. East wind clouds, which resemble fog spilling westward over the Wasatch crest, warn of these easterlies.

The Sierra creates its own winds as well. Warm downslope winds periodically roar through Reno and Carson City; like chinooks off the Cascades or the east face of the Rockies, they can melt a foot of snowpack in a day. Locals affectionately and respectfully call such a wind the Washoe Zephyr.

Mark Twain, in his Carson City journalist days, said "seriously" that a Washoe wind "is by no means a trifling matter." Not so seriously, he described what it hid within its dust clouds:

> Hats, chickens and parasols sailing in the remote heavens; blankets, tin signs, sagebrush and shingles a shade lower; doormats and buffalo robes lower still; shovels and coal scuttles on the next grade; glass doors, cats and little children on the next;

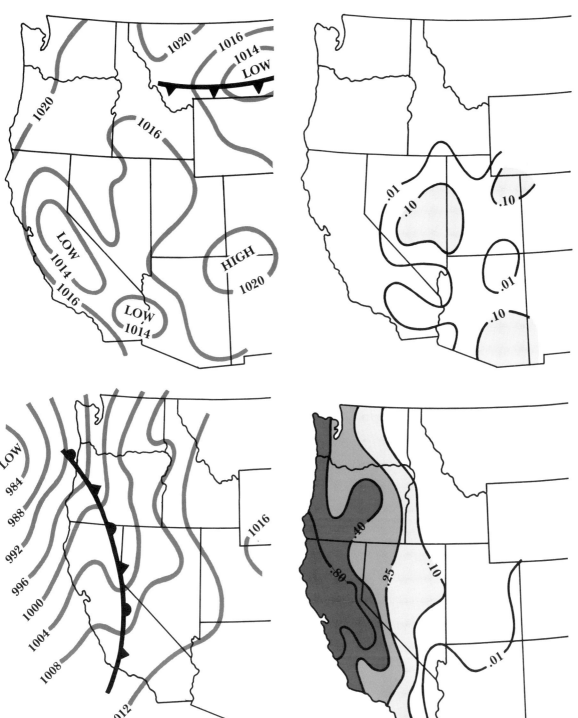

A typical August thunderstorm brings rain to the eastern Great Basin, moisture pulled inland from the Gulf of Mexico—but not far enough inland to shower western Nevada. (left: surface weather map; right: 24-hour precipitation measured in hundredths of inches.) (Based on Houghton, Sakamoto, and Gifford, 1975)

A typical Pacific winter storm-front sweeps over the Sierra Nevada in February, dropping most of its moisture in the mountains and leaving the eastern Great Basin cold and dry. (left: surface weather map; right: 24-hour precipitation measured in hundredths of inches.) (Based on Houghton, Sakamoto, and Gifford, 1975)

disrupted lumber yards, light buggies and wheelbarrows on the next; and down only thirty or forty feet above ground was a scurrying storm of emigrating roofs and vacant lots.

Downslope winds are by no means rare. Every night, cool, dense air flows down into basins, creating a pool of minimum temperatures *below* a more moderate belt: an inver-sion. As the sun warms valleys in the morning, upslope winds reverse air flow. But in winter, cold days can trap the cold air layer of an in-version, making for suffocating pollution in Salt Lake City and Reno.

These inversions are powerful ecological forces in the Basin. Minimum temperatures on valley floors can be up to thirty degrees Fahr-enheit lower than on side slopes, with a five- to ten-degree difference common.

Utah Valley shows what this can mean to the annual schedule of growth and reproduction in native plants—and fruit orchards. In this single valley the interplay of inversions, altitude, and proximity to the lake creates a forty-day difference in growing season between Provo (126 days) and Spanish Fork (167 days), only two hundred feet in elevation and ten miles apart.

In a strip of land immediately in the lee of the Sierra, from Tonopah north to Lovelock, the maximum effect of the rain shadow intensifies normal Great Basin aridity. Farther north, Pacific winter storms come more frequently; farther east, Great Basin lows bring an extra ration of moisture; and farther south, moist maritime air reaches inland to allow summer thundershowers. This dry, warm "banana belt" coincides with the low-lying Lahontan basin and allows some heat-loving Mojave Desert plants and animals to penetrate far northward.

Regional patterns bring an average annual precipitation to northwest Nevada basins of about 8.5 inches, the higher northeast plateau, 10.5, and the lower south-central section of the state, 6.25.

Sequences of mountain ranges compound the rain shadow effect and make for some of the driest places in the Basin. Andrews, Oregon, lies east of the Coast Ranges, Cascades, and Steens Mountain; spent clouds arriving in the Alvord Desert offer up only seven inches of precipitation annually at Andrews. Wendover, Nevada, manages only 4.5 inches after the Sierra wrings most moisture from storm fronts, and the Ruby and Pequop mountains and the East Humboldt and Toano ranges immediately upwind of Wendover finish off most of what moisture remains in the clouds.

Despite unpredictable storms, despite its unbarren, unsandy nature, the Great Basin is indeed a desert. It is dry, baked by the sun, eroded by flash floods that prevent water from percolating to plant roots, and subject to wild variability in climate from season to season and year to year.

Great Basin animals and plants must continually consider these facts. They live or die by them.

Every desert plant somehow must live and reproduce with only a fraction of the precipitation in which forest plants luxuriate. Most moisture disappears almost as fast as it arrives, victim of sizzling daytime temperatures, low humidities, and a sun and wind implacably drying.

The plant's adaptations, evolved through generations of successfully coping with stress, increase the odds of reproducing before its tricks to avoid death by dehydration fail. Annuals grow, flower, and set seed in the wet season, escaping the worst of the desert, the dry season, as tough seeds. They produce many seeds in a long-evolved compromise with the seed-eating ants, rodents, and birds; each uneaten seed germinates when it reaches its threshold of moisture and warmth, perhaps years after it fell to earth. It races to complete flowering and fruiting, risking a late snowstorm or a heat spell.

Perennials maximize water absorption and storage while minimizing the effects of the drying sun. Herbaceous perennials lie dormant in the extremes of summer and winter as roots or bulbs. Woody perennials send roots deep—some as much as sixty feet or more. They penetrate moist soil with wide-ranging nets of rootlets. Meanwhile, leaves need a constant water supply as they squander it in transpiration when they photosynthesize. To minimize this moisture loss, desert plants reduce the size and number of their leaves, shed leaves or even whole branches in the dry season, or eliminate leafy greenery altogether and photosynthesize in stem surfaces.

Waxy coverings and surface hairs reduce water loss; leaf color dulled to gray protects moist tissues from the evaporative power of the sun. Water can be stored, too, in the succulent stems of cacti and fleshy leaves of many shrubs; shallow fibrous root systems allow for quick uptake after a rain.

Plants also lose moisture when leaf "pores"

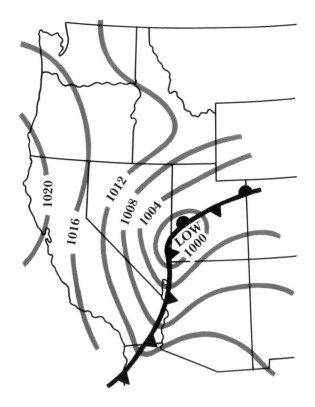
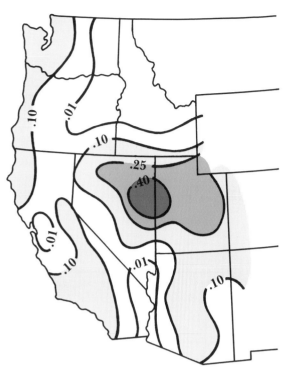

Tonopah low-pressure storms, like this March storm, originate in the lee of the Sierra and bring central and eastern Nevada and northwestern Utah their maximum yearly precipitation in spring. (left: surface weather map; right: 24-hour precipitation measured in hundredths of inches.) (Based on Houghton, Sakamoto, and Gifford, 1975)

(stomates) open to obtain carbon dioxide. Some plants open their stomates mostly at night, absorb carbon dioxide when air is cool, and store it until the next day when sunlight is available for energy to power photosynthesis. They thus avoid the dangerous dehydration risked when baring moist inner tissue during the day.

Evolution in some plants has taken an entirely different tack. They tolerate much higher than "normal" salt levels, modifying the delicate balance between survivable water loss and salt concentrations in tissues. They can absorb saline water fatal to moist-climate plants as well as cope with extreme tissue dehydration during drought.

Every dusty, gray-green Great Basin shrubland bristles with these botanical accomplishments. Plants that seemed static can make you giddy with their activity. These spiny plants have evolved along with the Great Basin Desert. They *are* the Great Basin Desert.

Desert animals, in contrast, have fewer options than plants in circumventing the blunt power of aridity. They cannot change their structure as freely. But they have one crucial advantage: they can move from place to place. No seeds

here? Fly to the next dune. No luck hunting jackrabbits on this hillside? Trot over the hill. Too hot? Search for shade.

They face the same challenge as plants: to obtain more water than seems possible, to hoard it once they have it, and to minimize its waste. At the same time they must keep down body temperature, or keep it relatively constant.

Animals take advantage of every available droplet: drinking dew, eating plants with high water content, avoiding plants with high salts, traveling to waterholes every day, storing seeds in moist burrows where they pick up a trace of extra moisture before being eaten.

Some arthropods (insects, beetles, and a myriad of others) can take water directly from the air when humidity exceeds 80 percent. An impermeable outer covering seals in water while also sealing in body heat. Even though arthropods and reptiles can survive (at least for short times) internal temperatures lethal to birds and mammals, they modify their behavior in a wide variety of ways that avoid dangerous overheating.

Birds and mammals have even more severe problems. With their need to maintain a constant internal temperature, they require water

*Borax Hot Springs
in the Alvord
Desert—crucial
water, alkaline
or not, in a
basin that receives
only seven annual
inches of
precipitation.*

26
―――
The Setting

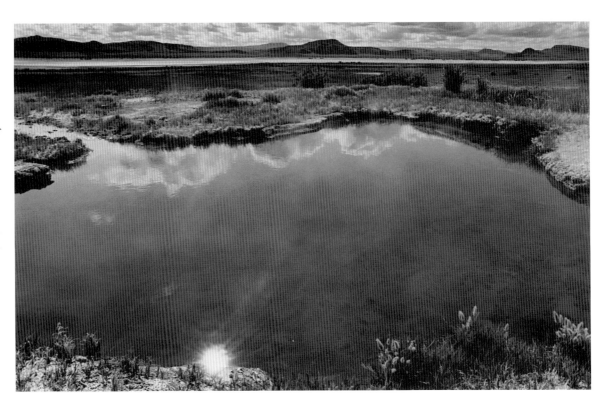

for cooling systems that rid them of excess body heat. Heat gain and water loss must be kept to absolute minimums. Light coloration helps reflect solar radiation. Hair and feathers create an insulating dead air space that helps keep heat out and water in. Resting in shade and in positions that avoid the full force of the sun helps in thermoregulation.

Small mammals, whose large surface-to-volume ratio heats them faster than large animals, mostly resort to avoiding daytime entirely, waiting for the cool night in shade and in burrows. Desert birds feed in early morning and late afternoon. Larger mammals pant or sweat and suffer dehydration until they can drink again. Birds pant as well.

Desert animals have remarkably efficient metabolisms. They use every possible molecule of water taken in or manufactured as they metabolize carbohydrates and fats. Birds and reptiles recover nearly all water in their kidneys before excretion of waste. They excrete semisolid uric acid and urates rather than the urea that in mammals must be dissolved in urine, using considerable water even when concentrated to the maximum.

When endurance fails as a ruse against the desert, animals can reproduce at favorable times and estivate (the summer equivalent of hibernation), escaping the intense desert summer. Burrowing toads and estivating ground squirrels, lizards, and insects all disappear in periods of extreme heat and aridity—in a way, the animal complements of the seeds of desert annuals, but with somewhat less staying power. Though they slow their metabolism to a near halt, they still slowly burn calories and sooner or later must revive and feed once more, dehydration risk or not.

To the Egyptian ecologist mentioned earlier, the Great Basin felt like a "botanical garden." But in this garden a chisel-toothed kangaroo rat must gnaw off the salty exterior of shadscale leaves before risking eating them. Clumps of iodine bush grow in soils so salty that no other plant competes with them. A mallow seed waits years for the momentary conjunction of moist soil and warmth that triggers sprouting. All Great Basin organisms deal with what Mark Twain described as the "only two seasons in the region . . . the breaking up of one winter and the beginning of the next."

The Great Basin is dry enough, hot enough, sunny enough, cold enough, salty enough, and difficult enough to qualify. It is, indeed, a desert.

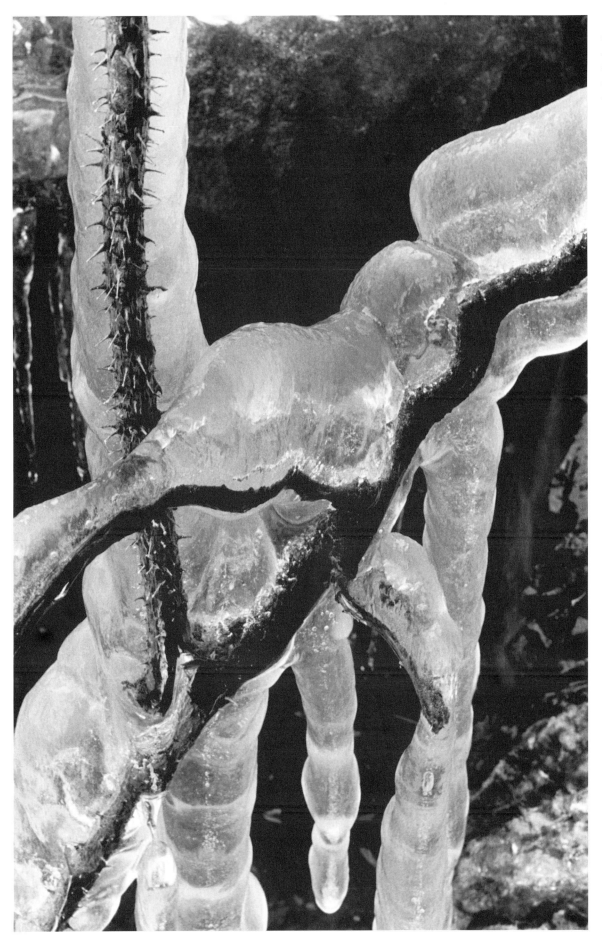

Winter ice covers a wild rose in McGill Canyon in the Jackson Mountains of northern Nevada.

II

Biogeography
Island Mountains and
Sagebrush Seas

The Relative Reality
of Natural Communities

3

*The interior of the Great Basin, so far as explored, is found to be a succession of sharp mountain ranges. . . . They are thinly wooded with some varieties of pine (*Pinus monophyllus *characteristic*), cedar, aspen, and a few other trees, and afford an excellent quality of bunch grass, equal to any found in the Rocky Mountains. Black-tailed deer and mountain sheep are frequent in these mountains; which . . . may be called fertile, in the radical sense of the word. . . . Sterility, on the contrary, is the absolute characteristic of the valleys between the mountains—no wood, no water, no grass, the gloomy artemisia the prevailing shrub. . . .*

Such is the Great Basin, heretofore characterized as a desert, and in some respects meriting that appellation, but already demanding the qualification of great exceptions, and deserving the full examination of a thorough exploration.

—John Charles Frémont,
Geographical Memoir, 1848

Pinyon Jay

As unvarying as it may seem at first glance from Interstate 80, as abrupt as many field guides are in their summary description of the Great Basin ("a monotonous stand of shrubs"), patterns in ecological communities mark this land. No one kind of plant can grow everywhere. Temperature, precipitation, soils, topography, interaction with other living things—all these and more determine where plants grow. And the plants, in turn, determine where animals can live.

As I drive along, I look for the patterns. It is a humbling experience.

I spot black sagebrush and sit back behind the wheel, complacent with my identification. My mind wanders, and the next time I pull over to stroll through the shrubs, I have descended imperceptibly into vivid green greasewood and dusty-leaved shadscale; iodine bush is holding out at the shore of the barren playa a few feet away. Along a wash I stare at an almost lifeless and leafless shrub. I know I should recognize it, but a name won't come. Finally I say, "rabbitbrush!" The white-green stems should have given it away.

The nature of the plant communities changes with remarkable subtlety. Why does shadscale spread across this basin when sagebrush filled the valley back over the last pass? Why does juniper grow where it does? What about this stand of winterfat?

Such questions can keep botanists busy for a lifetime and still leave them stumped. Add the hundreds of vertebrate and thousands of invertebrate species that have their own distribution patterns and the challenge begins to come clear.

In trying to understand why a particular Great Basin species grows where it does, every theory leads to another, every explanation is incomplete, everything is interconnected. Groups of plants and animals that favor the same environment live and reproduce as single individuals, adapt and differentiate as species. But they also confront similar opportunities and difficulties in any one environment—and in some ways evolve together as a community.

U.S. Highway 50, roller-coasting across the basins and ranges, rises into piñon-juniper woodland, drops back into sagebrush, then plunges on even lower to salt deserts. Up to the next pass, through woodland again, past bands of mountain brush and open forest to within sight of the bare mountaintops: alpine tundra. These basic patterns are undeniable.

A bit of knowledge makes a profound difference in the way you perceive the Great Basin. Botanist James Reveal met a family moving from Tennessee to California as they pulled into Ely, Nevada. They remarked in amazement that they had not seen a single living thing for two hundred miles!

To anyone accustomed to the overwhelming greens of the eastern deciduous forest, to the sheer bulk of plants, their reaction is understandable. To Reveal: "These eastern visitors had looked upon the vast expanses I had always relished as desolated vistas; those grayish shrubs and sparse low trees, which I had always considered a teeming forest, signified to them a bleak struggle for existence in a barren land."

I remember my own delight when I discovered in college the individuality hidden in the mass of greenery around me in Colorado. Suddenly, these were not just plants but specific and separate identities. Not just conifers, but Douglas-fir and limber pine and Engelmann spruce. Not just grass, but blue grama and ricegrass and sacaton. Not just flowers, but pinks and lilies and vetches. Each had distinctive qualities that made it as easily recognized as a Blue Jay, a grizzly bear, or a movie star. Graceful seed heads, pointed, square-edged needles, flowers with spurs and keels.

As you come to know Great Basin plants, the mass of dull gray shrubs pops into sharp focus. As your eye sharpens, animals, too, begin to reveal themselves: a dune that seems sterile becomes a metropolis of nocturnal rodents and their predators when you look for tracks at dawn before the wind whisks them away.

Once you recognize the residents of this desert as distinct characters you begin to notice them repeatedly in the same environments:

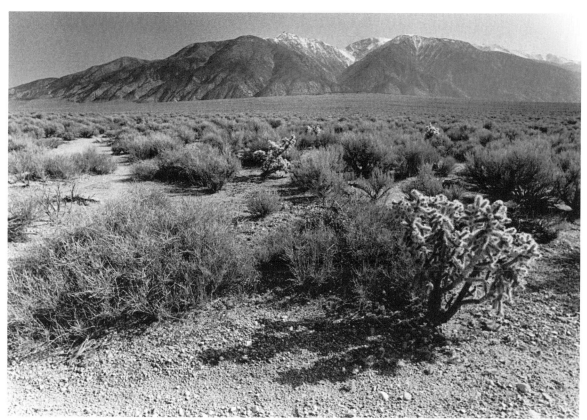

Cholla cacti grow in the shadscale country at the southern fringes of the Great Basin; below Boundary Peak, highest point in Nevada.

33

———

*Natural
Communities*

whitebark pines on windswept mountain ridges, muskrats in marshes, Pinyon Jays in piñon-juniper woodland. You expect to see them there; if they turn up somewhere else, you look for an explanation.

You have developed a naturalist's eye; you have begun to think like a biogeographer.

Even a single canyon in a single mountain range can dazzle with its complex ecological mosaic. In the twelve-mile drive through La-moille Canyon in the Ruby Mountains near Elko, the canyon floor rises from 6,200 feet to 8,850 feet. At the canyon mouth, valley sage-brush laps well into the gorge; only seventeen inches of moisture arrive annually. By the end of the road, precipitation doubles. In between, plant communities log these changes.

As I enter the canyon, on the left rises the sagey south-facing slope. On the right, beyond the creek, the more distant, shadowy north-facing slope begins to metamorphose into a mountainside. First, piñon and juniper trees begin to sprinkle dark green into the pale sage-brush, then aspen groves, puny and bent by winter snowpack, and curlleaf mountain-

mahogany. No need to strain to identify cross-creek species at this distance. In a mile or two, increasing elevation brings them to my side of the canyon, as the climate of the road-side south-facing slope comes to match the north face of two miles back.

White-barked aspen wind down gulleys sepa-rated by ridges of ragged sagebrush. Mountain-mahogany trees alternate and interfinger with the aspen, extending high up the canyon wall on the north slope in pure groves, patchy on the south-facing slope, clumps of mountain-mahoganies surrounded by aspen.

The aspen seem stately even when small, compared to the gnarled mountain-mahogany. The mountain-mahogany groves of middle La-moille Canyon look so evenly spaced, the indi-vidual trees so healthy, that they resemble care-fully tended orchards, their tufts of feathery fruits aswirl with magical light in late afternoon.

In the creek bottom grows a jungle. The scrubby aspen of the slopes give way to trees forty or fifty feet high. Aspen mix with willows and narrowleaf and black cottonwoods. They shade a lush understory of grasses, choke-cherry, dogwood, delicate columbine, and

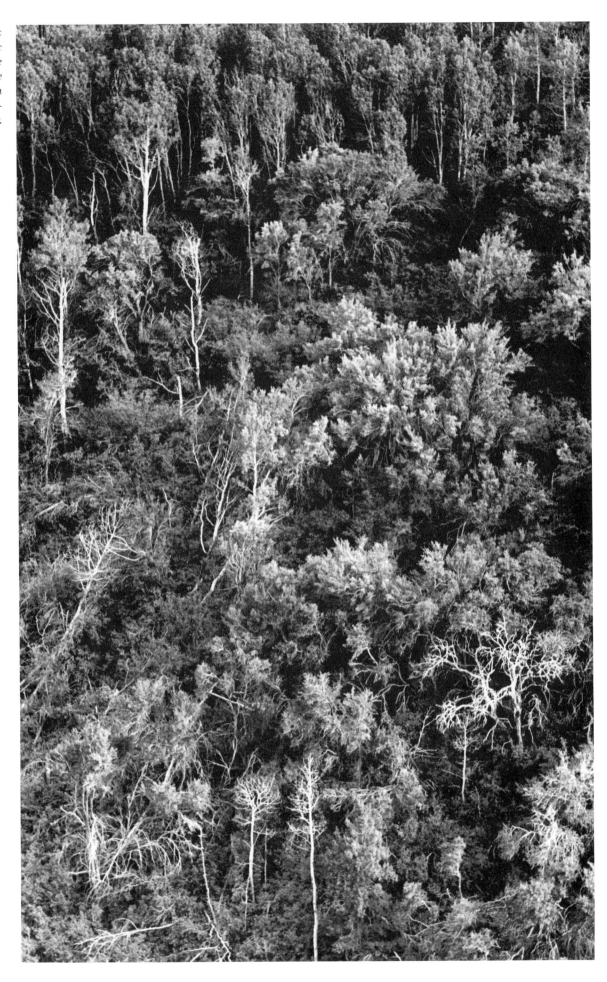

The complex ecological mosaic of Lamoille Canyon in the Rubies: aspen and mountain-mahogany.

Mountain Islands and Sagebrush Seas

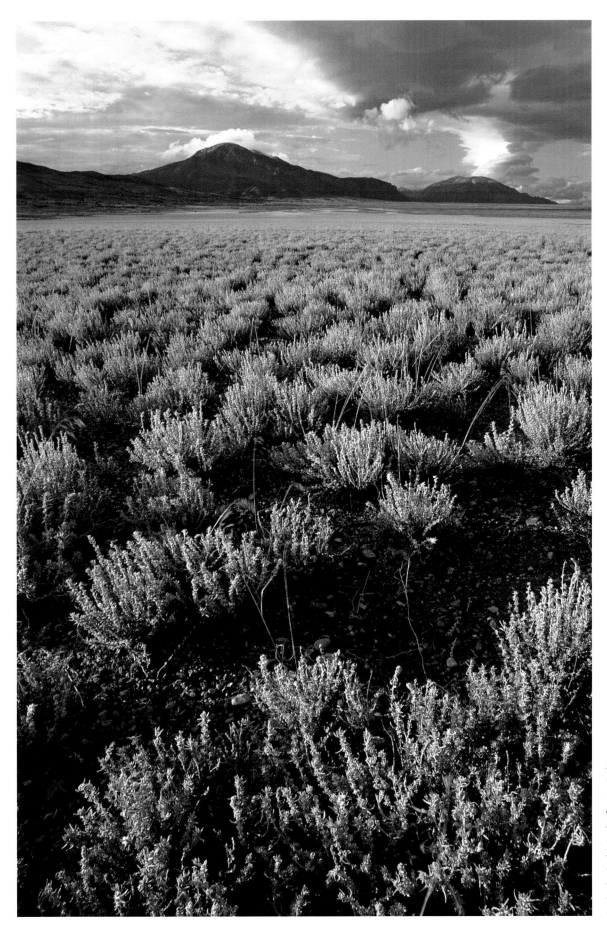

Pure stands of winterfat, Spring Valley, with the Schell Creek Range beyond; the metaphorical sagebrush ocean embraces currents, eddies, and embayments of other shrubs.

Basin and range,
basin and range:
the Deep Creeks
and Tule Valley
from the summit
of Notch Peak
(9,655 feet) in the
House Range.

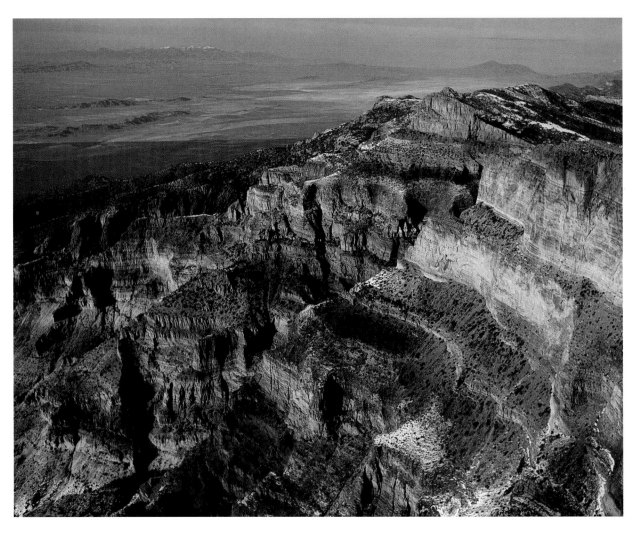

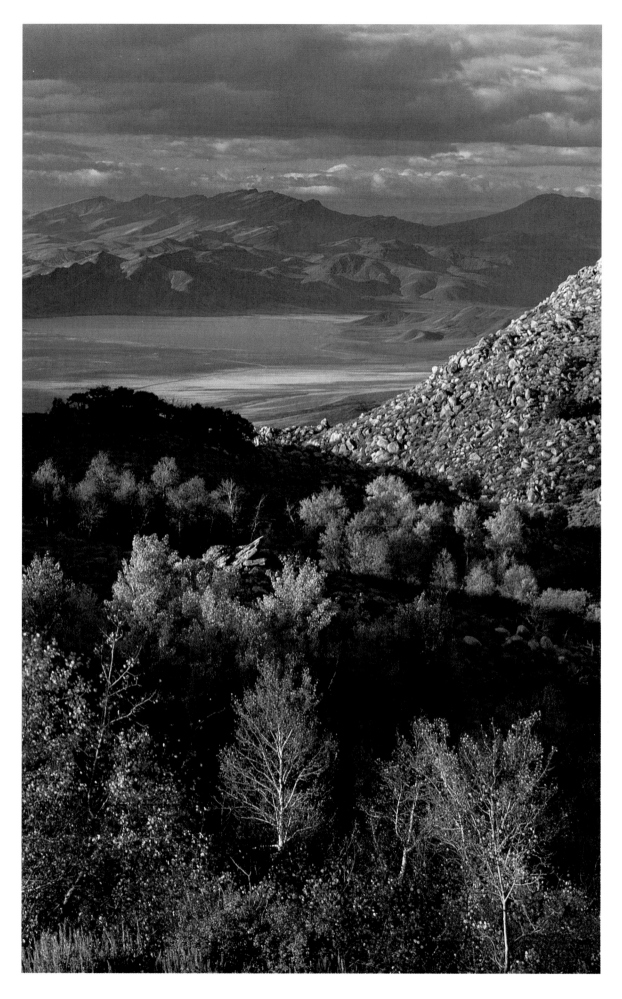

From an aspen grove high in the Pine Forest Range, bands of living communities pattern the desert north across a playa to the Pueblo Mountains on the Oregon border.

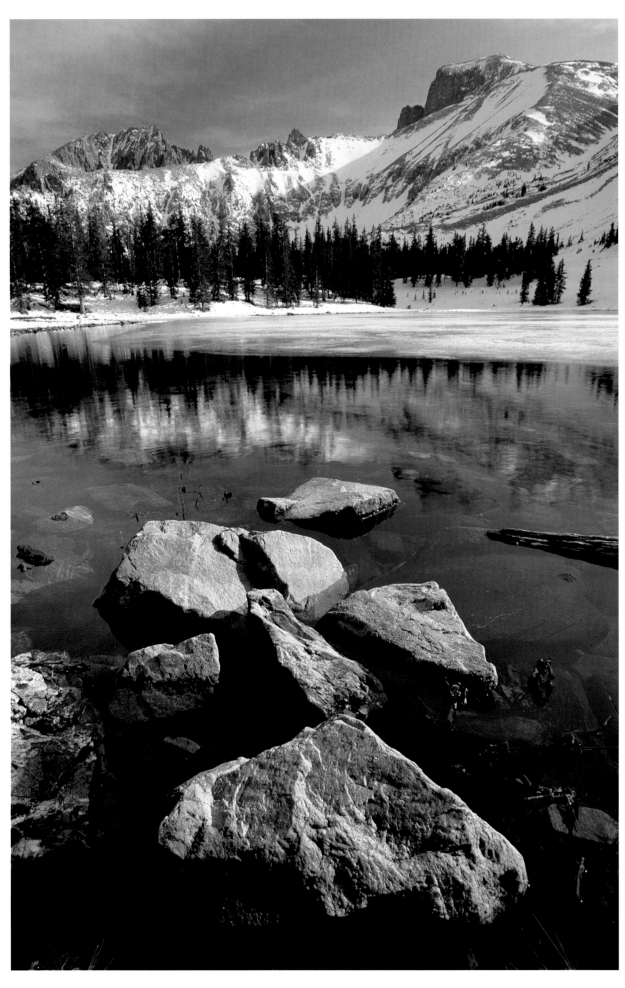

Wheeler Peak—centerpiece of the Great Basin National Park established in 1986 and highest point in Nevada's Snake Range; from Stella Lake.

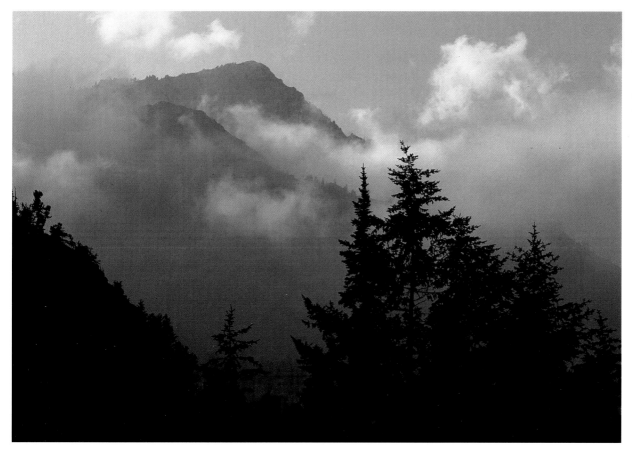

Clouds drift through dense subalpine forest on Deseret Peak in Utah's Stansbury Mountains.

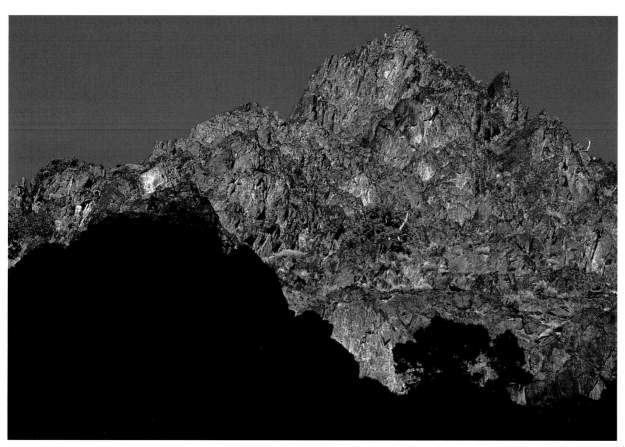

North of the Humboldt River, virtually no piñon grows, and some ranges even lack juniper. These solitary Utah junipers survive in the rocky crags of the Jackson Mountains.

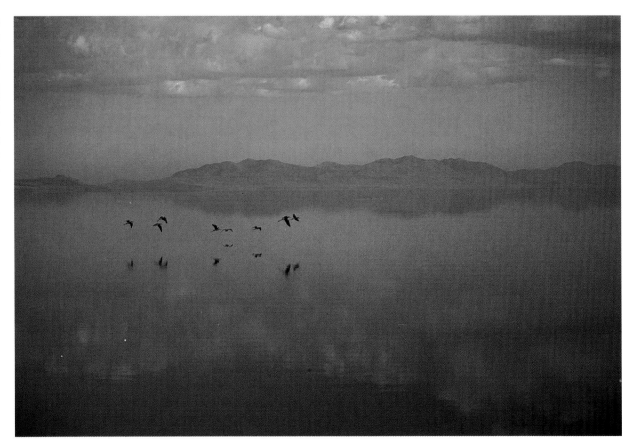

The heart of the hydrographic Great Basin is the Great Salt Lake, a strange, salty inland sea made more approachable by its birds, like these Black-necked Stilts.

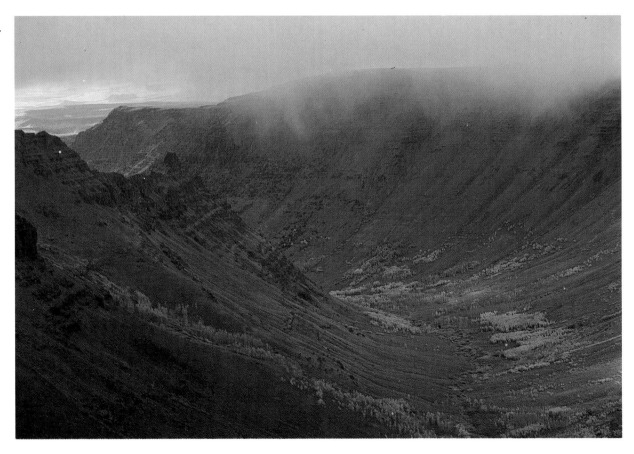

The glacially-scoured valley of Kiger Gorge on Oregon's Steens Mountain.

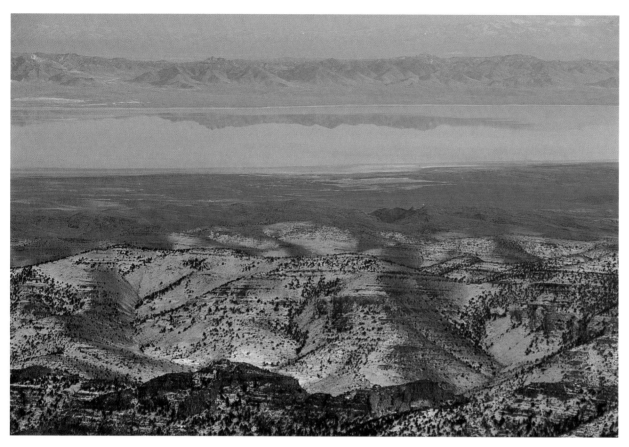

The view eastward from Notch Peak includes reflections from Sevier Lake, a fragment of once-enormous Lake Bonneville.

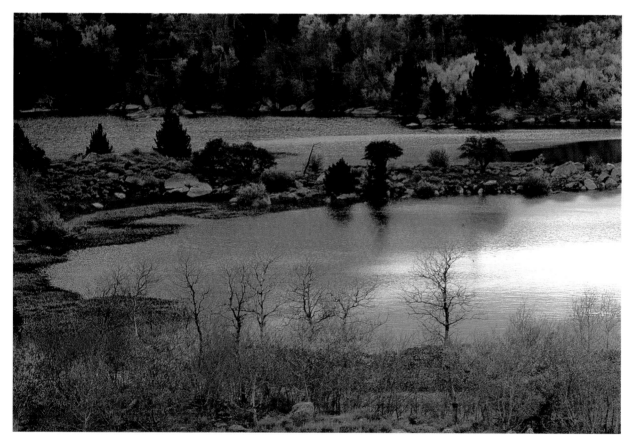

Blue Lake—dammed by a Pleistocene glacial moraine—glistens near the summit of the Pine Forest Range, small mountains isolated in the northern Nevada desert.

Unpredictability seems the most predictable characteristic of the Great Basin. The Great Salt Lake began to rise in the mid-1980s, flooding the resort beaches at Saltair.

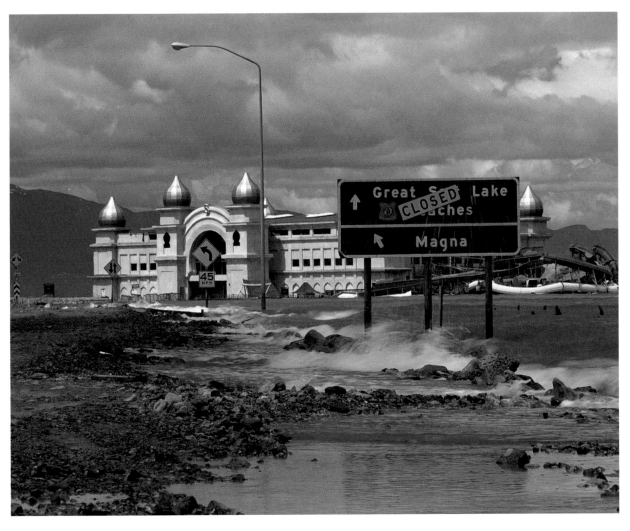

starry false-Solomon's-seal. Limber pine prospers along low-elevation streambanks but retreats to drier slopes in the higher subalpine areas.

The paved road ends near the upper limit of mountain-mahogany and aspen. From here on up, subalpine meadows and open-groved pine forest line the Ruby Crest Trail. No real tree line exists in the Rubies to separate subalpine and alpine communities. Conifers and alpine plants alternate up to the bare rock of the highest ridges.

To describe the limits of these communities precisely, ecologists have so many choices of factors to emphasize that the definitions have been restated dozens of times. What really controls these bands of life? Why are they so conspicuously changeable here, whereas in other parts of the world a single community may cover hundreds of miles without giving way to a second?

Simply deciding what to call any one community bounces us through a barrage of terms— and much of the history of biogeography in the last century.

Start with a stand of big sagebrush in the Reese River Valley of central Nevada, between the Toiyabe Range and the Simpson Park Mountains. We need some terms to characterize the group of plants and animals that live here. At the most basic level, the stand is an *association* of animals and plants. They live together and interact as an *ecological community*. Add all the physical factors that affect these organisms and the community becomes an *ecosystem*.

Some would include this sagebrush stand within the Upper Sonoran life zone. In the late 1800s, C. Hart Merriam noted that as one moved upward in elevation one traversed the same belts of vegetation that one encountered in moving toward the poles at constant elevation.

Merriam named these distinctive sequences *life zones*. He did his original fieldwork in northern Arizona, where plants and animals live in recognizable communities that change dramatically in the 10,000-foot rise from Mojave Desert in the bottom of the Grand Canyon to alpine tundra at the 12,700-foot summit of the San Francisco Peaks. To theoretically account for these life zones that banded the mountains he calculated two measures of temperature that he believed controlled the distribution of plants and animals. A statistic that measured the amount of heat available over the growing season gave Merriam the northward limits of a species. Southward, temperature averages for the six hottest consecutive weeks of summer indicated the maximum heat tolerance for each species. Groups of organisms seemed to share boundaries, and where their limits coincided, Merriam marked the divisions between life zones.

Merriam's recognition of definable elevational and latitudinal bands of natural communities made him a major pioneer of biogeography. Rigid adherence to his life zone concept elsewhere in the continent, where other factors clearly take precedence, discredited his system. His life zone names, however, remain in use in the West: Hudsonian and Canadian (boreal) for spruce-fir mountain forests whether at high latitude in the Yukon (boreal subarctic) or high elevation in Great Basin mountains (upper subalpine); Transition (montane) for the lower mountain forests of pine and Douglas-fir; Upper Sonoran, for piñon-juniper woodland and sagebrush; Lower Sonoran, for lowland hot desert shrub communities.

Merriam's life zones may not apply as broadly as he had hoped, but physical climatic factors nevertheless have a great deal to do with determining where plants and animals live. L. R. Holdridge made a later attempt at classifying worldwide vegetation into climatological life zones using annual averages of "biotemperature," precipitation, and a ratio measuring potential evapotranspiration.

One test of this system mapped Utah life zones according to Holdridge's three physical factors and came remarkably close to predicting the actual distribution of Utah plants and animals, doing best with mountain communities that change quickly with increasing elevation.

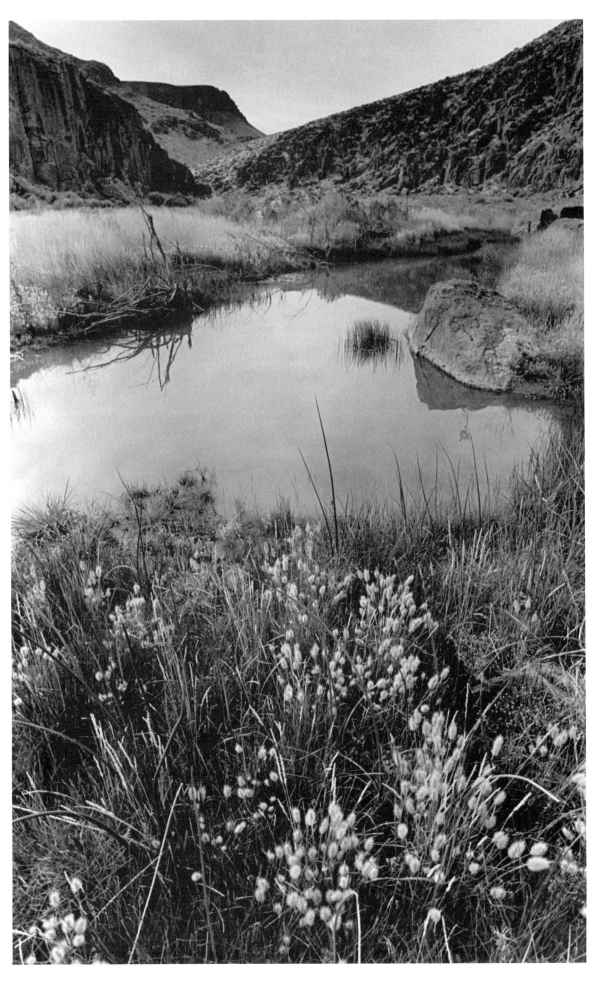

A small pool in an otherwise dry creek bed creates an oasis in Little High Rock Canyon west of the Black Rock Desert.

For our Reese River sagebrush stand, however, Holdridge tells us only that this stand lies in the subtropical montane steppe climatic zone.

Every attempt to classify vegetation and community types has its strengths and weaknesses. In the early twentieth century, Frederic E. Clements and Victor Shelford developed an approach based on the structure (life forms) of dominant plants (tree versus shrub versus grass). Their *biomes* (such as grassland, deciduous forest, and tundra) emphasized similarity. For example, they classed together geographically widely separated grasslands with completely different species compositions. At the broadest level, such concepts of worldwide biomes still give us a starting point in classifying terrestrial vegetation, with our sagebrush stand (and the entire Great Basin Desert) turning up as just that: "desert."

But by focusing on vegetation when it reaches a final "climatic climax," Clements and Shelford tended to ignore successional stages and discontinuous habitats, where some of the most abundant, strikingly adapted creatures reside: sand dunes, riparian forests, fire-adapted pioneer communities, and the like. Changes over time make for difficulties as well. In the Great Basin, a long-standing controversy exists about whether sagebrush always has been widespread or has only recently become common as it replaced grassland after overgrazing by livestock. Such uncertainties make decisions about "climax" biome boundaries difficult.

By comparing the geographic areas covered by species and by designating centers of evolutionary differentiation, Lee Dice would place Reese River sagebrush in the Artemisian *biotic province*. Dice's biogeography lends itself to animals as well as the plants dominating the schemes above. In this approach, however, communities with similar structure and species composition may be relegated to separate provinces because of geographic distance.

An emphasis on time leads to classifications emphasizing common evolutionary histories. Analysis of the entire flora of regions yields about ten *floristic provinces* for the continental United States, including a Great Basin province that would include our sagebrush stand. This expansive approach pays as much attention to rare plants as it does to common ones.

These are broad terms that do not differentiate the Reese River sagebrush community from Grass Valley sagebrush on the other side of the Toiyabe Range, or even from piñon-juniper woodland in the Wah Wah Mountains of Utah. All of these lie within the desert biome, in subtropical montane steppe in the Artemisian biotic province, related in their evolutionary history within the Great Basin floristic province, and all a part of the Upper Sonoran life zone.

Ecologists trying to narrow their sights have focused on dominant species within each of these stands of plants.

New problems arise. How many indicator species should be used? Should the canopy trees in a forest determine the community, or must the understory be taken into account? Is the type of tree (coniferous versus deciduous) all that matters, or is the species (ponderosa versus lodgepole pine) most important? Does this distinction matter to a chickadee in the Grant Range or a porcupine in the Raft River Mountains?

Federal land managers have adopted Rexford Daubenmire's classification scheme based on dominant species. These *habitat types* (h.t.s) allow mapping of presumed climax vegetation by labels that pair the dominant tree species with the dominant climax undergrowth species. These two plants may not currently grow in a designated stretch of the h.t., but at climax they would.

Foresters write with a prickly shorthand of h.t. acronyms. For example, you may hike through PSME/ACGL in southern Idaho's Sublett Range or in ABLA/BERE in the adjacent Deep Creek Mountains. Translation: *Pseudotsuga menziesii/Acer glabrum* h.t. (Douglasfir/Rocky Mountain maple); *Abies lasiocarpa/Berberis repens* h.t. (subalpine fir/creeping barberry).

Individual organisms continually defy our urge to generalize. What really matters is how an individual species or even an individual creature interacts with the environment. A single big sagebrush has no awareness about whether it grows where it is "supposed to grow" on a map of North American biomes or life zones or plant communities. The big sagebrush simply survives and reproduces.

A mountain may look to us like it has perfect pika habitat, with enough cool-climate meadows next to rockslides to support a viable population of the little rabbitlike mammals. But if pikas cannot reach the mountain or for some mysterious reason cannot survive as a self-sustaining population after they arrive, then a community where we would expect pikas will have none.

Sagebrush extends downward along a wash to penetrate deeply into a shadscale-filled basin. Rocky Mountain junipers thrive in the low Spring and White River valleys surrounded by sagebrush, well below the "normal" limits of junipers. On the west slope of Hancock Summit in the Delamar Mountains near Caliente, Nevada, Joshua trees grow among sagebrush and juniper well beyond the northern limit of creosote bush, co-indicator (with Joshuas) of the Mojave Desert.

Robert Whittaker believed that such exceptions should form our rules, that every plant is on its own. In his experiments along a gradient of elevation or climate each plant species seemed distributed independently of others. No groups of species had the same limits—their graphed occurrence along such gradients did not come in overlapping bunches. On this fine-grained level no recognizable natural communities seem to exist. Organisms seem to live independently of one another.

Yet animals and their obligate parasites, plants and their coevolved pollinators have exactly the same distributions. And sharp environmental boundaries indeed can occur. A change in rock formation shifts soils so abruptly that a single stride will take you into a new community. Pockets of unique vegetation growing on soils derived from the mineral serpentine are the classic example of such an "island" community. Soil derived from hydrothermally altered volcanic rocks on Geiger Grade near Virginia City, Nevada, produces almost as dramatic a change: from abundant piñon and juniper on most of the range to Sierran ponderosa pine on the altered soil. Increasing salinity near playas and alkaline hot springs produces similar sharp transitions.

The living world always throws monkey wrenches of complex reality into our too simplistic analyses.

This brief look at the troubles encountered in subdividing communities begins to show how hard it is to describe a single stand of sagebrush in a meaningful way—to keep "thinking like a mountain," as Aldo Leopold put it. All these hierarchies are arbitrary in some way. We see ecologists squaring off like taxonomists, as lumpers and splitters—the affectionately hostile camps who respectively combine varieties of organisms into a single group, emphasizing similarities, or divide them into seemingly endless categories, emphasizing small differences.

An additional problem arises from the profound changes wrought by humans on ecological communities in the Great Basin. Less drastic here than in other regions of the country, these still make actual plant and animal communities different from potential communities.

Notice I do not use the word "natural." Human intervention in the affairs of North American ecology dates back at least fourteen thousand years. Prehistoric events, like the loss of large Pleistocene mammals, seem natural enough to us now; the more recent losses of the wolf, bison, and wolverine seem unnatural.

Natural or unnatural, today's Great Basin differs from that of a century ago. In many places the bighorn are gone or severely reduced in numbers. Accidentally introduced weedy species like halogeton, Russian thistle, and cheatgrass have taken over vast acreages, a permanent transformation accelerated by livestock grazing on an unimaginable scale.

Humans continue to influence the Basin. Since the 1950s, hundreds of thousands of acres of piñon-juniper woodland have been chained—the trees uprooted by two Caterpillar

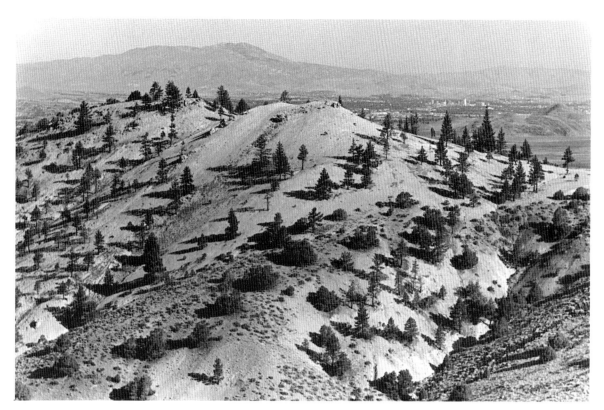

tractors dragging a battleship anchor chain—in hopes of increasing wildlife and livestock forage. Sagebrush "control" remains widespread under the same guise. These destroyed native communities are seeded with the exotic crested wheatgrass.

Do we now map these cleared areas as grasslands? What successional rules can tell us their true climax condition? From such enigmas comes a compromise: Kuchler's vegetation map of the United States—the standard—is labeled "Potential Natural Vegetation."

In the end, all these approaches produce maps with different labels (biomes, floristic provinces, biotic provinces, and others), but their boundaries are drawn in approximately the same places time after time: there *are* recognizable differences in communities. Even though species are distributed individually, even though most communities intergrade continuously, even though traits used in grouping organisms remain independent of one another—even with all these truths, we can still proclaim the additional truth that recognizable ecological communities exist.

We can drive from Beatty to Tonopah, Nevada, and watch the transition from creosote bush Mojave Desert to Great Basin Desert. We can say, accurately, these trees in Utah's Stansbury Mountains form aspen forest; the ridge beyond Stella Lake on Wheeler Peak is covered with bristlecone pine subalpine forest; above it stands a treeless alpine ridge.

Recognizing such real and observable differences, Dwight Billings has subdivided the Great Basin into vegetation zones that make sense. As he puts it:

> In mapping the extent of the vegetation zones of a given region, an ecologist must be guided by discontinuities in both physiognomy and quantitative floristics and draw the boundary lines on the map more or less arbitrarily according to his judgment.

In other words, all the factors favored by one or another classification system take precedence somewhere. Common sense and close observation are the guides, and Billings's broadly occurring Great Basin vegetation zones form the basis for the organization of this book.

First come valleys between the mountains. Shadscale covers desert basins in southwestern

*The Great Salt
Lake: largest
of the remnant
Pleistocene inland
seas; the alkaline
Great Salt Lake
Desert spirals
outward and
upward from the
lakeshore.*

40

———

Biogeography

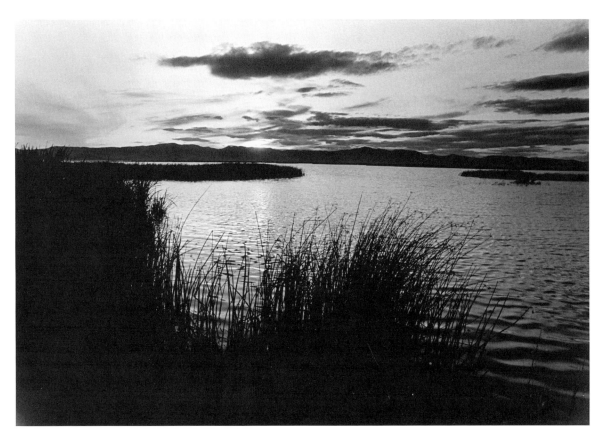

Nevada and the huge low-lying Lahontan and
Bonneville basins of Nevada and Utah, respectively. In most higher basins, sagebrush replaces it. These two communities fill the inter-
montane valleys with seas of desert scrub. In
saline areas at the edges of playas, salt-tolerant
plants like greasewood come to the fore where
salts foil shadscale and sagebrush. In sandy
areas, dunes form with their complement of
plants and animals adapted to this shifting
world. And in those few basins with permanent
water, riverbank forests or marshes survive,
both crucial to animal life.

Desert mountains rise from these oceans of
sagebrush and shadscale. Across most of the
Great Basin, mountain forest communities have
a distinct, depauperate island character in
comparison to the Sierra or Rockies on either
side. With increasing elevation and precipitation, sagebrush gives way to piñon-juniper
woodland. With still more moisture and shorter
growing seasons, Great Basin mountain brush
replaces piñon and juniper where in "normal" mountains pine and fir would grow. Sagebrush again dominates these communities, with

interspersed groves of aspen and mountain-
mahogany and a grassy understory. On the
highest summits, open subalpine groves of limber and bristlecone pines give way to alpine
tundra.

In the Carson Range between Reno and
Lake Tahoe immediately east of the Sierra
Nevada, many Sierran forest species extend
into the Great Basin. A few of these make it to
the next bank of ranges (the Virginia and Wassuk ranges and the Pine Nut, Sweetwater, and
White mountains); virtually none reach farther
east. Likewise, mountains west of Utah's Wasatch Range show Rocky Mountain zonation
as far westward into the Great Basin as the
Snake and Deep Creek ranges on the Nevada
border (though here only on the high, wet,
north-facing slopes; on upper south-facing
slopes and lower slopes in general these ranges
are typically Basin range in their life zones).

Not every ecologist agrees with this classification. But each of these zones of life has distinct meaning to its resident plants and animals. In the end, the living communities speak
for themselves.

The Dynamic Past
Great Basin Paleobiogeography

4

As the millennia had sped by and the tree-zones had rolled upward, the lake had shrunk back in the other direction. . . . Of all the plants that had grown there once—pines, firs, aspens, and berry-bushes, and lush grasses— not one had survived that death march upward.

Yet why should we call it death-march rather than life-march? If the pines died, the greasewood and the seepweed and the spiny-sage and the bunch-grass lived and prospered where they had not lived before. If the trout died, the pronghorns came to browse on the shadscale where once the trout had spawned, and where the otters had dived and sported in the shallows, now the kangaroo rats dug their holes in the dunes, and lived on the seeds of greasewood and seepweed, and flourished and multiplied.

—George R. Stewart,
Sheep Rock, 1951

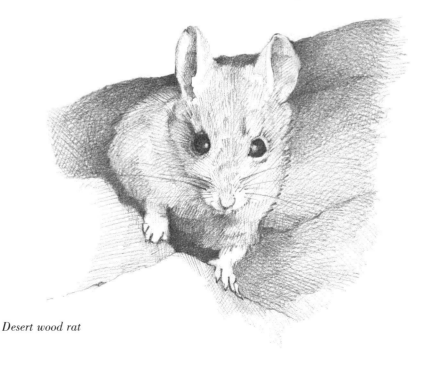

Desert wood rat

There are not just four Great Basins. There is an infinite number of them. The patterns of ecological communities in the Great Basin change constantly, and the current version is a recent innovation, decisively different from most times in its history. I sit in a camp chair in Stone Cabin Valley and try to comprehend this fact. Mountains surround me—the Kawich Range, gray-blue and craggy to the southeast, the Hot Creek Range, closer and rich in detail to the northeast, behind me the Monitor Range. The air is still and hot, and time seems indolent— the present the length of forever. I scrunch my toes in coarse gravel—bits of the mountains on the horizon brought down into the valley by millions of storms during millions of summers.

The piece of the North American desert that I see here has existed in its present form only during the last eleven thousand years. That covers only three ten-thousandths of one percent of the span of time during which life has existed on the North American continent.

During this longer span, North America has moved thousands of miles across the globe, from equatorial to temperate latitudes. It has crashed into other continents, then split away from them. Oceans have inundated it; mountain ranges have come and gone. Evolution has nudged living things into dominance, then replaced them with entirely new varieties. The "Great Basin" has seen ichthyosaurs, sequoia forests, camels, and lions.

How can we know such things?

The answers—the story of the distant past— lie in the fossil record trapped in Basin rocks: petrified wood from Pennsylvanian period forests, fossil leaves from the shores of Eocene lakes, skeletons of giant amphibians, primitive mammalian skulls. Paleontologists find other answers in less likely places. They sift weathered hillsides for tiny mammal teeth that tell the size and diet of our Cretaceous ancestors. The layering of fossil pollen grains in old marsh and lake beds yields a chronicle of climate, temperature, and plant community.

Of the billions of individual animals and plants that live and die, only a few become fossils. Decomposers and chemical weathering succeed well at returning even the hard shells and skeletons of animals to the elements. Given such poor odds for fossilizing, eroding out from the earth's surface, and being discovered by a paleontologist, we need not wonder at the fragmentary fossil record in the Great Basin. We can exult in knowing as much as we do.

In Pennsylvanian time, for instance, forests of fast-growing, soft-tissued trees, giant ferns, horsetails, and similar swamp-dwelling plants gave the continents a more uniform flora than at any other time in the earth's history. Their incredible bulk of organic debris gradually turned to coal, accounting for the period's alternative name, the Carboniferous. Though over much of its territory the formation is strictly marine, in central Utah, the 310-million-year-old fossils of the Manning Canyon Shale render a detailed picture of such early Pennsylvanian forests. This shale crops out in such arid modern mountains as the Oquirrhs.

The recent history of the Great Basin began about 140 million years ago, when flowering plants (angiosperms) first appeared at the beginning of the Cretaceous period. Angiosperms transformed the coniferous continents. Most early forms were trees, including Cretaceous versions of fig, poplar, sassafras, and magnolia. By 125 million years ago, flowering plants grew scattered throughout the earth's forests, and by Upper Cretaceous they dominated the world flora. Upper Cretaceous plant fossils from the Blackhawk Formation in central Utah include a mix of gymnosperms (sequoia, ginkgo, and araucarias—monkey puzzle trees), palms, and ferns, with angiosperms like walnut, cinnamon, magnolia, and willow.

The transition from Cretaceous to Tertiary (the first part of the Cenozoic era) was one of the great revolutions of life on earth. Dinosaurs—along with many other reptiles—disappeared. In the world's oceans, mass extinctions wiped out organisms in groups from invertebrates on up. Abruptly the world took on an

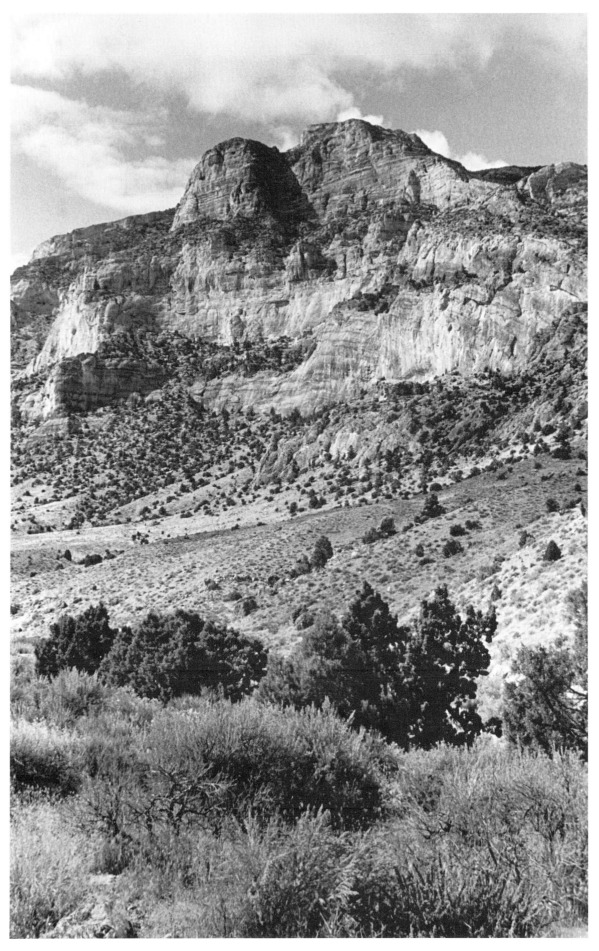

From caves in the Snake Range's Smith Creek Canyon come fossils of mountain mammals living far outside their current ranges.

almost modern aspect; the beginning of the Cenozoic ended the reptilian era and ushered in the age of mammals.

The Tertiary began with the Paleocene epoch and a Great Basin of low elevation and modest relief, forested by temperate trees not far removed from their Cretaceous ancestors. Indeed, well over half of the world's Paleocene genera of flowering plants have now become extinct.

In the succeeding epoch, the Eocene, the earth headed into the beginnings of modern times. The two great controlling factors in the evolution of today's living world began: the cooling and drying of the world climate. In the Southwest, an evergreen woodland appeared and diversified as aridity increased. Eocene woods included familiar-looking live oaks, piñon, juniper, and chaparral plants in dry places surrounded by a rich coniferous-hardwood forest. Only middle-sized mountains existed, but they nonetheless created a series of forest types with increasing elevation.

This Eocene Great Basin stood only slightly above sea level, with its highest ranges at the north end. Fossils from the Copper Basin in the Jarbidge Mountains of northern Nevada yield a glimpse of an Upper Eocene coniferous-deciduous hardwood forest close to modern montane evergreen forest. Here cedar, Douglas-fir, and sequoia towered over stands of maple, elm, and madrone in moist valleys and on lower slopes. Understory shrubs included rhododendron, sassafras, serviceberry, and hawthorn. The Bull Run Mountains forty miles west contain fossils from a purely coniferous spruce-pine-larch-hemlock forest from the same epoch. An extra few hundred feet (four thousand feet as opposed to Copper Basin's then thirty-five hundred to four thousand feet) eliminated the deciduous trees.

In lowlands, subtropical rain forest survived from earlier times. In the next epoch (the Oligocene, from thirty-eight to twenty-three million years ago) cooling and drying drove subtropical forest south, where it has remained ever since. Many present species originated at this time,

particularly conifers and woody plants.

With the Miocene the present landscape began to form. The crust of the earth between present Reno and Salt Lake City began to stretch, initiating the block faulting that created the Basin and Range province. The Sierra Nevada began its rise, though at the end of the epoch (some five million years ago) the range stood only one thousand feet above the Great Basin.

Through the Pliocene and into the succeeding Pleistocene, the Sierra and Cascades increased greatly in elevation, casting their long rain shadow over the land to the east. The crust continued to fracture, with long north-south segments dropping away relative to their surroundings, the high blocks forming mountains and the low, valleys. Meanwhile, regional uplift of the entire West from the Sierra to the Rockies raised the Great Basin five thousand vertical feet, mostly during the period from ten to five million years ago.

With this transformation of the land came another revolution in its life. The drying trends of the Miocene became extreme in the Pliocene. Precipitation decreased, particularly summer rains, and the Great Basin headed into the driest time of the Tertiary.

The northern forest fragmented, with many species going extinct. Woodland species took over the foothills; leathery-leaved evergreens that had long been developing to the south finally had their chance, mostly now-extinct species of oak, pine, palm, soapberry, and locust.

Temperate forest species found refuge in eastern North America on the coastal lowlands, but in the West they had nowhere to go. Squeezed between arid lowlands and cold mountains, they were squeezed out, surviving today only as isolated or rare species on the California coast.

By late Pliocene, savanna and grassland covered much of the Great Basin. Mammals reacted to these dramatic changes with radical measures, evolving with the vegetation: grazers (who eat tender shoots and grasses) re-

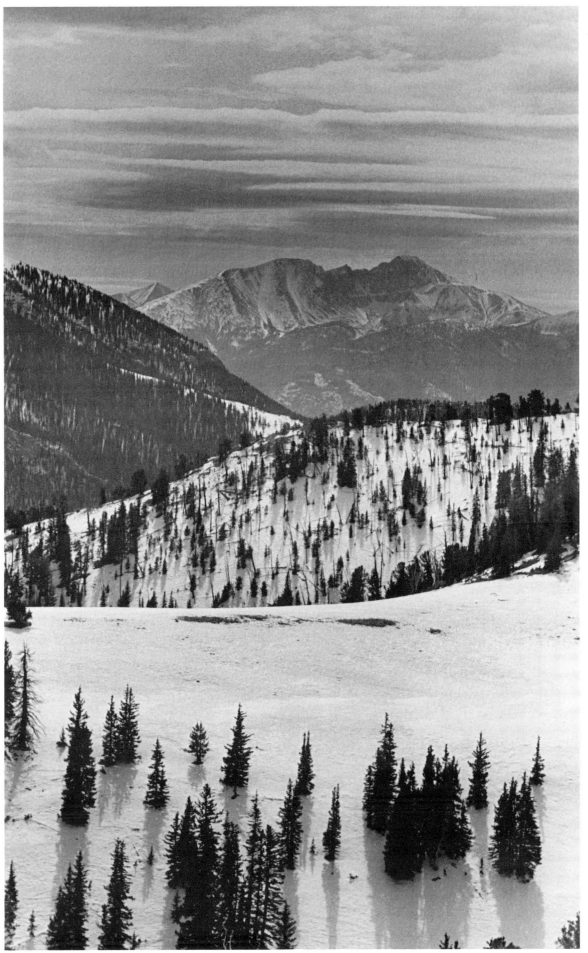

*Wheeler Peak
from Mount
Moriah: sheltered
under Wheeler's
north face lies
the Great Basin's
only remaining
glacier.*

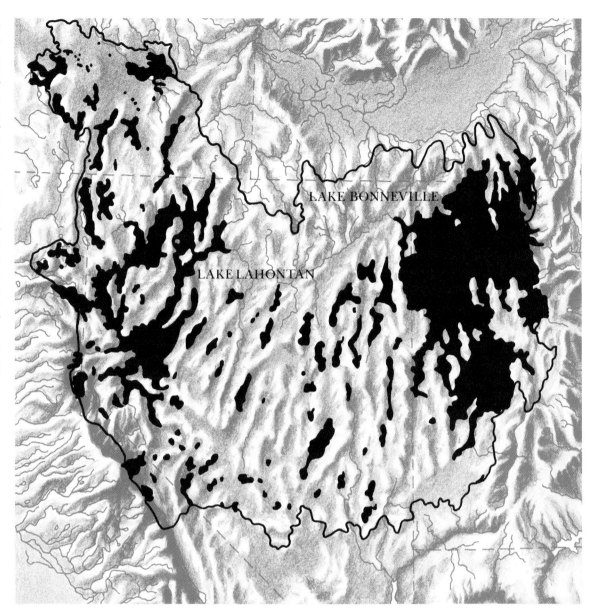

LAKE BONNEVILLE

LAKE LAHONTAN

placed many browsers (who eat mostly twigs and leaves).

Huge herds of Pliocene camels, horses, mastodons, rhinos, bison, and a dozen species of pronghorn ranged the North American plains. Camels, horses, and pronghorn evolved in North America. Other groups reached the New World over the Bering land bridge, exposed as the continent rose, and with them came Old World plants that would remain conspicuous in the Great Basin long after most Pliocene mammals had gone extinct. These mid-Pliocene arrivals included, according to some botanists, sagebrush, saltbush, Mormon tea, molly, and desert blite (seepweed).

In earlier times, both animals and plants fossilized easily in widespread swampy en-

vironments that preserved bones and intact leaves and trunks. With drier and drier conditions through the Miocene and Pliocene, macrofossils decrease in abundance while the fossil pollen record becomes more and more important. By comparing them to modern forms, specialists can classify these multiribbed, pyramidal, and spiky microscopic pollen grains trapped in ancient lake sediments, identifying the fossils sometimes even to species.

About two million years ago, the Quaternary began, its span divided between the Pleistocene and the Holocene, the latter the most recent ten thousand years since the last great Ice Age. Finally, the climatic changes accelerating through the Tertiary reached a climax.

The Pleistocene brought with it advancing glaciers alternating with warm, dry interglacials. In the last eight hundred thousand years there have been at least fifteen major periods of cooling and warming across the northern hemisphere. Changes in the jet stream dictate their rhythm, moving the subtropical high north or south to control storm patterns. In turn, cyclic changes in the earth's orbit control the jet stream and vary the amount of sun heating the planet.

In cool periods, snowfall builds up during years not warm enough to melt the winter's accumulation; the snow compacts to ice, coalescing and flowing downhill as glaciers. Four times the great Pleistocene ice sheets have crept down from the Arctic to cover much of North America and Eurasia, while the mirror image was perpetrated on lands in the southern hemisphere (though less than 20 percent of glacial ice occurred there). The Great Basin saw only mountain glaciers at these times; continental ice sheets lay to the north.

These glaciers owe their development largely to the sixteen-hundred-foot increase in continental elevation since the Eocene, creating not only cooler highlands but raising land into thinner air much more responsive to cycles in heat received from the sun. Pleistocene glaciers moved across 30 percent of the planet, including five million square miles of North America, with ice two miles thick in places.

With each advance of the ice, temperate-climate plants (with their attendant animals) moved south; when the ice retreated, they returned to the north. Each sweep up or down the continent changed the flora, mixing Asian (northern) species from across Beringia with southern-originated North American natives. But, as James Reveal has pointed out, the flora did not march forward as a "herd."

> Individuals of a species on its southern fringe were unable to survive in the warming and drying climate and died out. . . . At the same time, on the northern fringe of the plant's range, individuals of other species were dying and into these new open sites a more southern plant migrated, if it could, and survived when it was possible.

In this way, species either "moved" or disappeared.

The last major Pleistocene glaciation in North America was the Wisconsinan, which reached its maximum about twenty-five thousand years ago. From the late Wisconsinan on, we can examine the fate of Great Basin communities in detail.

Much of that detail stems from a single technique used only in the past twenty years. Pack rats (wood rats—*Neotoma*) live in southwestern woodlands (and elsewhere) and have done so for tens of thousands of years. Throughout this time these rodents have functioned as unknowing botanical researchers.

They thoroughly sample the rocky slopes where they live, collecting leaves, flowers, fruits, twigs, bones, and other small objects for a distance of about 325 feet to stash in their dens for food and as raw materials for nest construction and midden fortification. They periodically clean house, piling the discards in a midden, which becomes a trampled urine-cemented herbarium.

Ecologists, led by Philip Wells and Thomas Van Devender, have been hunting the Southwest's caves and ledges for such "fossil" wood rat middens. Robert Thompson has extended Wells's pack rat work in the Great Basin. The ecologists collect the hardened debris, wash and separate specimens (or sift through them layer by layer in dry "splits"), and identify plants growing on the site over the long span of collecting by generations of occupant rodents, dating the material by carbon-14 analysis. Their efforts give us an exact record of plant distribution over the last twenty-five thousand years, midden by midden, range by range.

The tree-ring record yields climatic detail datable to the year. This chronicle of annual growth from bristlecone pines extends back nine thousand years, and discoveries of pieces of dead wood with the right sets of overlapping

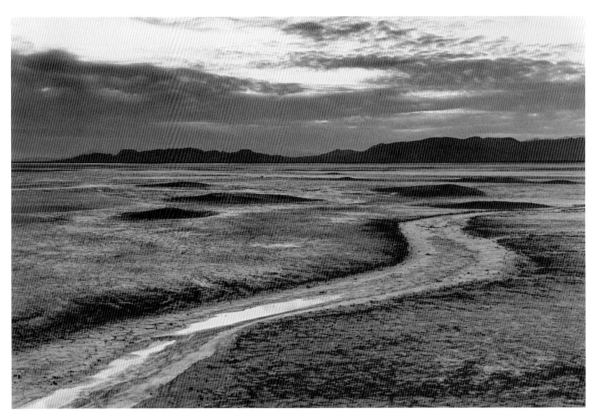

The Black Rock Desert, wet from melting winter snow, when it seems that Lake Lahontan has not quite disappeared from the big playa.

48

Biogeography

rings could push the record back several thousand years more. Rings mark droughts, early and late frosts, and temperature variations—a diary of the vicissitudes weathered by individual trees. Careful analysis yields occasional pockets of pollen enclosed by the growing wood. The bristlecone record also provides an invaluable cross-check for carbon-14 dates from pack rat middens and archaeological sites.

Geologists complete our picture of the Wisconsinan Great Basin. In the higher Great Basin ranges, alpine glaciers crept down valleys to as low as ninety-two hundred feet. At the same time, lakes filled many of the basins to depths of a thousand feet. These lakes resulted not so much from increased precipitation but from cooler temperatures that decreased evaporation, a climate known as "pluvial." The two largest, Lakes Lahontan and Bonneville, had profound impacts on Great Basin biogeography.

Picture Lake Bonneville filling today's Great Salt Lake Desert basin with a huge expanse of water gleaming in the Pleistocene sun. Or the narrow arms of Lake Lahontan, fjordlike, isolating range after range in western Nevada as long peninsulas and islands.

Though it may seem obvious, where either lakes or glaciers existed, no plants grew. Instead of an ocean of sagebrush and shadscale, the great Pleistocene lakes filled the basins with real inland seas. At the cold margin of ice—the upper limit of plants except for a few alpine species on higher rocky ridges between glaciers—a band of tundra left little room below for forests. In many basins, only three thousand vertical feet separated ice from inland sea.

This scene of ice white and lake blue is the unlikely stage for the desertification of North America.

From about twenty-five thousand to eleven thousand years ago, the Southwest began to warm, but changes came slowly, and the land that would become the modern North American hot deserts remained woodland. During these years the area within today's Mojave, Sonoran, and Chihuahuan deserts to the south of the Great Basin supported a typical modern Great Basin flora: piñon and juniper far more widely distributed than today, with sagebrush, shadscale, blackbrush, mountain-mahogany, and Joshua trees well south of their present range. Spruce and fir ventured much lower on

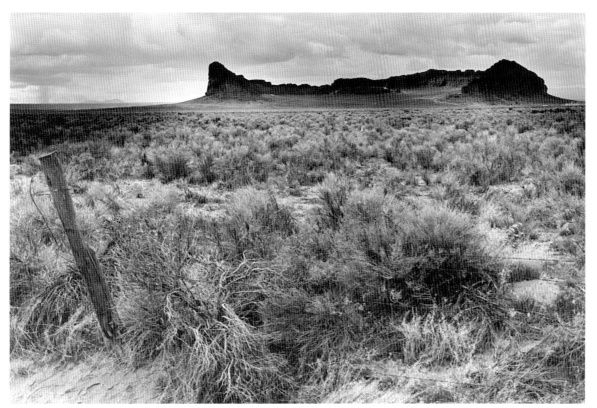

Fort Rock basin in Oregon: layered deposits of late Wisconsinan fossils in caves here show a gradual transition from white-tailed to black-tailed jackrabbits as the Hypsithermal warmed their world.

the flanks of the mountains than they do now.

In the Wisconsinan Great Basin itself, on the lower mountain slopes and on rocky islands in the valley bottoms grew subalpine conifers: limber and bristlecone pine, Engelmann spruce, and dwarf juniper. In southern and east-central Nevada, bristlecones reached to six thousand feet, more than three thousand feet below their modern limits.

Douglas-fir, white fir, and ponderosa pine grow today in a strip of montane forest below these subalpine conifers in the high ranges of the eastern Basin, but (according to the local pack rat midden register) in Late Wisconsinan they were rare or unknown. Climate, dry and colder than today by seven to eight degrees Fahrenheit, favored bristlecone/limber pine forest. Sagebrush dominated deeper soils in the valleys (perhaps with Rocky Mountain juniper). With no place to grow here, the montane trees survived only to the south.

Until eleven thousand years ago, changes came slowly. The great pluvial lakes maintained high levels. New plants moved slowly northward and upward, keeping pace with the gradually retreating glaciers. But starting about ten thousand five hundred years ago, the shift

sharply accelerated. Subalpine conifers gave way to sagebrush; shadscale and its allies expanded their range as lakes shrank. No single-leaf piñon grew in the Great Basin in late Wisconsinan; with the beginning of the Holocene, piñon began to move north. Nations of plants marshaled their forces and shifted their boundaries in a continent-wide march.

Drastic things happened to animals at this same time. Humans arrived in the Great Basin by at least thirteen thousand to twelve thousand years ago. They were hunters, and the land teemed with their potential prey: great herds of mammoths and mastodons, camels, bison, pronghorn, llamas, and horses (though only for bison and mammoths do we have absolute evidence of hunting). People competed for meat with saber-toothed cats, dire wolves, and other predators.

But in the centuries between thirteen thousand and ten thousand years ago, half of the genera of North American mammals went extinct; half the birds suffered the same fate at the same time. Of North American Pleistocene mammals weighing more than one hundred pounds, 70 percent disappeared.

We know that these remarkable events overlapped in time: the arrival of human hunters, the mass extinctions of mammals, and sharp climatic and vegetational changes. But untangling cause from effect is another matter. Paleoecologist Paul Martin believes that the wave of efficient human predators moving south through the continent wiped out the big mammals, an "overkill" that reproductive capacity could not surmount. Martin makes the case for overhunting as the sole cause of these extinctions. Many paleoecologists disagree vehemently.

Parallel changes in climate were shrinking the habitat of these open savanna and grassland species. Mountain species could retreat deeper into the forest. Smaller animals could survive by adapting to the change from grassland to desert scrub. But the pressures of disappearing habitat, reduced carrying capacity, increased competition, low reproductive rates, overspecialization, climatic extremes like drought and sudden storms—all must have had many larger animals teetering on the brink of extinction. Paleo-Indian hunting bands may simply have come along and pushed susceptible species off the edge of the cliff—literally.

About eight thousand years ago, a sudden increase in temperature started in the Mojave/Sonoran deserts, creating a wave of effects that spread northward through the Great Basin from seventy-five hundred to forty-five hundred years ago. This was the Hypsithermal (climatological jargon with the simple meaning "high temperature"). It was a worldwide event. But pioneer geologist Israel Cook Russell proposed it first in the Great Basin; James Reveal calls it "the molding influence of the biota of the Intermountain Region."

The Hypsithermal was not a single event but rather a period when seasonal temperatures reached maximum values, the particular maximum depending on the season. The relationship between the spring equinox and the closest approach of the earth to the sun changes cyclically, and as it does, the amount of solar heat at a given latitude reaches different maximums for different seasons. The Holocene

maximum for early summer (May through June) occurred thirteen thousand years ago, that for midsummer (July through August) about ten thousand years ago, and the late summer maximum (September through October) about five thousand years ago.

In southern Idaho, pollen records match these dates. Shadscale communities reached their highest elevation about eight thousand years ago, when August temperatures peaked. Tree line (the transition from fir forest to subalpine meadow) reached its highest level about five thousand years ago, when late-summer solar heat peaked. This makes sense, for summer drought limits low-elevation communities and the length of the growing season limits tree line forest.

The effects of these maximum temperatures were dramatic; they eliminated most of the vestiges of the cool Ice Age from the Great Basin and outlined the modern North American deserts. With even a 10 or 20 percent change in the precipitation/evaporation ratio (which this sharp increase in evaporative power surely could accomplish), the last holdouts among the drying pluvial lakes disappeared. Only remnants survived the Hypsithermal: Pyramid, Walker, Honey, Sevier, Utah, and Great Salt lakes. (And some of these modern lakes periodically dry and refill as climate fluctuates.)

Basin floors, impregnated with salt and heavy with mud and silt, opened to colonization by plants. Shadscale and other shrubs pioneered the move into these new habitats. Where they gained their foothold remains unclear: perhaps long resident on the fluctuating shorelines, these salt-tolerant plants may have first colonized the Great Basin around salty hot springs. Meanwhile, the Hypsithermal climate forced montane species to ever higher reaches of the ranges.

Finally, the northward-advancing flora reached barriers that blocked their march: the mountains of central Idaho and Oregon. Only a few of the full complement of plants that make up sagebrush country reach farther northward to the Columbia Plateau. In the Basin, the newly fragmented populations of high-elevation

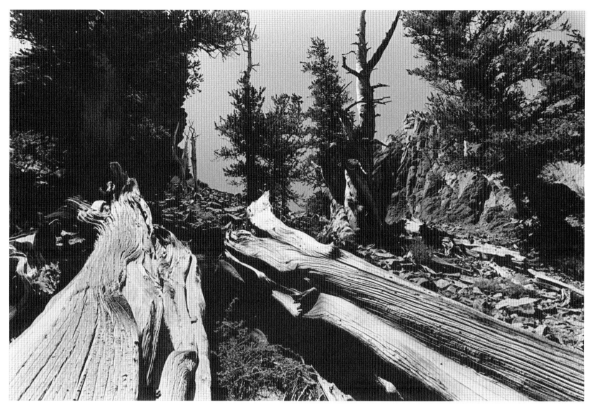

Bristlecone pines on volcanic rock in the Hot Creek Range, witnesses to the entire span of the "modern" biological world of the Great Basin.

51

____

The Dynamic Past

plants and animals began to cope with isolation.

The extremes of the Hypsithermal increased the mean annual Great Basin temperature about 4.5 to 9 degrees Fahrenheit over today's averages. This does not sound like much of a difference, but the subtle gradations in the patterns of life repeatedly show how fragile and fleeting is any one incarnation of reality. When temperatures moderated to the "normal" modern regime about twenty-five hundred years ago, the landscape of today had become recognizable.

The heat is still with us. It has presence and force. A summer storm may displace it briefly, but the next day dawns clear. The sun rises into the huge sky, and the desert returns as if from the ground, like an animal drawn to light.

That we cannot risk complacency about this landscape is obvious. We may simply be pass-ing through another interglacial, due for a fifth major Quaternary glaciation in a few thousand years. We have profound power to alter the land ourselves, changing whole plant provinces through livestock grazing or agriculture, snuffing out wide-ranging species of animals. Unpredictability seems the most predictable characteristic of this place. This book will not go out of date as fast as a newspaper. But that it will become obsolete is an absolute. Give it five thousand years.

The Great Basin Desert's youth is startling. Think of it this way: a single ancient bristlecone pine, more than forty-five hundred years old, has lived through the entire span of what we might call the modern biological world of the Great Basin. It has lived twice as long as what we call the modern historical world. And it still lives.

5

*Each range here is like a warship stand-
ing on its own, and the Great Basin is
an ocean of loose sediment with these
mountain ranges standing in it as if they
were members of a fleet without prece-
dent, assembled at Guam to assault Ja-
pan. Some of the ranges are forty miles
long, others a hundred, a hundred and
fifty. They point generally north. The
basins that separate them—ten and fifteen miles wide—will run on for fifty, a
hundred, two hundred and fifty miles with
lone, daisy-petalled windmills standing
over sage and wild rye.*

*. . . Discounting the cry of the occa-
sional bird, the wailing of a pack of coyotes, silence—a great spatial silence—
is pure in the Basin and Range. It is a
soundless immensity with mountains in it.*

—John McPhee,
Basin and Range, 1980

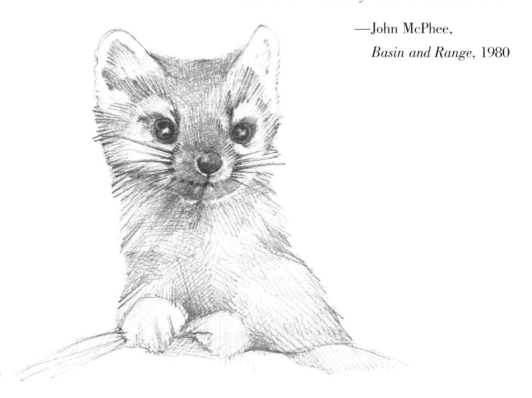

Pine marten

In the Great Basin, distances may be less fearsome than topography; isolation is a key word. A plant or animal finding itself isolated on an island mountain or in a basin walled in by mountains must cope with a surrounding sea of unlivable landscape.

In eastern Nevada, for example, the Snake, Schell Creek, and Egan ranges stand close-ranked, only fifteen miles separating their summits, which rise eleven thousand feet above sea level—and to thirteen thousand feet in the Snakes. But from the summit of one of the ranges, it is down, down, down into Spring or Steptoe valley, five thousand, six thousand, seven thousand vertical feet, from bristlecone pines and alpine meadows to salt-encrusted playas and iodine bush. From basin to basin or summit to summit is a voyage few animals or plants can make without flying—wind-borne or wing-borne.

If competition for resources grows too fierce, an individual forced out of the limited acceptable habitat on one mountain range cannot escape to an uncrowded neighboring range unless it can successfully travel across the desert floor of the basin. Likewise, if the population of a species on an island falls too low, with no new blood arriving from over the next hill, the local population may disappear.

Isolation and small (but not too small) populations can make for reduced competition and quick adoption of new genetic combinations as well. In small populations, individuals number too few for the statistical laws of natural selection to be all-important. Instead, genetic composition of the population "drifts" according to the happenstance of its founding members' inheritance and chance fluctuations in future generations. The population is not large enough for natural selection to cancel out the whims of chance and control the spread of mutant genes—even neutral ones. Thus, groups of islands—both oceanic and ecological islands—are famous for variation between populations and for the evolution of unusual species (the Galápagos Islands form a classic example).

Modern ecology and evolutionary biology began in the nineteenth century. It began on islands, with Charles Darwin alert and curious in the Galápagos and Alfred Russel Wallace wandering the East Indies. More recently, islands have kindled one of the flurries of research in the history of the science.

In 1963, Robert H. MacArthur and Edward O. Wilson proposed a theory of island biogeography that sought to predict the number of species on different kinds of islands. Their theory provided a set of predictions mostly proven wrong in subsequent research, but they stimulated biogeographers to come to the Great Basin to take advantage of its dozens of mountain ranges of differing size and isolation but with generally similar habitat—an uncommon natural pattern ideal for analysis.

Each researcher compared results with the MacArthur-Wilson model. They found that Great Basin mountain ranges do not often yield neat generalizations. But in these research results lie both new theoretical ideas and increased understanding of actual distributions.

It is not enough to say that the only conifer in northern Nevada's Pine Forest Range is whitebark pine, the neighboring Santa Rosa Range has only limber pine, while not far east, the Jarbidge Mountains support both these species plus subalpine fir. We also ask why.

In the Great Basin, such a simple question does not lead to a simple answer.

One Great Basin botanist, Arthur Cronquist, stated a "first approximation" of the answer:

> The vegetation of any region is controlled by the climate, and the taxonomic composition of the flora is determined by the climate and the history. The general nature of the fauna is in turn determined by the vegetation, and the taxonomic composition of the fauna is determined by the vegetation and the history.

Pithy diction like this requires rereading. The words are simple but full of ramifications, even in the most simplistic translation. Climate + history = vegetation. Vegetation + history = animals.

History as used here takes in more than

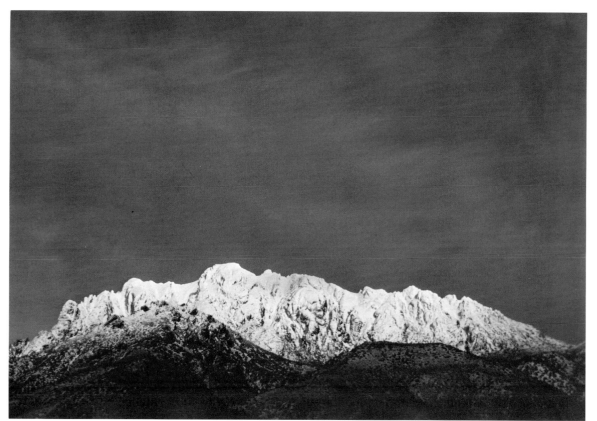

most single words can handle. It encompasses the entire span of geologic history that places the Great Basin where it is in relation to the equator, to mountain ranges, and to past continental connections. It includes the direct biological results of that long cycle: the list of animals and plants that had the opportunity to emigrate here and a parenthetical addendum of the ones that did not. History takes in all their subsequent successes and failures at surviving, as well as evolution and speciation in every region capable of launching colonists toward the Great Basin (either as fully grown immigrants or mere seeds with potential).

Finally, the history of the region involves time on a smaller scale: the daily interactions of organisms. The winners and losers of competition, the plants successfully pollinated and the ones left barren—all aspects of community ecology affecting the reproductive success of individuals (and therefore of species) and thereby controlling their distribution.

This is a considerable burden of meaning to ask one word to carry.

MacArthur and Wilson's model suggested that a constant, predictable number of species

will live on an island as colonization and extinction balance each other moment by moment. Organisms will reach an *equilibrium* species number, but since new species are always arriving and old ones going locally extinct, the *identity* of those present may change over time (species turnover).

In the Great Basin the theory met some of its major challenges. Most of the Great Basin mountain plants did not seem to arrive by long-range dispersal; most probably are remnants from the Pleistocene. They reached their current ranges when they could disperse much more easily across narrow barriers between montane islands enlarged by the cool climate. Today, colonization seems to be negligible. And yet *endemism* (distribution limited to a given geographic area) is low on Great Basin island mountains; for Basin plants, endemism on a given range always measures less than 5 percent of the total number of species.

Clark's Nutcrackers and Pinyon Jays busily caching seeds create a remarkably powerful exception to long-term sedentariness. They commonly feed on—and collect and cache seeds from—whitebark, limber, and piñon

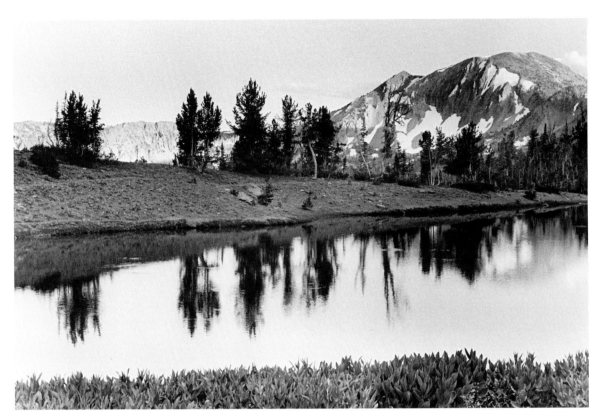

Emerald Lake and Marys River Peak in the Jarbidge Mountains, a range supporting just three conifers: whitebark pine, limber pine, and subalpine fir. A fossil marten from the range suggests once-continuous forest connections between these northernmost Nevada mountains and the northern Rockies.

pines, and less commonly, bristlecone, ponderosa, and Jeffrey pines. These birds can disperse conifer species to a new range in a single flight.

With the help of jays and nutcrackers, conifers have more access to isolated mountain ranges than most other plants. On eastern Great Basin mountains like the Snake Range, well stocked with a variety of Rocky Mountain conifers, immigration dominates extinction, and newly arriving conifers add to the forest of surviving Pleistocene relicts.

On smaller ranges, climatic fluctuations through the Holocene created drastic fluctuations in subalpine conifer populations. With remarkably detailed wood rat midden data, Philip Wells has even plotted some of the turnovers. Over a span of thirty-six hundred years, total species number on the Confusion Range of western Utah varied from two, to four, to five, to four, back to two. The last two (Rocky Mountain juniper and Douglas-fir) still survive and are different from the two (bristlecone pine and dwarf juniper) present at the beginning of the record, at full-glacial.

Great Basin island mountains have fewer bird species than cordilleran "mainlands."

Birds disperse so easily that they have colonized virtually all island mountains with suitable habitat regardless of isolation. The same impoverished habitats in several ranges support the same bird species. Ornithologists William Behle and Ned Johnson agree that habitat variety—not island area or distance from boreal mainlands—controls the number of bird species on Basin mountaintops.

The number of bird species dips lowest on the most isolated mountains. Johnson believes that this reflects isolation for all colonizing plant and animal species, resulting in general impoverishment of the island mountain's resources, particularly the plants and insects needed by birds for shelter and food. A mountain's *habitat diversity score*, measured by traits important to birds, depends primarily on coniferous tree diversity, with lesser contributions from moist communities like riverbank woodland, wet meadows, and streams and small lakes.

Permanent resident bird species, which have specific requirements not only for nesting but for food and shelter throughout the year, may have narrow habitat tolerances. Johnson gives an example: a set of ten birds, including

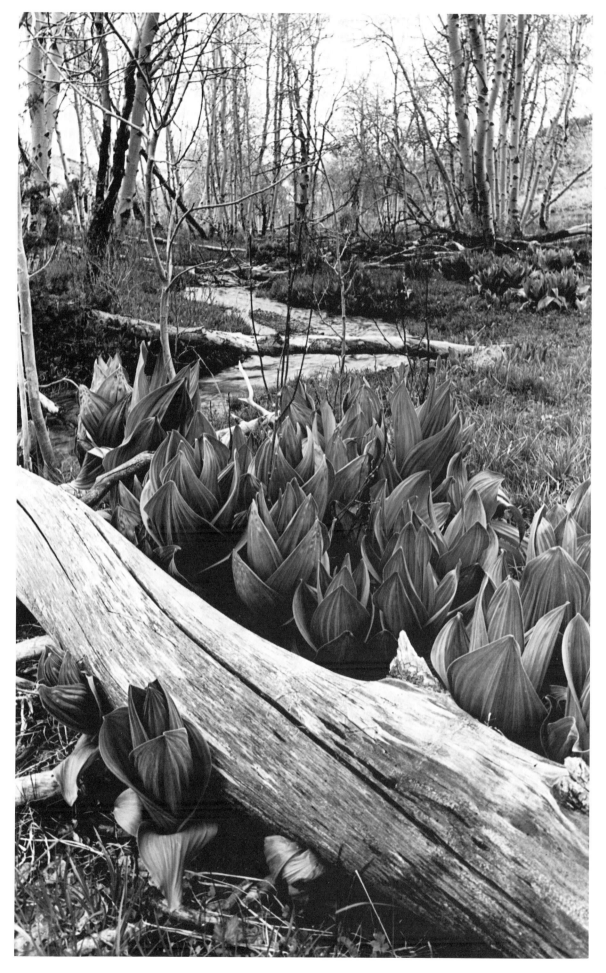

Wet meadows, like corn lily–lined Guano Creek flowing through aspen on Oregon's isolated Hart Mountain, are crucial to birds. Jays and nutcrackers may be responsible for bringing Hart Mountain its small groves of conifers.

kinglets, creepers, and sapsuckers, consistently prefer firs, and their distribution closely matches the range of the favored trees.

Boreal mammals, however, restricted to mixed coniferous forest or cool high-elevation habitats, are missing from the central Basin—species like mountain beaver, pine marten, Douglas squirrel, and heather vole. Only those boreal mammals that can survive in piñon-juniper woodland and habitats of comparable elevation live today on Basin ranges.

In his analysis of these "mammals on mountaintops," James H. Brown has tallied fourteen kinds of small boreal mammals on Great Basin island mountains; no single range supports all of them. Only six large ranges have ten or more boreal mammal species; four small ones have just three or four.

Large "islands" like the Ruby Mountains and Toiyabe Range still support mammals that need special habitats or food: the carnivorous ermine, relict on six island mountains, and the white-tailed jackrabbit, a six-and-a-half-pound herbivore dependent on large open meadows. Small plant-eaters, generalists both in feeding and habitat, persist on many islands—even small, resource-skimpy ranges in northeastern Nevada such as Spruce Mountain Ridge in the south Pequops and Pilot Peak. Uinta chipmunks survive on fifteen ranges, white-tailed jackrabbits on only two.

Mountain range area accounts for more of the variety in mammal species number than does any other single factor. There seems to be no current immigration at all to the islands.

So we have birds that avoid local extinctions by being good colonizers and mammals that cannot colonize at all, but still maintain their populations on larger islands and to a lesser degree on smaller ones. How did the mammals get here?

The answer depends on what we know of Great Basin paleohistory; Cronquist's word, "history," is all-important. When vegetation zones lowered in the Pleistocene, woodland mammals could emigrate across stepping stones of forest islands from range to range, stocking the Great Basin forest and woodland with boreal mammals. As the Basin dried out in the last eleven thousand years, woodland retreated and stranded the mammals on their newly isolated forest islands. On the smaller islands, as the forest disappeared so did the boreal mammals.

We know from wood rat middens that conifers grew much lower as recently as eight thousand years ago. And archaeologists have discovered direct evidence of past boreal mammal distribution. They have found heather vole bones in human middens about fifty-three hundred years old at Gatecliff Shelter in the central Great Basin's Toquima Range—185 miles east of the closest modern occurrence of the species. Here we have direct evidence of a restricted boreal mammal persisting on an island after Pleistocene colonization but going locally extinct before the present.

Gatecliff Shelter lies in sagebrush/piñon/juniper today, at seventy-six hundred feet. Late-Wisconsinan heather vole bones also have turned up at Smith Creek Cave in the Snake Range—even lower, at sixty-four hundred feet.

Other fossils from Great Basin caves show pikas, marmots, and pine martens living on many more ranges in late Wisconsinan than they live on at present. Pikas and white-tailed jackrabbits lived at lower elevations in Fort Rock basin, Oregon, until seven thousand years ago. Today, pikas no longer occur in this sagebrush/grass basin, and black-tailed jackrabbits have replaced white-tails as the dominant hare. Layered deposits of fossils in caves here show a gradual shift in relative abundance of the two hares through Hypsithermal times, from seven thousand to five thousand years ago. A similar decrease in the abundance of pika fossils in more recent layers at Gatecliff Shelter seems to document their gradual upward retreat in the Toquima Range.

Species such as heather voles and pikas, though generally subalpine and alpine in distribution, do not necessarily require conifers to survive; cool summers may limit their ranges. Both could have colonized Basin ranges in the cool late Wisconsinan—even across shrub-filled valleys.

On the other hand, mammals such as red squirrels, northern flying squirrels, and pine martens require continuous forests and probably needed an unbroken bridge of trees to make it into the Basin; they may have existed or may still exist undetected in the Basin (beyond the Carson Range, where the latter two still occur). A fossil marten from the Jarbidge Mountains suggests continuous forest connections with the northern Rockies.

All these factors combine to give each mountain island its distinctive personality. We interact with the nature of each range. For example, so much life exists in the lush Ruby Mountains that our visits have little effect on their spirit. So many organisms blossom and crowd and compete and clatter about here that a human presence is imperceptible. The Rubies go about their business, neither requiring nor bestowing acknowledgment.

As mountains become more alpine—from the Stillwater Range out beyond the Carson Sink, to the Carson Range, to the Sierra—they gain in power. But the number of people on their flanks, the sophistication of the trail system, the amount of resources they offer to be used—all these civilizing influences make the biggest, most powerful mountains more modified, more involved with humans than the puny, dry Basin ranges.

Major Sierra or Wasatch peaks—Mounts Ritter, Morrison, Timpanogos, or Nebo—have so many humans scurrying on them that each develops a reputation for unforgivingness or benevolence. The Goshutes, the Pueblos, or Newfoundlands have no need for such a reckoning. In this way the desert mountains remain wilder than the great peaks.

Mount Rose in the Carson Range occupies a position somewhere between. It has an instantly recognizable tone—major rather than minor, but not a heroic major like the Sierra. A secondary, spare, less important key. But absolutely not minor, like the Pancake Range or Jackson Mountains.

In the end, every island is unique, as is every kind of organism.

MacArthur and Wilson said, "The fundamental processes [in biogeography], namely dispersal, invasion, competition, adaptation, and extinction, are among the most difficult in biology to study and to understand."

Amen.

III

Between the Mountains
Valleys of Silence

Playas and Salt Deserts

6

Multitudes visit the Great Salt Lake daily during the summer. . . . Not one in a thousand knows of the weird horrors of its western coast.

There lies the only real desert of America. . . . Thousands of square miles as flat and void of vegetation as the cement floor of a warehouse; not even a sprig of sage brush, not a lizard, a spider nor a slinking coyote; not a drop of water—no moisture except seeps of liquid poison— no foothold to walk upon, for when dry the surface is a glittering, thin, crackling mosaic that crumbles at every step, and underneath the crust is like wood ashes. When wet it becomes the fatal gumbo clay. . . .

This desert is called "The White Death" . . . and . . . men dare the damned menace and sometimes cross it . . . without any apparent reason, unless—

Unless his soul demands the freedom of vast expanses filled with the verve and tang of untainted air, dry and electric, making the heart beat fiercely and the mind to work keenly. When he can be he. . . . If these thoughts prevail, then, for him, the rest of the world may go. . . . To him the desert is sufficient.

—H. L. A. Culmer,
The Scenic Glories of Utah, 1909

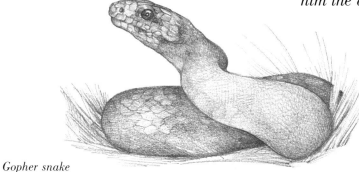

Gopher snake

A flat playa of clay, often salt-encrusted, gleams in the low point of a typical basin. Great Basin biogeography starts in the white glare of these centers and goes outward and upward. The story of colonization begins with the edge of the playa, created only a few thousand years ago, a frontier of salinity tolerable to only a few terrestrial plants.

Salts accumulate in the central sump of each internal drainage, making soils alkaline—and tough on plants. Where salt crusts over the surface, it poisons the land. When Dr. James Schiel penetrated the Great Salt Lake Desert with the 1854 Gunnison-Beckwith expedition, he proclaimed: "If the eye of a man of ancient Greece had seen this sight, he would have located the entrance to the underworld here."

The two largest basins hold the two largest playas: the Black Rock and Great Salt Lake deserts. Clay mostly surfaces the former, salt the latter. Both, strangely, were major overland routes in the 1800s, for though waterless they were flat, for which oxen and wagon masters gave thanks.

The Black Rock Desert seems a trifle more friendly than the Bonneville Salt Flats. A variety of people frequent its intense landscape. In a way, the same barrenness attracts them all. History buffs come to search for traces of the Applegate Trail preserved in the desert. In the mountains encircling the playa, rock hounds, often retirees, comb for geodes, fire opals, fossils, and the desert's strange and graceful crescentic arrowheads. Dirt bikers and off-road-vehicle rednecks find empty and rugged country for their machines. And desert rats in search of the ultimate solitary experience come close to finding it here. (The racing crowd brings jet-powered vehicles to the Black Rock Desert, as they do to the Bonneville Salt Flats, to run at record speeds. They do not camp; they stay in motels in Gerlach. The local cafe sells baseball caps with the town motto, "Gerlach, Nevada—where the pavement ends and the West begins.")

On the playa, no detail distinguishes one campsite from another. I do not turn the steering wheel sharply to angle into a sheltered canyon or choice streamside pull-out. I simply let the truck roll to a stop on the huge sun-baked mud pan, giving myself to the exhilarating freedom of its space.

Empty landscapes like the Black Rock playa seem somehow to pay attention to the entrance of a human. Each of us makes a difference; we make the land more alive. We feel a change in the reality of the place because we are there. Perhaps this is why writer Barry Lopez calls the Black Rock Desert "a stage."

People add an overlay of communion. They make the unearthly playa landscape more real by acknowledgment.

Elemental time and space play round every perception of the Black Rock Desert. Some say you can feel the curvature of the earth out in the playa's center. The sky becomes more than a dome over land, it becomes an envelope surrounding the sphere of the planet.

Playas form the flattest natural topography on earth. Nowhere else is the Great Basin Desert reduced to such simple elements.

Still, the dry surface varies remarkably with the light. With the first hint of dawn, the clay floor of the playa emerges from colorless starlight into a sweep of gray-blue. Then a slow shift from gray to deep tan. The wait from first color to actual sunrise feels like hours: it seems well into the morning when the sun finally pops up from behind Black Rock.

At first, the cracks in the mud all cast shadows, modeling the playa in sharp detail. Then colors blend and warm as the sun inches higher, and detail gives way to great hazy blocks of soft tints. Flat matte dominates in texture, accentuating the sharp angles and deeper tones seen only in the mountains and in the sunken polygonal mud cracks. Distances begin to deceive. Receding mountains float off into the haze. Only an hour after dawn, mirages have started. One desert devotee said to me of the Black Rock country: "It wouldn't surprise me a bit to see a dinosaur step out from behind a rock."

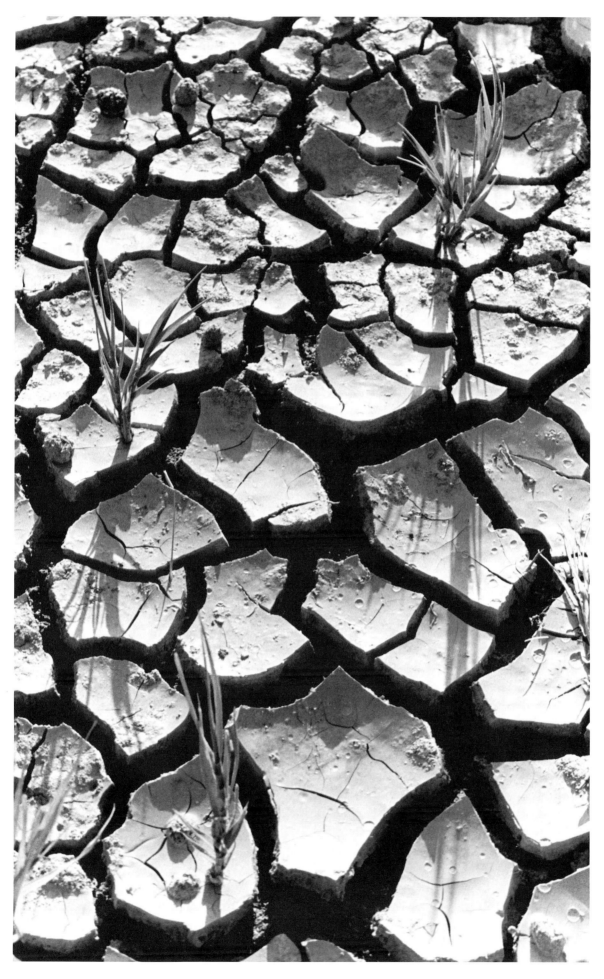

Stiff-leaved saltgrass—with the widest ranging salt tolerance of any salt desert plant—grows through brittle curls of clay along the edge of Nevada's Smoke Creek Desert.

Distribution of playas in the Great Basin Desert. (Based on Holmgren, 1972)

66

———

Between the Mountains

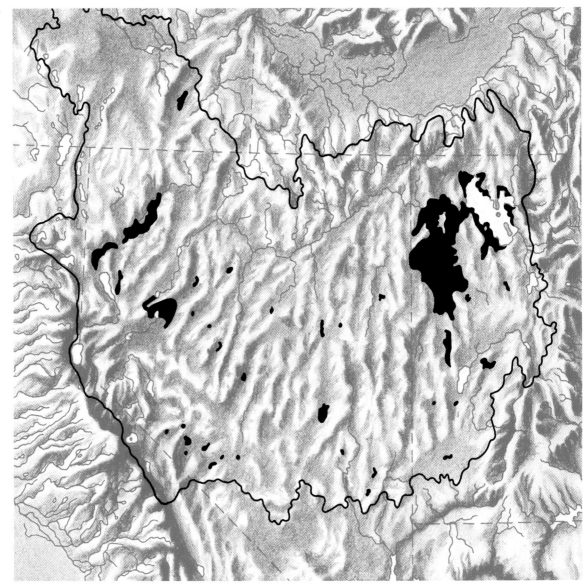

In the days when the Applegate-Lassen trail crossed the Black Rock Desert, teams of oxen sometimes stampeded toward such mirages, thinking they saw lakes shimmering out there. Their carcasses littered the lines of wagon ruts leading toward Black Rock Spring. The forty-niners called it the Death Route—"an abomination of desolation."

This one basin feels like a whole earth: the clean, white, hard-edged line of the playa rim circling round at eye level, the narrow band of sharp-angled mountains just above. Clockwise from Gerlach: the Granite Range, Calico Mountains, Black Rock Range, the Jackson Mountains, Pahsupp Mountain, and the Selenite Range. Three landmarks draw the eye: the dark focal point of the Black Rock itself, the

crags of King Lear Peak in the Jackson Mountains, and the pyramid of Pahsupp.

The mountains form a ribbon of familiar landscape separating two vast spaces, blue haze above, a mosaic of cracked mud below. The desert almost seems to mirror the sky in size. It complements it and completes it.

The boldest line of all is the sun track over the playa. It has the simplicity of a single wire stretched taut across the thirty-mile width of featureless mud. Only a jet's vapor trail, blown fuzzy, overwhelms it, splitting the blue dome of morning like a slash.

Other clouds sail over the playas: summer thunderheads and the dreary gray curtains of winter cold fronts. Summer storms come

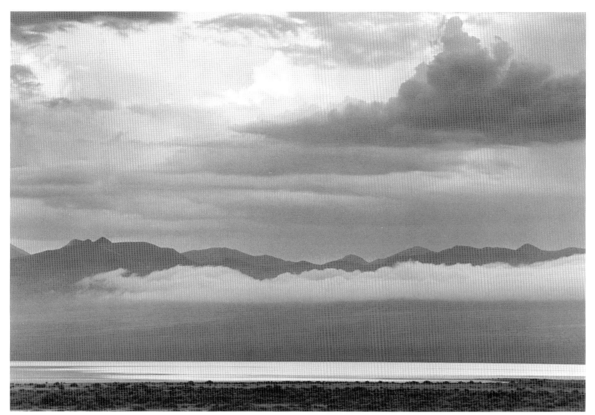

*Railroad Valley
playa, full from
summer rains,
a rule of silver
below blue clouds
hanging over the
Quinn Canyon
Range.*

67

---

*Playas and
Salt Deserts*

quickly and violently, usually not flooding a playa for long.

Dusk in Railroad Valley. The playa is full from summer rain, a rule of silver below blue clouds hanging low over the Quinn Canyon Range, the high peaks poking through the clouds in crags, like decorative carving on chair backs lined up around a table. The separation of the tops of the mountains from their bases increases their stature. They feel huge. The silver line of the wet playa seems strange and out of place, as if a graphic designer had retouched the scene, adding the line for some trick illustration in an annual report.

With winter rain and snow, however, the dry lake beds become real lakes—enormous still sheets of shallow water. With about two inches of precipitation, the playa comes to life. For in the mud lie seeds, spores, eggs, and estivating adult invertebrates, waiting for water and re-hydration to swirl into activity. A flooded playa has a wealth of living crustaceans, insects, phytoplankton, and algae—all furiously re-producing as quickly as they can. As the temporary lake dries, the water grows saltier and

saltier, and the playa community retreats into the mud to wait once more.

Fairy, clam, and tadpole shrimp most consistently inhabit playa waters. Their resting eggs have survived in dried playa mud for fifteen years. But the longer the flooding, the more insects invade, including winged insects drawn to the water. Plants provide little food for these islands of aquatic life. Most of the food for the bottom rung of the playa food chain comes from organic debris washed into the playa by floods.

Stormwaters drain quickly off the bare ranges. On their descent toward a basin, flash floods erode layer after layer from the mountains and deposit sediment in neatly sorted bands. Heavy boulders and gravels drop first from the flood, then pebbles, then silt, and lastly, fine clays. Such soil textures influence plant distribution as strongly as climate and elevation.

Each kind of soil has an inherent ability to hold water. Particle size—from larger sand grains to silt to finest clay—determines if soil can hold water, permit leaching, or raise moisture from the water table through capillary action.

When rain moistens dry clay, it swells and refuses to absorb more water. Any additional precipitation pools on the surface and drains in sheets to the lower basins, filling playas and flooding greasewood flats. Sandy soils drain, however, and salts can leach away, allowing plants to survive there that need deep, well-aerated soil (like sagebrush). Loam is the intermediate texture, containing mostly sand and silt in nearly equal amounts with only a small proportion of clay.

As rocks weather and release salts (and as Pleistocene lakes dry up and leave behind their minerals), meager precipitation in the Great Basin does not wash them away, as happens in wetter places. Salts remain in the soil; only their depth varies. Such salty soil may not be alkaline (as opposed to acidic). If the primary salt is sodium, however, the soils are both saline and alkaline. Most westerners use the two words interchangeably.

As salts increase in the soil surrounding the roots of a plant, water leaves the plant roots for the surrounding soil because the soil water is salty—much saltier than the water in the roots. In official jargon, the *osmotic potential* in the soil increases; the roots lose water until the water potentials on both sides of its cell membranes are equal. The roots have a tough time absorbing water in the other direction, and the plant finds itself dealing with physiological drought.

Some plants tolerate high salt intake and secrete excess salts from special cells (some saltbushes, for example), or have succulent leaves (as do greasewood and iodine bush) with more dilute salts in their cell tissue. Others cannot live in salty soil, stymied by both lack of soil moisture and toxic sodium. Each species has its own threshold.

Some plants have remarkably specific texture requirements. Big sagebrush grows in sands, sandy loams, or loams, but rarely in clays. Greasewood, on the other hand, will tolerate any soil texture encountered in a basin such as Dugway Valley.

The total soil moisture available creates the real limit on distribution of plants in Great Basin valleys. Effective precipitation depends not just on the amount of rainfall but also on the interaction of incoming water with the soil texture, depth, and surface slope; depth of water penetration and drainage; and the vertical distribution of salt.

Seville Flowers, who studied the Great Salt Lake Desert for many years, called it "one of the most forbidding deserts on this continent." Interstate 80, in its traverse of the Bonneville Salt Flats, passes by a last few shrubs on either rim of this absolute desert. Iodine bush, glasswort, desert blite, and saltgrass: these are their identities. Here there should be a roadside memorial to their difficulties and their success.

What makes a playa a playa is the presence of a seasonal lake bed. Even when the playa looks dry, wet mud often lies just below the surface, as many can testify who have tried to drive across what looks like a bone-dry crust on the Great Salt Lake or Black Rock deserts. Iodine bush fringes the lifeless playas, where the water table lies perhaps five feet below the surface. By one 1965 estimate, it covers 9 percent of the Utah section of the Great Basin.

Salt is the crux of the environment for succulent, segmented iodine bush. This plant can tolerate soil salt concentrations up to 5 percent as a full-grown shrub. But its seeds germinate only in concentrations of less than 0.1 percent.

The trick: iodine bush must find a way to germinate in a less hostile environment, then take advantage of its ability to survive in saltier soil. The plant does this by growing on sandy or silty hummocks where wind piles soil around an object or natural rise on the clay flats. As the iodine bushes become larger they build up litter and bind soil until their hummocks can reach two feet high and six feet in width. Here precipitation leaches surface salts sufficiently to allow germination of windblown iodine bush seeds. Deeper in the hummocks under the plants, soils contain up to 5 percent salt.

Between iodine bush clumps, however, cap-

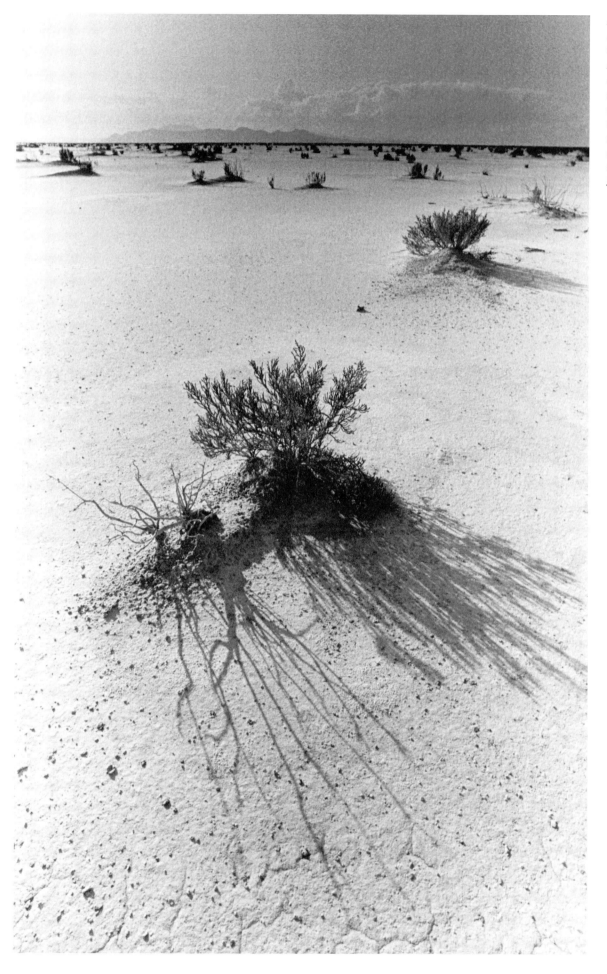

*Iodine bush
hummocks in the
Great Salt Lake
Desert: salt
concentrations
in the soil deep
under the plants
reach 5 percent;
the unvegetated
crust surrounding
them can measure
22 percent salt.*

illary action pumps groundwater to the surface, where it evaporates and leaves a mineralized crust that can measure an inch thick and 22 percent salt.

A few glasswort, greasewood, and, in places, a saltsage (*Atriplex tridentata*) survive on iodine bush hummocks. But they remain scanty and stunted. In an intensive study of the Great Salt Lake Desert's plant and rodent communities, E. Dean Vest found only two resident rodents in iodine bush flats in Dugway Valley: the deer mouse and Ord's kangaroo rat. Both animals burrowed in the mounds and fed on iodine bush.

Seville Flowers observed pioneering on the old Bonneville playa by both iodine bush and glasswort; they tolerated about the same degree of salinity. Glasswort, however, showed the narrowest range of tolerance for alkali, one form (*Sarcocornia utahensis*) growing where even iodine bush cannot, when pH measured an extremely alkaline 9.0 or more.

In succession, saltgrass commonly followed iodine bush, and desert blite followed glasswort; all but desert blite can reclaim a playa singlehandedly, forming pure stands. Tough little saltgrass seems to have the widest range of salt tolerance of any salt desert plant; saltgrass at a playa near Goshen, Utah, tolerated 1,211 to 26,533 parts per million total soluble salts.

Saltgrass has invaded freshly exposed beaches along the fluctuating shores of both Great Salt Lake and Pyramid Lake and thrives in the shallow water around the edges of some of the more dependably flooded playas. Since it sprouts from long underground rhizomes, shoots of saltgrass at the leading edge of an expanding meadow come up in ranks and files of new individuals. Still, not every playa succumbs to succession. Some remain bare and unvegetated.

Dwight Billings described alkaline communities in the Carson Desert region comparable to those of the Bonneville basin. In his Lahontan basin sites, perennial iodine bush—even at its densest—covered only about 6 percent of the total area. The annual red saltwort, on the other hand, grew as densely as 1,260 plants per square foot. It formed "a prominent zone along the edges of small channels of water running into a playa," where soils were strongly saline and wetter than those under iodine bush. Red saltwort, like iodine bush, turns orange or red in autumn and outlines these small streams in fall with a strip of succulent scarlet.

These are the true salt desert plants. Though they grow in saltier soil than most plants, they dominate here not because they require salt but because they can tolerate it. They can cope with a maximum of three to seven times the osmotic stress of their next closest competitor, greasewood.

Understanding greasewood distribution is tricky. The first two feet of soil under greasewood stands measure no saltier than under shadscale. At deeper levels, however, salt increases sharply to as much as 1.6 percent. Soils are not drastically different, precipitation measures no greater, but still, more surface moisture has carried salts lower in the greasewood areas.

This deeper salt layer tied to large amounts of surface moisture forms the key to greasewood distribution. For example, when rain or snowmelt floods the flats in the Dugway basin, the extent of water coincides perfectly with the limits of greasewood stands.

At the base of dunes that pool water after summer storms you find greasewood. Along drainageways from ravines outward to the flats, greasewood grows in a salt-tolerant diminutive streamside "woodland." On the most favorable sites it can grow fifteen feet high. The shrub can die back two-thirds in dry years, then recover with phenomenal growth when rains return, producing new branches up to three and one-half feet long in a single season.

Greasewood commonly taps groundwater at depths of twenty-five or thirty feet. Over the years, as water tables rise and fall, greasewood moves with them. On Hot Springs Flat, northeast of Fernley, Nevada, Dwight Billings found numerous dead greasewood bushes well out in a shallow lake on the rise. In a greasewood

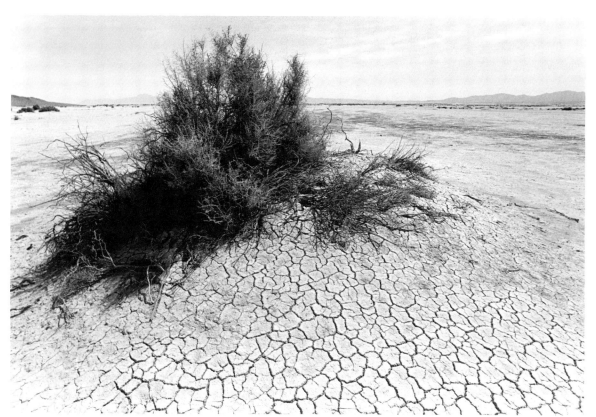

A rangy
greasewood in the
Black Rock Desert
can tap
groundwater at
depths of up to
thirty feet.

71

———

Playas and
Salt Deserts

stand near Fallon, Nevada, near land drained for agriculture, dead cattail rhizomes studded the soil between shrubs: greasewood was on the march here, taking over the drying lake.

Pure greasewood stands support many kinds of rodents, primarily as an overflow area when adjacent sand dunes are crowded. Greasewood maintains high jackrabbit populations as well. Resident birds and mammals closely resemble sagebrush communities, likely because plant cover, density, and height are similar in the two—both dominated by a single good-sized shrub. Sage Thrashers, shrikes, Sage Sparrows, and Brewer's Sparrows, for instance, favor both greasewood and sagebrush.

No need to count leaves or examine hairs with a microscope to identify greasewood—its color is unmistakable. In summer its bright green seems an anomaly: it excels in living in true salt desert where little else can, yet even here it looks lush. Salts or not, greasewood has the unmasked green of ferns and moss and cottonwood trees—the green bestowed by abundant water.

Greasewood shares its summer lushness

with deciduous trees, and it turns yellow-green in autumn, giving the basins their fall color. In winter, greasewood loses its leaves, making summer green that much more startling when the winter-gray shrub leafs out come April.

On the night of the summer solstice, I camped between greasewood bushes at the edge of the Smoke Creek Desert. At dusk it seemed that a remarkable event should happen. A shaft of light pinpointing a Paiute shrine, perhaps. The full moon sailing up over the playa. A glorious sunset.

But no special shows came to the desert that evening. As the sun set, the playa softly faded from gold to pale dun to muted blues and grays. Twilight. A star. Two stars. A third, then it disappeared. It came back, and I lay down in my sleeping bag.

The stars brightened as the darkness deepened. Sometime during the night I awoke and saw four great columns of colorless light in the northern sky. Northern lights? They flickered and disappeared, leaving me alone with space and time and pale starlight on the playa.

Shadscale

The New Desert

7

The highway went down into a narrow and immensely long, thunder-of-hooves valley, then, like a chalkline, headed north, running between two low mountain ranges, the higher eastern one still in snow. A sign: NEXT GAS 80 MILES.

. . . Squat clumps of white sage, wet from a shower out of the western range, sweetened the air, and gulches had not yet emptied. Calm lay over the uncluttered openness, and a damp wind blew everything clean. . . . there was no one. Listening, I walked into the scrub. The desert does its best talking at night, but on that spring evening it kept God's whopping silence; and that too is a desert voice.

I've read that a naked eye can see six thousand stars in the hundred billion galaxies, but I couldn't believe it, what with the sky white with starlight. I saw a million stars with one eye and two million with both.

—William Least Heat Moon,
Blue Highways, 1982

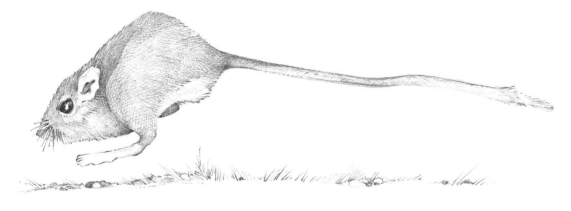

*Chisel-toothed
kangaroo rat*

There is something masculine about the Great Basin Desert—shadscale and sagebrush all compact, stiff, gnarly, and gray-green. Creosote bush of the hot deserts has more grace and animation with its willowy branches and decorative furry fruits. Hot deserts have the blooms of cactus; palm oases; Papago and Apache women. Southern heat, too, is feminine, in opposition to Great Basin cold.

In some places, you can sense the tension between cold and hot deserts. Along the southern rim of the shadscale desert you can still feel the dynamics of shrubs wheeling and dealing for a place to live. These brand-new communities are still evolving, still adapting to the environmental revolution wrought by the end of the Ice Age. The climatic transition is diffuse enough to make the resident array of plants unpredictable.

A creosote bush stand at Hiko in Pahranagat Valley lives north of its compatriots. On the passes west of Caliente, Joshua trees lap Great Basin Desert mountains. When I drive southward down Meadow Valley Wash from Caliente to Elgin, around one bend I come to a big arborescent cholla. The next turn brings the first Mojave yucca, then soon comes creosote.

Driving into the wheat and hay fields around Promontory Point after braving the Great Salt Lake Desert seems oddly jarring, almost disappointing. It feels like Holland, where the wild ocean has been diked and filled and turned into tulip fields. Here the Mormon farmers have domesticated Bonneville basin shadscale scrub—spiny and austere—and transformed it into cheerful green alfalfa.

T. H. Kearney and his colleagues described healthy shadscale stands in Tooele Valley in 1914: "No other vegetation in this valley gives the impression of being so nearly conquered by the environment. Even the few species which grow on the salt flats have the appearance of finding their habitat more congenial." Taken for sagebrush by the uninitiated, shadscale, *Atriplex confertifolia*, is not an *Artemisia*. In places, prickly gray seas of shadscale grow in nearly pure expanses. But most shadscale communities include large numbers of one or two other shrubs, all looking parched, like they were "crafted from cornflakes," in naturalist Elna Bakker's words.

Shadscale and its companion plants that tolerate even more salt dominate three great networks of valleys below about fifty-five hundred feet. Near Tonopah along the southern rim of the Great Basin Desert, shadscale forms an ecotone separating the creosote and sagebrush zones where winters are too cold for creosote bush and where the climate is too dry for sagebrush. Here shadscale—with a wider tolerance for extremes in temperature, aridity, and salty soil than either of these two dominant plants—looks out over the shimmering heat waves rising from the Mojave Desert. In most of this section, it looks outward without benefit of human companions, its range off-limits to the public in the Nevada Test Site.

Along this transition from Mojave to Great Basin Desert, the overall climatic change (from south to north, from drier to colder) controls the change from creosote bush to sagebrush. Especially on stony limestone soils, blackbrush rather than shadscale can form the ecotone between sagebrush and creosote. On a smaller scale within each basin, local topography (determining air circulation and inversions) and soils (textures and salt content) dictate the patterns in vegetation.

Farther north, shadscale covers vast areas open to colonization by terrestrial plants for just ten thousand years. Too dry for sagebrush, the Lahontan basin remains the domain of shadscale and its allies. In the Bonneville basin, physiological drought (maintained by salty soils) as well as climatic drought determines the limits of shadscale: soils may be wet enough for sagebrush but their salt content makes them unusable.

A century of livestock grazing and invasion by exotic plants has overlain a veneer of new pressures that shift this plant mosaic like an ever-changing puzzle. Trying to pin down the communities and put them on a map is like sorting jellyfish on glare ice.

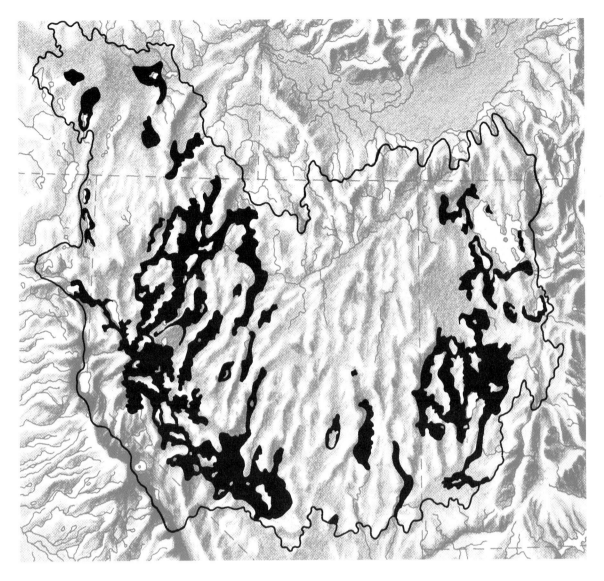

Distribution of the shadscale community in the Great Basin Desert. (Based on Holmgren, 1972; and Barbour and Major, 1977)

75

———

Shadscale

On the journey outward from the alkaline heart of a playa through concentric circles of plant communities toward enclosing mountain ranges, past greasewood comes shadscale. Shadscale ranges upward from where it grows as small plants on valley flats—where it may be three-quarters dead, barely tolerating summer drought and its maximum 0.8 percent soil salt concentration—to the tops of the smaller mountains on dry slopes. Along this spectrum, only dunes where sands reach deeper than ten inches lack shadscale.

Bailey's (little) greasewood dominates shadscale country in the Lahontan basin, totaling over 50 percent of the shrubby cover. Shadscale itself covers about 20 percent. Cooper's desert thorn, another shrub not found in the Utah basins, helps to make Lahontan valleys distinctive. These shrubs occur predictably on

mature soils in the region wherever annual precipitation drops below seven inches.

Bailey's greasewood has continued to grow where it did during the high-level lake stage: on the old Lahontan shoreline in soil not particularly salty nor with a high water table. Widespread big greasewood has invaded the Lahontan basin in its familiar habitats but does not grow where little greasewood does. The ancestors of Bailey's greasewood evidently were isolated here when most greasewood retreated south during the Pleistocene; when big greasewood returned, the stranded local population had become distinct physically and ecologically.

In the Bonneville basin, neither Bailey's greasewood nor Cooper's desert thorn occur, and shadscale dominates more authoritatively. Here its companion shrubs are green molly, littleleaf horsebrush, and bud sagebrush. These

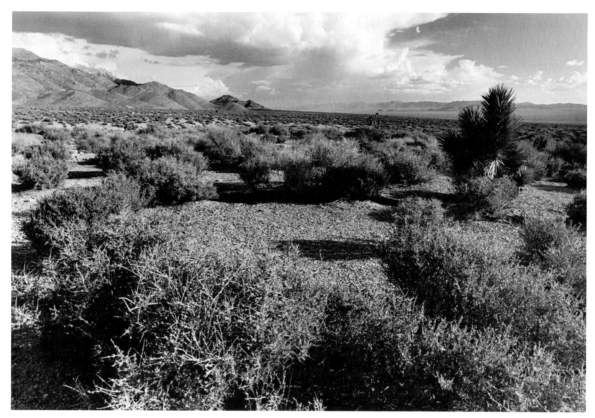

The tension between cold and hot deserts along the southern rim of the shadscale desert in Ticaboo Valley: here blackbrush and Joshua trees mark the last band of Great Basin vegetation before the Mojave Desert's creosote bushes.

shadscale communities cover 20 percent of the Great Basin in Utah.

In numbers, green molly rules many of the shadscale stands much as little greasewood does in the Lahontan basin. But molly is small and inconspicuous. It also has not fared well with the coming of civilization and seems considerably less abundant now than fifty or one hundred years ago, evidently as a result of disturbance from livestock or invading annual plants. Littleleaf horsebrush favors coarse soils—gravels at the heads of alluvial fans and dune sands.

In Dugway Valley, find any loam (never sand or clay) where the upper foot is low in salt and you will find bud sagebrush: in the foothills on shallow loams among shadscale, or in the flats in narrow bands a few feet wide within its tolerance for clays, sands, and salts. Elsewhere, its tolerance for soil textures seems a bit broader.

Bud sagebrush avoids summer drought by flowering and fruiting at the first chance come spring. Finished with its water-needy chores by early summer, it drops its leaves and goes dormant through the intense summer drought—

and suffers that intensity hardly at all. In mixed shadscale and bud sagebrush, chisel-toothed kangaroo rats are the dominant rodent: they burrow in soil with the same characteristics that meet bud sagebrush's needs, and they feed almost exclusively on shadscale.

In all these shadscale communities, if the water table is high enough, greasewood may occur, mixed in with the smaller gray shrubs. Loamy mounds at the bases of greasewood allow many more burrowing rodents than in pure shadscale stands. Billings found greasewood/shadscale communities particularly common around the smaller, drier playas at higher elevations around the Carson Desert.

Islands of winterfat lie in the matrix of shadscale throughout these valleys. Stock raisers gave winterfat its name, using its tender shoots as crucial winter forage for their animals. Also called whitesage, though neither a sage nor a sagebrush, this small, feathery, light-colored shrub stands out conspicuously in the darker grays and greens of shadscale flats. Its low stature makes a valley dominated by winterfat feel like a prairie or a manicured desert golf

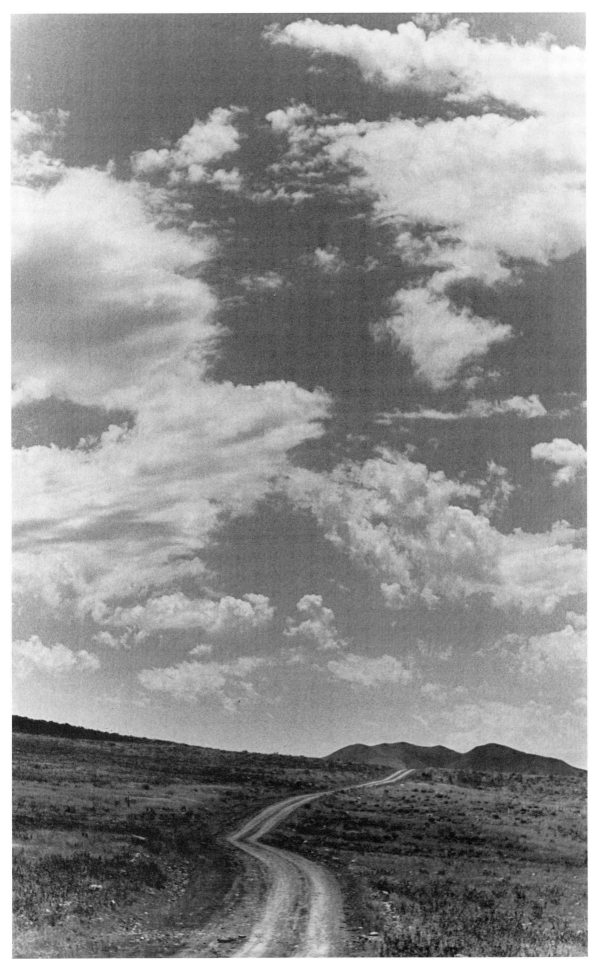

Driving a hundred miles on a dirt road without meeting another car is a likely adventure in Great Basin shadscale and sagebrush country.

course—much gentler than shadscale or sagebrush.

I have an inordinate fondness for winterfat, and I am not even a livestock raiser with an eye for good range. When I have been numbed by too many dusty miles of spiny gray, with humble molly and other anonymous members of the salt desert plant community demanding identification, winterfat's distinctive and surprising tenderness and softness of color and texture refresh my soul.

Long regarded as an indicator of less salty soil, recent work has detected considerable variation in the plant. It grows on well-drained soil but can handle a variety of low salt concentrations. Winterfat plants from different locations germinate at different levels of salinity, varying too much in tolerance to make much of a signpost for low salinity. Indeed, winterfat has the widest distribution of any salt desert plant, growing from Canada to Mexico and from Kansas to California, at elevations from two thousand to ten thousand feet, and living with annual average precipitation from four inches to forty.

When mixed with other shrubs, winterfat generally grows larger and woodier than in its pure stands. The latter—whitesage flats—may owe their abrupt boundaries to trace minerals or to changes in soil texture associated with shallow flooding from adjacent washes. Historic events, such as random colonization, may determine the pattern. As yet, we simply do not know why sharply defined winterfat islands break up the basins brimful of shadscale.

As they do everywhere from the driest valleys to alpine tundra, deer mice thrive in shadscale flats. Few other rodents do as well. One deer mouse cache in Dugway Valley consisted of 55 percent fresh shadscale leaves and leaf buds, 30 percent whole shadscale seeds, 5 percent shelled seeds, 4 to 6 percent freshly gathered terminal tips of shadscale, and a remaining 4 to 6 percent dried green molly leaves.

In Idaho's Raft River valley, deer mice live in both sagebrush and shadscale, but in pristine stands of the latter, chisel-toothed kan-

garoo rats dominate, sometimes completely. The chisel-tooth and deer mice populations counterbalance each other in shadscale: when grazing depletes shadscale, chisel-tooth populations go down and deer mice populations go up.

Chisel-toothed kangaroo rats have side-stepped competition with other desert rodents; they have adapted to eating shadscale leaves almost exclusively—an abundant resource few other animals want. The standard kangaroo rat has narrow, awl-shaped lower incisors; these rats have modified, flattened chisels.

In spring, when shadscale leaves are sweet and succulent, chisel-toothed kangaroo rats eat them whole. The rest of the year, the rats pass each leaf over their sharp incisors about ten times, shaving off and discarding the outer layers and eating only the inner tissue. In such dry shadscale leaves the sodium content of inner tissue measures only 3 percent of that in layers shaved off by the rat. In this way, the chisel-tooths not only reduce salt intake and ease water balance problems, they step out of the competitive struggle for seeds altogether.

In Dugway Valley, if a few greasewood plants occur in the shadscale, chisel-toothed kangaroo rats live in burrows at their bases (though feeding on the tips and leaves of the shadscale). Of the daytime-active rodents, least chipmunks and antelope ground squirrels also burrow under greasewood, the former dominating toward the flats, the latter toward the foothills.

Reed Fautin published an analysis of the animals of shadscale and salt desert communities in the Bonneville basin in 1946. He found patterns recognizable to naturalists all over the desert West. Only Horned Larks, Black-throated Sparrows, and Rock Wrens nested in these shrubs, the latter solely in rocky horsebrush habitat.

Fautin's reptile list included abundant side-blotched lizards, progressively scarcer from the base of the mountains to the valley floor. Leopard lizards thrived, eating everything from nine-inch whiptail lizards to grasshoppers. Gopher snakes and rattlesnakes lived in all the communities from shadscale to iodine bush.

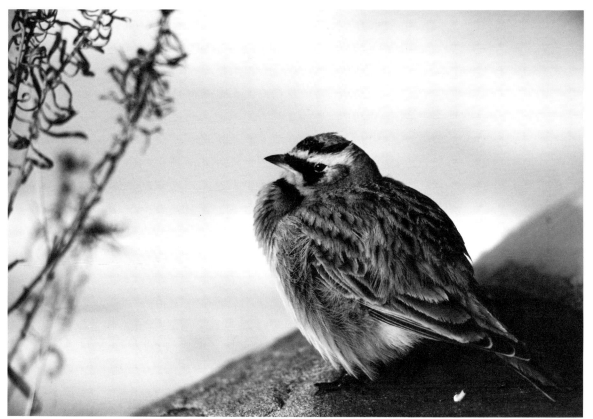

Along with this Horned Lark, Black-throated Sparrows and Rock Wrens are the only nesting birds in salt desert shrub communities in the Bonneville basin.

Eric Pianka, an expert on lizard diversity, suggests that the relatively stable pattern of rainfall in the Great Basin (compared with the unpredictable hot deserts) restricts the number of life forms in plants and that the simple vegetative structure (a sea of shrubs instead of the complicated cactus and Joshua tree forests with their understories) restricts the number of lizard species (no more than six of the twelve species common in the hot deserts).

Fautin tallied more than one hundred invertebrate species in the denser stands of salt desert scrub. Homopterans (cicadas, hoppers, whiteflies, aphids, and scale insects) were the most frequent and abundant insects. Some nine hundred arthropod species occur (in more recent studies) in mixed sagebrush/shadscale in Curlew Valley. But we know little of their ecology.

Tenebrionid beetles (including the common "stink beetles" in the genus *Eleodes*) are conspicuous, harvester ants even more so. The bare discs of the latter can account for up to 10 percent of shadscale landscapes, but plant productivity goes up along the edges of their feeding areas, so the loss of total potential veg-

etation is less than the simple area of their nests would suggest.

Heteromyid rodents (kangaroo rats and mice; pocket mice) dominated all shadscale and salt desert communities, except in greasewood, which they shared with deer mice and harvest mice.

Kangaroo rat burrows provided refuges for animals from scorpions to lizards. Rat burrows also broke up the hard alkaline caliche crust, allowing winterfat to grow where otherwise it could not. Within winterfat islands, the little shrubs grew twice as high on kangaroo rat mounds, where the rodents aerated and fertilized the soil. Several predators ate kangaroo rats as their primary diet: Burrowing Owls, kit foxes, badgers, and coyotes.

I often hear coyotes call from several directions when I stop to watch something— a storm, a sunset. I do not hear them on first stopping, only toward the end of the event— as the storm dissipates, as the color fades, as I quit photographing and relax. I cannot know for sure, but I always have the feeling that they, too, have paused to watch and that they strike up their chorus after they have finished

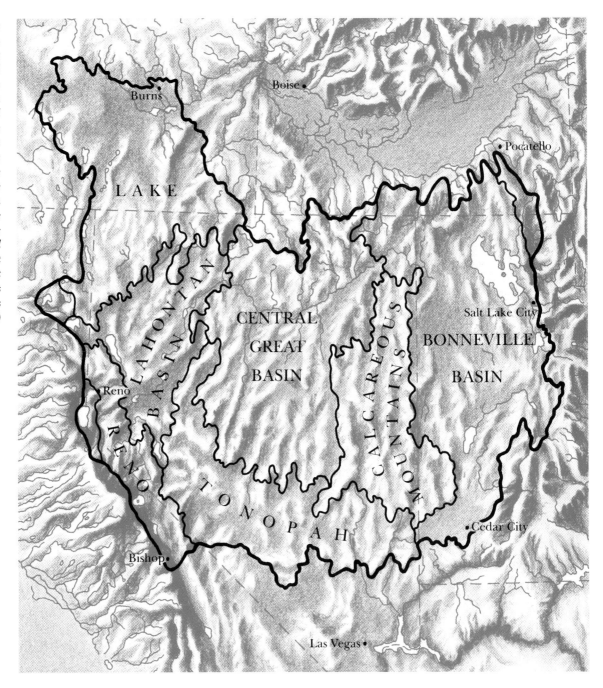

observing these events as dusk approaches and they prepare to trot out for the night's hunt.

Untangling the story of Basin biogeography resembles a game of multi-dimensional chess. At the beginning of the game the givens—the playing pieces—are the animals and plants present in nearby centers of dispersal. The crucial dimensions include the obvious—elevation, longitude, latitude, and climate. More subtle in their effects are time, behavioral interactions, speciation, colonization, and extinction. Just as in chess, a single, seemingly innocuous move along one dimension can dra-

matically change the outcome.

Botanists include the three great expanses of shadscale desert in three floristic sections reasonably congruent with the simple map of the shrub's dominance: the Lahontan basin, Bonneville basin, and Tonopah sections. Why shadscale dominates these areas in particular leads us to look at the Great Basin in sweeping perspective rather than valley by valley and to think in terms of change through time.

Mammalogists agree closely with the botanists about the distinctiveness of these areas. In 1977, David Armstrong slightly refined Stephen Durrant's 1952 map of Utah mammal

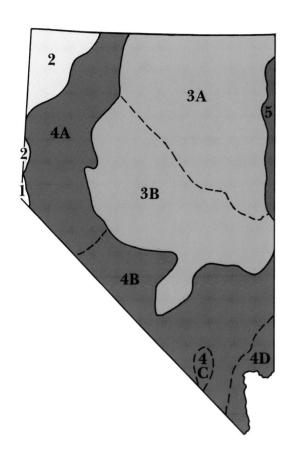

On Reveal's map of the 6,560-foot (2,000-meter) contour, the Lahontan corridor expands still further, a broad trough funneling southern species northward. The Bonneville basin barely opens in the southwest corner of Utah, remaining abruptly separated by the Pine Valley Mountains from the Mojave Desert to the south.

The Mojave Desert indeed ends below Tonopah. Regardless of physical ease of colonization, colder climates northward eliminate most hot desert plants and animals. Still, many move north into the recently opened habitats of the Lahontan valleys. From reptiles to mammals, a variety of animals have taken advantage of the dispersal route. Four species of lizards characterize all North American deserts. Of the eight additional species in southern deserts, only two range northward into the Basin, and the Lahontan trough forms their path.

Many plants, too, move north through the trough. Even Joshua trees extend into the Great Basin as far as Goldfield—at more than seven thousand feet on the Cactus Range. Some winter annuals, including buckwheats, four o'clocks, granite prickly-phlox, and phacelias, reach north toward Oregon and Idaho. Shadscale desert fills several basins in southeast Oregon (Alvord Desert and the Summer Lake and Harney basins); iodine bush reaches its northern limit in the Alvord Desert.

I felt the geographical power of the Lahontan trough at the east end of Honey Lake in California. With feet planted firmly among greasewood and shadscale, I looked west past the lake, a shallow remnant of Lahontan, to the gleaming snow of Lassen Peak on the horizon. I could see the Sierra Nevada end near Susanville and the Cascade Range begin with Lassen. Behind me, Mojave Desert plants made their way north through the Lahontan corridor; here their journey brought them within sight of the honest-to-god Northwest.

The Lahontan basin itself, northward outpost of many southern animals, has developed several unique subspecies. A distinct leopard lizard lives here. Among mammals, the huge areas of fine soil and sand opened up by the

distribution. They both define a faunal subdivision of Utah that encompasses the Bonneville basin. In Nevada, mammalogist E. Raymond Hall (in 1946) acknowledged the Bonneville basin and divided a great swatch of Lower Sonoran–Lahontan Lake Basin in two "centers of differentiation" that contain the two remaining shadscale deserts.

Hall's map makes clear a major biogeographical fact. The Mojave Desert of southern Nevada has intimate ecological connections to the Lahontan basin. The Bonneville basin is more isolated. James Reveal calls the obvious dispersal route through the low valleys of west-central Nevada the "Lahontan trough." He demonstrated this dramatically in a pair of maps based on simple elevation.

The first map shows the 4,920-foot (1,500-meter) elevation level for the Great Basin and surrounding country. High ground clearly outlines and thoroughly isolates the Bonneville basin. The Lahontan basin, on the other hand, *almost* connects southward to the Mojave through valleys west of Tonopah. Northward, the Lahontan basin has the same close ties to southeast Oregon and the Snake River Plain.

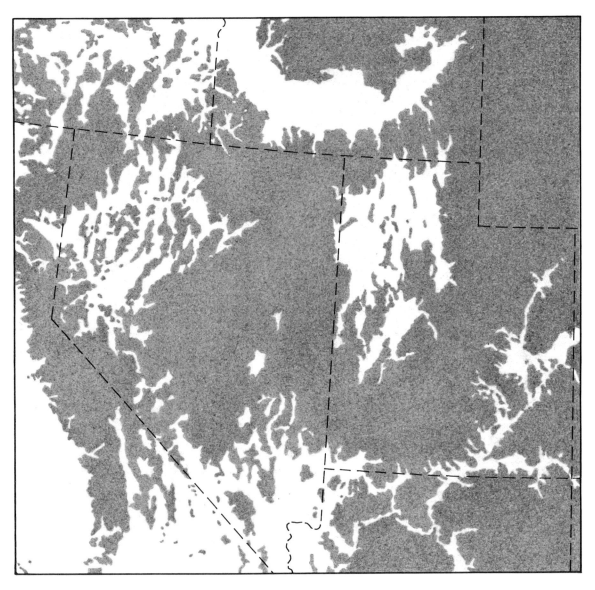

drying lake created potential habitat for many southern species, who could migrate to the area via the Lahontan trough and survive the northern winters because of the "banana belt" climate of the corridor. Mammals with Lahontan subspecies include the kit fox, long-tailed pocket mouse, dark kangaroo mouse, Ord's kangaroo rat, Botta's pocket gopher, and montane vole.

E. Raymond Hall calculated the effects of Lake Lahontan at its maximum: "If there were 20 mammals to the acre, the lake at its highest level reduced the population of land mammals by about 8,860,160." Since it dried, however, huge new areas of windblown sediments have created vast environments ideal for rodents; the lake's rise and fall may have *increased* mammal numbers.

The heteromyids favor sand dunes, and some kangaroo rats reoccupy land along receding lakes within a year or two after reemergence. Hall tells just how fast such transformations can occur:

> I was driving across the dry floor of Winnemucca Lake on July 21, 1941, incidentally noting abundant signs of small mammals, including burrows of *Dipodomys*, when I suddenly realized that at this same place in July, 1924, each of two fishermen in a boat about a half mile off shore caught his limit of Sacramento perch.

When E. Raymond Hall pondered which Nevada ecological province deserved the title of "typical" Great Basin, he judged the whole desert: Nevada includes a part of every Great

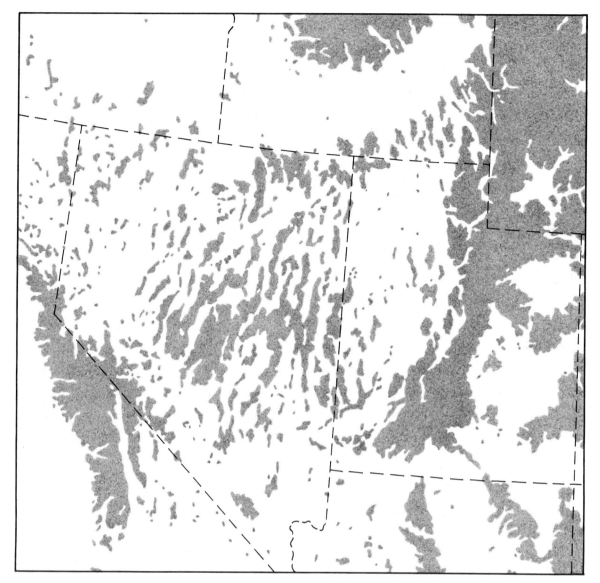

Basin ecological subdivision. The Lahontan basin? Too distinctive. The central Great Basin, with its island mountains rising from a sea of sagebrush, shares too much with the Rocky Mountains. The Lake section of southeast Oregon and northwestern Nevada resembles the Columbia Plateau and Snake River Plain lava country.

Hall evaluated his possibilities and chose the Bonneville basin.

Here, too, the land owes its story to the drying of a great Pleistocene lake. Lake Bonneville filled most recently from about twenty-five thousand years ago to sixteen thousand years ago until it reached the high shoreline mapped in geology texts. At 19,940 square miles— twice the area of Lake Lahontan—Bonneville at its maximum approached modern Lake Michigan in size. It fell about 325 feet some fifteen thousand years ago when the natural dam at Red Rock Pass in southern Idaho abruptly gave way.

By thirteen thousand years ago the lake had fallen below the "Provo terrace" cut after the great flood; by eleven thousand years ago it stood close to the level of today's Great Salt Lake (one thousand feet lower than maximum). Since then it has fluctuated constantly but has never risen more than forty feet above modern levels.

Much of the early drying of the lake took place during a time of major glaciation. Lake Lahontan was at a high level eleven thousand years ago, when Bonneville had mostly disappeared. These dates suggest that global cooling accompanying glaciation was not the sole

The Lahontan basin: rabbitbrush on the shore of Pyramid Lake.

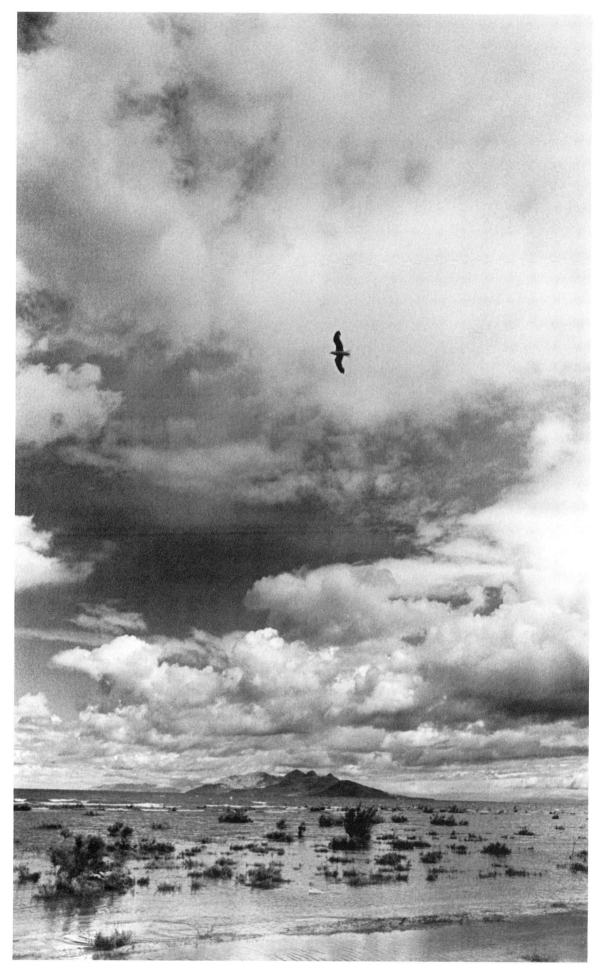

Open to colonization by terrestrial plants for less than 10,000 years, the Bonneville basin is too salty for sagebrush, but the fluctuating shoreline of the Great Salt Lake may still flood pioneering shadscale and its allies.

cause of major rises in Lake Bonneville. Shifts in storm tracks and resulting precipitation patterns must have had crucial effects as well.

The Bonneville basin is drier (due to lack of springs rather than lower precipitation) and saltier than the Lahontan basin. With its difficulty of colonization and longer immediate past as a desert it may have come closer to stabilizing in the number of its resident species.

Many annuals (buckwheats, penstemons, and lance-leaf scurfpea, for example) grow in species pairs: a low-elevation form in the old Lake Bonneville basin with closest relatives at adjacent high elevations. However, many of the plants pioneering on the salts and clays of the old lake beds are specialized genera with one or two species that vary little across their range. They belong to the goosefoot family, Chenopodiaceae: greasewood, desert blite, glasswort, iodine bush, spiny hopsage, winterfat, and the introduced Eurasian Russian thistle and halogeton.

Evolution has acted quickly here as plants took advantage of the new territory vacated by the shrinking lake. No living things demonstrate this better than *Atriplex*—shadscale and the many saltbushes. These plants form the exception to the Great Basin chenopod rule of stable, unvarying types. Botanist Howard Stutz describes them as "awesomely genetically rich," using "every known strategy for speciation," allowing us "to witness the evolutionary process at an unprecedented rate."

Stutz has studied the genetics of *Atriplex* in the Great Basin and has found numerous species and varieties, many of them still officially unnamed. He tells the following story.

Most older *Atriplex* species evolved to the south and emigrated northward as the deserts developed. They carried with them telltale signs of their origin: leaf anatomy associated with a type of photosynthesis adapted to hot, bright deserts.

A second holdover from the south proved useful in the north. In adapting to gypsum-heavy soils of northeastern Mexico, *Atriplex* evolved the capacity to tolerate high levels of salt. Not only could these plants deal with the climatic and physiological drought of the Great Basin, but their salty fluids worked as natural antifreeze in the colder north.

The saltbushes did not find every habitat instantly conquerable. In adapting to new pressures they have drawn on a wealth of evolutionary responses remarkable even for plants. One such route to diversity has been increasing the number of sets of chromosomes (any increase in chromosome numbers is known as *polyploidy*), according to Stutz, "a rather common accident in plants."

Races of shadscale with the normal complement of two sets of chromosomes usually grow in foothills above the old Bonneville lake bed. Races with twice or three times as many chromosomes show increased woodiness and reduced stature, which seems to make them better at invading the lowland clay flats: that is where they grow.

Four-winged saltbush (*Atriplex canescens*) has the widest distribution of any perennial member of the genus. It grows from central Mexico to southern Canada and from Nebraska to the Pacific. (From my house in the northern Rio Grande Valley in New Mexico I look out my window at a good-sized four-winged saltbush much frequented by juncos in winter.)

Over this huge area, with changing local environments the plant varies in the size of its leaves, capacity for root sprouting, tolerance of heavy clays, woodiness, stature, and palatability. In Stutz's words, "The variation is so extensive that some forms differ more from each other than they do from other species."

Polyploidy also occurs in four-winged saltbush. Plants with two sets of chromosomes live almost exclusively on sand dunes. Those with four sets (by far the most widespread) grow in sandy loams; plants with six sets inhabit heavy clay soils. In this species, with each increase in number of chromosome sets the plants become smaller, contrary to the general trend with polyploidy. Multiplication of chromosomes clearly has ecological as well as microscopic effects.

Even more important is hybridization between two species, followed by doubling of

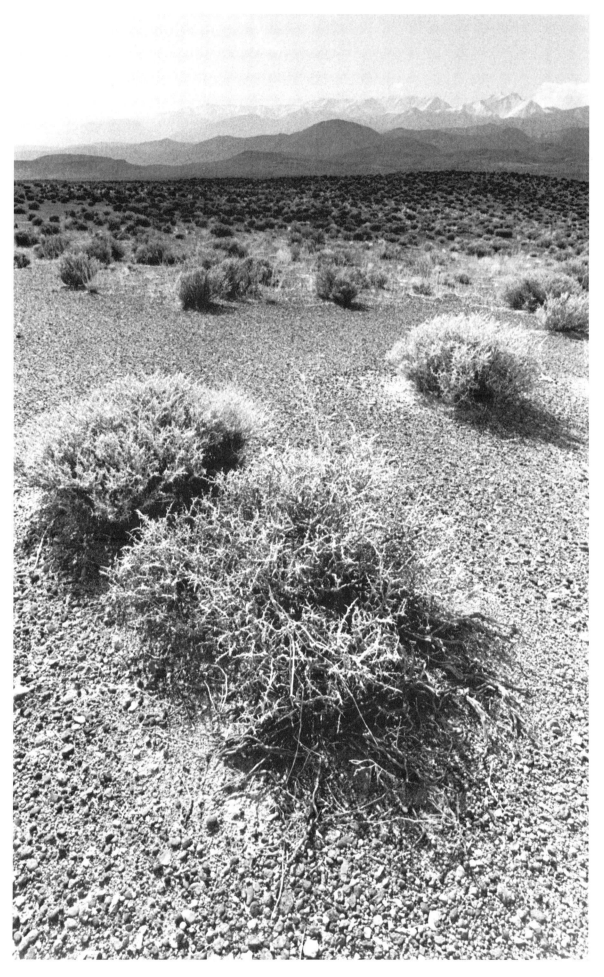

Shadscale and desert pavement in the Lahontan trough, Fishlake Valley, with the crest of the White Mountains on the western horizon.

chromosome number. This sequence of events has given rise to more than a third of the flowering plants on earth. In the Great Basin, the widespread four-winged saltbush has had opportunities to cross with nearly every other member of the genus. With the island-like nature of the landscape each new hybrid may evolve uniquely. Stutz claims they have, finding genetically distinct *Atriplex* populations in almost every valley in north-central Nevada.

Crosses between shadscale and four-winged saltbush grow in both the Lahontan and Bonneville basins, near Honey Lake, California, and at Garrison, Utah. The former is mostly saltbush, the latter mostly shadscale in character—products of further crosses of hybrids with pure shadscale or saltbush parents.

Two other hybrids show what all this confusing genetics can mean ecologically. Both have four-winged saltbush as one parent. The first derives from four-winged saltbush and the herbaceous sickle saltsage. This cross has not settled on a standard chromosome number; some have four sets, most have six. So many differing populations dwell in the north-south–trending valleys of Nevada that it seems the hybrid has arisen separately in most every valley. Its short stature, resistance to grazing, and apparent ease of reproduction give it the toughness and diversity to adapt to local conditions with remarkably fine tuning.

Four-winged saltbush also has crossed with *Atriplex tridentata*, a distinctive saltsage mostly confined to the alkaline Bonneville basin bottomlands. In Tooele Valley a population from such a cross covers about eighty acres. These shrubs stand upright and woody like typical nearby four-winged plants, but grow on heavy clays and bear soft-textured leaves and late-maturing flowers and fruits like saltsage. The hybrid seems better adapted to the valley than either parent and seems to be spreading.

Another four-winged saltbush/*Atriplex tridentata* cross has existed only since about 1970, for Stutz has found it only along the roadside of Interstate 80 in the Bonneville Salt Flats, and the plant evidently can be no older than the freeway. Both parents, hybrids, and

the new stabilized form occur. Stutz counted thirty-five thousand individual plants of the new form in 1977. Its unusually rapid growth rate makes it a fine pioneer. Still another small-statured hybrid covers thousands of acres in the Reese River Valley near Battle Mountain, Nevada, again on heavy alkaline clay.

These new saltbushes add a remarkable layer of possibilities to our understanding of why Great Basin plants grow where they do. Dwight Billings speaks of "tiles" of soil-determined communities within the greater "mosaic with its matrix of shadscale." But each "tile" of clay or sand can be invaded not only by existing species but by unpredictable new forms. Adjacent saltbushes can hybridize with ease. A chance doubling of chromosomes can generate just the right adaptation to forge a plant capable of moving into a hitherto unoccupied piece of the community mosaic.

Evolution is creating, changing, and refining the Great Basin Desert while we try to categorize it. The earth is dynamic, indeed.

On a June day in 1934, Selar Hutchings and Ben Stahmann were collecting plants one mile northwest of Wells, Nevada. Each time they put a new specimen in the plant press they took turns signing the tag as collector.

Working their way through the valley, they found a succulent annual resembling a new Russian thistle. Each fat little leaf on the plant resembled a tiny sausage with a projecting barb at its tip. It was Ben Stahmann's turn to sign for the specimen. By chance, he thereby became the first person to collect halogeton in North America.

It took a while to identify this new plant. Great Basin botanists had never seen anything like it. Stahmann and Hutchings had been hired by the Forest Service's Intermountain Forest and Range Experiment Station in Ogden, primary range research institution in the Great Basin, and in 1936 the experiment station shipped the sample to Washington, D.C. An expert on the goosefoots, the Chenopodiaceae, identified it as the genus *Halogeton* the next year. Not until 1941 did botanists pin

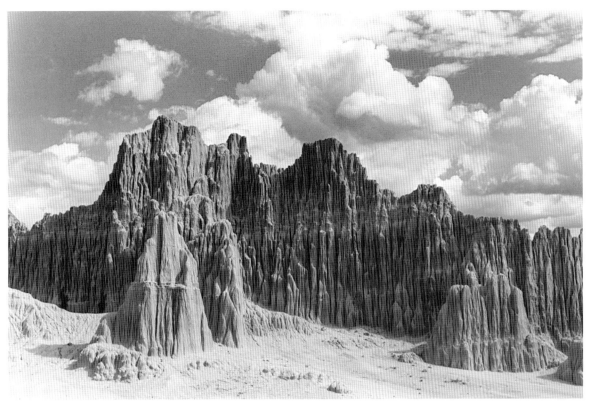

Some Great Basin
landscapes are
too extreme for
any *vegetation to
survive;* Cathedral
Valley State Park,
Nevada.

89

———

Shadscale

down the plant to species: *Halogeton glomeratus*, a native of the central Asian deserts.

With Ben Stahmann's specimen from Wells came the first official recognition of its presence, but it may have been here for years. No one knows how halogeton first arrived in North America, or when. Perhaps introduced with crested wheatgrass seed, or imported with Karakul sheep, the chenopod found the Great Basin to its liking.

At home in Russia, the plant grew on alkaline soils with Russian thistle and *Atriplex*. It favored the worst range, ranking as "fair to poor winter camel forage," the lowest grade possible in one Russian hierarchy of forage quality. In Nevada, halogeton invaded sparse or disturbed stands of shadscale and winterfat and pioneered clays heretofore unvegetated.

Range scientists abruptly began to pay attention to halogeton when Nick Goica lost 160 head of sheep from a band grazing near Wells in 1942 and veterinarians determined that eating halogeton had killed them. The plant contains high doses of oxalic acid, and when dehydrated and hungry sheep move through a patch of halogeton the results can be disastrous.

Botanists went looking for halogeton in earnest and found it in seven Nevada and four Utah counties in 1943. By the 1950s it had reached as far as California, Montana, and Colorado. It stopped there, evidently at the limits of its climatic and physiological tolerance.

Halogeton killed thousands of sheep (and lesser numbers of cows) in the 1950s, leading sheep ranchers to cease grazing some ranges altogether and to publicity that reached to *Life* magazine. In the midst of such public uproar, Professor J. H. Robertson of the University of Nevada brought halogeton salad to a faculty party, shocking the guests but insisting that the oxalate content was no higher than another tasty chenopod with the common name "spinach."

Sheep can adapt to halogeton, or, rather, the microorganisms in their rumen can adapt to dealing with the high oxalate intake. But with abrupt moves into halogeton, major sheep losses still can occur. The real problem: overgrazed range subject to invasion by such alien annuals as halogeton, Russian thistle, and cheatgrass. Range scientist Neil Frischknecht put it succinctly: "A vigorous stand of peren-

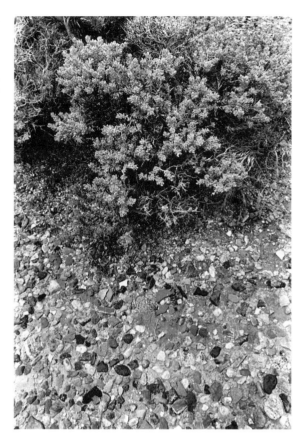

nial plants is the best insurance against halogeton invasion."

The Great Basin—like all the West—has been transformed by livestock in the last hundred years. It took only twenty years or so of heavy grazing to permanently reduce the numbers of fragile, highly palatable plants like molly, winterfat, and bunchgrasses. Shrubs replaced them, and then came halogeton.

In a classic 1947 paper, Walter P. Cottam asked, "Is Utah Sahara Bound?" He documented the remarkable changes in Utah vegetation since the coming of settlers.

Pioneer Americans simply did not acknowledge desert fragility. Cottam quoted a typical attitude from a Mormon patriarch's 1888 autobiography:

> When Parley P. Pratt concluded that Utah could supply pasturage for grazing animals "without limit" and "raise cattle and sheep to any amount," his knowledge of the drizzling rains and cold humid climate of Britain had not been tempered by the occasional drenchings and prolonged droughts of a dry, hot desert.

Some herbaceous vegetation exists, and in a wet spring, globemallow still may turn entire valleys orange. Grasses used to be common: old-timers insist on describing the basins as paradise pasturage with waving stands of ten-foot-high grasses. This description could only apply to wildrye bottomlands. In shadscale stands, considerably smaller bunchgrasses— Indian ricegrass, galleta, alkali sacaton, and bottle-brush grass (squirreltail)—offered summer forage for livestock.

Grasses grew sparsely in lowlands; the most palatable plants were abundant shrubs such as winterfat. Bunchgrasses grew more luxuriantly a bit higher in elevation, in sagebrush and piñon-juniper forest. Throughout, shrubs or trees have increased, and intense livestock grazing has drastically depleted grasses and tasty shrubs.

A best guess in 1940, based on work in the severely grazed Wah Wah Valley and lightly grazed Pine Valley, plotted winterfat at 25 percent of plant cover in the Bonneville basin in 1847; the plant totaled only 9 percent of the same area in 1937. The same scientists believed grass had accounted for 45 percent cover in presettlement days and in 1937 called it essentially absent. Big sagebrush, snakeweed, green rabbitbrush, shadscale, and juniper all had increased.

A 1965 estimate of winterfat cover in the Utah section of the Great Basin (which nearly encompasses the Bonneville basin) placed it at only 1.5 percent. Still, in 1979, Neil West found surprising resistance to grazing in individual plants of six species over thirty-four years of records at the Desert Experimental Range in southwest Utah. None of the six (shadscale, bud sagebrush, winterfat, Indian ricegrass, sand dropseed, and globemallow) varied much in survival between grazed and ungrazed populations. Small numbers of plants in these samples could have made the results untrustworthy, or the moderate level of grazing on this research area might have only minor effects.

West has also emphasized the fluctuation from year to year in species presence, productivity, cover—in every aspect of ecology. Drastic differences between wet years and dry years can confound the conclusions of short-term studies aimed at understanding succession. Insect outbreaks (such as snout moths and the scale insect *Orthezia annae*) can dramatically reduce shadscale populations. Still, heavy livestock grazing can have irreversible effects.

Russian thistle and, later, halogeton arrived in a Great Basin inevitably denuded by ranchers who practiced what Pratt preached. Both alien plants thrived on the disturbed lands and offered poor forage for wildlife and cattle alike. But these aliens have not taken over the salt desert valleys with the same tenacity as cheatgrass in sagebrush. The latter exotic dominates through a fire cycle. Halogeton and Russian thistle grow in sparser vegetation where plants remain far apart; fire does not often run wild here. These aliens depend on disturbed lands and overgrazed range to make inroads in new territory. If we graze livestock in moderation, we control their spread.

The Great Basin may be a sagebrush ocean, but within it lie shadscale seas. Nowhere in the Great Basin does a sense of ecological complexity surpass the shadscale desert.

In the central, higher Great Basin, sagebrush self-assuredly fills valley after valley. Sagebrush valleys share geographic supremacy with mountain ranges; they have the same weight.

But lower, in the old lake basins, mountains remain distant from glaring playas; the lowlands dominate. A lighter, brighter world persists, with black cloud shadows pooling like moving lakes on the basin floors, with paradoxically lush winterfat, tough spiny shadscale, and startling green greasewood pioneering at an arid and saline frontier.

Ocean of Sagebrush

8

Imagine a gnarled and venerable live oak-tree reduced to a little shrub two feet high, with its rough bark, its foliage, its twisted boughs, all complete. . . . It is an imposing monarch of the forest in exquisite miniature. . . . Sage-brush is very fair fuel, but as a vegetable it is a distinguished failure. Nothing can abide the taste of it but the jackass and his illegitimate child the mule. But their testimony to its nutritiousness is worth nothing, for they will eat pine knots, or anthracite coal, or brass filings, or lead pipe, or old bottles, or anything that comes handy, and then go off looking as grateful as if they had had oysters for dinner.

—Mark Twain,
Roughing It, 1872

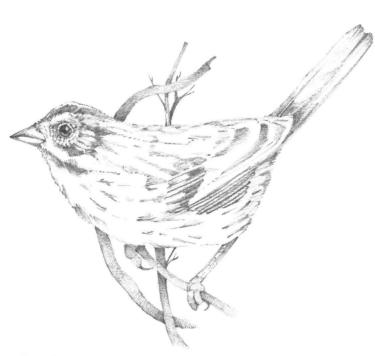

Sage Sparrow

During most of my time in the Great Basin I admit to having taken sagebrush for granted. It is always there; from its matrix rise the island mountain ranges, below it the rings of salt desert spiral toward barren playas. Its sharp scent, laced with dust and wind and sometimes a trace of rain, becomes so familiar that it no longer registers—until you leave this country and miss it.

Sagebrush indeed forms an ocean from which all other Great Basin places depart. If you picked the right line you could move through the entire length and breadth of the desert from north to south, from west to east, always walking through aromatic gray-green sagebrush.

This simplified view of the plant we so far have called sagebrush misleads. Misconceptions have plagued our understanding of the shrub since the first explorers wrote about it.

With remarkable variety in combinations of species, the metaphorical sagebrush ocean embraces currents, tides, eddies, and embayments. This is a complex and dynamic sea.

A single species, "sagebrush," does not dominate the Great Basin. Twelve sagebrush species (big sagebrush, *Artemisia tridentata*, and its allies) grow in the West, and several of these have distinct subspecies. Numerous other members of the genus occur (e.g., bud sagebrush) but are more distantly related to big sagebrush and thus not official sagebrushes. Most travelers through the Basin have not only lumped all sagebrush, but in their expansiveness have included shadscale and other shrubs unrelated to sagebrush.

Sagebrush has become a brand-name generic—like Kleenex and Scotch tape.

Further confusing its identity, sagebrush is not a true sage; it is a sage*brush*. True sages of the genus *Salvia* belong to the mint family and give personality to many a western image: "riders of the purple sage" ride through *Salvia*, not *Artemisia*. Woe to the creative camp cook who adds a few sagebrush leaves to the cookpot, again mistaking bitter *Artemisia* for the *Salvia* that flavors Thanksgiving turkey. Old World artemisias flavor absinthe, vermouth, and tarragon vinegar; in Europe, the common name for the genus, wormwood, refers to its use as a cure for roundworms.

Equally misleading is the implication that sagebrush exists in pure stands with no other participating plants. In reality, grasses played a crucial role in pristine sagebrush stands and still do, even in grazed communities. From south to north, from drier to wetter climates, grasses increase in density. Today, however, the identity of the grasses has changed in one of the most dramatic ecological revolutions the West has seen.

In the West, big sagebrush grows virtually anywhere that water and elevation allow, if soils are deep and sandy enough. Unlike salt desert shrubs with narrow soil tolerances, sagebrush will dominate if climate is right. Above about fifty-five hundred feet (in the south) and about forty-five hundred feet (in the north) and with seven inches of rainfall or more, sagebrush rims the shadscale basins.

In the Bonneville and Lahontan basins, the map of sagebrush goes sinuous, running in bands around low mountains above shadscale and below piñon-juniper woodland. In the central Great Basin, sagebrush fills valleys and carpets small mountains in huge continuous stands. Across northern Nevada and southeastern Oregon, with cooler and wetter climates, it reigns supreme—and continues to rule far beyond the Great Basin, covering the Snake River Plain and Columbia Plateau and reaching into the Wyoming Basin. The grand total within the United States for communities in which some sagebrush species play an important part passes a billion acres. Sagebrush communities blanket at least 45 percent of the Great Basin.

Pioneers looking for useful land made the first distinction between sagebrush plants. They determined that tall sage indicated arable land; low sage did not. This basic separation dominated the thinking of range managers until the 1960s, when the diverse ecology of the plant first began to come clear.

Biologists had seen big sagebrush in a gamut

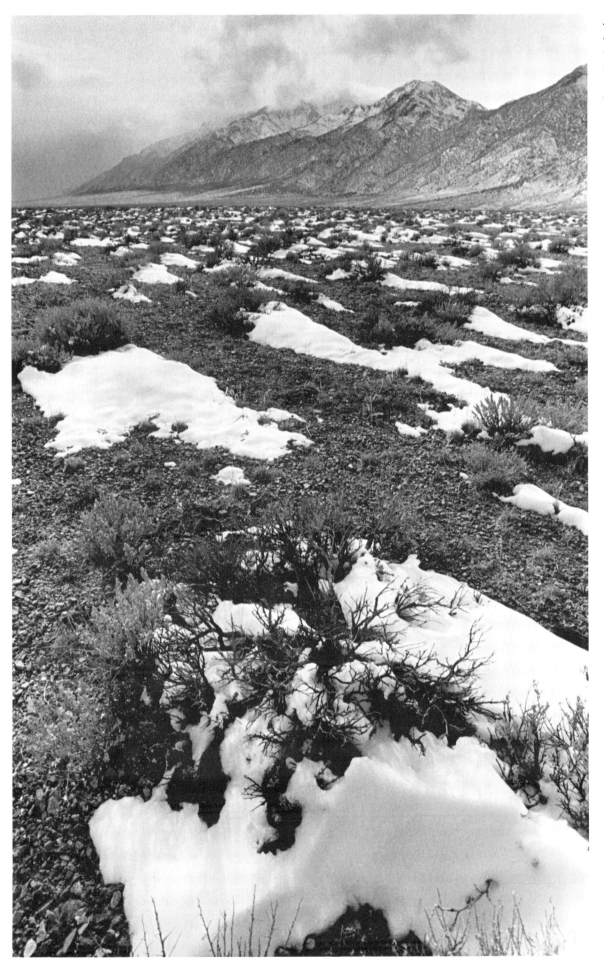

Zen gardens of snowdrifts and black sagebrush below the stormy Toiyabe Range, Big Smoky Valley.

*Distribution of
the sagebrush
community in
the Great Basin
Desert. (Based on
Holmgren, 1972;
and Barbour and
Major, 1977)*

96

———

*Between the
Mountains*

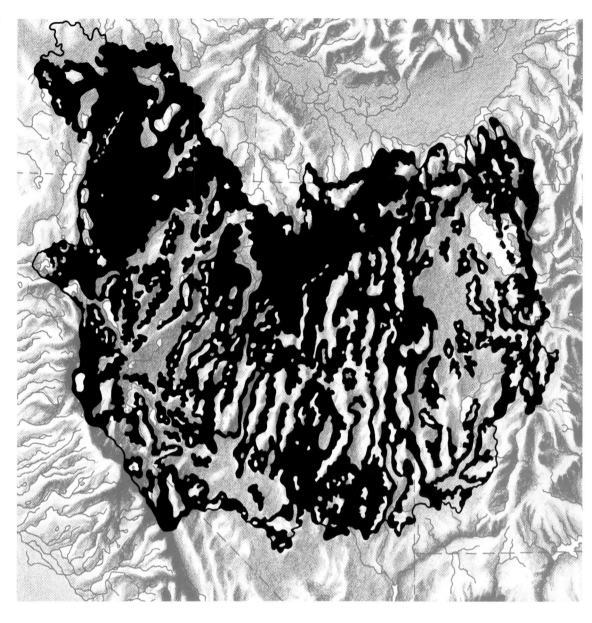

of soils and temperatures, growing dwarfed by
the desert and luxuriant in subalpine forests.
Yet not until recently did they recognize varieties, revealing a remarkably dynamic plant.
Like *Atriplex*, it has evolved with the changing
climate. Sagebrush is an opportunist.

Alan Beetle proposed a classification for
sagebrush in 1960 that has since been verified
and refined by A. H. Winward and E. Durant
McArthur. To understand their scheme, start
with big sagebrush itself.

The familiar smell of big sagebrush—the
most common western shrub—powerfully
evokes the Intermountain West. At least four
kinds of big sagebrush have evolved to take
advantage of the diverse environments across
its enormous geographic range:

Wyoming big sagebrush, *Artemisia tridentata*
subspecies *wyomingensis*
Basin big sagebrush, *Artemisia tridentata* subspecies *tridentata*
Mountain big sagebrush, *Artemisia tridentata*
subspecies *vaseyana*
Subalpine big sagebrush, *Artemisia tridentata*
subspecies *spiciformis*

A wealth of variation in the plant (size;
flower and leaf shape; flat or uneven tops to the
shrubs) identifies the various types and allows
sagebrush to live where otherwise it could not.
Natural (and heritable) variation exists—as
a given. Plants hybridize. Mutations occur. And
a new version of sagebrush—one that survives
and reproduces better in the habitat—may

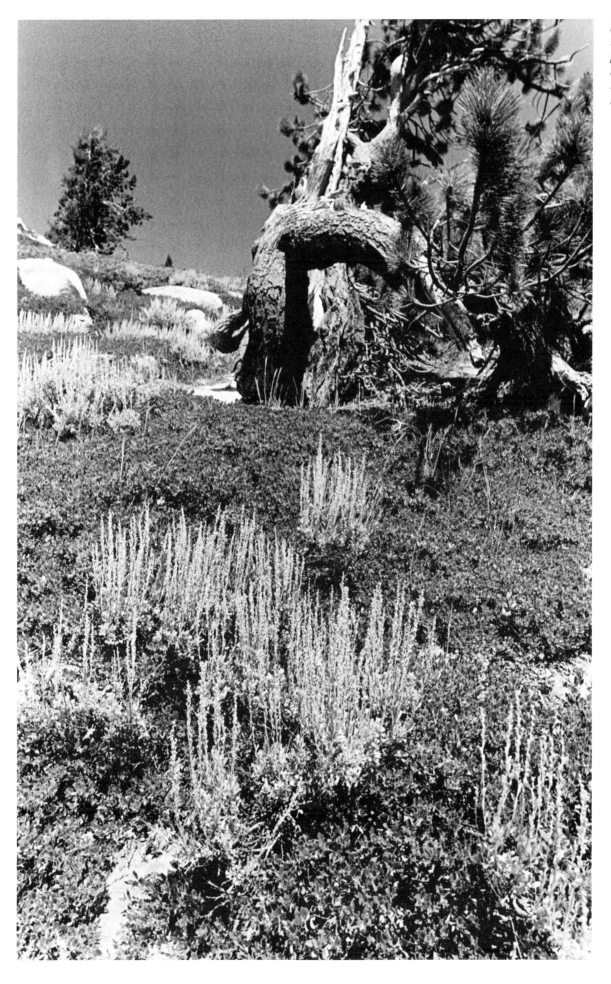

*Dwarf sagebrush,
manzanita, and
pine at Marlette
Lake, near tree
line in the Carson
Range.*

come to exist next to an old one. With time, the new type replaces the old because it leaves more offspring.

With the end products fine-tuned to their homes (whether alkaline clay or subalpine stream-side meadow), we tend to think plants strive to accomplish such goals. But evolution works with raw material generated by chance mutations or hybridizations resulting from a limited number of possible forces. Natural selection gives evolution direction. Sometimes, success comes. To us, modern plants and animals look perfectly adapted. But they did not "know" where they were headed when the variation first developed.

On the other hand, plant geneticists can manipulate sagebrush species with definite goals in mind. Through artificial selection they can breed species capable of reclaiming soils devastated by strip mining, or hone a palatable species for use in reseeding destroyed wildlife habitats.

They have remarkable diversity to work with. Even the distinct subspecies of big sagebrush vary widely with location. Every stand has unique combinations of volatile oils that determine its scent and palatability. Each varies in growth form, color, flowering cycles, soil tolerances, and susceptibility to insect depredations (most commonly the sage-defoliating webworm moth).

Most researchers believe that the genus originated in Eurasia and that the big sagebrush complex evolved recently in North America. Hybridization is rampant (big sagebrush is wind-pollinated), and many modern forms owe their existence to natural crosses. Wyoming big sagebrush, for instance, seems to have origins in three older sagebrushes: basin and mountain big sagebrush and black sagebrush. Chromosomes in the group behave similarly, though polyploidy commonly occurs.

Increasing elevation orders the list of big sagebrush types: each successive subspecies lives in moister and cooler environments, forming a series of distinctive plants from 6,000 to 10,800 feet. Subalpine big sagebrush favors the highest elevations, sites even cooler and

wetter than the mountain variety. On Steens Mountain in Oregon, it dominates the upper one-third of the mountain (above 7,000 feet).

The most primitive form (genetically) is mountain big sagebrush; this plant now grows in mountains and foothills with deep, summer-moist, well-drained soils (its fragmented range evidently a relict from more continuous range in pluvial times). Unlike the simpler communities of valley sagebrushes, forty species of other plants commonly grow with it. Crushed leaves of mountain big sagebrush smell fresh and minty rather than sagey.

Below, in drier valleys, grow basin and Wyoming big sagebrush. Basin big sagebrush reaches maximum size for the species—usually three to seven feet and sometimes fifteen feet high. Probably the most abundant of the sagebrushes, this form fills valleys below seven thousand feet on dry, deep soils. On drier sites yet, Wyoming big sagebrush takes over. This smaller shrub evidently evolved most recently: it grows in the newest of the dry big sagebrush habitats in southeast Oregon (where it is the most common sagebrush on the High Desert) and in southern Utah and Nevada.

Above its threshold for aridity, clays, and high temperatures, where does big sagebrush *not* grow? On steeper, rockier soils, piñon and juniper compete well with it. On deep, moist mountain soils and in colder canyons, conifers and aspen overtop the shrub. Below, in the climatic zone it dominates, rainfall remains too low for trees; in these deeper soils the pungent shrub outcompetes rockbound piñon and juniper.

A second series—low sagebrush—has taken over on even drier sites, on the frontiers of the salt desert and on the thinnest soils and windiest ridges at higher elevations. The sequence of these low-growing shrubs begins with bud sagebrush, which we already encountered in shadscale country. With increasing elevation come black sagebrush (*Artemisia arbuscula* var. *nova*) and then dwarf sagebrush (*Artemisia arbuscula*). Of the two, dwarf sagebrush favors consistently wetter and higher-elevation sites. Alkali sagebrush (*Artemisia longiloba*), an ad-

Valleys of Silence

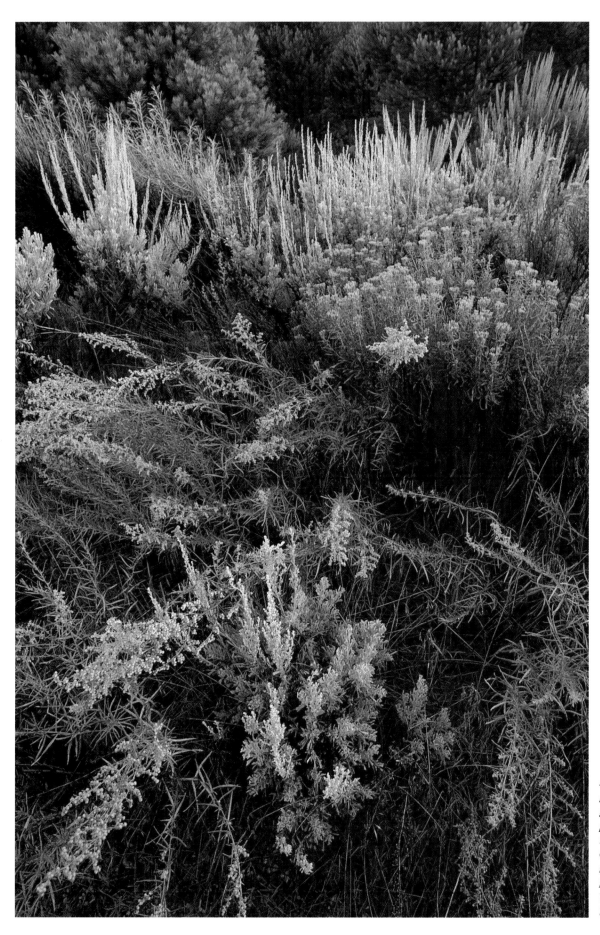

An untended garden of gray-green sagebrush, piñon, and rabbitbrush along Granite Creek in the Deep Creek Range above the West Desert in Utah.

The flattest natural topography on earth—the exhilarating freedom of space in the center of the Black Rock Desert. The desert mirrors the sky in size; it complements and completes it.

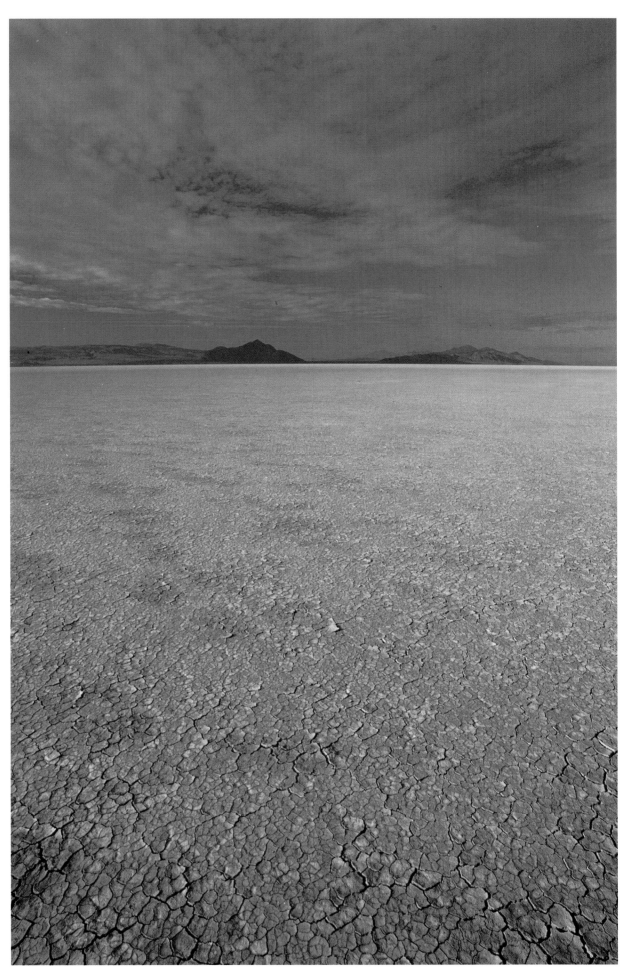

The salt-encrusted Bonneville Salt Flats at the heart of the Great Salt Lake Desert— one of the most forbidding landscapes on the continent.

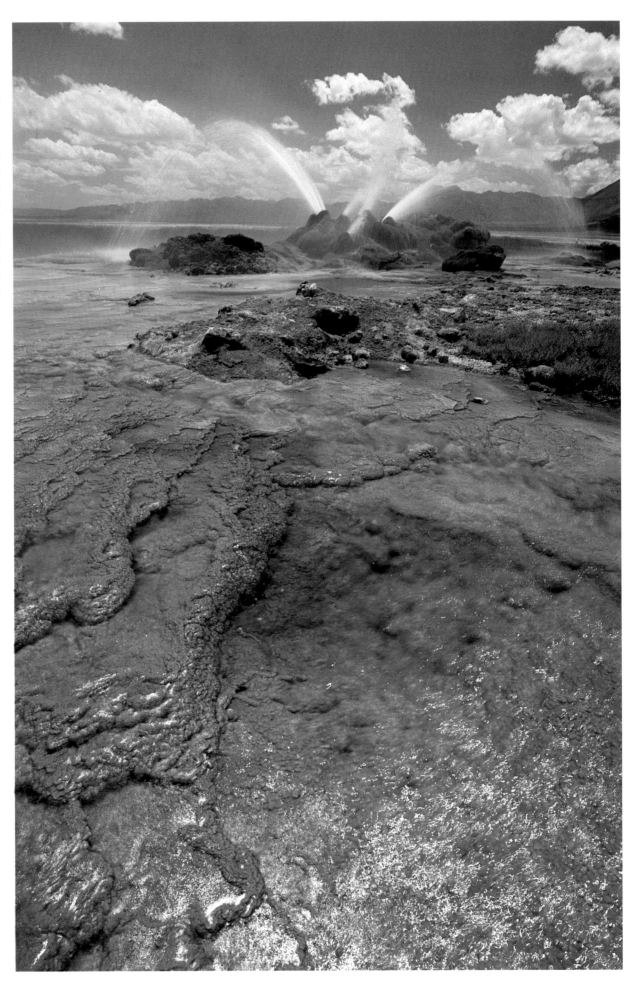

Salt-tolerant plants may have first gained a toehold in the Great Basin around salty hot springs like Geyser Hot Springs in the Black Rock Desert. When the Hypsithermal opened Basin floors to colonization by plants, these alkali-tolerant species were already nearby to do the colonizing.

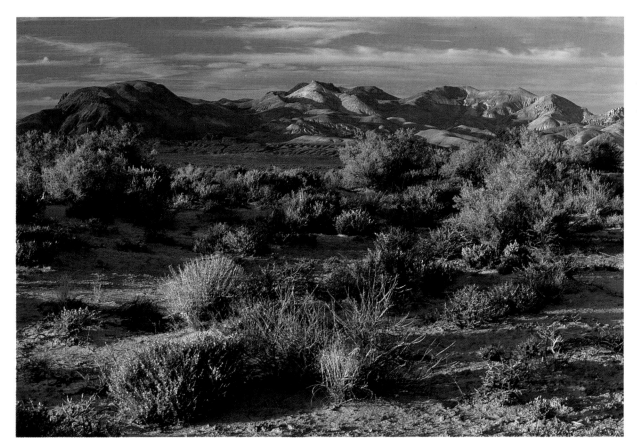

Greasewood turning yellow in autumn, below the Calico Mountains at the edge of the Black Rock Desert.

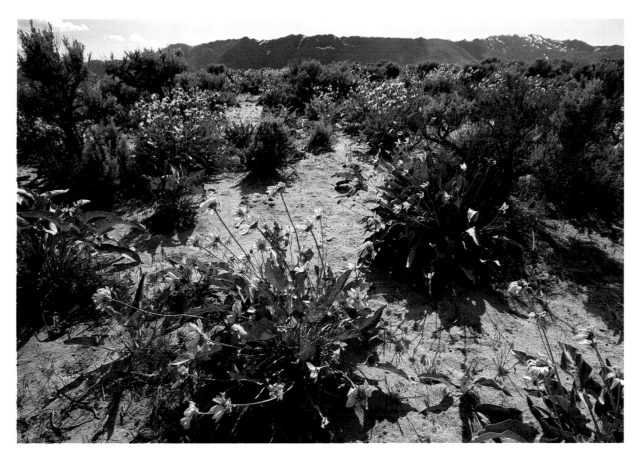

Big sagebrush and balsamroot below the Granite Range, Nevada.

From the matrix of sagebrush rise island mountains, like the Monitor and Toquima ranges.

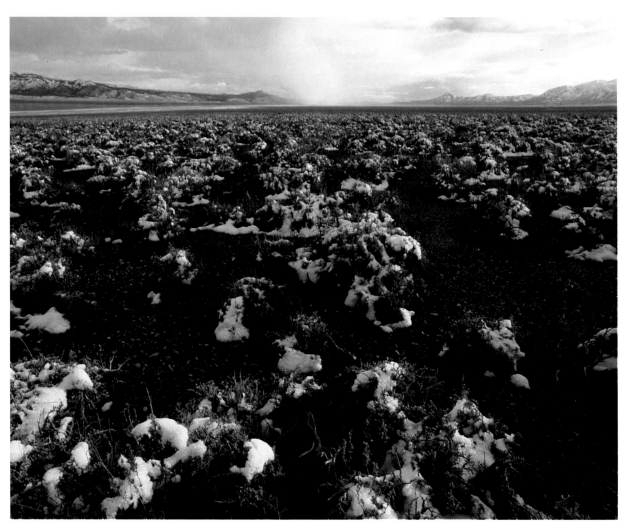

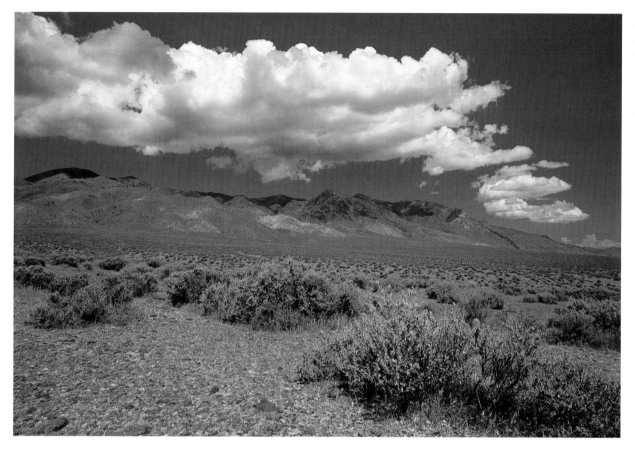

Shadscale and greasewood in Dixie Valley; cloud mountains mirror the peaks of the Stillwater Range.

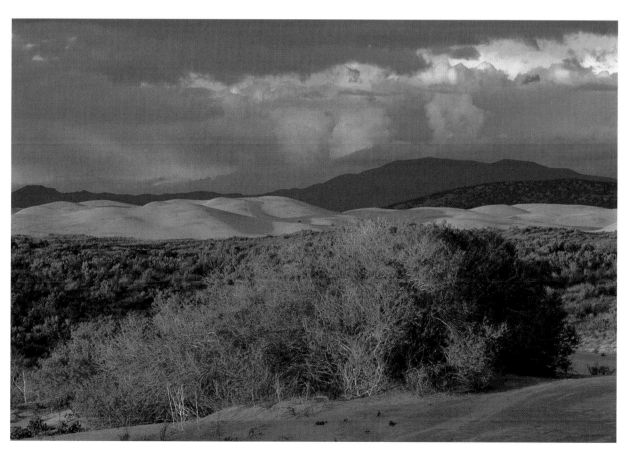

Last relics of the ancestral form of the species, giant four-winged saltbushes in Utah's Little Sahara Dunes grow new twigs three times as fast as other members of the species, keeping ahead of deepening dunes.

Tumbleweed tracks on the Crescent Dunes, Big Smoky Valley.

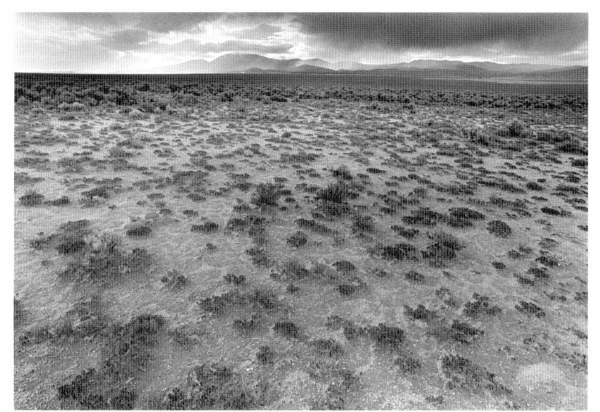

ditional low sage, occurs widely in the central Great Basin. The tiny pygmy sagebrush grows in nearly barren small meadows in limestone soils in eastern Nevada and western Utah.

Black, dwarf, and alkali sagebrush dominate half of Nevada's sagebrush vegetation. Soil differences set these short sagebrushes apart.

Dwarf and alkali sagebrush communities occur on shallow, stony soils where clay prevents water from penetrating around the roots of the shrubs. Abundant in northern Nevada, dwarf sagebrush retreats upward in elevation in the southern Basin—above the piñon-juniper woodland, commonly to tree line at 11,500 feet and often beyond to 12,800 feet.

Black sagebrush favors shallow gravelly soils with high carbonate content on rocky pediments and foothills, as close as sagebrush comes to the prehistoric lake deposits where shadscale dominates. Black sagebrush plants often grow on desert pavement; decorated with their persistent reddish-brown flower stalks, they look like small desert bouquets arranged in a Japanese Zen garden. North-south roads in central Nevada valleys frequently run along

the black sagebrush belt—above lowland salt desert and below the big sagebrush-covered foothills.

These valleys are bigger than you ever remember, and so are the mountains that bound them, each one popping up sequentially from below the horizon—a landmark. The basins feel more like oceanic fjords (temporarily dry) than valleys. There appears to be nothing in them, just a low growth of black sage and grass, with less conspicuous plants next to the playas. Every few miles a grove of cottonwoods and poplars up against the foot of the range marks a ranch, situated where the creeks flowing from the mountains can be tapped before they dissipate in the basin. And here and there a mining operation makes raw the mouth of a canyon. Nothing else. That's all.

The Big Smoky Valley is one of the biggest, some 120 miles worth of silent sky between two of the Basin's most imposing ranges. The Toiyabe Range stands to the west, rising to rounded summits faced with crags called the Wild Granites. On the east, the Toquima Range crests at the long level tableland of Mount Jefferson, a broad catwalk of alpine grassland

Sagebrush made useful: the lush wheatfields of Cache Valley, Idaho.

scooped into by cirques that do not meet, leaving a high, rolling, remnant horizon.

Sagebrush scientists have long argued about how much grass existed in Great Basin sagebrush communities before the introduction of livestock. Again, we have created problems with our stubborn and parochial insistence that every sagebrush stand is pretty much like the next one. In reality, a gradient exists from nearly pure sagebrush to prairielike grassland.

Perennial bunchgrasses and herbaceous plants become ever more numerous along the gradient toward moister sites—higher or farther north. At the arid end of the sagebrush spectrum, the gray-green shrubs make up over 70 percent of the plant cover and 90 percent of the biomass (weight per unit area of living material).

On such drier sites, and south into the Lahontan basin, needlegrasses form a series, with Thurber's needlegrass the standard companion to big sagebrush, *Stipa occidentalis* in wetter stands, and sewing needle-and-thread on low, sandy areas. On still drier sites, shadscale-zone bunchgrasses turn up: bottle-brush grass, Indian ricegrass, and, in the south, galleta.

Shrubs other than sagebrush characterize this same moisture gradient. Bitterbrush grows with sagebrush at higher elevations, blurring into the zone better described as mountain brush. At the other extreme, spiny hopsage and Mormon tea bridge the boundary between sagebrush and salt desert.

Bluebunch wheatgrass forms the classic companion for big sagebrush in the northern Great Basin, often joined by Sandberg's bluegrass. In the High Desert in Oregon, big sagebrush/wheatgrass communities dominate. On lusher sites, Idaho fescue is the characteristic grass. The same grasses characterize moisture gradients in black sagebrush and dwarf sagebrush communities.

At this lush end of the scale, in an area completely protected from grazing (the Mona, Utah, cemetery), native grasses total 92 percent of the cover. This fenced (and probably irrigated) reserve measures potential viability

of the grasses, but not of the effects of grazing, for local residents weeded sagebrush from the cemetery as it invaded.

Bluebunch wheatgrass turns parts of Cache Valley, Utah, into a variant of true Palouse prairie. Novelist Thomas Wolfe described just how lush Cache Valley seems after a long drive through the desert; in *A Western Journal* he wrote of the view from the flanks of the Wellsville Mountains as the road from Brigham City gently eased into the valley:

> Suddenly, cupped in the rim of bold hills, a magic valley plain, flat as a floor and green as heaven and more fertile and more ripe than the Promised land . . . a valley that makes all that has gone before fade to nothing—the very core and fruit of Canaan—a vast sweet plain of unimaginable riches—loaded with fruit, lusty with cherry orchards, green with its thick and lush fertility.

Few animals make sagebrush the center of their universe in the way chisel-toothed kangaroo rats rely on shadscale. Least chipmunks live consistently in sagebrush stands, though they eat mostly seeds; sagebrush voles and pygmy rabbits use the shrub as primary food. But sagebrush's volatile oils inhibit microbe action in the rumens of hoofed browsers like deer and sheep. Of large mammals, only pronghorn eat large quantities of sagebrush in winter, and of birds, only Sage Grouse.

In the past, Pleistocene browsers like North American camels and ground sloths may have made better use of the abundant forage. Though big sagebrush matches alfalfa in protein content and surpasses it for carbohydrates and fats, today most sagebrush browse goes uneaten.

Ecologist James MacMahon groups sagebrush desert mammals of jackrabbit size and smaller in seven "guilds" determined by diet and adult size: seedeaters; a carnivorous mouse (the predatory grasshopper mouse); large browsers (jackrabbits); small browsers (cottontails); a micro-omnivore (a deer mouse); a woodrat; and a daytime-active medium-sized omnivore (a ground squirrel). Across the Great Basin the species representing each of these guilds vary. But they remain ecological equivalents, filling the same roles—one way to understand how animals and resources mesh to make a community.

We can apply the same concept in miniature to spiders living on sagebrush. Predators all, one way to subdivide their world is by their hunting methods—though we never know whether the spiders see it in the same way. These spider guilds include ambushers, nocturnal hunters, agile hunters, runners, and web builders.

Likewise, spiders (and other arachnids like scorpions and solpugids) can be ecological indicators for communities just as can birds or mammals. Along the Great Basin–Mojave transition in southern Nevada, spiders were most common in blackbrush and mixed brush communities; solpugids were least common in blackbrush and most common in piñon-juniper and spiny hopsage–Cooper's desert thorn, where spiders and scorpions were not abundant. In southern Idaho, spiders were most abundant in sagebrush, least in rabbitbrush, where solpugids dominated.

Black-tailed jackrabbits outnumber every other sagebrush vertebrate. In Curlew Valley in the northern Bonneville basin, the biomass of all rodents combined did not match jackrabbit biomass, even with jackrabbit numbers at a low. In such terrain, jackrabbit populations fluctuate from about 155 per square mile to 1,550 per square mile. Their primary predator, the coyote, cycles with them, its maximums and minimums lagging behind the hare's by a year or two.

For detailed analysis of sagebrush animals, from mammals to mites, Reed Fautin's 1946 study has few peers. He did most of his work in Fernow Valley, at the east edge of the Bonneville basin, but compared many other valleys in western Utah. His results verify patterns seen elsewhere. For both resident mammals and birds, sagebrush met crucial nesting and cover requirements rather than providing food.

Fautin found long-tailed pocket mice most frequently in black sagebrush communities, which meshes with E. Raymond Hall's conclusion about the mammal: it favors "stony ground"—the same ground favored by the shrub. Another small mammal favoring rocky ground, the canyon mouse, replaced the nearly ubiquitous deer mouse in black sagebrush, especially near ledges. Wood rats, too, concentrated here.

Mourning Doves nested only in sagebrush areas, and Fautin saw nighthawks here most often. Sage Thrashers, shrikes, Sage Sparrows, and Brewer's Sparrows used both sagebrush and greasewood, the two communities akin in vegetation density and life form. Sagebrush lizards showed the same distribution pattern, though most abundant in sagebrush, feeding on insects living on the shrubs.

We know little of the ecology of the more than one thousand additional insects and other invertebrates observed on a sagebrush/grass site (and the hundreds more undetected species), but they have enormous impact. In sagebrush stands near Reno, harvester ants moved underground vast quantities of leaves and seeds—between sixty-three and ninety-two million annual plants per acre annually. And webworms can defoliate large numbers of sagebrush. Their larvae concentrate on terminal leaves early in the season; the adult moths eventually emerge in time to feed at rabbitbrush flowers later in the year.

Many biologists have added to our understanding of sagebrush animals since Fautin tried to analyze them all. A sampling of their discoveries reveals still more of the inner workings of the community.

Sagebrush voles eat mostly grasses but can girdle vast numbers of sagebrush in winters with heavy snowpack; montane voles also girdle sagebrush. Then there are the predators. Badgers total about one-half the biomass of coyotes, the masked mustelids feeding largely on rodents whose burrows they excavate with nearly unstoppable power. Bobcat populations total only one-twentieth the biomass of coyotes. And as conspicuous as they seem, the great predatory birds that feed on jackrabbits—the

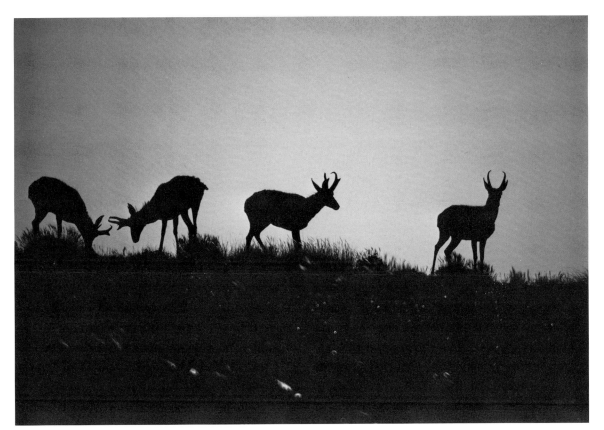

Pronghorn prefer open country and therefore frequent dwarf sagebrush and black sagebrush. They trace a thread of movement through vast and still basins of unmoving plants.

Golden Eagle, Ferruginous Hawk, and Red-tailed Hawk—each add a biomass of only 1 to 3 percent of the remarkable coyotes.

When Lewis and Clark first wrote of the pronghorn in 1804, fifteen million or more (some say forty million) of the unique North American antelope roamed the West. By the turn of the century, ten thousand survived. Like so many other large animals moving in herds they made easy targets for market hunters. Pronghorn need large expanses of unfenced habitat, which disappeared quickly as the frontier receded. Nevertheless, pronghorn biologist Jim Yoakum estimated numbers at more than four hundred thousand in 1980.

The largest pronghorn herds lived on the Great Plains, and today, even with universal protection, the antelope still do best in the plains states. Great Basin sagebrush always has been peripheral range. Pronghorn prefer open country and therefore favor dwarf sage-brush and black sagebrush over big sagebrush. The latter makes perfectly good forage, but any time it grows more than thirty inches tall it stands too tall for these animals of the short-grass, big-sky, western spaces.

I watched a group of pronghorn amble through low-growing black sage below the Reveille Range. It was sunset, and the antelope were the same golden color as the backlit grass, haze, and dust. Life, speed, the gamboling of the kids—the herd traced a narrow thread of movement through the vast basin of unmoving plants. Though unhurried, they traveled fast and disappeared westward into the amber light of the sun.

Sage Grouse make a better emblem for the sagebrush world. These birds rely on sage-brush for virtually every facet of their daily needs. They feed on it, take cover under it, and nest beneath it. Yet a monotonous stand of dense big sagebrush will not support the grouse. They need small-statured shrubs for nesting, here and there a meadow with succulent herbs, water in summer, and open spots for strutting. For the first three months, the diet of young grouse includes 50 percent insects, gleaned from wet meadows or upland sagebrush in prime condition. Dwarf and black sagebrush stands with islands of big sagebrush seem nearly perfect, with density of cover neither too high nor too low.

The size of small turkeys, the males—called "cocks of the plains" by Lewis and Clark when they introduced them to science—gather on communal strutting grounds. Once as many as four hundred males gathered to vie for female attention. Today a dozen or so males make for a good show. Visit them during breeding season on a cold April morning at the edge of a meadow in Nevada's Sheldon Antelope Range or on Oregon's Hart Mountain.

Fanning his spectacular tail feathers and swishing his wings back, the male inflates his chest sac—an extension of his esophagus—with more than a gallon of air. When he deflates it, the air balloons into two bare patches of olive yellow skin on his chest; these are his noisemakers, collapsing with sharp pops. The sound rings through the still, crisp air for a third of a mile.

The watching females mate only with males holding territories that include a mating center. A young male, with luck, acquires a territory on the fringes of a breeding ground and gradually makes his way toward a center, where he finally mates after waiting several years.

Once, Sage Grouse range matched that of sagebrush. Today, they inhabit much of that area but in greatly reduced numbers. Excessive stock grazing has increased the abundance of sagebrush in some areas but not the populations of Sage Grouse. A pure stand of sagebrush, with few grasses and herbs, does them little good.

Livestock graze some 70 percent of the land within the eleven western states, at least during part of the year. The public owns much of this land, and federal biologists manage it. The interplay of native plants and animals with introduced species from cows to cheatgrass has more effect on sagebrush communities than any climatic or geographic factor. Range managers control the future of the Sage Grouse as they control the ecology of most of the sagebrush ocean, islands and all.

After the Paiutes and Shoshones made it their home, mountain men saw this desert first. Peter Skene Ogden knew the sagebrush country. So did Jedediah Smith. In the Intermountain West they found a new sort of wilderness.

This was the arid country, the land of little rain; the Americans had not known drouth. It was the dead country; they had known only fecundity. It was the open country; they had moved through the forests, past the oak openings, to the high prairie grass. It was the country of intense sun; they had always had shade to hide in. The wilderness they had crossed had been a passive wilderness, its ferocity without passion and only loosed when one blundered; but this was an aggressive wilderness, its ferocity came out to meet you and the conditions of survival required a whole new technique.

In this passage from *The Year of Decision: 1846*, Bernard DeVoto was looking back after a century. He could see the ferocious necessity for a new way of living with a dry land. Yet even today, westerners pooh-pooh DeVoto and try mightily to ignore this truth.

To the overlanders of the mid-1800s, the Great Basin was desert and Great Basin Indians were all "Diggers." Shoshones on the northern fringe of the Basin had acquired horses, but unmounted Paiutes and Goshutes farther south lived where resources barely supported tiny bands of humans. Bison disappeared from even the lushest sagebrush ranges before 1830; pronghorn never had been abundant. But still the Indian people lived with the land, cycling from resource to resource with the seasons.

In 1847, Mormons moved to the Great Basin. Their symbolic beehive meant "industry," and they set about putting the desert to good, God-fearing use. The California gold rush in 1849 and the Comstock strike in Virginia City, Nevada, a decade later gave ranchers an instant, insatiable market for meat. One more decade and the transcontinental railroad bisected the Great Basin, making it easier still to get cattle to market. It took just fifteen years from the start of grazing before the best grasslands within the sagebrush desert were grazed

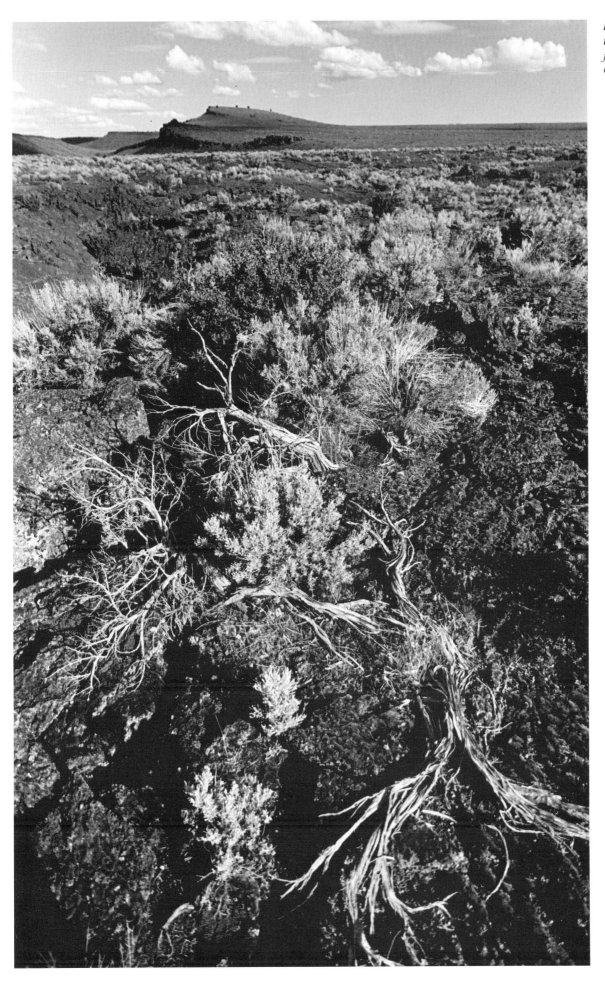

Big sagebrush on the rough lava flows of Diamond Craters, Oregon.

*Sheepherder,
Harney Basin,
Oregon; livestock
graze some 70
percent of the area
of the eleven
western states.*

106

*Between the
Mountains*

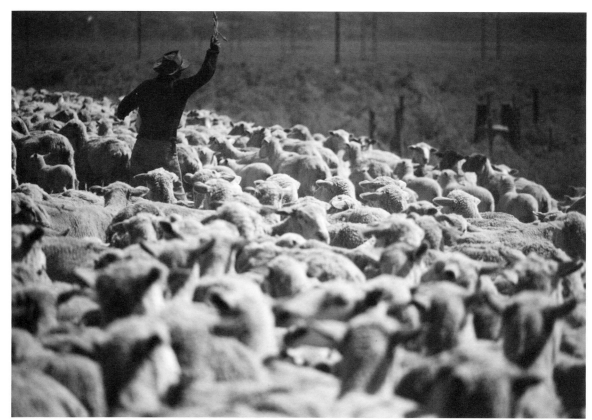

out. Unfortunately, they do not recover with fifteen years of rest.

James A. Young, Raymond A. Evans, and their colleagues at the University of Nevada in Reno have traced the successive disasters in the sagebrush range. Young summarizes what happened: "The plant communities did not bend or adapt, they shattered." The story reads like a Dickensian morality play, complete with good guys, bad guys, heroes, and villains.

*Act One: wherein livestock come to
the pristine Great Basin, beginning a
tragic tale of doom for our native heroes of
the sagebrush ocean.*

For the first time, English-speaking ranchers adopted Mexican open-range tactics for raising livestock on marginal land. They stocked the range with as many animals as could survive and determined this number by overstocking and allowing winterkill to tell them when they had reached their limit. Cattle eat grass, and when the grass began to thin, ranchers added more sheep, who browsed the shrubs.

The perennial grasses and herbs stood no chance. They had adapted to the long cen-

turies of drying since the Pleistocene by putting all their energy into flowering and fruiting in spring, after the wet winter and before summer drought forced dormancy, waiting for the occasional wetter-than-normal year for big pay-offs in reproductive success. The lack of grazers gave them time to be patient; using up all their food reserves at once remained a safe risk.

With a half-million animals on the spring range, the grasses inevitably gave way. Sagebrush, on the other hand, retains a set of winter leaves that photosynthesize year-round; it has a head start on reproduction come spring. It taps water deep below ground. And its evil-tasting leaves save it from livestock.

When the frigid winter of 1889–1890 (harshest in five hundred years) followed the drought of 1888, hundreds of thousands of sheep and cattle died. In 1885, Elko County rancher John Sparks branded thirty-eight thousand calves; in the spring of 1890, the same range yielded sixty-eight calves.

By the end of the nineteenth century these calamities combined to reduce sagebrush ranges to dust beds—a near-monoculture of remnant sagebrush in a denuded, erosion-prone wasteland. Even with the beginning of grazing control after the creation of the U.S. Forest Service, the perennial grasses did not recover. And no native annuals existed that had adapted to such environments.

End of Act One: which saw our heroic pristine sagebrush/grassland destroyed in forty years. Stage setting for Act Two: an empty scaffold, a biological vacuum.

With the introduction of domesticated animals and Eurasian crops like wheat, the accidental introduction of an occasional foreign seed became inevitable. Only those plants that found favorable environments sprouted, survived, and spread. But at the turn of the century the bare ground of the degraded sagebrush ranges was up for grabs. The first accidental arrivals to spread were broadleaf species: Russian thistle, redstem heron-bill, and several mustards.

Russian thistle pioneers bare ground by rapid germination. Mustards succeed in such harsh seedbeds by protecting their seeds with a mucilaginous coat. Heron-bill has a twisted tail on its seeds that accomplishes self-burial: as humidity increases, the coiled midsection of the seed relaxes. When the desert sun dries it out, it tightens and twists like a screw, driving the seed into the ground, planting itself.

These alien species began to colonize bare ground under sagebrush before 1900. They flourished in summer, when many native grasses and herbs went dormant. The natives found their resources usurped by competitors they had never before encountered.

Just after 1900, the problems for native species multiplied beyond imagining when another Eurasian immigrant turned up in the Great Basin: downy brome (*Bromus tectorum*)—cheatgrass.

Cheatgrass evolved in Eurasia under constant pressure from large grazers. Native perennial bunchgrasses had escaped such pressures. Not only did heavy spring grazing confound the natives' reproductive success, but they fared poorly with trampling, incapable of filling in wounds as sod-forming grasses can do.

Domesticated animals grazed the steppes of central Asia—the ancestral home of cheatgrass—in a climate similar to the Great Basin. Cheatgrass had grown, and evolved, with heavy grazing for millennia. An annual, it survived summer drought as a seed, germinating in pulses through autumn and winter whenever moisture was sufficient, establishing a root system that prepared it for rapid seed-set come spring. On some plots about fourteen hundred cheatgrass seedlings per square foot popped up through the litter of the broadleaf plants. Grazing and trampling might wipe out numerous seedlings, but cheatgrass numbers prevailed.

After 1900, cheatgrass spread widely along railroads, in livestock fur and straw, and on its own powers of dispersal. Wheat farmers unwittingly sowed contaminated seed in autumn and watched their fields blossom with cheat the following spring, "cheating" them of their crop and giving the grass its common name. The *Idaho Statesman* ran a story on May 1, 1928, about the replacement of bunchgrass by cheat. The Boise newspaper said of the alien grass: it "grows in a day, ripens in a day, and blows away in a day."

The sharp points on dry cheatgrass seeds gave cows more pain than nutrition. And cheatgrass competed so successfully, it could invade native bunchgrass stands ungrazed and unburned for fifty years. That latter factor—fire—dominates the next segment of the story, a tale unraveled first by R. L. Piemeisel in the 1930s.

Act Three: wherein the villainous weed signs a pact with a force greater than itself, and in league with fire marches to empire.

We cannot know how frequently fire swept through the pristine sagebrush/grassland. But we have a clue.

Sagebrush dies after fire and must resprout from seed. Burned perennial grasses tend to weaken initially but later gain in vigor from reduced competition with shrubs. Green rabbitbrush, snakeweed, and littleleaf horsebrush and lesser numbers of currant, desert peach, and Mormon tea all sprout from roots after fire. These latter shrubs make poor forage for browsers, whether native or domestic. But they dominate burns for ten or fifteen years before sagebrush again grows large enough to regain its domain.

Intense widespread fires could have come no more frequently than every few decades, or else the root-sprouters, not sagebrush, would have characterized the Great Basin. Lighter fires must have come frequently enough to keep the ever-increasing sagebrush in balance with bunchgrasses. After denudation by excessive stock grazing but before cheatgrass invasion, the sagebrush lands became virtually fireproof, with shrubs too far apart to carry flames and no burnable understory. This allowed sagebrush to increase in abundance more than ever.

Cheatgrass, however, created a new cycle. The little annual filled in the gaps between sagebrush, curing tinder-dry in summer. Fires became common. And with weakened bunchgrasses on most of the sagebrush ranges, fire removed sagebrush, favored root-sprouters, and gave cheatgrass a chance to use its boundless germination energies and deplete the bunchgrasses still further.

Today, cheatgrass quickly builds up the tinder again, and fire comes before sagebrush can grow back. If fire does not come too frequently, root-sprouting green rabbitbrush and littleleaf horsebrush may replace sagebrush as the dominant shrubs. With frequent enough fires, cheatgrass can take over completely, in Aldo Leopold's words, covering the "ruined complexions" of the hills with "ecological face powder."

James Young and Raymond Evans liken the dominance of cheatgrass after wildfires to "the phoenix of an alien life form rising from the ashes to haunt the post-burn environment." Their image is not overdramatic. Native bunchgrass species cannot invade pure cheatgrass stands. Relict native grasses can suppress the alien only with absolute protection from disturbance and fire; even the activities of native rodents can slow down succession.

Russian thistle pioneers the most disturbed sites, succeeding to the broad-leaved alien mustards, then to cheat. Increase the disturbance and cheat reverts to tumbleweed, but all these annuals prevent the perennial native grasses from flourishing.

And in places, new exotic annuals have managed to displace even cheatgrass. Medusahead, an annual grass that favors heavy clay soils, has crept from central Oregon south into California and remains poised on the fringes of the Basin along the Nevada border. It can successfully invade cheatgrass stands and offers half the already poor forage potential of cheat.

Act Four: wherein range scientists ride into the valley to do battle with the denuded land and the alien weed. The buckaroo biologists come armed with platoons of bulldozers, buckets of herbicides, and torches of fire. They carry as peace offerings wreaths of Russian wheatgrass.

The 1930s forced recognition of the disastrous results of overgrazing by livestock. Sodbusters on the plains created the Dust Bowl; throughout cattle country, drought in combination with overgrazing brought about similar disasters, and in 1934 the Taylor Grazing Act initiated federal regulation of the public range. Eventually, the Bureau of Land Management took over management of these lands—by default, for these were the leftovers after homesteaders, foresters, and park preservers all had done their best to carve their heart's desires from the public domain.

By the time management began, the sagebrush range was overgrazed, eroded, and invaded by alien weeds. The biologists knew their only hope: to free bunchgrasses from spring grazing pressure so they could reproduce. But what would ranchers do with their stock during this season?

Bunchgrasses had deteriorated in most places to the point where simple reduction of grazing or change of season brought little change. Native grasses did poorly in reseeding attempts. Mechanically destroying sagebrush

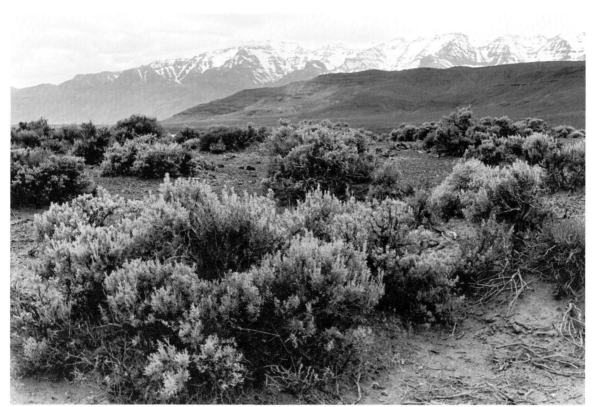

*Big sagebrush in
the Alvord Desert
below Steens
Mountain.*

109

———

*Ocean of
Sagebrush*

stands with cables or disc plows encouraged
root-sprouters and annuals.

Range managers turned to exotic perennial
grasses evolved in communities similar to the
intransigent cheatgrass—communities long
grazed. Russian wheatgrasses (*Agropyron*)
proved to be resistant to heavy spring grazing,
capable of lush growth in the Great Basin, and
(once established) even able to suppress cheatgrass. Drought-tolerant desert wheatgrass
worked best on lower, drier sites; crested
wheatgrass thrived higher and to the north.
From the 1930s to the 1960s enormous areas
of gentler slope and deeper soil were plowed
and seeded to exotic wheatgrass.

Ranchers had their spring pastures. Range
biologists had enough work to keep them in research money for forty years. And conservationists and wildlife biologists had begun a
long cycle of skeptical eyebrow raising.

Range scientists became better and better
at restoring degraded range to productivity for
livestock. After World War II they began using
herbicides like 2,4-D to kill sagebrush and
rabbitbrush. They developed precise application techniques in hopes of controlling side
effects of the poison. Under growing pressure

from wildlife biologists concerned about the
glaring single-mindedness of their efforts, they
began reseeding with mixtures that included
wildlife browse and forage species.

But the outcry from a public finally wise to
the fact that the Intermountain West was being
managed for the exclusive use and profit of the
livestock industry slowed the "golden era of
range improvement" in the 1960s. Spraying
had increased in cost and its effects proved
short-lived: sagebrush and rabbitbrush frequently reinvaded quickly. Increasingly du-
bious wildlife biologists challenged the value
of pure wheatgrass stands to native animals.
And yet wheatgrass seedings did make it easier
for ranchers to stay in business—and to provide for a nation exceedingly fond of steaks
and hamburgers.

Today the debate goes on, a face-off between two alliances: the livestock industry and
western politicians on one side and federal
land managers, conservationists, and wildlife
biologists on the other.

One hundred and forty years of tampering
with the delicate balance achieved between
shrubs and grasses in the sagebrush community has altered it irrevocably. We may well

have permanently reduced its nutritional capabilities. Whatever tactics we choose now, we have set forces in motion that will not stop while we pause and ponder our next move.

Livestock grazing continues and will not cease unless Americans modify their devotion to eating vast quantities of red meat—an unlikely revolution in diet. Wild horses, recently protected and ever increasing in numbers, add additional grazing pressure where they roam. Sparse grasses may recover not at all with general reduction in livestock numbers. A recent evaluation of pastures of basin big sagebrush in Utah's Tintic Valley found that the standing crop of perennial grasses actually decreased after thirteen years of rest from grazing. On the other hand, late-autumn sheep use of sagebrush range enhances grasses, since sheep will browse sagebrush at this season. Without some means of reducing brush, sagebrush continues to invade wherever grasses weaken.

Dense stands of big sagebrush are just as useless as wheatgrass pastures to most wildlife traditionally designated "sagebrush/grass species." To maintain the diversity of cover and food favored by most animals, including Sage Grouse, some brush reduction is necessary, whether by grazing, fire, or herbicides. Neil West points out that the best method might be to herd sheep specifically on areas in need of moderate pruning. Or introduce an exotic browser, like the Asian saiga antelope, capable of living on sagebrush. But these gambles would have unknown effects on wildlife and watersheds, and the economics do not work out well.

Fire can open sagebrush stands but must be used with great care to avoid encouraging cheatgrass. Meanwhile, range scientists now believe they can eliminate cheatgrass with her-

bicides, allowing perennial grasses to reclaim still more land. With chemical poisons creating rampant problems for wildlife, other biologists are skeptical.

Still, cheatgrass has reclaimed ranges otherwise completely degraded. It helps prevent erosion, serves as livestock forage in spring if nothing else is available, and supports the Great Basin's most important upland game bird, the Chukar.

Chukar introduction paired this Asian partridge with an environment similar to its home—rugged country dominated by cheatgrass, its most important food. Like cheatgrass, Chukars filled a void, and today the bird's popularity with hunters adds yet another dimension to range and wildlife management decisions.

Aldo Leopold said in *A Sand County Almanac:* "This ecological ring-around-the-rosy merits long thought." Through livestock grazing and introduction of weedy exotics, we have modified this ocean of sagebrush as surely as we have transformed tall-grass prairie with the plow. Far more than an Iowa cornfield, however, the sagebrush desert still looks and feels like wilderness—a wilderness with cows.

Unlike pristine wilderness, it requires management. One recent evaluation of the Humboldt River basin found a depressing 1 percent of the sagebrush range in "fairly high" condition. The rest was degraded. Without management, it will remain degraded.

The challenge: juggling a billion acres worth of ecologic, economic, and political realities with deftness, wisdom, farsightedness, and tolerance.

We should wish ourselves luck.

Unlikely Oases
The World of Dunes

9

The ant is wrestling the husk of a seed. She watches him. He pulls the seed into the shade of a gray stone and leans against it. She can see the swirl of dust snaking over the desert floor toward them. It takes a long time, stopping and disappearing, then starting again, puffing the dust with sighs; the sun begins to fall before the swirl arrives. It comes suddenly over the grey stone like a wave breaking, bowls the seed from the ant's grasp into a foreign crevice and tumbles the ant away. Then it flattens out. It evaporates. It brushes her hips. . . .

The ant emerges slowly from a cul-de-sac of dust. He walks across the desert. He disappears into the crevice after the seed. . . .

She is asleep. The ant emerges from the crack in the floor of the desert. He has the seed. The yellow light of the full moon glints on his round smooth belly.

—Barry Lopez,
Desert Notes: Reflections in the Eye of a Raven, 1976

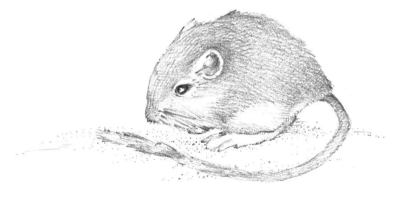

Pale kangaroo mouse

Humans like rhythm. And sand dunes are rhythmic, their winding S-curves moving back and forth with the wind, alternating lee side and slip face, light and shadow.

Their smoothness is striking—even playas are marked by mudcracks. But smooth sand in the larger dunes of the Great Basin contrasts with the spiny surrounding shadscale. Smooth and feminine curves of sand; angular and masculine shrubs.

In parts of the Sahara and Arabian deserts, sand seas indeed can be barren. Sand. Endless sand. The wind stirs up squalls, sending them pluming off dune crests in sinuous roostertails. No tracks mar the pattern of wind ripples. Nothing lives. No lizards, no beetles, not a blade of grass.

Great Basin sand dunes, however, turn out to be precisely the opposite. In low valleys with inhospitable alkali and clay, a small dune offers an island of livable soil. It holds water deep in protected reservoirs, tappable by plants with long-enough roots. The soft cups of coyote tracks in the sand contain small windfalls of dried plant debris: bits of shadscale leaves and broken pieces of lance-leaf scurfpea rhizome.

In turn, this island of rich plant resources becomes a hotbed of small animal populations. Kangaroo rat burrows lace blowouts, patches of heavier sand, and stabilized dunes. Walk along the base of the dune and lizards scatter to either side, taking off across the hot sand like bottle rockets ignited by your footfalls.

Sand dunes occur only where a source of sand exists, where winds have the power to move the sand, and where a topographic trap stops the wind-bounced grains and allows them to accumulate. In the Great Basin, dry lakes provide rich sources of sand, particularly the huge old Bonneville and Lahontan lake beds with delta deposits from larger rivers like the Carson, Humboldt, and Sevier. And with mountain ranges ever on the horizon, barriers to windblown sand come easy.

A few dunes pile high enough to remain barren at their summits, too shifting and too deep for plants. The prevailing westerly winds build these on the east sides of valleys. The Crescent Dunes in Big Smoky Valley just north of Tonopah and Little Sahara Dunes near Delta, Utah, both rise to impressive stature. Extensive smaller dunes dot Oregon's High Desert and the country north of Winnemucca. Sand Mountain, just off U.S. Highway 50 east of Fallon, Nevada, on the edge of Four Mile Flat, probably is the biggest Great Basin dune. In *Blue Highways*, William Least Heat Moon describes it as "a single massive mound of tawny sand . . . of such size that, while it wasn't perhaps big enough to be a mountain by everybody's definition, it was surely more than a dune."

Surrounding these active dunes, and in many other places in the Basin, plant-stabilized dunes cover huge areas. They really do not look like dunes but create a humble, hummocky topography of sandy soil.

Stabilized-dune communities in the Carson Desert region lie on the gravel flats and clay hardpans of the Lahontan lake bottom, superimposed on the vast stands of shadscale and Bailey's greasewood. The latter two shrubs may even act as dune formers, catching blowing sand, which builds up around them. The shadscale and greasewood may keep pace for a time, elongating their roots to cope with deepening sand. They may die, buried too deep to survive. Either way, other shrubs invade the growing dune.

First comes smokebush, the dominant shrub on Lahontan dunes. Four-winged saltbush is next. When wind piles the sand ten to twenty feet deep, littleleaf horsebrush takes root. Many dune herbs range northward into the Lahontan basin from the southern deserts. Of all lowland Great Basin communities, dunes seem most clearly a northern counterpart of the hot desert.

Their piles of silica grains can certainly radiate heat like the southern deserts. I walked into the Big Smoky Valley's Crescent Dunes on a cloudy summer morning, streaks of deep brown showing where the sand held moisture from yesterday's rain. I started barefoot, but af-

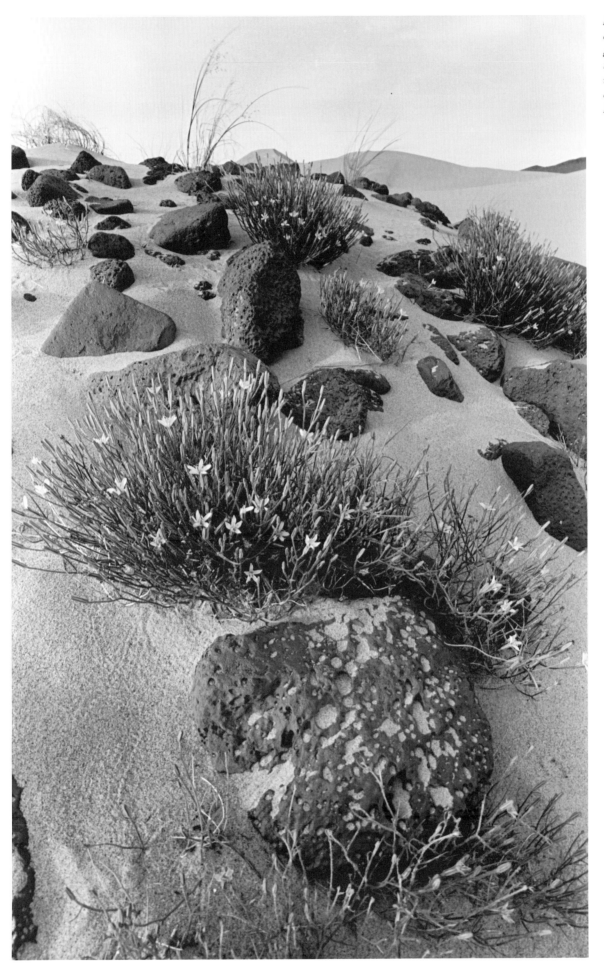

*Boulders provide
a foothold for
grass and shrubs
in the shifting
world of dunes
around Sand
Mountain.*

Wind ripples and scurfpea shadows pattern the surface of dunes north of Winnemucca.

ter only a few minutes of sunlight as the clouds burned off, on went my sandals.

Comparable islands of sand support the greatest diversity of plants on Bonneville basin valley floors. Though many species grow in other places, they assemble on dunes in distinctive combinations.

In Dugway Valley, for example, herbs pioneer first on swales and ridges of sand: lance-leaf scurfpea and buckwheat. Delicate Indian ricegrass, sturdy sand dock, and green rabbitbrush come next. Once sand has piled deep enough, large shrubs dominate: rabbitbrush, four-winged saltbush, littleleaf horsebrush, greasewood, and spiny hopsage.

At the base of these dunes, sand combines with clay to make hummocks of sandy loam that also support distinctive plant and animal communities. Here green rabbitbrush, shadscale, granite prickly-phlox, and bud sagebrush grow luxuriantly, with airy stands of alkali sacaton.

Smokebush does not grow in the Bonneville basin, but dunes in the two old lake beds share many other resident plants. Indeed, some of these characteristic species, whose adaptations enable them to grow in deep, moving sand, live on dunes all over the Southwest. Urban people enshrine dunes as romantic symbols of aridity; Great Basin Indians knew otherwise. They knew that dunes symbolize abundant moisture to desert plants and cool, wet sand to burrowing desert animals. For the Indian people this meant rich harvests of everything from ricegrass seeds to grasshoppers and rodents.

Dune plants have an easy time taking up water—far easier than plants rooted in fine-textured clays that bind water tightly, but not so easy as in sandy loam, seven times more permeable than sand. Nitrogen-fixing bacteria and root fungi that help capture phosphorus ease the problems of low nutrition in pure sand.

Depth and movement of sand create difficulties at odds with this easy access to water. Many plants living in dunes show a consistent adaptation: they can grow long stems and roots, and can do so rapidly. Though dunes trap precipitation and harbor groundwater reservoirs, capillary action can raise water only about sixteen inches above the water table. Dune plants must grow long taproots to anchor themselves and to keep their roots in wet sand in an advancing dune. If they do not, their food-producing leaves and seed-producing flowers cannot stay above accumulating sand. Buried, they die.

Moving sand not only buries plants at the leading edge of a dune but excavates plants at its trailing edge in blowouts. Dune plants fare poorly with such deflation of their home. Dozens of feet worth of twisted stems, roots, and runners of lance-leaf scurfpea trail across depressions where the shoots have been killed by dunes moving on. For a time smokebushes remain perched on pillars of sand held by their roots; when the sand blows out from under them, they perish.

These adaptations happen through the statistical process of natural selection, not by design. Plants commonly double or triple their sets of chromosomes (in the process called polyploidy), as we have seen in saltbushes. This provides variation and creates new versions of saltbushes that may possess more successful adaptations to a local environment.

Four-winged saltbush grows widely on Great Basin dunes. Botanists recognize only one species, but this one species varies phenomenally across its range. The widespread varieties have mostly four sets of chromosomes, with some at six sets. One population, however, has maintained itself on Utah's Little Sahara Dunes as the only four-winged saltbushes with just two sets of chromosomes.

Atriplex expert Howard Stutz believes that the dune population with two chromosome sets survives as the last relict of the old, ancestral form. Newer forms, with their multiple sets of chromosomes, grow more slowly—smaller, hardier plants evidently better adapted to the drying desert of the past ten thousand years. The Little Sahara saltbush has several adaptations that work spectacularly well in the dunes but would make it dangerously attractive to browsing animals elsewhere. The widespread form of four-winged saltbush generally does not survive on such high, active dunes and indeed cannot invade Little Sahara.

These remarkable dune saltbushes grow to giant size, twelve feet high and up to fifteen feet across. Normal four-winged saltbush rarely exceeds four feet in either dimension. The giant saltbushes can grow new twigs forty inches long in one season—three times the rate of normal plants. Leaves and fruits measure larger as well. Early flowering isolates the relict plant from surrounding populations with four chromosome sets.

The giant saltbushes favor the leeward bases of dunes, which hold more moisture; this also places them in the path of encroaching sand. To survive they must grow at least fast enough to keep ahead of deepening dunes. After coping with moving sand through generations of evolving four-winged saltbushes, modern giant saltbush seedlings grow twice as fast as normal plants. As the dune moves on they add new roots easily, in whatever layers of sand lead to water. Previously buried stems and roots develop chlorophyll and may become photosynthetic if exposed anew.

Stutz attributes the survival of these plants to their near-complete isolation from grazing. Too luxuriant and too palatable, other ancestral populations disappeared; in the dunes, natural selection gradually refined this old form's adaptations to the moving world of sand.

Throughout the Great Basin, plants on dunes form a community composed of such local specialists, along with plants from adjacent habitats and widely distributed species that favor sandy soil. Dune animals live in distinctive combinations as well.

These islandlike concentrations of rodents in simple environments make for the kinds of experiments ecologists love to call "elegant." But even here, with what appear to be simple ecological problems, nature confounds us with hidden complexities.

E. Raymond Hall introduced his 1946 classic *Mammals of Nevada* with a walk around Sand Mountain just after dawn, where small mammals occur in "a density equaled in few other habitats." By day,

> the sand's smooth surface is relieved only by sharp-edged, cut-out hollows where the wind races round a bush and fires out a sandblast that stings the cheeks, tortures the eyes, and coats one's teeth with grit. The sun's reflected heat, which burns through the soles of stout boots, drives even the lizards and antelope squirrels to the shade of bushes.

But by night the dune comes alive with the comings and goings of small creatures. At dawn, "before a person's curiosity is half satisfied about the burrows and the dozens of stories told by the tracks, the sun is up—and with it the wind, the wind that obliterates every telltale mark and burrow opening."

What do these myriads of pocket mice, kangaroo mice, and kangaroo rats find to eat in this barren world? "It lies there buried in the sand for all those who have keen noses to find it and the will to dig it out—seeds of grasses and other desert plants."

Anyone who has trouble believing that such a rich source of food could lie hidden in the dunes must return to Sand Mountain, or some other sandy Great Basin valley, after the crucial conjunction of winter rain and warm spring that triggers a spectacular year for blossoming desert annuals. Evening primrose, mallow, prickly-phlox, phacelia, penstemon, and many others mark the gray-tan desert with sprays of blazing color—sprouted from the seeds the rodents left uneaten.

Hall knew the habits of the seed-eating rodents well enough to predict confidently where they would live and when they would be active. He noted the dependence of the pale kangaroo mouse on fine sand with scattered plants; the desert kangaroo rat's requirement of sand at least twenty inches deep; the little pocket mouse's ability to wait out in torpor times of climatic stress or low food availability. He discussed the dynamic evolution apparent in Lahontan basin rodents still adapting to the newly

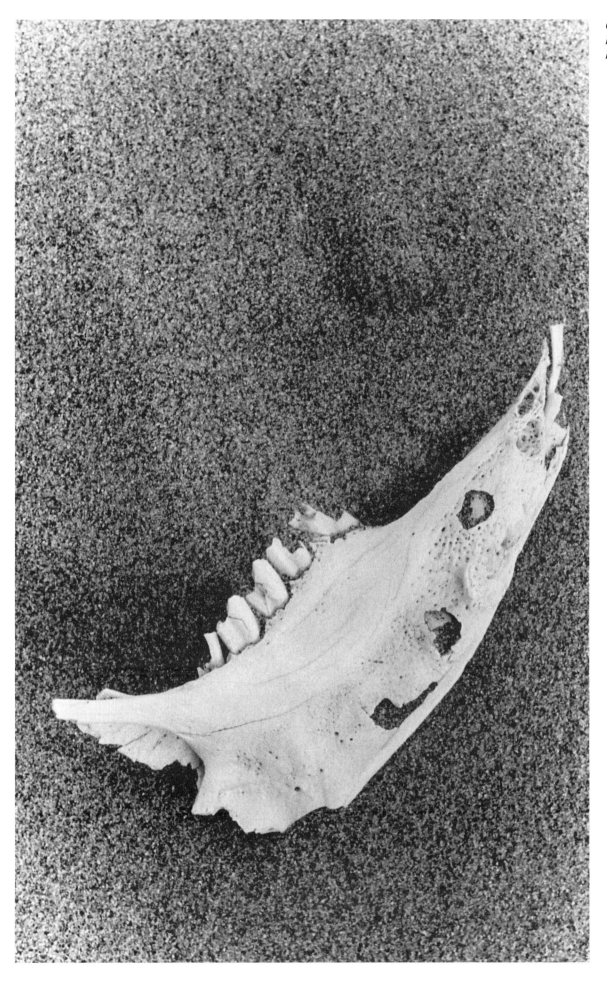

*Cottontail jaw,
Little Sahara
Dunes.*

created dry flats on the old lake bed.

In 1946, after trapping in Nevada for years, Hall knew the basic story of Great Basin dune communities. After extensive trapping in the fifties, E. Dean Vest summarized similar patterns in the Bonneville basin, stating: "It would be difficult to emphasize a single factor that would influence the distribution of any of the rodents, largely because of the unknown effects of high populations and interspecies relationships."

From the late sixties to the present, ecologists have done their best to unravel that single factor and have come up with a gamut of conflicting answers. The broad answer is "water." The dunes support rich life because they trap the water necessary to nourish a dependable larder of plants. But forty years after Hall we are still struggling to understand just how so many rodents of such similar habits manage to live on the rich resources offered by Great Basin dunes—and coexist in what seems a simple habitat difficult to subdivide.

To be successful, an animal needs to live long enough to procreate. If it can fit into a spectrum of resources where no other animal exists, then times are fat, living is easy. If the animal competes for exactly the same resources with several other animals, then it will need some distinguishing adaptation to allow it enough food/shelter/space to survive and reproduce.

Divide and conquer. Mountain lions eat bigger prey than bobcats eat. Predatory birds kill food, scavengers eat carrion, vegetarian birds stick to seeds, leaves, or fruits.

On a sand dune in the Great Basin fewer choices exist. Rainfall is unpredictable, and leafy plants offer slim pickings. Two rodents slip into unique slots in the resource spectrum by taking sidetracks not favored by other rodents. Grasshopper mice hunt; they are tiny predators living mostly on insects but capable of bringing down lizards and mice. And chisel-toothed kangaroo rats—shadscale specialists—avoid competition with their fellow heteromyids by dropping out of the seed competition entirely. In spring, Merriam's kangaroo rats could

compete with the chisel-tooths, for during breeding season these seed-eaters need green vegetation. With their separate reproductive seasons the two avoid conflict.

In 1970, James H. Brown began a series of experiments aimed at understanding how seed-eating rodents in the Southwest deserts maintained their incredible abundance and diversity. He trapped in dunes in the hot deserts to the south as well as in eleven sites across the Great Basin. The patterns he found in resident rodents are remarkable, his conclusions controversial.

He found a basic pool of seed-eating rodents living on dunes throughout the Southwest: Ord's, Merriam's, and desert kangaroo rats; pale kangaroo mice; little pocket mice; deer mice; and western harvest mice. Other species occurred more rarely. Still other rodents were common at times but did not compete for seeds (e.g., the predatory grasshopper mouse and the omnivorous antelope ground squirrel).

These seed-eating rodents, ranging from .25 ounce to 3.5 ounces, showed remarkably regular spacing of body weight on any one dune. Common species coexisting always differed considerably in body weight by a ratio (larger/smaller) of at least 1.5. The fewer species on a dune, the greater their differences. What underlying resource dictates that dune residents cannot be too close to the same size?

Brown found that the number of species on his dunes correlated strongly with annual precipitation, which he linked to plant productivity. With more rainfall, more plants grew; they produced more seeds, and rodent diversity increased. So far, so good.

Brown believed dune rodents subdivide these seeds and avoid competition by "feeding on seeds of different sizes and by foraging in different places." This final conclusion seemed innocent enough but has generated years of research, challenge, and counterchallenge. It is remarkably hard to test.

All heteromyids have external fur-lined cheek pouches that they use to store and transport seeds. Brown assumed seeds in cheek pouches reflect actual diet, and analyzed cheek

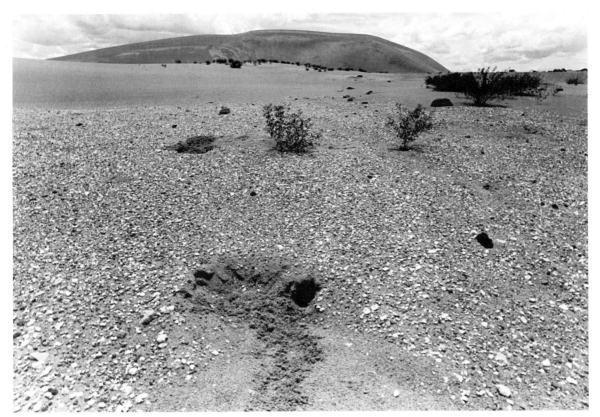

pouch contents from the heteromyid rodents he trapped. Large kangaroo rats indeed collected bigger seeds than smaller ones, and small kangaroo rats collected larger seeds than kangaroo mice and little pocket mice. Because deer mice and harvest mice have no cheek pouches, Brown could say nothing about their seed size preferences.

To determine where the animals foraged, Brown placed his traps in a series from the center of plants to adjacent open areas. In open areas he usually caught the highly specialized kangaroo rats and mice (with powerful hind legs for moving quickly and greatly enlarged auditory resonance chambers in their skulls for super-sensitive predator detection). Pocket mice and harvest mice seemed to stay close to clumps of vegetation. Deer mice foraged everywhere equally—or at least the trap data suggested that they did.

Brown's theory was simple, even elegant. But does it truthfully show the world according to kangaroo rats?

Over the years, other ecologists found differing results, and each offered a new explanation for how the rodents divided up their resources.

Even definitions prove difficult, however: what is the proper way to measure a large seed usually collected husked (and therefore smaller) by pocket mice and unhusked by kangaroo rats? If a desert kangaroo rat collects a large fruiting head filled with many small seeds, is this a large seed or a clump of small ones? Forced to refine his original theory of seed size preference, Brown proposed that rodents collect "food packets" providing net energy returns consistent with their body size.

More goes on than just difference in body size. Foraging at different times through the night would minimize face-to-face confrontations and ease competition. Staying active at higher (pocket mice) or lower (deer mice) temperatures gives these species an edge at climatic extremes. Deer mice alone remain active when snow covers the Basin. And many other explanations seemed possible for the difference in body size. The ability to safeguard food caches could depend on burrow size and, hence, body size. Different body sizes might be related to different methods of predator avoidance.

Competition with other distantly related

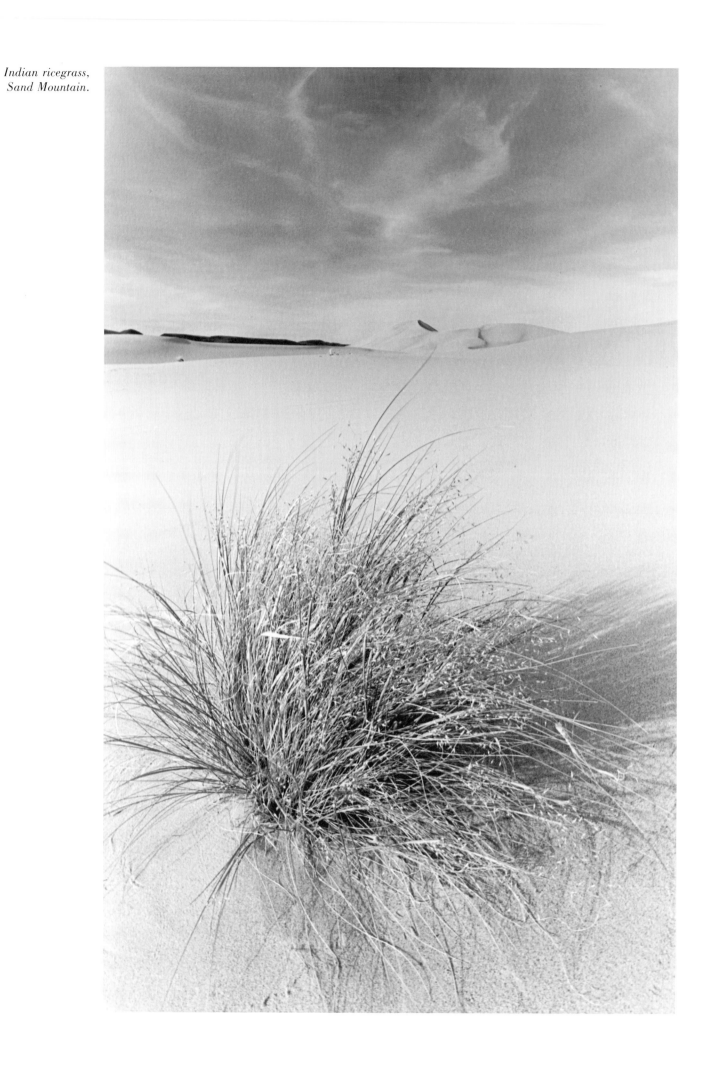

Indian ricegrass,
Sand Mountain.

seed-eaters further complicates matters. Dune grasshoppers may eat annual plants before they produce the seeds sought by the rodents. And harvester ants eat vast numbers of the same sized seeds as rodents and forage in the same places both during the day and by night, depending on the season. Heteromyids may even excavate ant mounds to raid their seed caches. Seed-eating birds have their biggest effect when great mixed-species flocks of finches and sparrows migrate through the deserts in good seed-crop years.

The rodents also seem to influence their seed resources by coevolving with the reproductive systems of their food plants. The ecological literature on "behavior" of seeds in soil is almost as rich as that detailing behavior of rodents. We know most about the intricate relationship between heteromyids and Indian ricegrass.

Two facts set the stage for this story. Though Indian ricegrass grows abundantly on dunes, its seeds usually will germinate only when the outer seed covering is removed. And heteromyid rodents cache vast quantities of ricegrass seeds.

In Desert Queen Valley in the Carson Desert, four species of heteromyids buried an average of 250 ricegrass seeds per cache, one cache per 7.8 square feet, each a little more than two inches deep. The rodents cached some 8 percent of the total ricegrass seeds produced here in a good year. They chose the biggest, plumpest, most highly germinable seeds and took no empty seeds at all (though ricegrass produces 28 percent empty-shelled seeds).

Before caching (at the ideal germination depth), the rodents usually removed the outer covering that induces dormancy, and thereby enhanced germination from the cache and provided themselves with fresh seedlings to feed on in spring—crucial nutrition during breeding season. Other seedlings growing from the cache survived and helped maintain the ricegrass population.

During the July ricegrass harvest, all four rodents took mostly ricegrass seeds. They ate a total of 35 percent of the filled seeds produced. The rest of the year, they took mostly Russian thistle seeds, but in July they ate none. The similarity in diet of every rodent from the little pocket mouse and pale kangaroo mouse to the desert kangaroo rat is striking, but these researchers did not detail the differences in the remaining 35 to 40 percent of the seeds taken. Since we never know which environmental factor the heteromyids see as crucial, we never know for sure what to measure—or if our measured differences and similarities, however statistically significant, matter to the animals.

Every conclusion from trapping experiments can be misread. For instance, if a rat is caught most frequently in the open, does it necessarily forage most frequently in the open? Small and nocturnal, these rodents remain hard to observe directly.

In 1982, Steven D. Thompson published the results of a clever effort to spy on the mice. He worked with a community of desert and Merriam's kangaroo rats and little pocket mice in the Mojave Desert. His trick: to the skulls of each animal live-trapped in his plot he glued "beta lights," which glowed with constant light. He then simply let the rodents adapt to his presence and stood and watched them feed— tiny points of color-coded light moving through velvety darkness.

He discovered that all three species foraged under bushes. The pocket mouse continuously sorted and sifted the sand while moving slowly underneath a shrub. Kangaroo rats moved quickly from bush to bush, but did their foraging under the shrubs. When he set out traps, however, he obtained the same results as Brown and others: pocket mice were trapped under bushes, kangaroo rats mostly in open areas.

Does competition exist at all? Perhaps we cannot pin down how the rodents subdivide their sandy resources because they simply do no such thing. Perhaps there is enough to go around.

Species distributions clearly controvert this.

In the Lahontan basin and just to the south in the Lahontan trough, desert kangaroo rats (the largest of Great Basin heteromyids, at

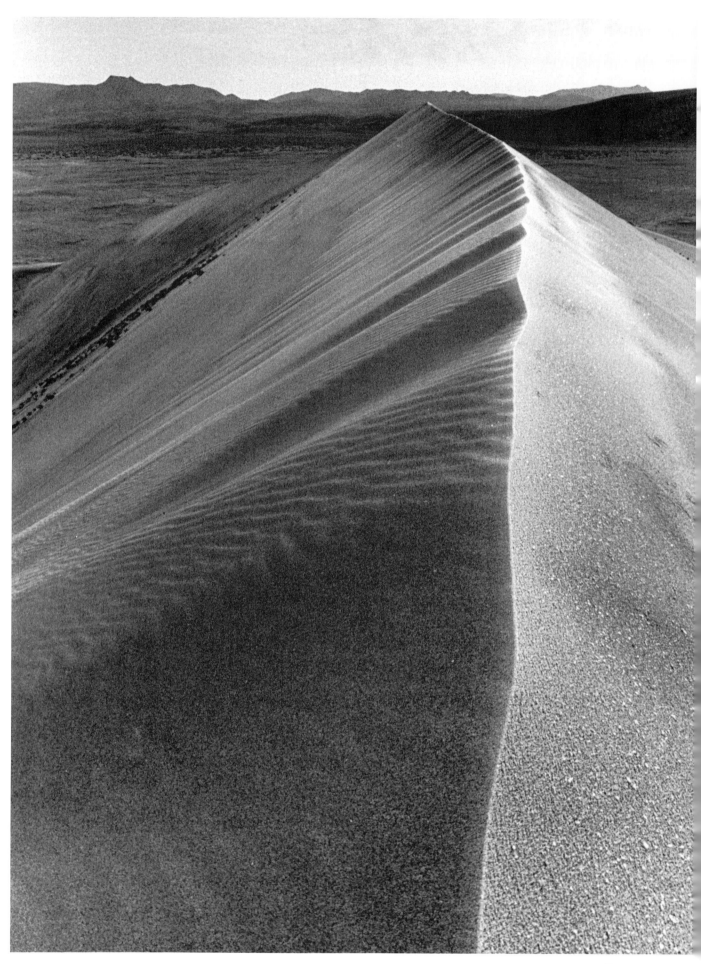

Frost on the
Crescent Dunes,
Big Smoky Valley

3.5 ounces) lived on every dune sampled by Brown. Smaller Merriam's kangaroo rats lived with them as common residents on every dune but one (where they occurred but in smaller numbers). Little pocket mice, pale kangaroo mice, and deer mice lived in abundance on five of the seven Lahontan dunes Brown studied. Harvest mice and Ord's kangaroo rats only lived on dunes with four or more species.

The Bonneville basin, isolated Railroad Valley in central Nevada, and Mono Lake all lie outside the ranges of desert and Merriam's kangaroo rats. These dunes all had Ord's kangaroo rats and deer mice, with sometimes one or two additional species.

Outside the range of the pale kangaroo mouse, the dark kangaroo mouse "replaced" it on two dunes. Likewise, outside the occurrence of the desert kangaroo rat at Mono Lake, the Panamint kangaroo rat (also quite large at 2.8 ounces) "replaced" it. Similar-sized harvest mice and little pocket mice never were common on the same dune.

Brown concluded that coexistence of seed-eating dune rodents depends more on their body size than on their identity.

In the western and southern Great Basin, sand dunes are easily colonized, yet not every potential colonist lives on them. In isolated basins where limited numbers of species can colonize dunes, the few that do live there increase in abundance. Something controls these variations in density and diversity. Competition for resources indeed seems to exist.

After all these years of research we still cannot fully explain the structure of rodent communities living on Great Basin dunes. A great exhilaration comes whenever we understand the tiniest process in nature—or believe we do. On dunes, similar wonder comes from being mystified and awed by the subtlety of these creatures.

We still do not understand how this small world of sand and seeds supports a greater diversity of rodents than many grasslands, forests, and marshes. No matter how simple, stark, or barren an ecological world seems, be prepared to have it baffle your best efforts. Never underestimate life.

Water in the Desert
Great Basin Wetlands

10

He remembered the ceremony of joy as practiced by the wild birds of Pyramid Lake.

All afternoon the sunlight had lain like burning dust upon the mountains and the palisades, and the still lake had been a mirage. . . . The birds were still. . . . Then all at once they went up. They flew in clouds around and around the islands, a huge aerial dance. . . . They chattered and cried and called in the air, so that the mountains cried back as if, in their canyons, invisible clouds of other birds were also celebrating. They were full of the madness of life. They were trying to relieve this tremendous energy and joy before the dark came and they had to settle. . . . Then the sun was gone. . . . The ritual cries of the birds stopped. In the dusk their pale cloud fell apart and down, and the islands were still. . . . Low over the darkling waters a lone cormorant sped home to Anaho.

—Walter Van Tilburg Clark,
The City of Trembling Leaves, 1945

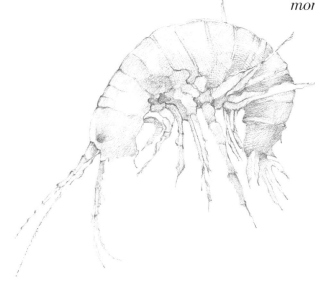

Brine shrimp

reat Basin wetlands gentle some unlikely places: shadscale valleys, the
edges of barren sinks. No matter
that the lakes are salty, the rivers
short-winded, they nonetheless harbor remarkable concentrations of plants and animals.

Flowing water attracts us just as powerfully
as it does wildlife. We build Great Basin towns,
farms, and roads close to water. Hikers gravi-
tate to canyons with the reassuring sound of a
creek bouncing through boulders, where sunlight and green leaves dapple the streamside
strip of rich soil, with here and there a bloom-
ing monkeyflower or columbine.

Along the northern rim of the Basin, the
ranges from the Jarbidge Mountains to the
Bannock Range drain north to the Snake River.
Elsewhere, most higher mountains in the Basin
feed a few creeks that run yearlong, and some
of these flow a short distance onto the neighboring plains before dwindling to dry channels
and sinks. Only the Humboldt builds a major
river system with both headwaters and sink in
the Great Basin.

Streams created in the high bordering ranges
reach out to give life to Basin lakes. From the
Sierra the Walker River feeds Walker Lake.
The Carson River runs to the Carson Sink; the
Truckee River runs from Tahoe to Pyramid
Lake. On the east edge of the Basin the Wa-
satch feeds Utah and Great Salt lakes via the
Bear, Logan, Weber, and Provo rivers; the Se-
vier River dies in Sevier Lake.

Here and there, other remnants of once-
huge Pleistocene lakes survive: Malheur, Harney, Summer, Abert, and the Warner lakes in
Oregon; Mono, Honey, Eagle, and the Alkali
lakes in California. Springs and groundwater
keep the Ruby Lakes fresh. Outlets are a rar-
ity: Utah Lake flows into the Great Salt Lake
via the Jordan River; Malheur overflows into
Harney Lake.

Surrounding many of these lakes are marshes
filled with waterfowl—hot spots of life, cities
of birds. Great Basin rivers flow through bottomlands lush with grass. Forests mark their
course—broad-leaved trees free to extrava-
gantly waste water. Great Blue Herons lift

away from streambanks and flap deliberately
downstream. No place in the Great Basin feels
more lush.

A single cottonwood leaf tapping in the breeze
embodies all the lushness of Great Basin wetlands. I heard a single note in this music of
life, struck by a cottonwood tree in winter on
King Lear Peak above the Black Rock Desert.

The Quinn River flows along the east side
of the Black Rock Range. Even in winter it
barely runs, never making it past its sink at
the base of the right arm of the Y-shaped playa.
On this November day, melting snow kept the
playa wet. Smooth and muddy, with none of
the dry cracks of summer, it felt like the five
hundred feet of water in Lake Lahontan had
drained just the week before.

Five thousand feet above loomed the greatest mountain in the neighboring ranges, King
Lear Peak, 8,910 feet high. In winter, with
wisps of gray cloud and snow plumes trailing
off high white turrets, it *looked* like King Lear
in torment.

McGill Canyon leads into the western flanks
of King Lear, a mountain stream hidden a
scant two miles from the intensity of the playa
below. Within the enclosing walls of rock,
junipers and cottonwoods shade mosses and
horsetails. As the sun hit the bank of the frozen arroyo on this cold day, pebbles began to
roll down the melting bank, loosened by the
touch of warmth—erosion made audible. The
sound suggested a vision that made me smile:
ants and beetles gleefully rolling pebbles off
the rim.

I surprised a flock of Chukars, the Asian
partridges introduced in the West years ago for
sport hunting. They raced across the arroyo in
front of me, climbing up the cliff—not flying
at all, but scaling steep rocks like miniature
bighorn sheep, deliberately and confidently.

The note of mystery, of cycling life, came
from a cottonwood tree. A single leaf remained
on the stark white branches, dryly tapping in
the wind. Downstream, already-fallen cottonwood leaves piled against a cobble in the creek,
stacked neatly one on another in a precarious

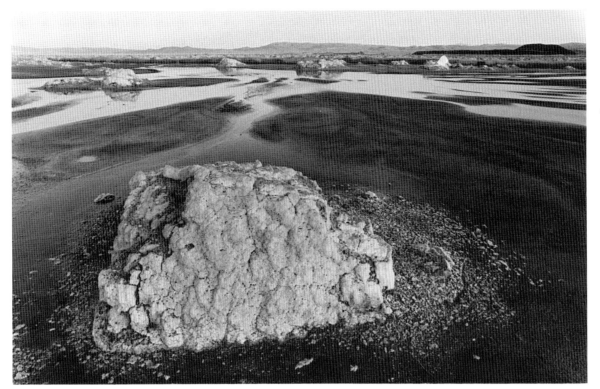

The unquenchable thirst of Los Angeles for distant water has lowered Mono Lake more than forty vertical feet and halved its volume. Salinity has doubled, and shorelines have been transformed into alkali flats.

drift of autumn. The wavering leaf on the tree marked the last fragment of a year of growth, the final bit of a desert summer. When it falls, the year will end, and time will jolt ahead into another season.

Unmappable on regional-scale vegetation maps, such riverside (riparian) woodland has an importance out of all proportion to its tiny area. Tangles of shrubs beneath cottonwoods are crucial to wildlife. In the Great Basin of southeastern Oregon, for example, 80 percent of the 363 terrestrial vertebrate species either depend directly on streamside woodlands or use them more than other plant communities.

Here they find not only permanent water but also luxuriant vegetation—useful both as cover and food. All over the West, willows dominate this understory, cottonwoods this forest. In most of the Great Basin, Fremont cottonwood lines the lower-elevation streams; in the western and northern Basin, black cottonwood takes its place. At higher elevations comes narrowleaf cottonwood, replaced still higher by aspen. Alder and river birch accompany them. Shrubs include Wood's rose, silver buffaloberry, chokecherry, American (red-osier) dogwood, and the exotic tamarisk.

Less exotic plant communities outline less dependable streams, each next-more-moist community penetrating the next-drier community where it can. Sagebrush and rabbitbrush line arroyos in shadscale flats; piñon-juniper "stringers" wind through sagebrush stands along sometime-watercourses. Along streams with permanent water, at least permanent underground water, willows and other riparian shrubs take over, then come trees—"gallery forests" flanking the watercourse. With more meandering streams, floodplains broaden and wet meadows develop.

Rocky Mountain juniper favors wet sites and often grows along streams; it rarely turns up in the piñon-juniper woodland. The most surprising stands of this anomalous montane juniper are the "swamp cedars" of Spring and White River valleys. Here the juniper grows at less than 5,600 feet in groves of vigorous trees as much as 650 feet below the piñon-juniper woodland on the nearby ranges—1,600 feet below the nearest Rocky Mountain juniper.

Some biologists suspect that the Spring Valley junipers survive because of an uncommonly high water table rejuvenated yearly by discharge from the mighty Snake and Schell Creek ranges on either side. Inversions keep tem-

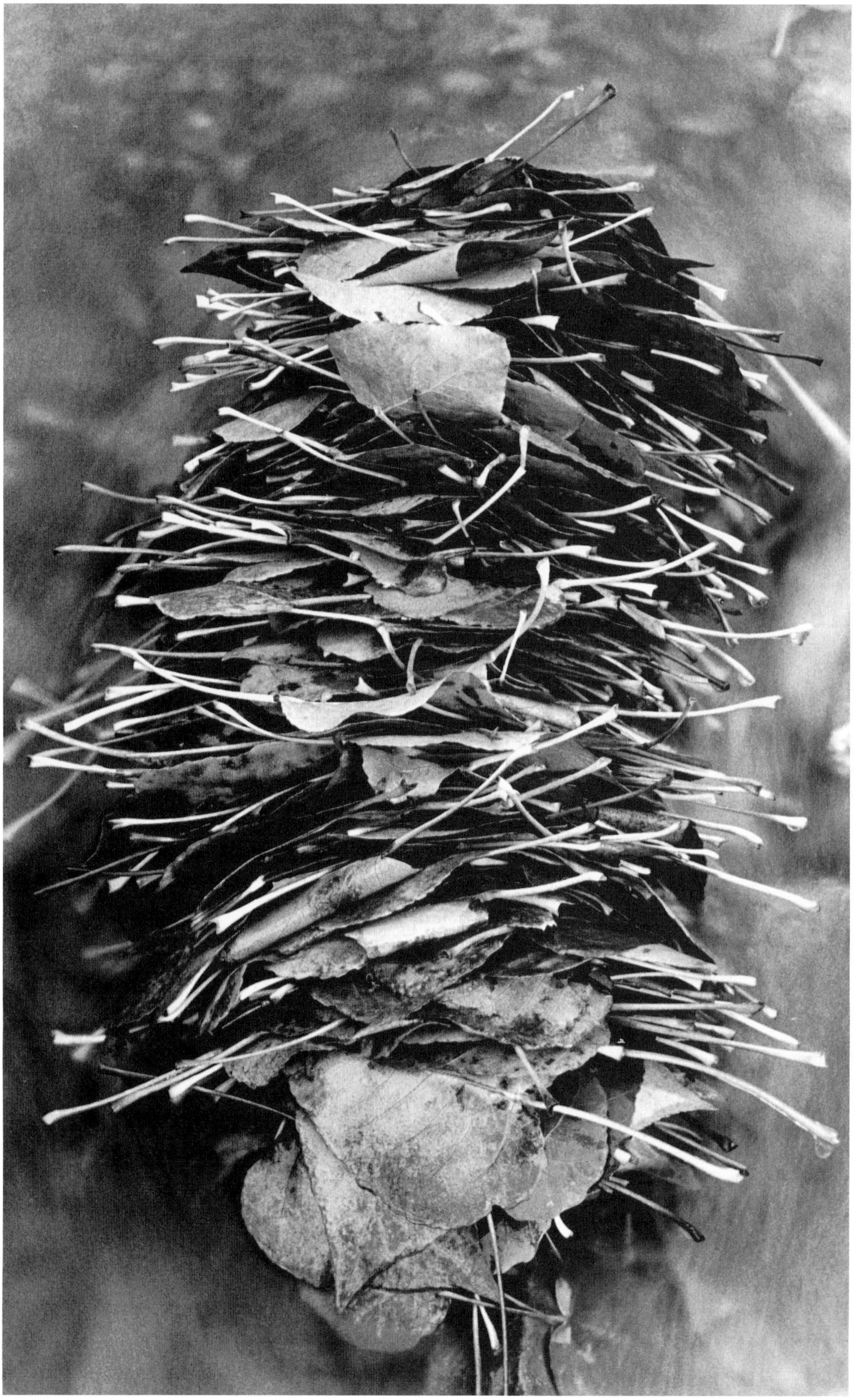

A precarious drift of autumn: cottonwood leaves in McGill Canyon on King Lear Peak.

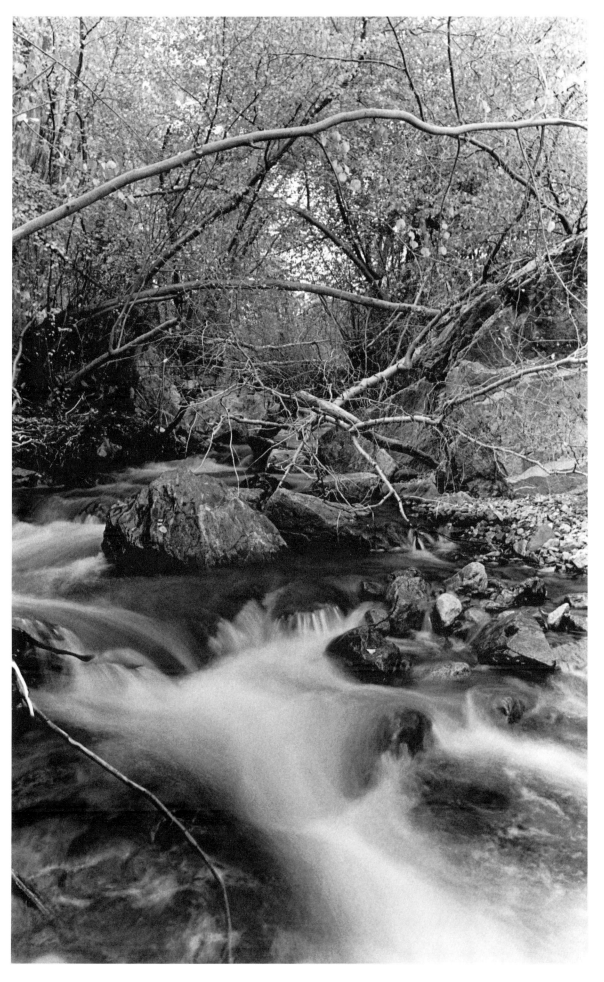

A riparian jungle, mostly river birch, along a mountain stream—South Twin River, Toiyabe Range.

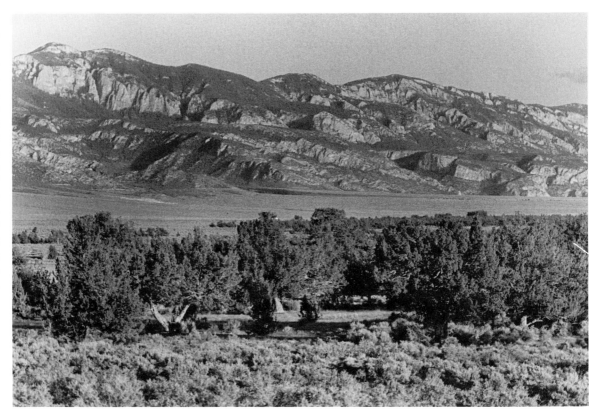

In Spring Valley, below the Snake Range, moisture-loving Rocky Mountain junipers grow at less than 5,600 feet— 1,600 feet below the nearest members of the species. These "swamp cedars" may be relicts of a Pleistocene woodland, or they may survive because of an uncommonly high water table.

peratures bearable for the trees. Paleoecologist Philip Wells believes the junipers pioneered this site in late-glacial times as pluvial Spring Lake disappeared, and they survive as relicts of this ancient woodland.

Birds concentrate in riverside woodlands like nowhere else in the West. In the Great Basin a standard group of widespread riparian birds turns up even in ranges as arid as the Kawich: kestrels, flickers, Western Kingbirds, Yellow Warblers, Yellow-breasted Chats, Northern Orioles, and Song Sparrows.

Other species accompany them—birds of northern forests, with biogeographical connections to the rich communities of the Snake River system. Ned Johnson tallied twenty-eight species in central Idaho riparian woodland. The totals dropped as he moved south to Great Basin streams: to twenty-one near Elko, fifteen in the Toiyabe Range, and twelve in the Kawich Range.

These widespread standard species form a core community. Slimmer and slimmer resources—not isolation—seem to keep diversity down: high-flying birds have little trouble colonizing appropriate habitat. Like the heteromyid rodents on sand dunes, with increasing

resources increasing numbers and kinds of birds can coexist.

But these streamside birds subdivide resources in much clearer ways than the seed-eating rodents on dunes: the diverse core group of birds ranges from seed-eaters to insect-eaters feeding in the vegetation, on the ground, or in the air to birds of prey. In Ned Johnson's words they have "fundamentally different body designs." Only the two warblers belong to the same family, and the chat is larger than the little Yellow Warbler by 1.5 times.

Here in this complicated tangle of vegetation many species find ways to make a living that will not bring them head-to-head with some other creature bent on taking over the same resource. Paradoxically, we understand this complex place better than the "simple" dunes. Or we think we do.

The coming of civilization has confounded Great Basin streams at every level—mountain meadow beginning, middle course woodland, and final valley bottomland.

Geologists have documented alternating natural cycles of erosion and deposition on floodplains since late Pleistocene. Alluvial de-

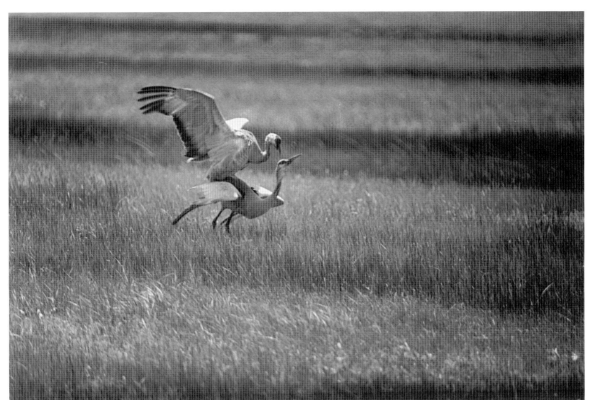

posits form during wet periods; arroyo cutting happens naturally with a drying climate and with uplift of a young and active mountain range. But excessive stock grazing has triggered most of the erosion of the past century.

In almost every valley this recent erosion began within ten or twenty years of settlement. Streams that once meandered through meadows now run in deepening arroyos (the steepwalled, flat-bottomed channels of ephemeral streams) with vertical headwalls. Once started, the cycle is hard to stop.

Unlimited numbers of livestock kill plants and trample the mosses and algae crusting the soil surface between them. Soil loosens, runoff increases. Erosion accelerates, carving deeply through a meadow. Confined to its channel, a stream ceases to inundate its wide floodplain; trees depending on nourishing backwaters begin to die. The arroyo deepens, the water table lowers. Still more plants die. Sagebrush and rabbitbrush invade once-lush wet meadows.

In lower reaches of rivers like the Humboldt and Truckee, intense livestock grazing has combined with river channelization and reclamation projects to transform the floodplains. As natural meandering streams, these rivers usurped potential agricultural land. Unchanneled, they flooded homes and fields. So we took control of the rivers. We tamed, diverted, and groomed them. In the process, we have destroyed their wildlife resources.

Robert Ridgway studied birds along the lower Truckee in the spring of 1868, when he came through with Clarence King's Geological Survey of the Fortieth Parallel. He described "exceedingly dense willow-jungles" banking the stream and sloughs, the latter filled with rushes and other aquatic plants. "Most of the valley consisted of meadowlands, interspersed with velvety swards of 'salt-grass' and acres of beautiful sun-flowers." Cottonwood groves studded the meadows, generally with a dense shrubby undergrowth dominated by silver buffaloberry.

University of Nevada ornithologists looked for birds along the same stretch of river from 1972 to 1981. Ridgway's "jungles" and "sloughs" have disappeared with farmland development, river channelization, and overgrazing. With them have disappeared forty-two of Ridgway's total of ninety-one breeding bird species; twenty-six species have declined in abundance. This bird checklist did not change randomly: nearly two-thirds of the lost species require riparian shrubs (like the raucous Yellow-breasted Chat and Yellow-billed Cuckoo) or wet meadows and marshes (including the elegant Northern Harrier and American Avocet and the buzzy little Marsh Wren).

Other early visitors to Great Basin valleys spoke of grass belly-high to their horses. In arguing about the historic prevalence of sagebrush, some have fastened on this line to prove that grasses once dominated Great Basin valleys more powerfully than we can imagine.

Only one Great Basin grass truly achieves such luxuriance: Great Basin wildrye. This magnificent grass can grow six feet high or higher (the related giant wildrye grows even taller).

Great Basin wildrye has an unusual distinction: the grass can grow both on well-drained upland soil and on alkaline/saline bottomlands. Today, small stands remain in the uplands (growing mostly where badger-churned soil aids in germination). Once the grass covered vast floodplains along major Great Basin rivers. On the Humboldt it kept alive the overlanders' animals. In winter, when snow covered short grasses, wildrye became a crucial resource for ranchers. W. B. Todhunter wintered ten thousand to twelve thousand steers in Long Valley in northwestern Nevada on nothing but Great Basin wildrye in 1871.

The devastating winter of 1889–90 taught Great Basin ranchers that they would have to feed their stock supplemental winter forage. Wildrye made excellent hay. Trouble was, it withstood neither grazing nor mowing. With much of the wildrye stands destroyed over the years by such overuse and the rest converted to agriculture, one must look long and hard today to find a place to ride through grass brushing one's boots.

Great Basin lakes and marshes always surprise me. Coming on them is like coming on a human city in the desert. After miles of alkali and greasewood, the greens of rushes and sedges, the noisy concentrations of avocets and phalaropes and coots and blackbirds create the same contrast of activity and emptiness—a village midst countryside.

The greatest Basin marshes spread along the margins of lakes. Smaller patches of water, bulrushes, and birds turn up at springs. Some marshes survive in managed refuges like Malheur, Bear River, Ruby Lake, and Fish Springs. Malheur by some estimates is the nation's largest freshwater marsh.

Others have disappeared, particularly the smaller sloughs along rivers. And reclamation projects have created some new marshes, such as Stillwater Marsh on the south edge of the Carson Sink. Stillwater pumps some water and receives runoff from fields around Fallon watered by the Newlands Reclamation Project—water once bound down the Truckee to Pyramid and Winnemucca lakes and into Carson Lake via the Carson River.

Bulrushes (tules) dominate marshes in shallow open water. Spikerush grows densely on peat soil. And baltic rush, cattails, burreed, and common reed grass make up the intervening mosaic in still shallower water. Saltgrass fringes most Great Basin marshes, for they lie in alkaline basins and only huge amounts of water can vanquish the ever-present salts.

With variations these patterns hold up throughout the Basin. Common reed grass does not grow in the Lahontan basin. At Fish Springs, isolated deep in the Great Salt Lake Desert, baltic rush lines slough shorelines and grows in "meadows" in depressions among saltgrass; common reed grass marks the dry marsh edges.

Tamarisk, the Eurasian exotic, first reached the Great Basin at Utah Lake in 1926. Today it grows throughout the Basin, common along watercourses and on dry marsh edges.

These patches of marsh and open water exist as tiny islands in the sagebrush ocean. Water birds return to them unerringly year after year in great migrations. Submerged vegetation in shallow lakes produces unbelievably rich food resources.

Waterfowl productivity at Malheur Lake depends directly on the abundance of pondweed

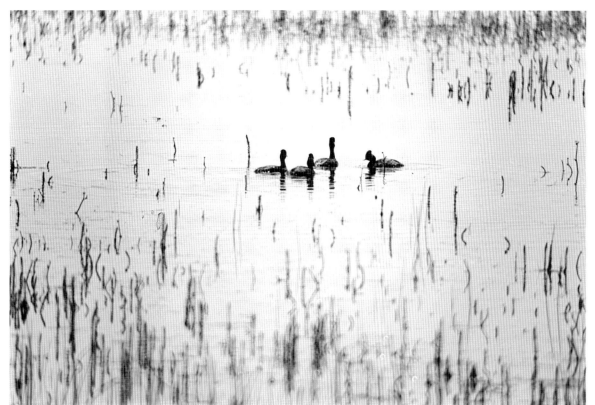

and horned-pondweed and water milfoil. In good years the lake can produce fifteen thousand ducks, one thousand Canada Geese—and fifty thousand muskrats! Good years still cannot be guaranteed through management, and, indeed, Malheur Lake has remained largely free of fancy stabilization procedures. In the past fifteen years it has varied from five hundred to fifty thousand acres in size.

In talking of such protected marshes I automatically slip into the lingo of wildlife management. Here, ducks do not simply nest and raise young; they *produce* offspring—a harvest for hunters.

Wildlife refuges have a complicated history in the United States. Established to save waterfowl from the decimation of market and plume hunters, they rescued many species from extinction. Refuges also protected marshes seen as useless land to be drained and farmed.

By managing natural marshes, diking ponds, planting grain, and selectively grazing, haying, and timbering, potential productivity has greatly increased. Half of our wildlife refuges are hunted. Exploitation by mining, grazing, and overcrowding threatens many. Even after

protection, upstream water diversions can dry up downstream wetlands.

Ruby Lake sees seventy-five thousand recreationists a year. In years past they came to circle the lake, motorboating and water-skiing. Unwittingly, they shredded underwater vegetation and distressed waterfowl to the point of abandoning nests. After a court battle, the U.S. Fish and Wildlife Service now strictly regulates motorboat use. This refuge supports even more nesting Canvasbacks than Malheur in a much smaller area.

Even with all our tampering, managed marshes still feel like remnant wildlands. In saving habitat for huntable species, we also preserve nesting sites for egrets and herons, grebes and gulls, terns and killdeer. At Malheur and Ruby lakes we see nesting Trumpeter Swans, North America's largest bird. During migration on Bear River Bay we get as close as we can to reliving the wild sound of millions of waterfowl that John Charles Frémont heard in 1843 as "distant thunder." We still can see here a half-million ducks and geese, with mind-boggling totals of single species: 40,000 Tundra Swans, 180,000 Northern Pintails, 28,000 of the nationally declining Redhead.

Or we could until 1983. The Great Salt
Lake is on the rise, and in 1984, runoff from
the Bear River completely drowned Bear River
refuge. Even with no further increase in water
levels, vegetation for nesting and feeding will
need at least ten years to recover. Meanwhile,
geese have virtually ceased to nest in Bear
River Bay; only Western Grebes, which build
floating nests, are thriving.

Unlike any other Great Basin environment,
in surviving marshes animals dominate both
landscape and plants. Sandhill Cranes leap
and bow ceremoniously in their annual mating
dance. Great flocks of avocets make crazy
noises as they swing their bills through the rich
soup of shallow pondwater. White-faced Ibises
shine iridescent in the hot summer sun. They
look exotic and Egyptian, though they are perfectly respectable natives.

These birds have distinctive character.
Though the birds certainly do not perceive
each other in this way, if we relax our scientific
vocabulary their demeanor fits human types.
Blackbirds click and whistle, their serious commentary a background chorus to the cheery,
lively Marsh Wrens in the lower rushes. An
American White Pelican swimming at a distance looks like a gull (the pelican's great bill
and neck) perched on an island (its body). It
rises with slow wingbeats, with presence and
power. Like owls, it seems wise. Black-necked
Stilts and American Avocets, in contrast, seem
vapid—like the stereotypical willowy high-
fashion model.

The marsh feels like the Galápagos Islands,
like the East African plains, like a Walt Dis-
ney wildlife movie. Hardly ever do we find
ourselves anymore in a world where other creatures match our conspicuousness, our distinct-
ness, our force of personality.

The Great Basin offers two extremes for rare
perspective: the playa and the marsh. On playas we isolate ourselves from other life. Here
in the marsh—regardless of how much we
have manipulated it—we feel a little of the
old world where humans and animals lived
together.

Moving into the open water of lakes and streams
reveals still another world: of relict fish, of microscopic creatures with incredible salt tolerances, of islands in dying inland seas where
birds breed safe from predators—for now.

The Great Basin's lakes share the extremes
of its land. Lake Tahoe holds the record depth
for algae, more than twice the common maximum: Tahoe *Chara* grows at 450 feet, where
light intensity—even in Lake Tahoe at its
clearest—is only a tenth of a percent that of
full sunlight. Shallow and severe Great Salt
Lake lies at the other extreme; before the lake's
1984 breaching, only the Dead Sea was saltier.

Great Basin fish merit a biogeography book
of their own, and have received such attention
from several specialists. Clark L. Hubbs and
Robert R. Miller spent decades unraveling the
relationships in fish populations isolated by
drying Pleistocene lakes. Like James Brown's
boreal mammals isolated on mountaintops, fish
communities have lost many members; extinction has overwhelmed colonization. Thus, most
Great Basin valleys have smaller numbers of
species than the habitat could support if not so
isolated and fragile.

Bonneville basin fish have close ties to the
upper Snake River, reflecting the long-ago
spillover of Lake Bonneville into the Snake
drainage at Red Rock Pass. The Lahontan
basin has similar closely related groups. White
River and Meadow Valley Wash, draining
south to the Colorado, differ drastically from
northern drainages. Small isolated basins in
Oregon's High Desert and in east-central Nevada contain unique and depauperate combinations of species.

Many drainages have been isolated enough
to evolve distinct species: the Alvord chub,
the desert dace (which lives only in Soldier
Meadow, Nevada), the Railroad Valley springfish, the Tahoe sucker, and the cui-ui sucker
of Pyramid Lake. Many other of the Great
Basin's fish have distinct varieties in several
drainages—notably local strains of the widespread tui chub and speckled dace and the
threatened native cutthroat trout.

Adapted to such alkaline waters as Walker

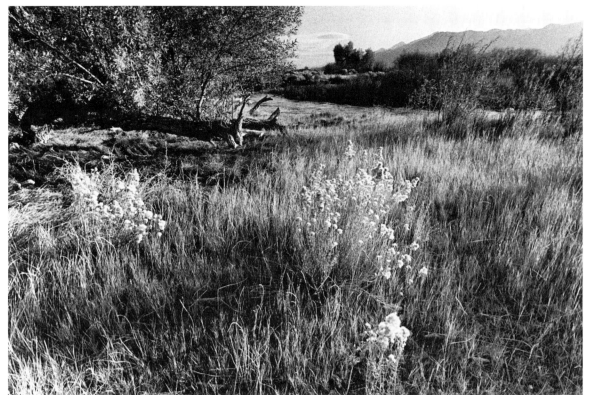

The Owens River at Bishop, California; like so many Great Basin streams, the Owens begins in mountains, ends in a sink, and harbors unique and endangered fish.

Lake, Lahontan cutthroat once thrived throughout the lakes and rivers of the Lahontan basin. Most populations have disappeared as rivers crucial to their spawning have been polluted, diverted for irrigation, or have silted in, drying to undependable trickles. Remnant natives have hybridized with introduced rainbow trout.

Today only Summit Lake, Nevada, Independence Lake, California, and tiny creeks in the headwaters of the Walker and Carson rivers have pure reproducing populations of Lahontan cutthroat. High in the Black Rock Range, isolated Summit Lake with its spawning stream, Mahogany Creek, harbors the major pure stock used for transplants.

A separate cutthroat subspecies lives in the Humboldt River basin and still survives in some twenty streams. Although these drainages have been stocked for years with rainbow, brook, brown, and Yellowstone cutthroat trout, the Humboldt cutthroat has not interbred with the nonnative fish. Evidently better adapted to the harsh alternation of floods and drought in the desert streams, the Humboldt cutthroat has persisted pure and widespread. Its home has the familiar potential dangers from human interference, however. In some small streams,

during late-summer droughts the entire trout population concentrates in a few fragile pools and beaver ponds.

Isolation has saved these fish. Commercially important lake populations have not fared as well. Lovely Utah Lake once supported a dozen native species of trout, suckers, and minnows. It teemed with distinctive Bonneville cutthroat weighing fifteen to sixteen pounds. When the Spanish explorer-priests Domínguez and Escalante visited Utah Valley in 1776, this place with its "Lake of the Timpanogos" enchanted them; they proclaimed it the "most pleasant, beautiful, and fertile in all of New Spain."

Since colonization of Utah Valley in 1850, irrigation diversions of inlet streams have blocked trout and suckers from their spawning areas. Water quality in the lake and its streams has deteriorated with years of careless agriculture and sewage pollution. Introduction of twenty-five exotic fish species transformed the competitive world of the natives. Today, the trout are extinct. Suckers have decreased drastically. Thirteen of the introduced species have survived; carp and white bass dominate Utah Lake.

Similar stories unfold at Walker, Tahoe, and Pyramid lakes. Each supported great native fisheries; each now has been irrevocably altered. Pyramid Lake's band of Paiutes lived on Lahontan cutthroat and cui-ui, the unique native sucker. Other Paiutes knew the Pyramid Lake people as *Kuyuidokado*, the "cui-ui eaters." Pyramid Lake produced the largest of all western trout, an official world record forty-one pounder, and an unofficial monster fish of sixty-two pounds.

After 1905 and the diversion of the Truckee in the Newlands Reclamation Project, Pyramid cutthroat began to decline. By 1938 they were extinct. Cui-ui fared better, for they can spawn in the lake's shoreline shallows, and their forty-year life span allows them to make full use of occasional wet years when they can reach the lower Truckee. But with the continued diversion of Truckee water, the lake—and all its fish—will eventually dwindle to extinction. Its companion, Winnemucca Lake, already has.

Pyramid Lake carries an air of poignancy, risking the same fate as Winnemucca Lake. In drought it shrinks, exposing the tufa formed in its underwater brine—The Needle, the Pyramid itself. On the rim of its basin, concentric circles of its old shorelines ring the lake. When Frémont and his men discovered it, "it broke upon our eyes like the ocean." Today, just when it began to look like a dwindling pond, several wet years have rejuvenated it, and the Pyramid again stands as an island.

Tahoe's Lahontan cutthroat disappeared in the forties, victims of damming, pollution, and siltation of tributary spawning grounds. Sixteen holdout trout trapped at Walker Lake in 1948 gave rise to the present brood stock used (with Summit Lake eggs) to stock all three lakes (Walker, Pyramid, Tahoe).

Of the major Great Basin lakes, Great Salt Lake and Mono Lake have become too salty for fish. Instead, their rich soup of invertebrates feeds a wealth of birds.

Great Salt Lake generates legends like fantastic sparks struck from the metallic shimmer of its waters. Chronicler of the lake Dale Morgan called it "an ironical joke of nature—water that is itself more desert than a desert." People have believed it to be an arm of the Pacific Ocean, home to sea serpents, whales, and boat-swallowing whirlpools. An early Mormon expeditioner called it "the briny shallow." The salt makes the lake water so dense that sailing in it resembles a voyage through solidifying gelatin. Dive into it and risk breaking your neck. In storms, it batters boats and pilings with a power not usually associated with mere water.

Blue-green algae (which turn the lake pink rather than blue-green!) form the basis of a short food chain that leads quickly to the brine shrimp *Artemia* and two species of brine flies, called buffalo gnats by locals. These little arthropods thrive in the saline water, where their parasites cannot. With no fish preying on them they reach enormous numbers, reproducing to the limit of the food supply.

In July, windrows of rotting brine fly pupal cases ring the mucky lakeshore, prompting Captain Howard Stansbury in 1849 to describe it as being "impregnated with all the villainous smells which nature's laboratory was capable of producing." Yet such "foetid & offensive sulphureous" odors bode well for birds; piles of fly pupae denote healthy Great Salt Lake water and abundant food for ducks and gulls.

Considerable variation in saltiness occurs throughout the lake. Bear River Bay receives enough freshwater inflow to support colonies of algae intolerant of higher salinities in the central lake. The Lucin Cutoff railroad trestle bisected the lake in 1903, creating a northern saltier arm effectively isolated from the inflow of fresh water reaching the main southern arm. With 34 percent dissolved salts (ten times saltier than sea water), the northern arm reached concentrations almost three times that of the southern lake. Breaching of the causeway in 1984 (to ease flood danger on the more heavily populated south shore) reduced this figure drastically.

With the lake on the rise in recent years (reaching a hundred-year high), inflow dilutes

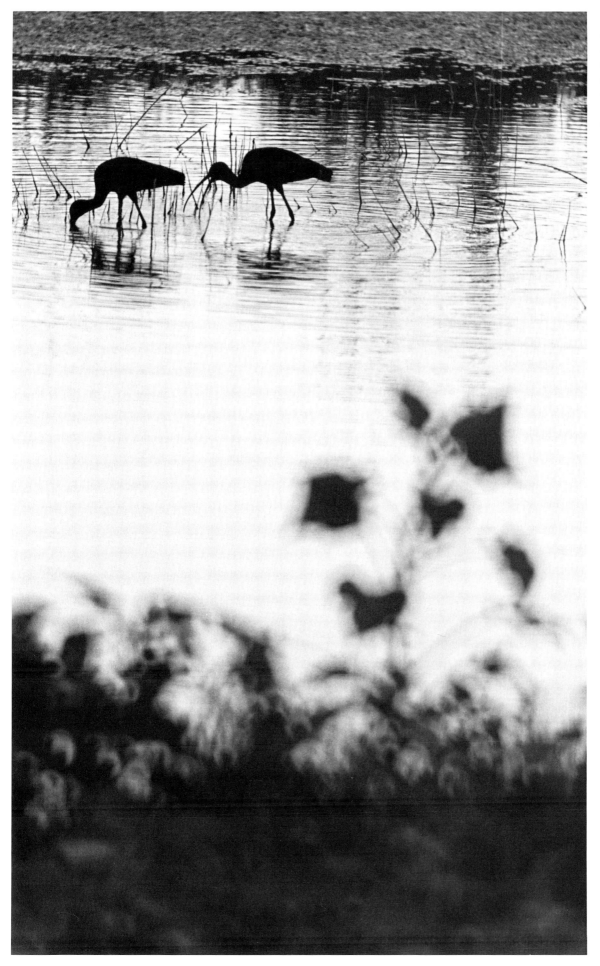

White-faced Ibises shine iridescent in the sun at Great Salt Lake's Bear River Migratory Bird Refuge, looking exotic and Egyptian, though they are perfectly respectable native birds.

the south section and even with the breach maintains variation in salinity. Each ten-foot rise floods an additional 240 square miles. In *Basin and Range* John McPhee saw the reason: "The basin flatness just ran to the lake and kept on going, wet. The angle formed at the shoreline appeared to be about 179.9 degrees."

Rising salt water has contaminated three-fourths of the surrounding freshwater marshes and drowned millions of dollars worth of property. The Utah legislature has funded the breaching of the Lucin Cutoff and the pumping of Great Salt Lake water west into the desert that hasn't seen such freshets since Lake Bonneville's heyday. The Great Salt Lake remains alive and capricious—a climatic barometer as dynamic as the Great Basin Desert itself.

Stark and barren islands sit mysteriously in the shallows of Great Salt Lake, surrounded by a moat of strange water that resembles a slightly dangerous chemical. Instead of fish, the lake generates shrimp too small to eat and flies known mainly for the disgusting smell of their rotting pupae. Coming on the island nesting colonies in such a place makes them seem almost magical.

The Stansbury expedition first described the bird islands of Great Salt Lake in 1850. They found pelicans, California Gulls, Great Blue Herons, and cormorants nesting densely enough to cover some of the small islands, "makeing a very confused & amuseing heap of moveing matter" and ensuring that whole islands reeked of rotting fish.

The gulls and Great Blue Herons continue to thrive. Double-crested Cormorants and pelicans have had less success. Pelicans abandoned Hat Island when low water connected it to the mainland, allowing coyotes to reach the colony. Only Gunnison Island today supports a pelican colony.

Gulls, grebes, phalaropes, and ducks feed on Great Salt Lake invertebrates. Herons, cormorants, and American White Pelicans nesting on islands in the lake must fly to bordering marshes to fish for their young.

Herons nest on the ground or in the tops of greasewood bushes. Pelicans must keep a wary eye out for gulls ever intent on stealing eggs and chicks. Those pelicans not on guard duty join fishing parties. Platoons of the solemn birds lift off ponderously, making daily trips to marshes up to one hundred miles away.

Pyramid Lake's Anaho Island supports another great colony of pelicans, cormorants, gulls, Caspian Terns, and herons. Also in danger of connection with the shore as the lake dries, Anaho nonetheless has been the continent's largest American White Pelican colony, supporting many thousands of birds. Here, too, for food the pelicans fly as far as Walker Lake, one hundred miles away.

Mono Lake has become the symbol of all Great Basin lakes in recent years. Not only has it decreased in size from its Pleistocene heyday, but diversions of its feeder streams to Los Angeles suddenly have put its very survival in doubt.

Like Great Salt Lake, Mono is too salty for fish. Its waters teem with brine shrimp and brine flies; its resident band of Paiutes were called *Kuzedika*, the "fly-pupae eaters." "Mono" itself means fly-people in the Yokut language.

Mono's brine shrimp have adapted to water even more challenging than the salty Great Salt Lake. Mono Lake water is less salty (chloride content) but a hundred times as alkaline (determined by concentrated carbonates) than the Utah brine. In *Roughing It*, Mark Twain described Mono Lake—"this solemn, silent, sailless sea"—and its alkaline waters: "If you only dip the most hopelessly soiled garment into them once or twice, and wring it out, it will be found as clean as if it had been through the ablest of washerwomen's hands."

Great Salt Lake brine shrimp cannot survive in Mono Lake water, as Mono shrimp—tuned to Mono salt and carbonate concentrations—likewise perish when placed in other brines. Mono brine shrimp overwinter as eggs on the lake bottom. They hatch in spring, begin eating their way through the winter crop of algae, and move to the warming surface layer of wa-

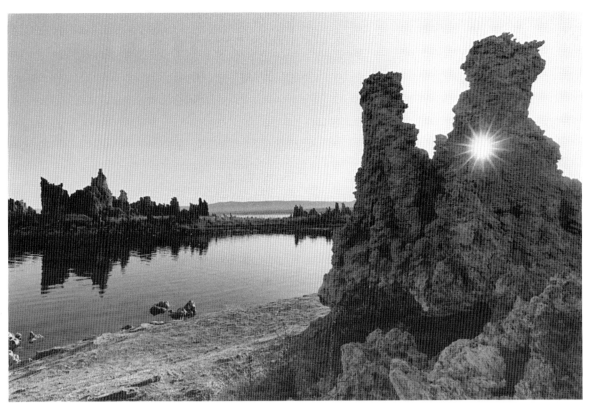

*Tufa towers—
time itself
crystallized
in fragile,
changeable shapes
at Navy Beach,
Mono Lake.*

139

---

*Water in the
Desert*

ter. They and the brine flies occur by the trillions in summer—food enough to support Mono's clouds of birds.

The California Gulls come to breed, fifty thousand of them—95 percent of California's nesting population. The lake provides endless food for hungry young; the islands protect eggs and chicks from four-footed predators like coyotes, raccoons, and weasels. Other nesters include Snowy Plovers, their coastal breeding habitat wiped out, the birds dependent now on inland sites like Mono.

At midsummer come migrants, headed south from breeding grounds and pausing at Mono to feed for weeks or months, laying in fat reserves from the harsh waters alive with brine shrimp and flies. No freshwater lake, where birds must compete with fish for invertebrate resources, can compare. Ninety thousand Wilson's and Red-necked Phalaropes and seven hundred thousand Eared Grebes drop out of the sky to feast. Mono Lake naturalist David Gaines describes the phalaropes as "numerous, graceful, and trusting."

These days, their trust seems misplaced.

Los Angeles has an unquenchable thirst for water. Seeking farther and farther afield for what Will Rogers once summarized as "more water for its Chamber of Commerce to drink more toasts to its growth, more water to dilute its orange juice," the city extended the Owens Valley aqueduct to the Mono basin in 1941. In 1970, a second aqueduct began siphoning southward still more of Mono's inlet streams.

Since then the lake has fallen over forty vertical feet, its volume halved, its salinity doubled, and its shorelines transformed into seventeen thousand acres of alkali flats. Much new tufa precipitated underwater has been exposed and left far inland. Mark Twain thought these frail columns of rock resembled "inferior mortar, dried hard." Others have likened them to "giant towers of cemented cauliflower." To me, they feel like time itself, crystallized in fragile, changeable shapes that embody the provoking mix of past, present, and future.

In 1979 the shrinking lake exposed a landbridge. Coyotes crossed to Mono's Negit Island, destroying the entire nesting colony of thirty-four thousand gulls. Even after construction of a predator-proof fence, the gulls failed to recolonize the island. In 1981, the lowest water level yet reached, brine shrimp numbers plummeted when overwintering eggs failed to hatch normally; twenty-five thousand gull chicks starved.

Since then, record-setting runoff has filled the aqueducts. The surplus has replenished the lake and resurrected Negit Island. Gulls, however, have returned slowly to the Negit rookery, for the rising water stranded coyotes there, predator-proof fence or not, along with a dependable larder of rodents and rabbits. The rising lake has eroded many of the islets, overcrowding gulls on the remaining ones. If diversions continue at their current rate, Mono will become too salty for its brine shrimp and flies; its islands all will become peninsulas; its birds will disappear. This unique living world will become a sterile sump.

In 1984 the U.S. Congress established a Mono Lake National Forest Scenic Area, re-quiring the Forest Service to "protect . . . geologic, ecologic, and cultural resources." But the scenic area does not reduce water diversions. The battle between conservationists and the Los Angeles Department of Water and Power continues in the courts. Its result will determine Mono Lake's future.

Mono Lake represents all Great Basin wetlands. Delicate, surprising islands of unbelievable vitality in the gray-green sagebrush sea, these lakes and marshes survive as fragments of the fjord-like world of birds that enlivened the Pleistocene Great Basin.

In the last century we have sped them along toward death at an ever accelerating rate. We also know how to stop.

We have a choice.

IV

The Basin Ranges
Forgotten Mountains

The Piñon-Juniper Woodland

11

These curious woods . . . though dark-looking at a little distance, are yet almost shadeless, and without any hint of the dark glens and hollows so characteristic of other pine woods. . . . The entire State seems to be pretty evenly divided into mountain-ranges covered with nut pines and plains covered with sage—now a swath of pines stretching from north to south, now a swath of sage; the one black, the other gray; one severely level, the other sweeping on complacently over ridge and valley and lofty crowning dome.

—John Muir,
"Nevada Forests," 1878

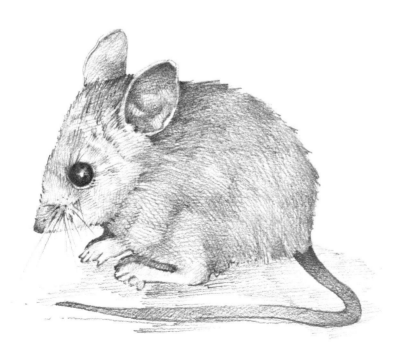

Piñon mouse

In this ocean of sagebrush, piñon pines and junipers form the only dependable woods, the only widespread forest community. These two trees rarely grow taller than twenty feet—a scale comprehensible to humans. They twist into singular shapes, stand in isolated dignity, or grow in dense and friendly concentrations. Covering more than seventeen million acres, dwarfing in area if not in stature the patches of full-sized pines, spruce, and fir that reign on the highest mountains, the Basin piñon-juniper "pygmy" woodland needs no apologia.

The Great Basin is sufficiently short on trees that here people rely even on the gnarly trunks of these two humble conifers for lumber. Both woodland trees give fuel, fence posts, and small poles. Juniper and piñon woodsmoke scent memories of the mountains as sagebrush perfumes Great Basin valleys. Westerners love the trees.

In part because other trees are uncommon, in part because the dwarf conifers have strong presence, the people who live around them pay attention to them. In Oregon, cowboy philosopher Reub Long suggested a fine goal to High Desert travelers: to see how many shapes of western juniper they could photograph. Teetotaling Utahans may not turn Utah juniper into Tanqueray, but its blue-green berries taste just as pungent as the Old World junipers that flavor gin.

And everywhere in singleleaf and Colorado piñon country, in late summer, weekend piñon nutters eye the crowns of the pines as cones develop, timing their harvest to beat squirrels and jays to the crop. Before settlement, nutritious piñon nuts made winter survival possible for Great Basin Washoe, Paiute, and Shoshone Indian people. Any one grove does not produce a huge crop every year; they cycle, surpluses coming about every three to seven years. The Basin's Indian people kept track of these cycles and scheduled the location of their annual piñon harvest festival a year in advance by watching the cones' two-year development in the various groves.

Junipers are more widespread than piñons,

and some ecologists consequently insist on the term "juniper-piñon woodland." Felicitous phrasing, however, as well as the traditional spiritual attachment of native peoples to piñon, favors the reverse.

The piñon-juniper woodland always feels friendly to me, perhaps because of the scale of these dwarfed trees, perhaps because of our old dependence on piñon nuts. For whatever reason, the woodland feels approachable; these trees are our peers.

Though the woodland looks similar across the Basin and, indeed, varies little in structure from Texas to Idaho to California, the identities of the pine and juniper species change. In most of the Great Basin, singleleaf piñon grows with Utah juniper. From Oregon southward into California and northern Nevada, the larger western juniper replaces Utah juniper. And in southwestern Utah, Colorado piñon takes over from the single-needled pine.

Mapping piñon-juniper woodland is straightforward: simply map where the trees grow. To avoid calling one or two solitary trees "woodland," one research team required a minimum density of ten trees per acre and the presence of at least one mature tree before a stand gained official status as mappable "p-j."

Simplicity distinguishes this forest. When piñon and juniper crowd together densely, few other plants survive in the woodland. Only the two conifers grow there exclusively. Understory species range through adjacent sagebrush/grassland and mountain brush. Shrubs and cool-season grasses dominate the understory to the north; southward and eastward, progressively fewer shrubs and more warm-season grasses appear as more rain comes during the growing season. But throughout, the woodland trees dominate a depauperate flora and fauna.

Sagebrush goes about its business, one or another sagebrush codominating from valley to mountaintop. Where they can survive, piñon and juniper simply overlay the shrub communities, superimposed on the primary sequence of life zones.

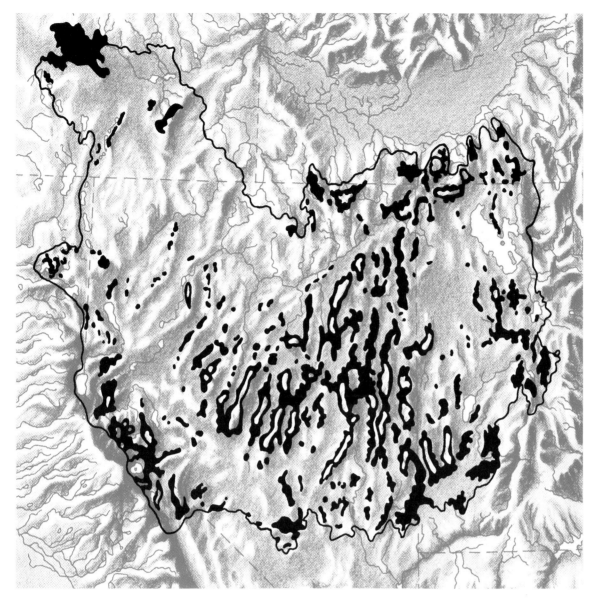

Distribution of piñon-juniper woodland in the Great Basin Desert. (Based on Holmgren, 1972; and Barbour and Major, 1977)

145

The Piñon-Juniper Woodland

The catch is that misleadingly simple phrase, "where they can survive." A group of range ecologists (C. Dwight Beeson, Kenneth Rea, Robin Tausch, Paul Tueller, Neil West, and their associates) have traced out many ramifications of this simple phrase, but the story still has its mysteries.

Piñon and juniper do best where annual precipitation totals twelve to eighteen inches. The trees survive at extremes of eight and twenty inches. They favor elevations of about five thousand to eight thousand feet, but grow below four thousand feet at the edge of the Mojave Desert and as high as ten thousand feet in the White Mountains. Temperature also limits their distribution, as we shall see.

The trees grow on a variety of soils but can tolerate rocky places with practically no soil at all. On level ground, surprisingly, rocks, gravel, and hardpans trap extra moisture. Even on cliffs, runoff funnels into cracks, increasing effective moisture for outpost piñon and juniper rooted in crevices, wedged precariously onto cliffs like rock climbers with their fists jammed boldly in cracks.

Since juniper can handle drier sites than piñon, you usually meet it first when moving up from valley bottoms. Piñon becomes more common with increasing elevation, dominating above about 7,000 feet, until at the upper limit of woodland it grows alone. The band of woodland on most ranges averages about 1,150 feet in elevational width. At its broadest, woodland spans twice that. In the colder north the woodland narrows until finally it disappears.

*Only in its
moistest reaches
does piñon-juniper
woodland support
such understory
species as
mushrooms and
lupine; Mount
Moriah, Snake
Range.*

146

*The Basin
Ranges*

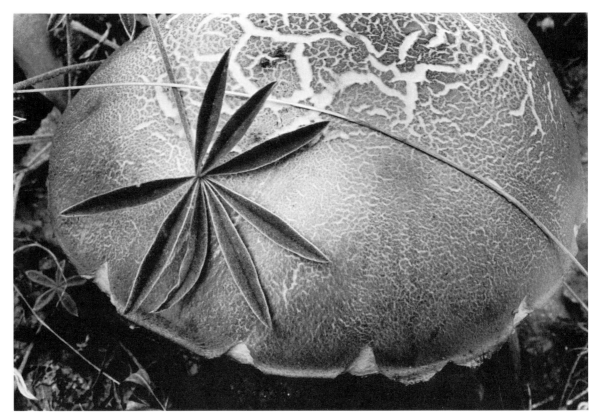

A great gap exists between the true mixed piñon-juniper woodland of the central Great Basin and the rim of western juniper woodland along the northwest frontier. Virtually no singleleaf piñon grows north of the Humboldt River. The Santa Rosa, Pine Forest, and Black Rock ranges have neither piñon nor juniper. Why?

Piñon-juniper forest moved south during cooler, wetter glacial times. No singleleaf piñon grew in the Great Basin, necessitating reinvasion of these northern ranges once the climate warmed—reinvasion perhaps still taking place.

Patterns in most valley communities—when understandable at all—seem tied to soils and local variation in precipitation, with soils in the Lahontan and Bonneville basins intimately related to their pluvial history. Modern climate, however, can account for the pattern of piñon and juniper on the mountains.

In the west-central Great Basin, inversion layers develop in winter. Cold air pools in valleys. Mid-elevations on adjacent mountains consistently measure warmer than slopes above and below them, warmer by some seven to eight degrees Fahrenheit. These thermal belts

above inversion layers match almost perfectly the extent of piñon-juniper woodland.

But Pacific winter storm fronts grow stronger to the north. As they sweep through with regularity they break up inversions, lowering minimum temperatures and increasing the duration of cold spells, evidently past the tolerance of singleleaf piñon. First, woodland diminishes on north-facing exposures. Then, northward, with sufficiently cold winter average temperatures, it disappears.

Across the southern Great Basin, woodland changes more subtly. Utah juniper increases to the east. Across southwest Utah, Colorado piñon replaces singleleaf piñon. Here, too, summer rains increase, thundershowers generated from moist air pulled in from the Gulf of Mexico. In the southeast corner of the basin, along the Utah/Nevada line west of Cedar City, woodland stretches across rolling hills and valleys alike, with a feeling like Colorado Plateau woodland, complete with cliffrose perfuming the breeze.

Aridity controls the lower boundary of woodland here in the south, with piñons and junipers first diminishing on dry south-facing slopes. With weaker westerly fronts and abun-

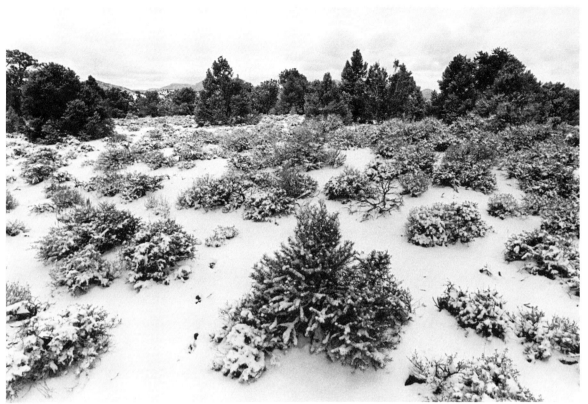

dant gulf low-pressure systems, winter temperatures do not plummet as far and inversions rarely form. As temperatures go up, it takes more rainfall to support piñon-juniper woodland.

In his fine book, *The Piñon Pine*, Ronald Lanner sketches the story of piñon evolution. The two piñon species diverged some twenty million years ago when a mutation in an ancestral two-needled Colorado piñon transformed it into a single-needled tree. The tree reproduced; its inheritors dispersed in a stand of two-needled trees.

Then, the climate changed. Some characteristic of the single-needled form made it better able to cope. It gradually expanded into territory unlivable for the Colorado piñon, country generally to the south of today's Great Basin, with hot, dry summers.

After the glaciers retreated for the last time (so far) and piñons invaded north into the drying Great Basin, it was singleleaf piñon that conquered the summer-dry western Basin. Both Colorado piñon and Utah juniper are southwestern trees, and they need the touch of the Southwest's summer rains to survive. Colorado piñon moved west from its stronghold on

the Colorado Plateau, but drying summers stopped its advance in western Utah.

Today, along the eastern edge of the Great Basin, the two piñons meet and hybridize. Below a threshold of three to four inches of summer precipitation (July–September total), Colorado piñon begins to give way to singleleaf piñon. Colorado piñon pierces singleleaf country as far as the Confusion Range and to Pioche, Nevada—mostly on rock and soil with lower phosphate content. But the Great Basin really is the domain of singleleaf piñon.

At this point in the story, a chorus of community ecologists raise their eyebrows, as they do whenever purely physical factors seem to account for where an organism lives: "What about competition?"

The Pleistocene seems to have eased the competitive struggle of woodland trees. Pluvial times eliminated the montane white fir, Douglas-fir, and ponderosa pine from the Basin just as surely as piñon and juniper. When the dry Hypsithermal of a few thousand years ago parched this huge piece of land, piñon and juniper swept northward into mountain ranges where they mostly competed with shrubs. Montane species have reinvaded timidly; most of

*Western junipers
dot the vast plains
of big sagebrush
in southeast
Oregon.*

148

*The Basin
Ranges*

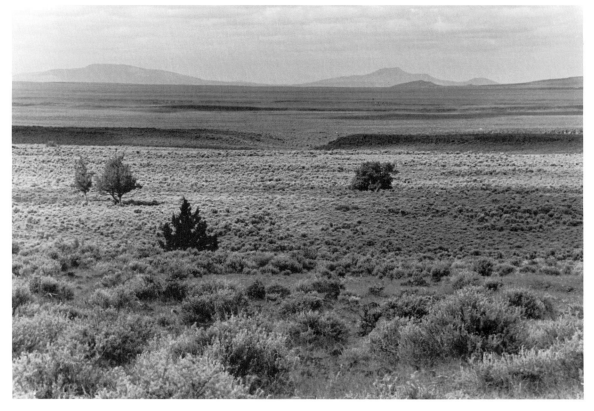

their primeval range now is too dry for them. Only on the bordering Sierra Nevada and Wasatch Range do chaparral and montane forest compete more fiercely, sharply narrowing the woodland.

In the Basin, piñon and juniper compete mostly with each other. The competitive dominance of piñon at elevations where both trees live longest (about sixty-five hundred to eight thousand feet) seems to confine juniper to the lower and more marginal elevations where only juniper (more tolerant of cold and aridity) can grow. Tree density and cover is highest in the center of woodlands. But at the more open fringes, the high and low borders, individuals grow fastest, evidently released from intense competition. Where only these solitary trees survive, each struggles at its climatic threshold. Competition with neighboring conifers decreases until there are no other trees, only one last twisted and dwarfed juniper or piñon.

Paleohistory and competition suggest why the little trees grow where they do. The shape of a range has its effect, too. Smaller ranges have the narrowest belts of woodland, for larger mountains catch more moisture. Big, long mountains protected on the west (like the Monitor Range) have wide belts. On ranges larger than about 270 square miles, the widest woodlands grow on the highest peaks regardless of further increase in mountain area. But extrahigh mountains like Arc Dome in the Toiyabe Range create environments *too* cold and wet; here woodland grows lower and in a narrower band.

The woodland flora includes plants associated with the Sierra, the Rockies, and the Mojave Desert. Ranges with highest plant diversity rise along the Mojave/Great Basin transition (the Silver Peak and Toquima ranges, and the Shoshone Mountains, for example). These mountains also have some of the most extreme elevational differences from valley to summit, making for great variety in habitat and many hideaway crannies for diverse plants.

Even Joshua trees mix with junipers on the west side of the Delamar Mountains west of Caliente and on Hancock Summit. Here grows a disorienting mix of plants: juniper, Joshua tree, sagebrush, green rabbitbrush, Palmer's penstemon, white prickly-poppy. (In this part of Nevada, place names, too, teem with *p*s: Pahroc, Panaca, Pioche, Pahute, Pahranagat.

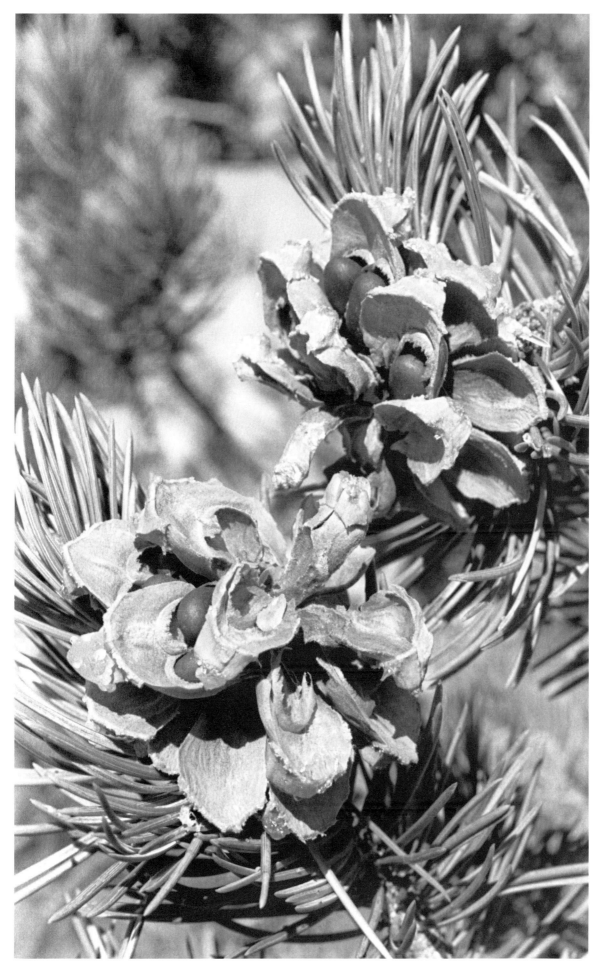

Piñon nuts (from Colorado piñon trees)—lifegiving staple of Great Basin wildlife and humans. Pinyon Jays can carry twenty of these seeds at once while flying to their seed caches.

These are mostly Paiute names; *pah*, in Paiute, means water.) Somehow the mix of plants suits these ranges that straddle two deserts.

Still, the location of a range in relation to climate seems the crucial factor for woodland. The northern Rubies suffer the full brunt of Pacific fronts and have no woodland on their west slope. But the southern Rubies, the south tip of the East Humboldt Range, and Spruce Mountain—all shielded by ranges "upwind"— have fine woodlands. In one section of the Virginia Range, opposite a low section of the Carson Range, moist cold air penetrates past the barrier of the higher western range and removes the inversion over that section; no woodland conifers grow there.

Any one tree either survives and reproduces in the spot in which it takes root or it does not. But each juniper and piñon *species* lives in a shifting, dynamic world.

Beyond the northernmost piñons and on low ranges in the Bonneville basin (the latter presumably too dry for piñon) Utah juniper rules alone. The juniper, in turn, gives way at the extremes of summer drought; Utah juniper does not closely approach the Sierra south of Mono Lake. On mountains like the Excelsiors along the California border only singleleaf piñons grow.

At the northern frontier, where winters run cold and summers sere, western junipers take over, their ragged-topped rows mirroring the ragged draperies of clouds hanging down from the big Oregon skies. One of its subspecies (mountain western juniper, *Juniperus occidentalis* ssp. *australis*) grows high in the Sierra and with Jeffrey pine along the upper Owens Valley. Only the ranges across northernmost Nevada lack junipers and piñons altogether, leaving a gap between singleleaf piñon/Utah juniper and western juniper.

One startling alternative reason exists for the missing piñons north of the Humboldt. Jays disperse piñons, and they simply may not yet have reintroduced the trees to these ranges.

Arguably the most conspicuous animal in piñon-juniper woodland, Pinyon Jays are unmistakable. Their calls sound like the audience hooting at sardonic humor in the most offbeat of off-Broadway theatres. They look more like blue crows than jays. And they move in flocks that may number up to several hundred.

Piñons and Pinyon Jays have lived together for a long time. Fossils exist from the Miocene (some fifteen to ten million years ago) of ancestral piñons and jays similar to Pinyon Jays. Ronald Lanner sums up succinctly the interwoven, coevolved bargain struck by bird and tree: "piñons were invented by jays."

Piñons have large wingless seeds that fall to the ground immediately under each tree if unharvested. If this constituted their only chance, few new piñons would sprout. But the trees present their cones like a bouquet—scattered across the tree crown when mature, opened wide, each seed exposed on a small shelf of scale tissue, readily pluckable by harvesters lured to the feast.

The strategy works well on their clientele. Pinyon Jays spend late summer and fall collecting and caching piñon nuts. They hammer apart green cones but can take seeds more easily later in the season when the cones have opened to present their wares. Capable of packing into its bulging esophagus up to twenty seeds at once, each jay flies with its harvest to the flock nesting area (frequently miles away), where it caches seeds in soil and ground litter. Come spring, nesting jays have a ready food source.

When the normally dependable piñon forsakes them in the undependable round of desert weather and the nut crop fails, Pinyon Jays do not breed in spring. But if a normal summer follows they will breed late, using the new crop for food. Indeed, the mere sight of green piñon cones (paired with the right day length) stimulates testes enlargement in male Pinyon Jays.

Steller's and Scrub Jays cache piñon seeds as well. Clark's Nutcrackers live mostly at higher elevations, where they cache seeds from whitebark and limber pine. But they too sometimes come down to the woodland to work the piñon groves.

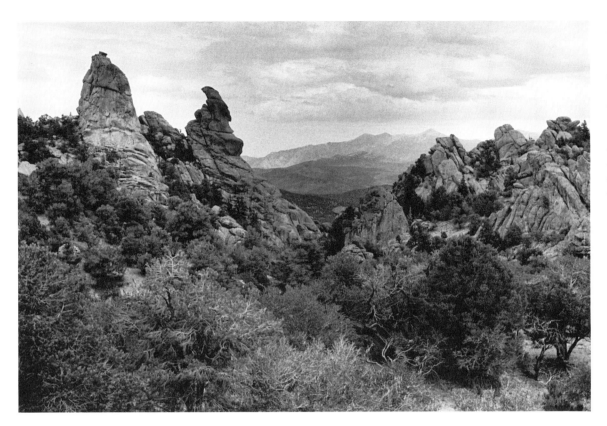

Piñon-juniper woodland cloaks the crags of Blue Mass Canyon in the Kern Mountains—a small range between the Snake Range and the Deep Creek Range, the latter seen here to the north.

These jays know their craft. Pinyon Jays ignore tan-shelled nuts, which rarely contain fully developed seeds. The jays search for dark brown nuts but test them for weight and resonance with their bills before bothering to cache them, knowing the exact feel of plump seeds that warrant their energy expenditure.

Biologists watching jays and nutcrackers have seen single flocks cache hundreds of pounds of seeds. One group of 150 nutcrackers cached a ton of seeds one fall—two to three times their winter energy requirements. Piñons clearly can sacrifice huge numbers of their nuts as jay food when the birds carefully disperse and bury so many more seeds fated to rejuvenate the piñon stand.

Pine and jay have struck a fair bargain.

One August I passed through a meadow in piñon-juniper woodland in the Snake Range. I rested against a tree and watched a cliff chipmunk through my binoculars.

The little rodent was feasting on a big meadow goat's-beard seed head, climbing to the top until its weight bowed down the whole plant stem, then eating the seeds one by one. With its cinnamon brown tail wrapped around the stem, just before the chipmunk toppled the foot-high plant it looked like a big furry fruit or a parasitic growth—a plant with a live "chipmunk-skin" hat, Davy Crockett–style.

Next came a long grass with bushy panicles of winged seeds. The chipmunk bit off the brush of seeds, then sat back on its haunches and chomped through the seed head bite by bite. Its look of sharp concentration, focused on some distant object but not attending to anything but its feeding, reminded me of people feeding corn-on-the-cob past their incisors. The ear of corn is too close to focus on, so while munching away you gaze fixedly at the white china mandala of your plate.

I passed though this meadow, still in cliff chipmunk country, but as I headed up the canyon, ponderosa pine and aspen replaced piñon-juniper and Uinta chipmunks came into their own.

Ecologist James H. Brown studied cliff chipmunks and their high-altitude neighbors, Uinta chipmunks, in the Snake Range below Wheeler Peak. Normally, cliff chipmunks live in open piñon-juniper woodland, Uinta chipmunks in denser forest where the branches of neighboring trees interlock.

In the Ruby Mountains, only the Uinta chipmunk occurs, on Pilot Peak only the cliff chipmunk. On ranges where only one is present, either chipmunk can expand into the habitat usually appropriated by the other, living throughout the forests. Since they are about the same size and eat the same foods, elsewhere some mechanism of competition must separate the two.

In observing the narrow zone where their ranges abut, Brown unraveled a simple behavioral difference that divides the mountain between them. Cliff chipmunks behave much more aggressively than Uintas, an adaptation useful for defending scattered resources in open habitats. Uintas spend more time climbing in trees but are less aggressive, and they are also more tolerant of numbers of other chipmunks nearby.

At a rich food source, Brown watched cliff chipmunks spend so much time chasing away Uinta chipmunks, which escaped easily into the trees, that they had little time left for feeding. Uintas would return to the food source whenever a cliff chipmunk scampered off on a chase. In this way they captured the prize even though they consistently lost individual aggressive encounters with the rowdy cliff chipmunk. With decreasing elevation, the trees become too far apart to allow easy escape and the cliff chipmunk's aggression succeeds; the Uintas retreat up the mountain to denser forest.

This interplay of food and tree and open space affects other piñon-juniper animals. Since the two conifers favor rocky soil, the coincidence of rocky cliffs with woodland makes for concentrations of ledge-dwelling mammals here. Other animals live in woodland largely because it suits their requirements for open (but not *too* open) habitat. Since all may feed on piñon nuts or juniper berries, unraveling exactly which factors keep them here is difficult.

Aromatic piñon phloem (moist tissue just beneath the bark) draws porcupine. Open habitat is crucial not only to cliff chipmunks but to wintering mule deer; at times both feed from the trees. Bighorn sheep range here but never

far from cliffs that offer escape cover. Wood rats, too, live in the woodland in abundance largely because of the rocky denning sites.

Piñon mice are one symbol of the woodland. Either piñon or juniper serves them well. They may even favor junipers and could as accurately be christened the "juniper mouse." Junipers offer hollow branches for safe travel, fibrous bark for nests, berries (really cones) for food.

Piñon mice choose where they live with more discrimination than their cousins, the ubiquitous deer mice, also common in woodland. In Nevada, piñon mice live in rocky areas with piñon or juniper trees. Piñons without rocks or rocks without piñons evidently will not do: E. Raymond Hall found no piñon mice living in such alternate renditions of habitat.

Besides Pinyon Jays, common year-round woodland birds include Bushtits and Plain Titmice. Along the Nevada-California border, southern woodland birds meet species more typical of northern coniferous forest. In mountains like the Sweetwaters—nearly continuous with the Sierra—such higher-elevation nesters as Steller's Jays and Brown Creepers breed in piñon groves. And farther south, in the Silver Peak Range, southern birds like Scott's Orioles and Gray Vireos turn up in woodland. Many other birds occur in both ends of this spectrum of latitudes, but their densities change from one end to the other or they switch habitats as their preferred cover disappears or becomes too dry.

Birds also distribute junipers to new territory. Fruit-eating species like American Robins and Townsend's Solitaires harvest juniper berries in huge numbers, passing seeds through their intestines intact and planting new stands in their travels. Junipers growing in a neat row record an old fence line, where flocks of these thrushes perched over the years, leaving behind freshly dropped juniper seeds in as true a line as corn in a carefully plowed furrow.

Insects often destroy 90 percent of the piñon cone crop. And these moderate-elevation rangelands serve as reservoir for the eggbeds of

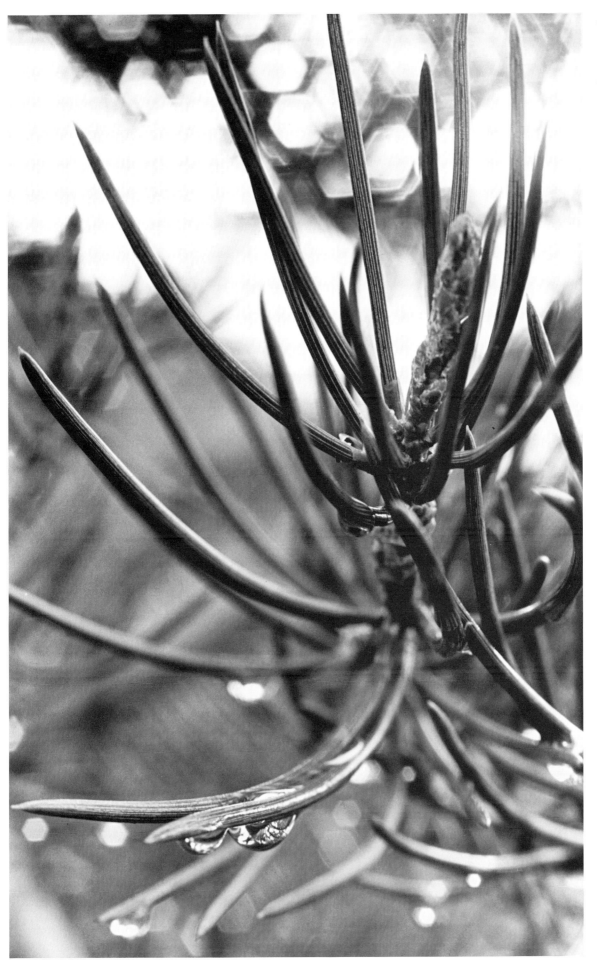

*Singleleaf piñon
after a summer
rain shower,
Quinn Canyon
Range.*

the Mormon cricket, actually a shield-backed grasshopper. From the first famous outbreak observed by horrified farmers, when the crickets threatened the crops of Mormon pioneers newly arrived in the Great Basin in 1848 and sea gulls saved them, crickets periodically have descended into valleys in great bands, devastating fields.

Mormon crickets usually remain where they hatch. But in years when many eggs hatch and many nymphs survive, the flightless insects move in bands, defoliating every plant in their path. In the 1930s, huge outbreaks infested two million acres in Nevada, one band in Elko County advancing along a twelve-mile front. Another Elko County band piled against a barrier fence for five days. Since the 1950s, annual surveys determine where insecticides must be applied to prevent cricket population explosions.

Bighorn sheep spend considerable time in piñon-juniper woodland. Since bighorn depend on acute vision to detect danger, they will not use dense woodland. Open woodland and sagebrush communities offer fine forage, but sheep will use them only if cliffs are near.

Sheep numbers have dropped so low since the coming of settlers that we cannot know just where they once occurred. One effort at documenting their historic range in Nevada mapped petroglyph sites depicting bighorn. From a variety of early sources, it seems clear that bighorn lived on most, but not all, of the higher Basin ranges. Today, most live in the Mojave Desert, in ranges so dry and rugged that hunters did not favor them and competition with livestock never eliminated native herds.

Bighorn will eat an enormous variety of plants. They need waterholes in summer and never stray too far from such sources. But more than anything else, cliffs for use as escape routes and safe lambing areas limit their ranges. Bighorn rarely move more than a half-mile from such broken and precipitous terrain. Even in annual migrations, as on the Toiyabe and Grant ranges (with subalpine summer range separated from winter range in sagebrush and woodland), cliffs determine the travel routes.

Such cautious sheep rarely pioneer new habitats. They *have* crossed valleys to new ranges, but to restock empty historic range today we must transplant sheep and manage their range with great care. Bighorn also fall victim to cycles of disease; the blue tongue virus, native to North America, seems to keep always one step ahead in its evolution of new forms, with the small gene pool of the sheep unable to evolve resistance at a speed to match.

Moving up from valley floors to woodland and then still higher into forest, the Great Basin ecological world rises into the sky like a pop-up book. In dunes, mammals dominate, living on—or in—the ground. Shrubs multiply the number of different ways to make a living, offering a new set of feeding and nesting sites. Birds increase. In the piñon-juniper woodland, birds increase still more, dominating other vertebrates in diversity, though reptiles do well in this rocky habitat. At higher elevations and along creeks, full-sized trees multiply bird diversity yet again, while the kinds of mammals and reptiles decrease.

Woodland forms an overlap area, where habitat generalists thrive and where desert creatures meet mountain creatures. The trees themselves give the pygmy forest its personality and define its extent. But even with such a simple definition, Great Basin woodland proves to be as dynamic as shadscale or sagebrush. A goodly number of ecological papers speak of juniper "invasions," and range managers are serious about this war.

Humans have leapt into the fray without fully understanding the powers at odds. Junipers have increased in the past hundred years, at their lower limits moving into sagebrush valleys and at their upper limits moving higher on mountains. Piñon follows, as the more drought-tolerant junipers prepare the way as "nurse-trees," shading the seedbed for piñon. Where piñon grows alone, as on the Pine Nut Mountains, it has expanded upward on its own. Throughout much of the woodland, tree density has increased, mostly in the form of small bushy trees sprouted since 1860.

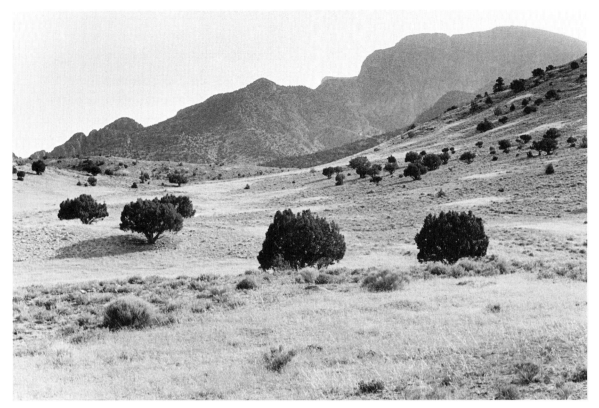

We would be delighted with this if the trees happened to be good forage for livestock; "invasion" would become "expansion." But as the trees increase in density, forage decreases. The real war is not ecological but political, part of the complicated interplay in the West between ranchers, local politicians, federal land management agencies, range biologists, wilderness advocates—and the land.

That the conifers have increased in numbers is irrefutable. Modern photographs composed to exactly match pioneer photographs show considerably more woodland than in the last century, even where nineteenth-century miners did not clearcut the forest for shaft props and firewood. The reasons woodland trees have expanded their range, however, remain unclear.

By coring and dating trees on many mountains, Great Basin ecologists have traced the history of succession in east-central Nevada since 1725, when juniper already was present in what would become the dense woodland stands of today. Junipers in modern open woodlands sprouted by 1869. Piñon occurred in denser stands after 1800 and in all stands after 1921.

The latter year seemed to be a key year; "in-vasion" accelerated about then in all communities in a pattern evidently unrelated to moisture availability. In the early 1900s, enormous numbers of livestock overgrazed these ranges, reducing other plants competing with piñon and juniper and dispersing juniper seeds in their feces. Little fuel accumulated and fires decreased. Increase in density of the conifers coincides with this peak period of overgrazing.

A 1981 analysis of woodland density across the entire Great Basin reached similar conclusions. The oldest stands, and those with trees most decisively dominating other vegetation, grow on intermediate topography. Younger stands of both singleleaf piñon and Utah juniper dominate less decisively above and below these densest stands.

Piñon outnumbered juniper in more than two-thirds of the stands. In more than half of the sample woodlands, trees younger than 150 years old dominated—trees sprouted since ranchers and miners came to the Great Basin. The trees (primarily piñon) established themselves at highest rates between 1870 and 1920, the time of greatest pressure on the Basin by settlers.

Juniper and piñon have increased; invasion

is a fact. But we know that during the mining booms of the nineteenth century, entire mountains were denuded of trees for fuelwood and charcoal to stoke smelters and cookstoves and to heat mining camps. For example, the Comstock district surrounding Virginia City burned 120,000 cords of firewood in 1866; woodcutters soon had to move to the Sierra to support such demands.

In central Nevada no neighboring forest could relieve the pressure on piñon-juniper woodland. Smelters at the Austin mines in the 1860s burned a cord of wood per ton of ore. Fuelwood constituted about 60 percent of milling costs. Woodcutters had harvested all the piñon and juniper within twenty miles of Eureka by 1874, and by 1878 within fifty miles. Similar harvests took place around every mining camp on virtually every mountain range in Nevada.

Today we cannot document the extent of woodland before this period of intense harvest. The woodcutters left no stumps: they took the trees right down to the ground. Evidence from dead trees simply does not exist. Fires swept the woodland frequently, both before settlement, in Indian-set game-drive blazes, and after, when fires often were set for no reason other than to clear a path for sheep herds. Such fires thinned the stands: for example, western junipers less than fifty years old have a poor chance of surviving wildfire. And fires cleared litter that contained chemicals that inhibit grass growth under the conifers.

Overlapping these catastrophic changes came intense stock grazing that depleted the understory and, hence, eliminated the tinder to carry wildfires. Fires dropped in frequency and land managers began to suppress those that did start. Suddenly, fire no longer played an active role in the woodland.

Of all the factors controlling succession in woodland, these changing fire cycles seem crucial. Without fire, sagebrush increased on grassland; juniper and piñon increased in both historic sagebrush stands and in piñon-juniper savannas.

Today, in woodland as well as sagebrush, cheatgrass has further complicated the cycle. With little understory in dense woodland the forest becomes virtually fireproof. Cheatgrass reverses this trend, and battalions of invading juniper may lose in the end to the alien weed adapted to frequent fires best of all.

Long-term climatic change may influence the expansion of woodland as well. Temperatures warmed in the Great Basin from 1850 to 1960, and the last half of the nineteenth century was wetter than normal. Are piñon and juniper responding to long cycles of global climatic change, simply reclaiming the land they held before nineteenth-century deforestation, or truly invading into new territory? All these factors likely affect the expanding woodland.

Even this exceedingly fuzzy picture has holes in it—holes punched by the controversial practice of chaining.

Chaining started after World War II, when wartime industrial success had galvanized enthusiasm for technological management on a grand scale and a population freed of wartime restrictions hungered for red meat. Too many trees? Too little forage? Not enough browse for mule deer? Trouble with the rural economy? Put America to work and *do* something about it: eliminate the trees and reseed with more useful plants.

To destroy woodland, battleship anchor chains were dragged between bulldozers, uprooting trees. South of the Great Basin, federal land managers used an eighty-ton tree crusher in Arizona and New Mexico projects. Elsewhere they tried herbicides and fire. By one estimate, between 1950 and 1964 three million acres of woodland became newly minted pastureland. Between 1960 and 1972 over a third of a million acres of Forest Service and Bureau of Land Management (BLM) land in Utah and Nevada were chained.

Fully half the papers presented at a 1975 Utah State University symposium—the best source available on piñon-juniper ecology—concerned the techniques and ramifications of purposeful destruction of the woodland. One paper was entitled "Pinyon-Juniper Forests:

Asset or Liability." Any Paiute, Shoshone, or Washoe family thriving on piñon nuts through a long Great Basin winter could answer that question, though they might wonder about the perception and ethics of the man who asked it.

The range scientists who spoke at this symposium understood the paradoxes of the woodland. The author of the paper mentioned above argued for accepting piñon-juniper forests "as they are" and managing them for "multiple-use." In the management actions lies the controversy.

Chaining began enthusiastically, without regard for our poor understanding of the reasons behind woodland expansion. The federal agencies chained stable permanent stands as well as young invading ones, paying little attention to where juniper or piñon had increased in density or invaded open range.

Thirty years later, manipulation of piñon-juniper woodland has fallen into disfavor. At the 1975 symposium, the range managers who had supervised the chaining concluded that their results were confusing, and that most chainings failed to deliver on their promises.

Livestock forage does not increase permanently, as hoped. In most economic analyses, expensive woodland conversions barely break even—at best. Most of the chainings have begun to revert to woodland, requiring "additional treatments." The tractors and chains do not kill saplings. And Pinyon Jays are always busily at work caching nuts; thrushes leave juniper seeds behind them on their journeys.

Still, forage has remained high on some chainings for up to thirty years, and with tight control of piñon-juniper reproduction some of these chainings may be economically viable (measured by cost of chaining versus livestock production, without regard for the value of trees).

Mule deer usually do not take to the huge open pastures created by chaining. On some chainings in Utah the State Department of Wildlife documents increased local use by mule deer, but nowhere have total populations in herds of game animals increased on chainings. The effects of woodland conversion on the myriads of other creatures remain unknown.

Chaining has ambiguous effects on watersheds in dense woodland. Some scientists believe that the cryptogamic crust of fungi and algae naturally growing on soil prevents erosion. Even in woodland with little understory, in stands protected from overgrazing the crust ponds rainfall and snowmelt. This may either increase or inhibit infiltration, enhance or slow runoff, be mostly positive or negative for other plants—no one yet knows.

Cryptogamic crust may prevent seedlings from sprouting until the crust is broken by grazers or burrowing rodents; we need to compare disturbed sites to ungrazed pristine rangelands (which exist only in tiny relict areas). Chaining destroys the cryptogams, but whether chaining and reseeding ease or increase erosion problems we cannot yet say. With conflicting research results swirling around them, many people reach their opinions about piñon-juniper chaining on emotional and ethical grounds.

Well-intentioned as attempts at woodland conversion might be, the perpetrators reckon with a powerful affection. Westerners hold all trees in great esteem. Even ranchers obsessed with grass tenderly nurture cottonwood windbreaks around their houses. The first thing a Mormon family did when founding a new colony was to plant Lombardy poplars; Wallace Stegner calls them "Mormon trees."

Native Americans from Paiutes to Pueblos revere the piñon as the giver of first food to the first people. Its nuts continued to keep Great Basin people alive through winters up to a few decades ago. Groves outside normal piñon range almost always mark old tribal trails— "orchards" planted accidentally or deliberately. For centuries, in the Great Basin and the Southwest, juniper wood has burned clean and hot in the cookstove while blazing lengths of pitchy piñon warmed camps and cabins.

Clearcutting virgin Douglas-fir in the Northwest arouses great outrage. The last patch of Kansas tallgrass prairie has its defenders. Humble piñon and juniper, too, nourish the

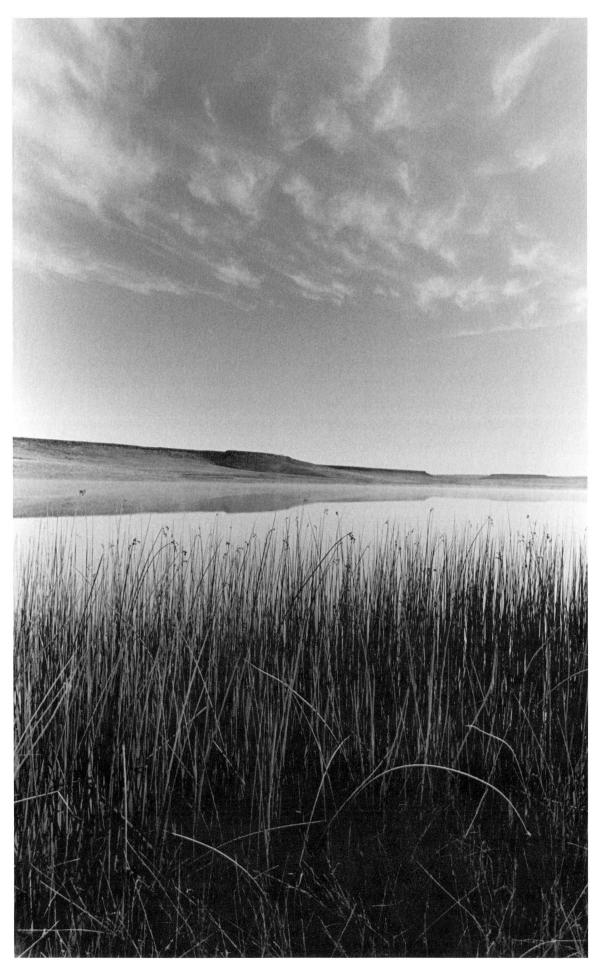

Not all Great Basin water sources are alkaline lakes or ephemeral rivers. Resource management creates as well as destroys: this is Catnip Reservoir on the Charles Sheldon Antelope Range.

souls of those who live with them. And sound and pragmatic reasons exist to cease their persecution: economics, maintaining the great pool of continental ecological diversity that holds answers to our unspoken questions.

This does not preclude management. The woodland is neither static nor pristine. Piñon and juniper trees have swept in tides across the Great Basin for millions of years. They respond to changing climate with sensitivity, and their populations shrink or expand accordingly. They survived the exploitation of pioneer days when huge areas were clearcut, and an unknown percentage of their current "invasion" is simply the retaking of this historic range.

But the permanent loss of understory has created a fireproof woodland except in the case of firestorms that wipe out everything; the trees increase in density unchecked. Piñon and juniper rapidly grow roots and begin dominating the shrubs and herbs when only sixty to seventy years old. With present trends, all but the extremely marginal woodland sites in the Great Basin will lose most understory productivity by the year 2000. Erosion will increase, and so will the danger of firestorms.

Simply decreasing grazing will not reverse this pattern; too few grasses remain. We have permanently transformed the primeval woodland and now have an obligation to manage the woodland trees and their world of grass, mule deer, Pinyon Jays, nut crops—and cows. Deciding the course of that management weaves the political and practical with the desirable.

Range managers have nearly ceased chaining. If they truly seek effective "multiple-use," a variety of choices remains. Woodland trees can be farmed for nut crops and harvested for fence posts, fuelwood, and Christmas trees. To increase forage for livestock, the best bets seem to be prescribed burning in small patches, retreatment of already-chained areas, and reseeding after wildfires (seeding both with grass for livestock and browse and herbs desirable to game animals). With careful consideration of side effects, herbicides can help thin unburnable stands.

It will keep managers on track as they sit in air-conditioned urban offices if they can smile with the remembered sense of sharp woodland fragrances, feel again the relief of shade beneath these trees in the heat and glare of a summer day. Let us hope that the people who make the decisions to determine the woodland's future know what it feels like to brush against stiff-needled small trees enduring with tenacity on the dry frontier of forest.

Let us hope that they have been here.

Mountain Brush and
Aspen Glens

12

*May 12, 1859: Descending the west
slope of the mountain . . . along a pure,
mountain-gushing stream, which I call
after Lieutenant Marmaduke, of the
Seventh Infantry, brought us to the
mail-station on the east side of Steptoe
Valley, in the vicinity of which we en-
camped. . . .*

. . . what the Mormons call mountain
mahogany *. . . grows generally at the
summit of the passes. It is somewhat
scrubby in appearance, ramifying in several branches from the ground, and in
form resembles the apple-tree. Its greatest
height is about 20 feet. . . . Its wood is
very hard, and is used for cogs, journals,
gudgeons, &c.*

—Captain James H. Simpson,
Report of Explorations, 1859

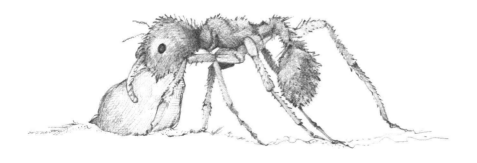

*Harvester ant with
bitterbrush seed*

The trouble with being a mountain conifer in the Great Basin is that these desert mountains are not continuous. Each range rises from dry valleys useless to any moisture-loving tree, and the ranges themselves can be almost as dry.

On the Rockies or the Sierra, successive belts of forest ring the mountains above piñon-juniper woodland and chaparral right up to the tree line. But in the central Great Basin many ranges have no forest above the woodland. A subalpine fringe of limber or bristlecone pine crowns the highest peaks. Except for a few pockets of ponderosa pine and Douglas-fir that spill over from the Rockies and Sierra, brush covers the slopes above woodland and below windblown subalpine pines.

Ranges whose summits fall between about seventy-five hundred and ten thousand feet lack subalpine forest, and on them, mountain big sagebrush, bitterbrush, snowberry, western serviceberry, and other shrubs extend right over the top of the mountain. Such "bald mountains" dot the map of the Great Basin. Only groves of curlleaf mountain-mahogany and aspen rise through this expanse of shrub-statured plants.

A rancher driving through this relatively wet, luxuriant brush country in the Santa Rosa Range said to me, "Nice country up here . . . for desert country."

The climate of these brush slopes seems just right for montane conifers like ponderosa pine. But the Pleistocene eliminated these trees from the Great Basin, and even with jays to help with distribution, beyond the cordilleras they have yet to reinvade in numbers. Conifers currently dwelling in the central Great Basin have temperature and moisture tolerances that keep them either lower (piñon and juniper) or higher (limber and bristlecone pines) on the mountains. In between, the brush feels like desert because the expected forest is missing.

Sagebrush remains abundant. On the Santa Rosa Range, for example, beyond the northern boundary of piñons and junipers, sagebrush dominates up to the summit of the range at about ten thousand feet. Only pockets of aspen and limber pine break its reign.

A community by default, mountain brush nonetheless has unique combinations of species. Bitterbrush and, in the southeastern Basin, cliffrose form distinctive communities much favored by mule deer. Bitterbrush ranges from a small, low, layered shrub at the top of Hart Mountain, Oregon, to near tree size in country with a longer frost-free season along the western edge of the Honey Lake basin in California. Cliffrose grows just as tall at the eastern foot of the Grant Range in Nevada. Perhaps most distinctive is the related curlleaf mountain-mahogany, which grows at higher elevations in pure stands or forms a more open woodland with snowberry and bunchgrasses beneath.

Curlleaf mountain-mahogany is a small tree with great character. Perched on dramatic outcrops, often limestone, mountain-mahoganies look exotic: evergreen and Mediterranean, like ancient olives or oaks. Usually about eleven feet high, mountain-mahoganies along Baker Creek in the Snake Range reach thirty feet plus. These stable communities grow on steep, arid, warm, rocky ledges and plateaus where conifers do not thrive. Cottontails eat seedlings and seem to limit reproductive success.

On the arid White Mountains, big sagebrush and black sagebrush form the background community from 6,000 to 12,800 feet. Forests of piñons below and bristlecones above overlay the sagebrush, but the two bands of conifers rarely meet. A high-elevation band of sagebrush and mountain-mahogany separates them.

Here curlleaf mountain-mahogany grows mostly above nine thousand feet on deeper soils; the more shrubby littleleaf mountain-mahogany grows mostly below on steep limestone slopes in piñon woodland. At sites intermediate between these extremes, hybrid mountain-mahoganies form a continuum—plants closest to one or the other parent dominating places most like the parental habitats. These hybrids concentrate between nine thousand and ten thousand feet in the transition from piñon to bristlecone forest, intermediate

Wetlands and Woodlands

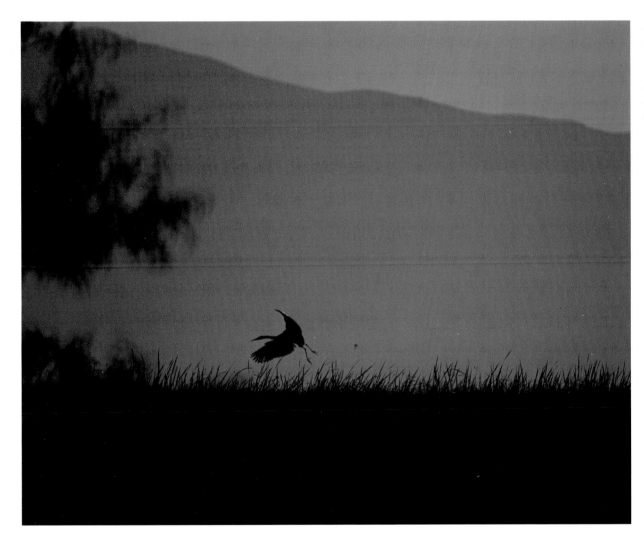

A Great Blue Heron flaps down into the tules at Bear River Migratory Bird Refuge, Great Salt Lake.

*Salt-laced
Pyramid Lake,
largest remnant of
Lake Lahontan,
named by John
Charles Frémont
in 1844 for its
great pyramid of
rock.*

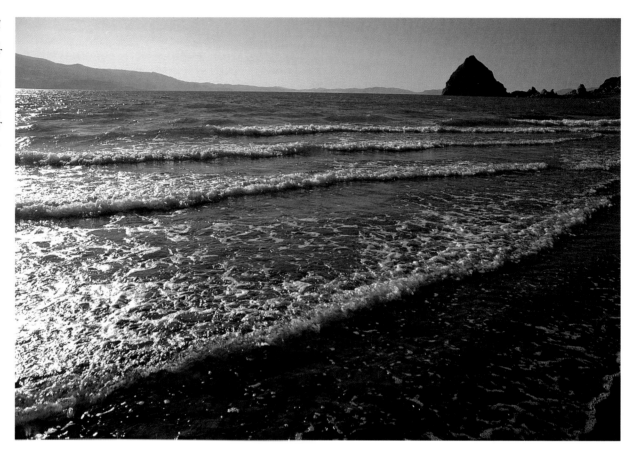

*Mono Lake lies
at the base of the
Sierran wall—
the range that
intercepts Pacific
moisture, leaving
the Great Basin
in a rain shadow,
as a desert.*

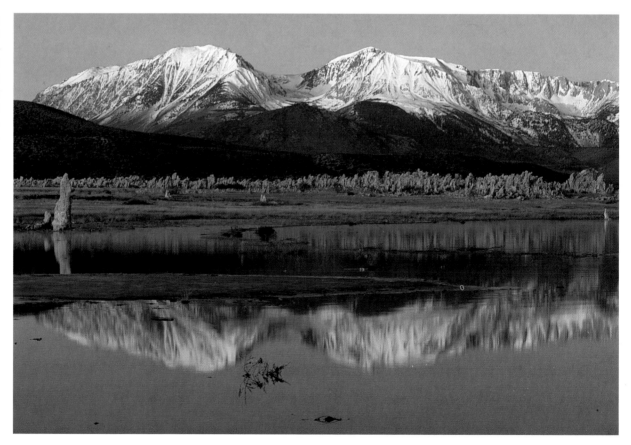

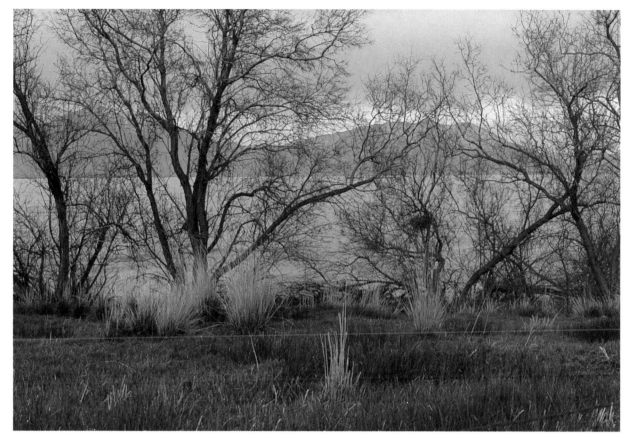

*Leafless
early-winter
cottonwoods line
the west shore
of Utah Lake.*

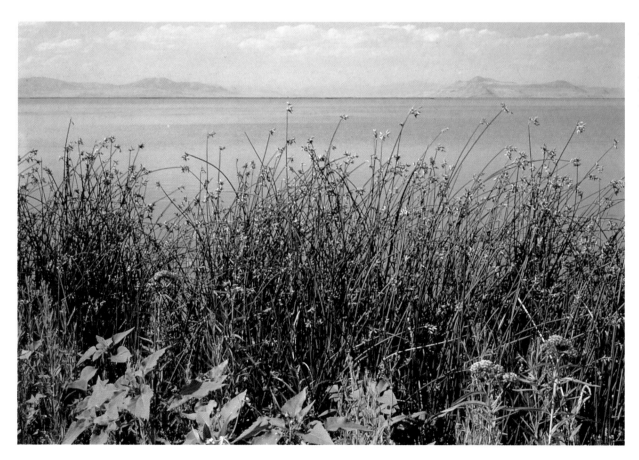

*Bulrushes and
milkweed fringe
the Great Salt
Lake at Bear
River Migratory
Bird Refuge.*

Flowing water attracts humans just as powerfully as it does wildlife; Hendrys Creek, Mount Moriah, Snake Range.

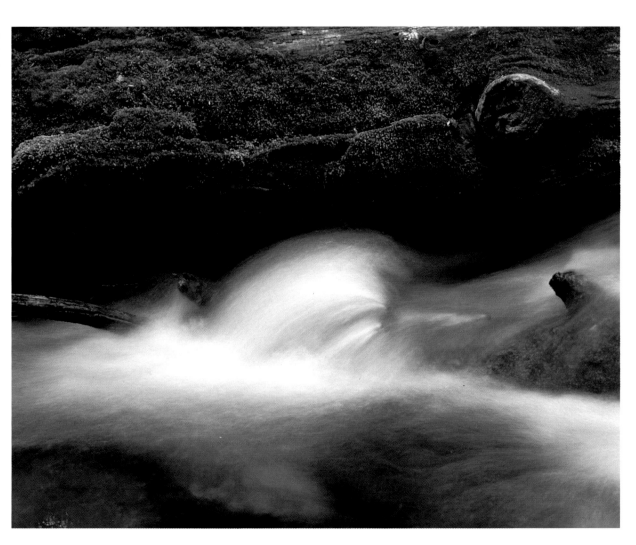

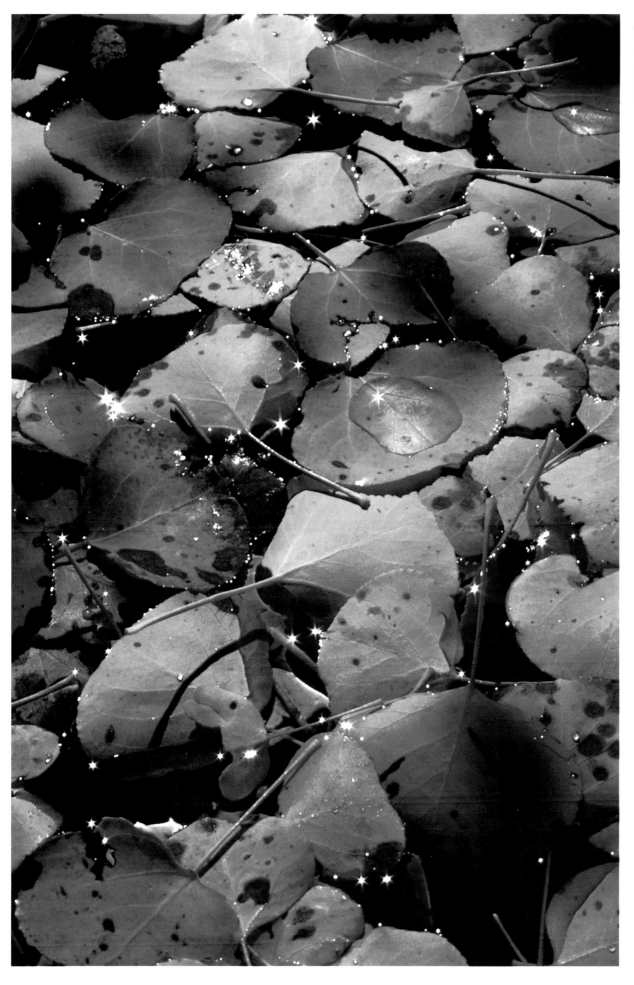

Autumn aspen leaves floating on the glittering surface of Pine Creek, Toquima Range.

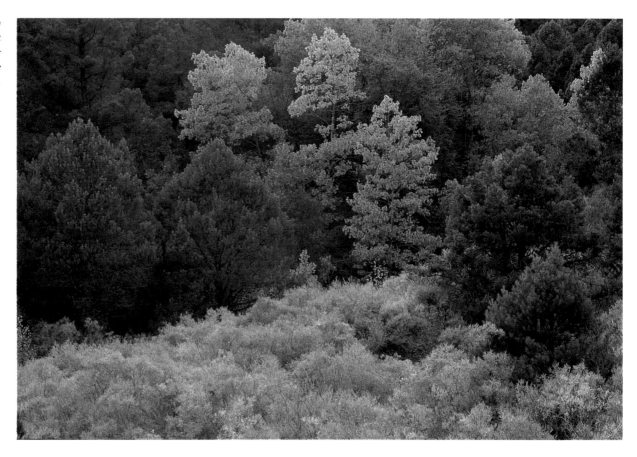

Piñon and willow in the last light of evening; Ophir Creek, Toiyabe Range.

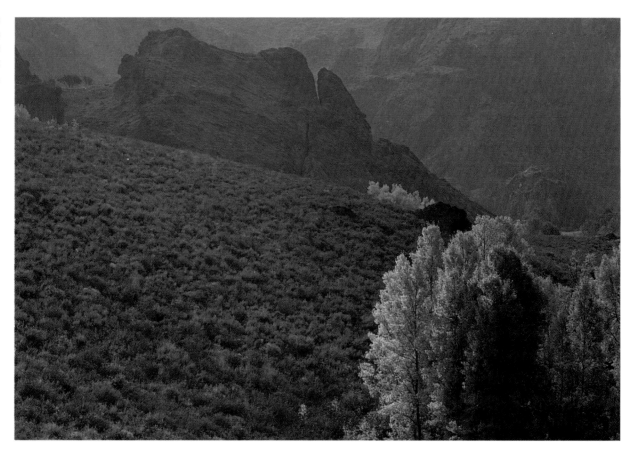

An aspen grove along Indian Creek in the Santa Rosa Range.

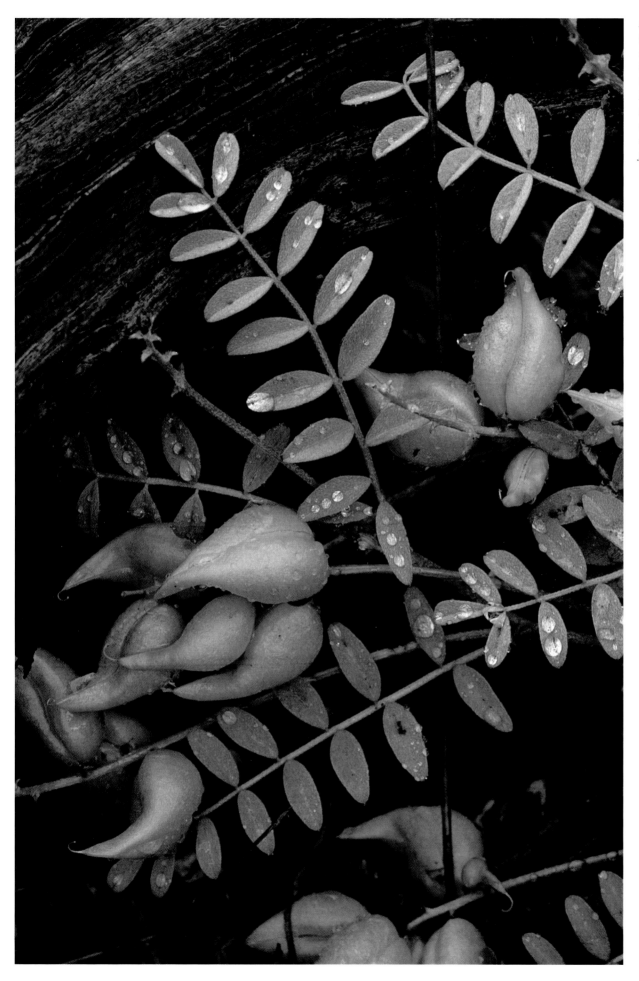

Annual plants like this astragalus along Cherry Creek in the Quinn Canyon Range are rare enough to be conspicuous in dense piñon-juniper woodland.

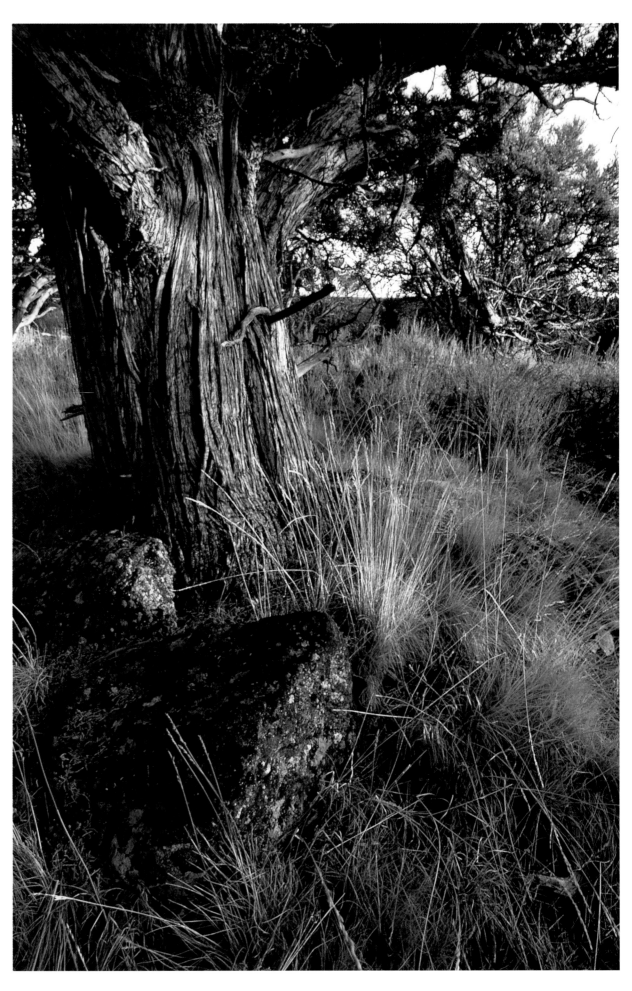

A robust, grassy understory beneath western junipers on Steens Mountain.

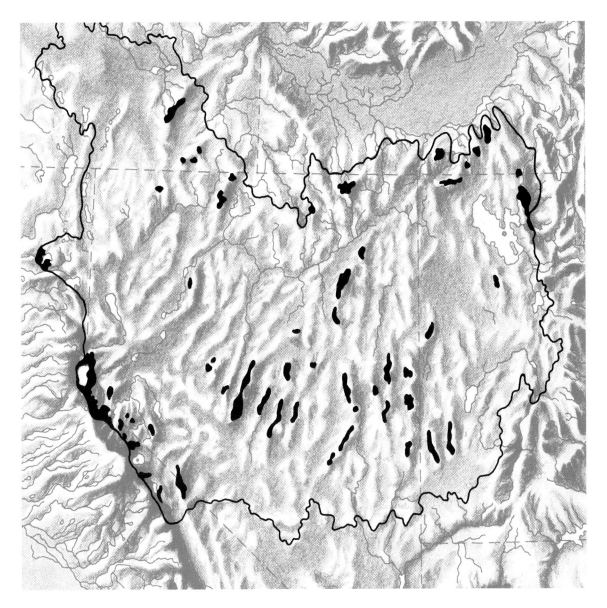

Distribution of montane plant communities (mountain brush, pine and fir forest, alpine tundra) in the Great Basin Desert. (Based on Holmgren, 1972; and Barbour and Major, 1977)

environments that are recent and still gradually changing. The White Mountain mountain-mahogany hybrids seem adapted in a startlingly precise way to the intermediate sites.

Like cliffrose their fruits have feathery tails. Mountain-mahogany trees in fruit, backlit, shine brightly, like desert Christmas trees. Weatherbeaten and solitary or in small groves, they form one emblem of the Great Basin.

Each life zone in the Great Basin has its characteristic family: goosefoots (Chenopodiaceae) in the salt desert, sunflowers (Asteraceae) in sagebrush, woodland junipers (Cupressaceae), and roses (Rosaceae) in mountain brush.

Mountain-mahogany, bitterbrush, cliffrose, Apache plume, western serviceberry, fern bush, tufted rockmat, ninebark, cinquefoil,

wild rose, chokecherry—all are roses. Virtually the only important Great Basin mountain brush plants not in the rose family are snowberry (a honeysuckle), and deerbrush (a buckthorn)—and Sierran and Wasatch species that reach partway into the Intermountain region, and whose story appears in later chapters.

Bitterbrush and cliffrose have an intertwined evolutionary history. Some botanists believe that antelope bitterbrush, a northern species, arose from the southwestern cliffrose. Today they have met in the Great Basin after long isolation and still can interbreed freely, producing many combinations and crosses, including one new species: desert (waxy) bitterbrush.

All Utah bitterbrush show influence from earlier hybridizations with cliffrose, and though such traces decrease to the north, even in Brit-

The long, feathery
tails of mountain-
mahogany seeds,
White Mountains,
California.

164

The Basin
Ranges

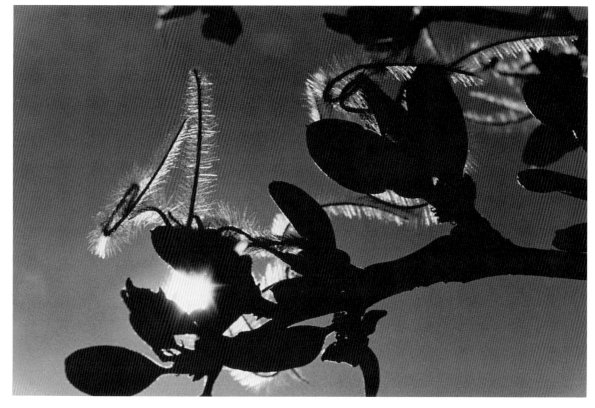

ish Columbia a few bitterbrush stands have cliffrose characteristics. Such a wide spectrum of adaptations fine-tunes each stand for its particular climate. These plants, full of variation, can deal successfully with climatic surprises, with one population somewhere in their range likely able to cope with a given set of new rules.

All these related plants provide crucial winter browse for big game. Since elk and bighorn now are rare or missing from Great Basin mountains, big game usually means mule deer here. Deer eat an enormous variety of plants through the year, including grass, herbs, shrubs, and trees. When snow piles deep, deer move down into sagebrush. In summer and fall, and during light winters, they concentrate in mountain brush, where bitterbrush is their favorite.

Western serviceberry, snowberry, and young mountain-mahogany become important for deer where bitterbrush does not grow. Old mountain-mahogany offers little forage, since it often raises its live branches in "umbrellas" too high for browsing animals to reach. When these tasty plants become rare, deer eat many other shrubs, including big sagebrush. Mule deer need escape cover just as they need food. Bit-

terbrush growing within piñon-juniper woodland or along the edges of aspen groves meets both needs.

Ecologists sensitive to the economic importance of mule deer herds have paid considerable attention to bitterbrush. Encouraging bitterbrush reproduction, however, proves complicated. The papery seed covering inhibits germination; evidently this covering rots away in winter, allowing germination come spring. Rodents and harvester ants collect and cache almost the entire crop of bitterbrush seeds; their activities are crucial to bitterbrush reproduction.

Heteromyid rodents cache ten to one hundred seeds in tight clusters buried about two inches deep. In spring the sprouting bitterbrush rosettes are a favorite food of kangaroo rats, kangaroo mice, and pocket mice; deer mice, too, seem particularly fond of them, perhaps because of their high vitamin A content. Insect predation and disease take their toll. All these combine to thin the sprouting plants, allowing a few survivors to grow with minimal competition.

Bitterbrush usually does not sprout after the hot, intense blazes that follow long-term fire

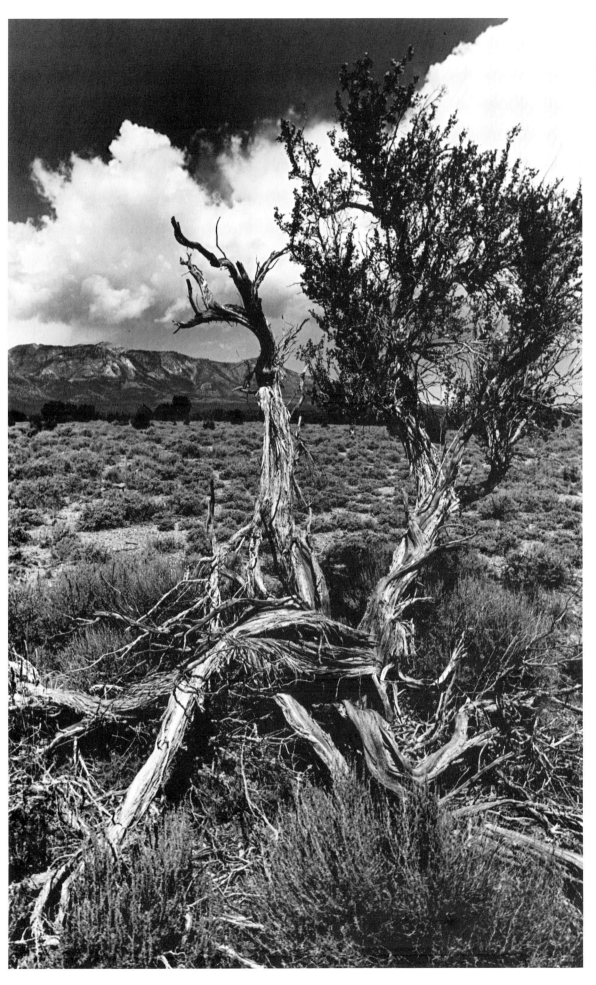

Unusually large cliffroses grow below Troy Peak in the Grant Range.

prevention. In dry places, fire may promote cheatgrass. Less-intense fires clear litter and encourage rodent caching. But rodents cache many seeds, including cheatgrass and crested wheatgrass as well as bitterbrush. Big-game biologists want to see thriving stands of bitterbrush; livestock range managers want to see fields of wheatgrass—and not cheatgrass. The rodents simply want to survive and reproduce.

Evolution and paleoclimatology determine the general extent of bitterbrush and cliffrose species. Reproduction is intimately tied to fire cycles and seed predators. And every change wrought through grazing and fire management interacts with these old patterns and with the new ones woven by the introduction of aggressive alien species.

Once again, trying to understand the distribution and successful reproduction of a single Great Basin plant quickly expands almost without bounds into time and space.

After years of research, we feel confident of predicting the effects of prescribed burns on Sage Grouse or mule deer. We know that huge chained clearings of piñon-juniper do little for deer. Punching small clearings into the woodland to encourage mountain brush and shrubs while preserving escape cover indeed increases deer numbers. But a single-purpose management has effects on every other community member. We know little of the ramifications of any management technique for Green-tailed Towhees, Merriam's shrews, or rubber boas. It takes dedication, cleverness, insight, time, energy, and money to tease out even a few such details for every creature in a community.

Only one "real" tree grows commonly in mountain brush communities: aspen. Quaking aspen has a range greater than any other North American tree, but in the Great Basin its distribution is spotty, its growth forms an almost infinite variety of shapes. It survives only on wetter slopes and in canyons in higher mountains, where moisture requirements center it in the same zone as mountain brush.

Compared to the huge aspen forests of Colorado, New Mexico, and central Utah, Great

Basin stands are puny. But in the ocean of desert shrubs and tough little woodland trees that surround them, these few aspen bring a rare touch of brightness and luxuriance to the Basin mountains. Even the most hard-bitten prospector gentles when passing through the white-trunked glens of trembling-leaved aspen.

Along Hendrys Creek on Mount Moriah in the Snake Range, I walked up the canyon, always in aspen, always with the rushing creek. The sound stayed with me for two days, the constant churn of water tumbling down to the desert. When I hiked above it past the spring where the creek starts, the silence startled me. Only when I did not hear the stream did I realize how my ears had adapted to it.

I was last here in August. It is now October. Several weeks ago came a fierce early storm that left four feet of snow in the high country.

Deciduous plants like aspen had their schedules abruptly thwarted. They slowly had been preparing for winter when I saw them in August, gradual changes in day length and in temperature controlling their hormonal secretions. Their streaming fluids carried commands to the leaves to begin to prepare to drop. At the same time, buds, seeds, and other vegetative parts readied for dormancy. Then came the storm.

Leaves froze, turned brown, and fell to the ground. Where each leaf was amputated, plants plugged wounds with cork or gums that prevent entrance of disease-causing organisms. Capricious continental weather patterns jolted to a halt careful cycling of hormones. But the plants long ago evolved adaptations to such variation in growing seasons. This early loss of leaves is irritating only to me, for it foils my plan to photograph a blaze of fall color in the canyon.

It also proved irritating to a rancher I met near the base of Mount Moriah. The snow caught him high up, moving cattle off the mountain. The storm slowed the herd and forced him to move down in darkness he described as "blacker than the inside of a cow."

The man had been grazing his cattle above eleven thousand feet on Mount Moriah's unique

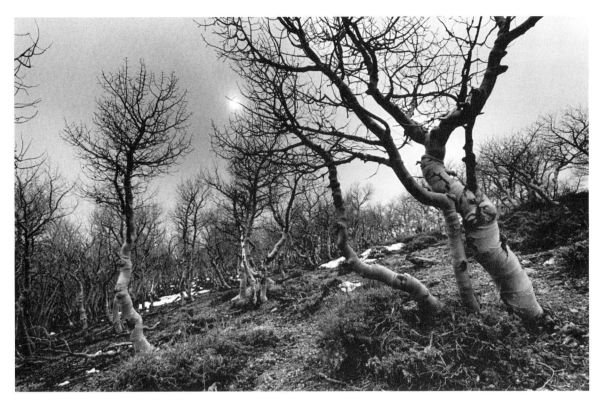

Table, a three-square-mile plateau of alpine grasses and wildflowers dotted with stands of bristlecone pine. This was my destination, about ten miles up Hendrys Creek from the trailhead at six thousand feet.

Hendrys Creek, like many places in the West, has a touch of paradox in the feel of its wilderness. Rarely do you meet anyone in such little-known and isolated places. Wildness remains intact. But cowboys and cattle have almost always been there before you. Like most Great Basin ranges, cattle still graze The Table every summer, and aspen up and down the creek record fifty years of local cowboy history in their carvings.

Most are just initials or names and dates. But on August 20, 1924, Willard F. Sorenson recorded that "it's snowing like hell."

Cliff and Emeron Ballender were the most prolific of Hendrys Creek aspen carvers. They worked the canyon from 1929 to 1933 and left their names everywhere along the trail. Cliff tended to write short messages, keeping a laconic journal: "Headed for The Table"; "Riding down Henry's [*sic*] Creek Today."

Emeron favored extremes. Either he wrote only his initials or name, leaving it at that, or he carved long stories with introduction, com-

mentary, and conclusion. Most of the longer inscriptions are overgrown, but one still can be read:

> Emeron R. Ballender
> Aug. 30, 1929
> Followed my donkeys from the bottom
> A hell of a long ways to walk alone
> Goodbye and Good Luck
> Till We Meet Again
> Adios.

Above nine thousand feet I caught up to the snow, the remains of that four-foot blanket. Aspen leaves had melted down into the drifts like rocks, the dark leaves absorbing heat from the sunlight at a faster rate than the snow. Miniature wells pockmarked the banks, at the bottom of each a single leaf. Here, too, the ponderosas and white fir of the lower canyon gave way to Douglas-fir and Engelmann spruce. As I climbed out of the main creek toward the ridge leading to The Table, the aspen showed the difficulties of higher elevations: stunted aspen gave way to limber pine on exposed knolls, then to bristlecone.

In dense coniferous forest, aspen pioneers clearings and burns. The sun-loving aspens

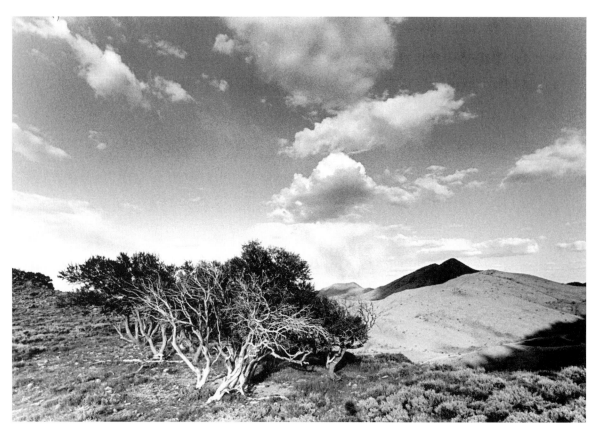

Elfin groves of mountain-mahogany have a bit of fantasy about them, like a forest from a Tolkien tale; below Currant Mountain in the White Pine Range.

shade sun-intolerant spruce and fir seedlings, which flourish beneath them. Gradually, over fifty to four hundred years, aspen gives way to the dominant conifers. Most Great Basin mountains, however, lack such evergreens. With no spruce and fir at their feet inexorably growing toward takeover, aspen stands remain stable, rejuvenated by fire and other disturbance, or become decadent and succeed to brush or grass.

Animals may help maintain aspen groves, even on ranges with more kinds of conifers, by feeding on conifers and thus reducing competition. Deer and hares browse young white firs, and porcupine and sapsuckers work them over when older. The sapsuckers excavate in aspen trunks as well, and other hole-nesting bird species thrive in this forest, nesting in the holes provided by sapsuckers.

Western aspens rarely reproduce directly by seed. Aspen seedlings require constant moisture, their seeds too fragile for much success, viable for only two to four weeks and dispersed in June and early July, when seedbeds are dry.

Instead, aspens send up suckers from their roots by the thousands. This allows them to bounce back immediately after fire, insect outbreaks, blowdowns, or (these days) clearcuts. Over generations, root suckers spread a single aspen "individual" over many square feet—or even many acres. This genetically identical clone sends up aspen trees that look alike, turn the same color in autumn, and flower, leaf out, and drop their leaves at the same time. Blocks of different colors in autumn outline precisely the mosaic of clones on a hillside.

Stems produce a hormone that suppresses sucker formation. When a fire wipes out the stems, the supply of inhibitory hormone in the roots drops and stimulates suckers to shoot up in densities that reach thirty thousand per acre. One big clone in the Sevier basin measured more than one hundred acres, with forty-seven thousand stems. Utah and Colorado possess the largest aspen clones in the West, and therefore probably the oldest.

Over most of their range, single aspen trees rarely live longer than sixty years, just as they rarely grow more than sixty feet high. But is a single trunk in a clone really a separate individual?

Starting from a single seedling, the clone itself continues to live for hundreds or thousands of years. Today's aspen clones may date to the Pleistocene or earlier, when the climate favored seedling establishment. Rejuvenating fire cycles could have kept gradually expanding aspen clones alive. Sometimes displaced at the surface by coniferous forest, each clone survived underground, sending up suckers here and there, patient roots waiting for a fire or windstorm to clear the evergreens and give aspen shoots their chance to reach light.

Ancient aspen clones may be as old as the creosote bush clones currently considered the oldest living things on earth.

Mountain brush communities share much with the chaparral of the Rockies and the Sierra. Fire, aridity, and lack of competition from conifers perpetuate these open mountain slopes and bald summits. Open to the sun, where one expects closed forest, dense and lush, where from a distance one expects barrens, they surprise, one of the distinctions of the Great Basin.

In the sagebrush ocean they are the high tide of shrubs. Above them lie the windblasted subalpine forest and the alpine tundra.

Mountain Brush and Aspen Glens

Tree Line Ancients
Great Basin Subalpine Forest

13

I got on a higher ridge, among some tough little wind-warped pines. . . . the knotty fingers of pine roots bulged out of shape from their long and agonizing grasp upon the crevices of the rock. I lay under the pines in the sparse shade and went to sleep once more.

It grew cold finally, for autumn was in the air by then, and the few things that lived thereabouts were sinking down into an even chillier scale of time. In the moments between sleeping and waking I saw the roots about me and slowly, slowly, a foot in what seemed many centuries, I moved my sleep-stiffened hands over the scaling bark and lifted my numbed face after the vanishing sun. I was a great awkward thing of knots and aching limbs, trapped up there in some long, patient endurance that involved the necessity of putting living fingers into rock and by slow, aching expansion bursting those rocks asunder. . . .

I had . . . moved with the century-long pulse of trees.

—Loren Eiseley,
The Immense Journey, 1957

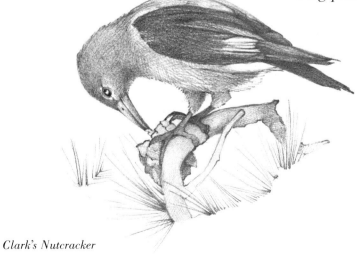

Clark's Nutcracker

reat Basin mountains have few dense forests. They lost them thousands of years ago. Only relics remain from once-dense subalpine full-glacial woods—a light fringe of venerable trees rooted near the summits of the highest Basin ranges. They grow in the same cold, harsh climate they favored in the Pleistocene. Such places come sparingly in the Great Basin Desert.

On northern mountains, limber pine dominates this subalpine forest; in a few ranges, whitebark pine takes its place. To the south, Great Basin bristlecone pine—symbol of Great Basin mountains—grows on high peaks from the White Mountains in California to Utah's Stansbury Mountains.

For bristlecones, adversity begets longevity: bristlecones surviving on the most difficult sites grow very, very slowly. The oldest of them approach five thousand years in age, the earth's most ancient individual beings that have not renewed themselves vegetatively but have sprouted once—and survived.

Like the piñon-juniper woodland below, trees alone define subalpine woodland. Above about ninety-five hundred feet, this open woodland grows on the windswept ridges to tree line at eleven thousand feet or more. Other resident plants and creatures range into the woodland from sagebrush and mountain brush below or tundra above. Understory species are inconspicuous; in one open bristlecone grove in the White Mountains, plants shaded only 35 percent of the ground and bristlecones accounted for more than 80 percent of this total.

Here and there between the trees is a full-fledged subalpine meadow. More than any other animal, pocket gophers characterize these patches of soil. They lead extremely sedentary lives, tunneling through perhaps an acre of soil during their lives, remaining underground 99 percent of the time. These stay-at-homes have gradually differentiated in isolated mountain ranges; no other genus of Nevada mammal has evolved so many taxonomic races (at least

according to E. Raymond Hall, a taxonomic splitter).

In Nevada, Botta's pocket gopher is widespread in lowlands (but in places spans the range of habitats from valley to high mountain meadow), mountain pocket gophers occur at high elevations in the Sierra and Carson Range, and northern pocket gophers live in intermediate climates between the two. Gophers are crucial to the ecology of high mountain meadows, binding soil to the surface in "pushups" and dirt cores left over from winter tunnels under the snowpack. They create new habitats for those plants that favor disturbed sites, including an assemblage of alpine species known in the Rockies as "gopher garden" plants.

In high mountains of eastern Nevada like the Snake Range, Botta's pocket gopher lives from low elevations to high. As the glaciers retreated and the higher elevations of the peaks opened up for gophers, E. Raymond Hall suggested Botta's must have been the only pocket gopher living at the base of the mountains. The gopher "worked slowly upward, developing populations with individuals adapted to living at these higher elevations as it went." These pioneering Botta's pocket gophers still are not abundant on their newfound high-elevation territory.

Though they live on the most rugged ridges, or perhaps *because* they live here, limber pines are the most widely distributed subalpine conifer in the Great Basin. These pines thrive in the dry, sunny, and cold environment. They can grow in wetter areas but usually do not, for plants that have to grow in such areas compete with them and exclude them. Where bristlecone or whitebark pine occur, limber pine grows below them.

Like lower-elevation pygmy forest, the ecology of at least two of the subalpine trees, limber and whitebark pine, is orchestrated by a bird, the Clark's Nutcracker.

Along with piñon pines, these qualify for Ronald Lanner's designation "bird pines." Both whitebark and limber pine have large,

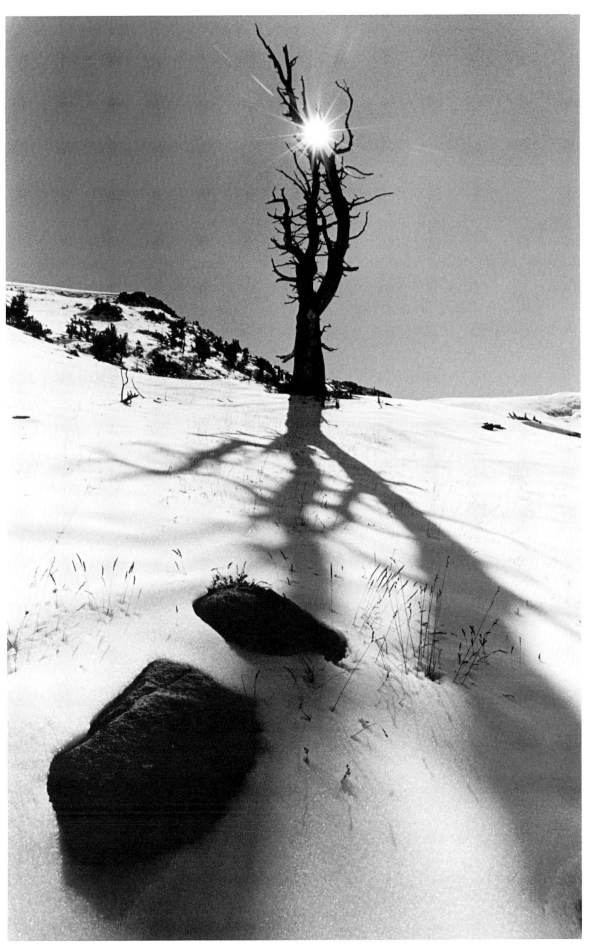

A lone limber pine snag at tree line on Mount Jefferson, Toquima Range.

wingless seeds useless to the trees in distributing them to new territory via the wind but wonderfully attractive to birds. Both have evolved their own ways of balancing their needs with those of the seed-seeking, seed-sowing nutcrackers.

Sparrows can scratch for seeds any time of year, and Sage Grouse nibble on sagebrush leaves continuously through the seasons. Nutcrackers, however, eat seasonal food—pine nuts that ripen only in fall. They must store their yearly harvest.

The nutcrackers collect most of the seed crop (as much as 90 percent) while limber pine cones are still green, taking no chances on losing too much of their harvest to squirrels and chipmunks. Even after cones open, nutcrackers continue to gather seeds.

They move through the limber pine groves in boisterous flocks, hammering apart cones and then flying as far as several miles to cache the nuts, for the high-energy nutcrackers need food throughout the year. The nutcrackers have a pouch under their tongue for seed transport and can carry one hundred or more seeds at once.

They fly to ridges likely to be snow-free in winter and hop across the weathered rock, placing four or five seeds in each cache about an inch deep. In a good fall, each bird will make thousands of caches. Through the winter and spring they return to the storage sites, dig up the seeds (some buried under snow), and feed on their larder.

Nutcrackers cache far more seeds than they can eat. Perhaps they do this to insure against forgetting a few cache locations. Some uneaten caches will sprout, and thus the birds renew the limber pine stand. The pine sacrifices most of its seeds in trade for the remarkable efficiency with which Clark's Nutcrackers disperse, plant, and forget the few caches necessary to keep the limber pines broadly distributed.

Whitebark pine also depends on nutcrackers for successful seed dispersal. It presents its bright purple cones at the tips of upswept branches like a bouquet arranged for feasting,

each cone filled with fat, nutritious seeds.

When mature, the dry cones do not open immediately to cast their seeds on the ground. At first their scales loosen just enough to make easy pickings for nutcrackers, each scale continuing to support its seed even after a nutcracker has exposed it. Nutcrackers can despoil a cone without ever changing position. When they flap away with the nuts, they leave behind piles of discarded cone cores and scales.

Whitebark pines clearly have evolved cones that make a fine food supply for nutcrackers, even more so than piñon or limber pine. The birds take full advantage: one biologist watched a nutcracker flock cache an estimated ninety-eight thousand seeds per bird in a harvest season of eighty days. Many of these go uneaten, to sprout and replenish the whitebark pine forest.

Whitebark pine barely enters the Great Basin from the northern Rockies and Sierra. The Carson Range has whitebark, and so do a few ranges along the northern Nevada state line: the Pine Forest and East Humboldt ranges and the Independence, Jarbidge, and Ruby mountains.

Whitebark pine is the only pine of the Pine Forest Range. The Santa Rosa Range, on the other hand, has only limber pine. In the Jarbidge Mountains both occur, but limber pine is rare above sixty-six hundred feet. Both pines grow in abundance in the Ruby Mountains and East Humboldt Range.

Modern precipitation gradients cannot explain such spotty distribution. Though much wetter than central Great Basin ranges, these northern ranges support fewer kinds of subalpine conifers. The warm Hypsithermal, perhaps less drastic in northern ranges, may have spared depauperate remnants of these original high-elevation stands of conifers. Elsewhere, rises in Hypsithermal tree line pinched them out.

The Rubies' glacial history set them apart. Ice covered one-third of the central Rubies at the glaciers' maximum advance. With tree line evidently depressed as low as seven thousand

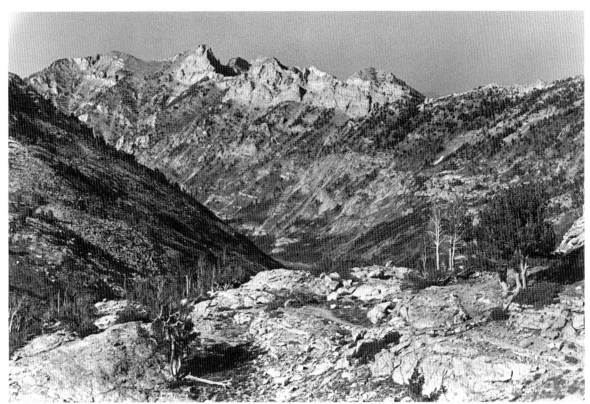

feet, cold winds blowing off the glaciers must have prohibited forests for several miles below the ice. The band of subalpine forest was narrow indeed.

Where today dense subalpine forest grows in ranges like the Snakes and Schell Creeks, the full-glacial climate was much less severe, glaciers less extensive than in the Rubies, and the Pleistocene subalpine forest much less compressed. With reinvasion rates to the now-isolated Rubies low again, conifers cloak only about 1 percent of the range, and their number of species is small. An unusual whitebark pine forest remains, largely a testament to the climatic history of the mountains.

With nutcrackers busy dispersing these pines, some of the surprising range-by-range distributions may simply reflect the erratic plantings of these far-flying birds. In years of high nutcracker populations and poor seed crops, the nutcrackers go in search of food as far as four hundred miles from their traditional territories. The wanderings of nutcrackers carrying a few stray pine seeds may account for some of the isolated stands of subalpine conifers in the northern Basin.

Once carried to a specific mountain range,

other factors control just where the pines sprout from forgotten caches. On the Pine Forest Range, whitebark pine seems to be confined to soil weathered from granitic rocks. In the East Humboldt Range and northern Ruby Mountains, whitebark dominates at higher elevations (8,500 to 10,600 feet—particularly around Lamoille Canyon) and limber pine dominates below (between 8,000 and 9,000 feet). Here whitebark rarely grows on deep soils; competition with shrubs and herbs probably restricts it to rocky ridges with shallow soil.

In late summer I walked from the Lamoille Canyon roadhead up into the high Ruby Mountains under the constant harangue of Clark's Nutcrackers. Intent on pillaging the local crop of whitebark pine cones, the birds perched on high branches blowing in the clean mountain breeze while they shredded the cones to obtain seeds for their yearly cache. Indeed, when William Clark first discovered "Clark's crow" on August 22, 1805, along Idaho's Lemhi River, the bird was "feeding on pine burrs."

Unlike ravens, who pay humans no heed, the noisy nutcrackers interact with us. They caw, chirr, and chatter, demanding acknowledgment. I found the nutcrackers working the lower whitebark groves in early August, where the cones had just matured. One bird flapped down to the shadowed duff between the roots of a big pine and began to cache seeds as deliberately as if planting wheat in contour furrows, piercing the soil with its sturdy bill in a swift plunge.

Hopping over each root to the next cache site, the nutcracker kept glancing over its shoulder, looking surreptitious, for all the world like it wanted to make sure its fellows had not observed the hiding places it had chosen for its seeds. Perhaps it was only checking landmarks, for nutcrackers relocate their seed caches by memory, months after making them. It is from forgotten caches that pine seedlings sprout. Thus, the nutcrackers' plantings maintain their food-producing trees. Pine plantations at tree line: overseer, William Clark's crow.

Whitebark, whitebark, and more whitebark. The only pine in this section of the subalpine Rubies, whitebark forms an open forest unique to the range, the trees and groves spaced nearly as far apart as the truck stops on U.S. Highway 6.

The raucous nutcrackers frequenting their crowns lighten the demeanor of the pines. Whether or not a nutcracker shreds them, whitebark cones shed and disintegrate, each scale falling from its core to drift in piles at the base of the tree. I found no well-turned, intact whitebark cones in the duff around my camp in the Rubies, only dejected-looking cores and piles of singular scales.

Whitebark pines do not live much past four hundred years. Though they sometimes look at first glance like bristlecones, their youth shows. No hoarding of life juices for four thousand years for whitebark—they have more energy, to me, a more wanton personality. With more pliant branches, these pines do not develop the weathered, mostly dead trunks of old bristlecones. They remain fully vital, and the ranges topped with their forests feel less eerie and more approachable than ranges holding groves of ancient bristlecones.

Summer 1953. Edmund Schulman was working in the Sawtooth Range above Sun Valley, Idaho, looking for old pine trees to expand his tree-ring record. He and a few fellow dendrochronologists—beginning with A. E. Douglass—had invented their science from scratch over the previous fifty years. By matching rings in overlapping cores they gradually extended datable chronologies of narrow and wide rings deep into the past.

In the Sawtooth Range, Schulman found an old limber pine that contained a seventeen-hundred-year record. Then he heard tantalizing rumors of bristlecone pines in the White Mountains that suggested the possibility of older trees and longer chronologies. He set off for California to investigate.

Within two years he discovered living bristlecones more than four thousand years old. And they met the needs of the tree-ring readers: bristlecones showed extreme sensitivity to wet and dry years, varying the width of their rings but rarely skipping a year. Sadly, Schulman died just as his landmark article went to press in the March 1958 issue of *National Geographic*, telling the nonacademic world the story of the trees. But his discovery remains the most widely known Great Basin ecological story.

A fact less widely understood: Schulman by no means discovered bristlecone pines. Known to science since the mid-1800s, they were praised by John Muir in 1878 as "preeminently picturesque." Muir climbed through "a thick spicy forest" of eighty-foot-high bristlecones on Troy Peak in the Grant Range and described on neighboring ranges "old giants, five or six feet in diameter, that have braved the storms of more than a thousand years."

Not until Schulman, however, did anyone realize how *much* more than a thousand years the old pines could live. Other bristlecone biologists followed. Today the tree-ring record built from living, dead, and fallen pines extends back nine thousand years.

Bristlecones continue to surprise us. Until 1970, botanists called all bristlecone pines from Colorado to California by the same spe-

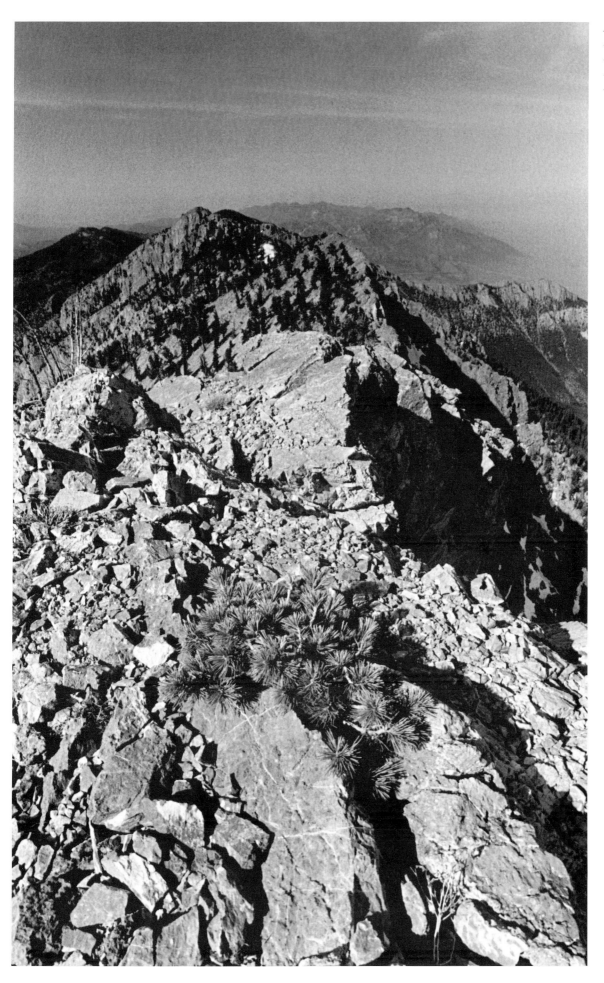

A bristlecone seedling on the summit of Troy Peak in the Grant Range.

*Bristlecones in
the Methuselah
Grove, White
Mountains. These
trees, the oldest
known living
pines, grow in one
of the harshest
environments
of the range:
"adversity begets
longevity."*

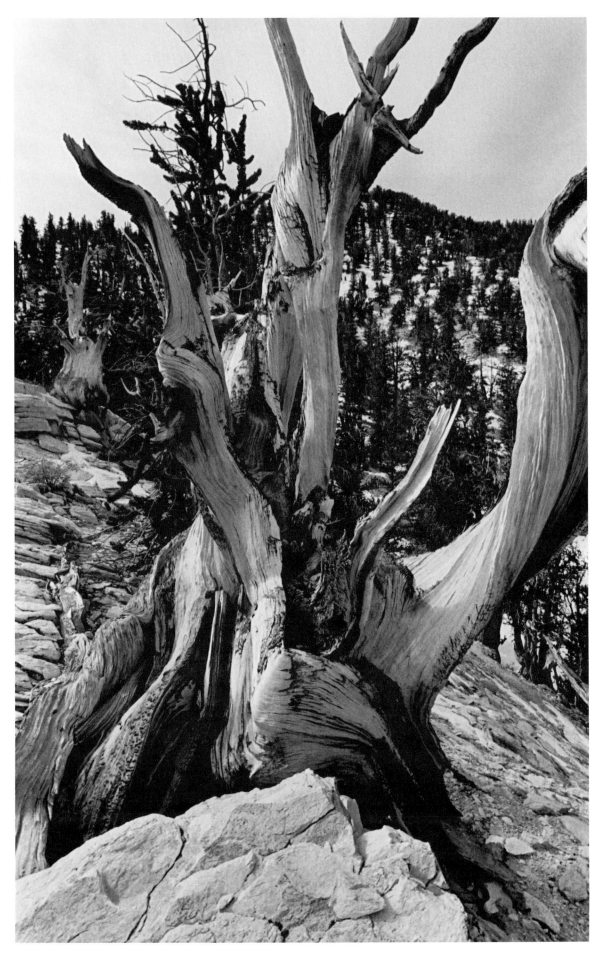

cies name, *Pinus aristata*. Then D. K. Bailey noticed that Snake Range trees from Nevada lacked the white resin "dandruff" dusting their needles that characterized Colorado trees. He divided bristlecone populations into two species, the shorter-lived Rocky Mountain bristlecone (*Pinus aristata*) and the long-lived Great Basin bristlecone (*Pinus longaeva*), with slightly different needle and cone anatomy.

The oldest trees discovered so far live on the White Mountains and on eastern Nevada's Snake Range. Only here do the bristlecones rank in the official age category "ancient": four thousand years plus. The oldest of all living trees—and the only "ancient" so far discovered outside the White Mountains—was cut down by an overenthusiastic researcher in 1964, a tree on the Snake Range's Mount Washington whose rings petered out at forty-nine hundred years, muddled by heart rot.

To kill the earth's oldest living thing is a unique responsibility to bear. A few minutes with a chainsaw snuffed out a life that began in the same years that head any list of "major dates in world history." This bristlecone pushed up through blocks of quartzite on a Great Basin ridge about the same time that Sumerians built Ur, Menes founded the first Egyptian dynasty, and the Indo-Europeans arrived in Greece.

When cut, only a narrow strip of living bark remained, carrying water from a few functioning roots to the single, living, needled shoot, which still photosynthesized, feeding the bark and roots.

Most bristlecones older than fifteen hundred years adopt this strip growth, which allows them to bypass the demands of supporting huge amounts of living tissue endlessly accumulated. Only two ways exist to tell a three-thousand-year tree from a four-thousand-year ancient: use an increment borer and read the rings from its core. Or cut the tree down and count rings in cross-section.

No one knows why bristlecones live so long. Or why, in Ronald Lanner's words, they take so long to die. But the most ancient trees grow on the poorest sites, where any growth at all comes slowly. Fast-growing trees on wetter sites often develop heart rot when they reach eight to ten inches in radius; they rarely live more than a thousand years.

Bristlecones keep their needles for up to forty years, far longer than most conifers. In a drought year they can bide their time: with no need to produce new needles, they photosynthesize at a bare minimum, add a few cells of new wood (a narrow band in the tree-ring chronology), and wait for a better year. Some trees add as little as a half-inch to their radius in a century, and this only on the strip of living bark.

As trees age, their roots erode and dry out. Their ability to maintain their whole crown diminishes. And the strip-growth habit becomes essential. Bristlecone wood added in tiny increments is incredibly dense, aromatic with resin, and resistant to decay. This resistance of wood exposed to the elements seems a key to longevity. For most species, if a tree restricted itself to a single strip of bark and living branch, the wood exposed would rot and topple the tree.

In the dry White Mountains, precipitation increases little even at the highest elevations. Temperature determines where most shrubs and herbs grow. Bristlecones and limber pines share the subalpine forest, wherever sagebrush does not dominate. The oldest bristlecones grow on cool, dry ridges with little competition. Methuselah Grove, with the oldest trees of all, has one of the harshest of bristlecone environments.

Bristlecone seems tied to moisture requirements, and its personal demands and tolerances combine to map its distribution. Soils matter more (and nutcrackers matter less) to bristlecones than to the other subalpine pines.

The White Mountains, where nearly all the research on bristlecones has been done, offer a jumble of rock types to live on, from limestone to sandstone to granite. Distribution of each plant species depends on the underlying rock and on temperature, moisture, and elevation. Sagebrush and limber pine do best on sandstone and granite soils; neither seem to tolerate the poor nutritional content of soil formed from dolomite (limestone with high magnesium content). Bristlecone can.

Granite supports twice the total vegetation of sandstone or dolomite. On soils derived from granite and sandstone, sagebrush accounts for almost 80 percent of the shrub cover, but on dolomite it totals only 13 percent of the sparse shrub layer. Sagebrush, of course, grows much lower than bristlecones, which do not survive much below ninety-five hundred feet. Bristlecone forest develops best on north slopes, sagebrush on south. Big sagebrush clearly can tolerate drought better than bristlecones. It, too, may reach its maximum age on the White Mountains, with rings tallying more than two hundred years.

Uncommon here, limber pine grows best on granite-derived soil, poorest on dolomitic soil. Above 11,200 feet, limber pine gives way entirely to bristlecones. Bristlecone can grow well on granite, as it does on Boundary Peak at the north end of the White Mountains; with the favorable Hypsithermal climate, bristlecones grew in abundance on quartzite on Campito Mountain, and a few still do. But in the southern Whites, dolomite is extensive, and here grow the oldest bristlecones.

The preference for dolomite is clear, but the reasons for it are not. Bristlecones need considerable light to photosynthesize and reproduce. This may keep them on dolomite away from most other competing plants, for young bristlecones grow in forest openings, and fifty-year-old "seedlings" photosynthesize fastest at high light levels. It takes at least half the summer to produce enough carbohydrates to replace the energy drain of a normal winter, when respiration continues but photosynthesis halts.

On dolomite, sparse ground cover keeps ground fires to a minimum. Perhaps most crucial, the light-colored dolomite reflects 25 percent more light than darker rocks, keeping summer soil temperatures lower and ground moisture higher.

Measured rates of photosynthesis show that tiny differences in soil moisture create enormous differences in bristlecone growth. The consistent moisture difference between dolomite and sandstone soils may not be great, but it brings bristlecone beyond a crucial threshold. Bristlecones reach furthest down into the White Mountain sagebrush zone on dolomite. Likewise, these pines grow at their highest limits—11,800 feet—where dolomite carries them higher than the average tree line. Even here they stand as full-sized trees.

Only on Nevada's Snake Range does bristlecone form the windblown mats of *krummholz* that make tree line distinctive on ranges where limber pine, Engelmann spruce, or subalpine fir form the last outposts of trees. On the Snake Range, the bristlecones grow on quartzite, where glaciers piled blocks of rock loosely. Water drains through them rapidly; they have little organic carbon, clay, and nitrogen. On these nutrient-poor, arid sites grow the oldest bristlecones in the range.

Elsewhere, most bristlecones prefer limestone. Botanist Noel Holmgren defined a floristic section along the Nevada-Utah state line, the Calcareous Mountains section, by the dominance of limestone-capped mountains and limestone-loving plants. Bristlecones grow on most of these mountains—from Spruce Mountain and the southern Rubies south to the Quinn Canyon Range and the Wah Wah Mountains.

Outside this section, bristlecone groves occur infrequently: west to Morey Peak in the Hot Creek Range (where they grow on volcanic rocks) and the Monitor Range, then a long gap before the Silver Peak Range and White Mountains at the extreme west. Eastward, bristlecones grow on a few ranges in the central Bonneville basin: the Deep Creek and House ranges and the Stansbury Mountains. On the latter, the three bristlecone stands total only about 180 trees.

Most bristlecones reproduce unassisted from small winged seeds blown to new sites by the wind. Some isolated bristlecone groves, however, may be nutcracker-planted. In the White Mountains, bristlecones grow in multistemmed clumps, just as if they sprouted from nut-

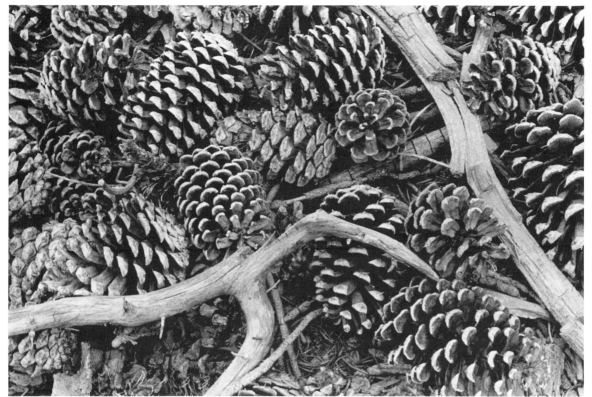

*Great Basin
bristlecone pine
cones, Duckwater
Peak, White Pine
Range.*

181
———
*Tree Line
Ancients*

cracker caches. Though the nutcrackers prefer larger seeds, they surely deign to feed on bristlecone seeds when piñon and limber pine crops fail. A few forgotten bristlecone caches could be crucial to the tree's distribution.

Bristlecone wood remains undecayed on the ground long after the trees have died. Such remnants can document directly the elevation of tree line at the time the trees germinated. Many pieces of bristlecone wood from the summits of Great Basin mountains date to more than four thousand years ago. At least one nine-thousand-year-old piece has been found.

These remnants of old trees consistently occur above today's tree line—up to five hundred feet above it in the White Mountains. By dating them we know that trees could germinate higher during the Hypsithermal; some survived until about two thousand years ago. The many seedlings taking root above today's adults suggest that with summer temperatures warming during the last century, once again tree line has moved upward.

Information on older bristlecone distribution comes from wood rat middens. Both limber and bristlecone pine grew down to the valley floors in the late Pleistocene, though probably only on rocky outcrops. With no piñon present and no lower-elevation mountain conifers (like white fir and ponderosa pine), when paleo-ecologists suggest that Pleistocene mammals could move from range to range through bridges of coniferous forest, they mean bridges of bristlecone and limber pines. These may have been islands of pines in seas of sagebrush—not so different from today's sagebrush valleys. But the islands made the difference for animals dependent on evergreens; they expanded their range accordingly.

Geologists measure rates of erosion by examining the soil around bristlecone roots. Archaeologists check radiocarbon dates against the precisely dated tree-ring chronology, matching up events at the beginnings of civilization with rings from trees still alive.

These trees look out on Great Basin valleys barely changed from when they sprouted: here and there a ranch, a few roads (mostly dirt), tiny specks of cows—scarcely different (from the lofty perspective of a bristlecone) from the scene several thousand years ago.

Bristlecones cannot find reassurance in that fact. But I do.

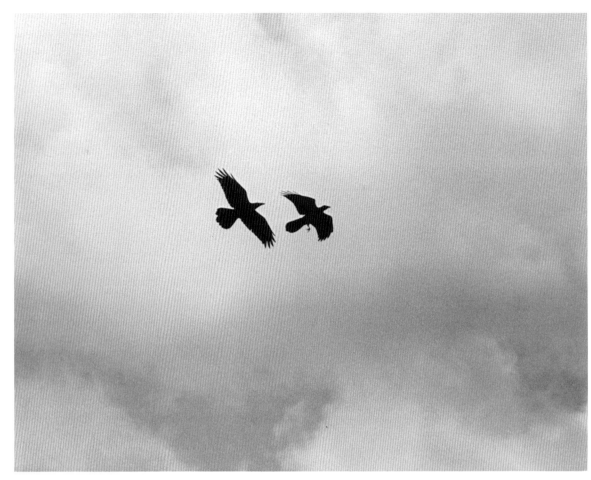

The great wall that rims Utah's West Desert rises 8,000 vertical feet in three mountain masses: the southern Snakes, northern Snakes, and the Deep Creek Range. Each culminates in one of the highest peaks in the basin: Wheeler Peak (13,063 feet), Mount Moriah (12,050 feet), and Ibapah Peak (12,087 feet), respectively. On lower slopes these mountains have Rocky Mountain forests, dense and diverse. Near their summits they are more typically Great Basin: bristlecone pines grow on each.

High on Mount Moriah, I crossed The Table, a perspective-fooling flat expanse of pure white snow at eleven thousand feet. Stands of bristlecone dotted its edges. I headed for the rocky outcrop in its center.

Even in winter the streamside forest in Hendrys Creek below me had an undercurrent of action—the stream itself, aspen leaves pausing only for a season in their shimmering and quaking. But bristlecones have a slow, still feel to them all year.

They do not share much. Bristlecones give almost as little of their personalities as lichens or starfish. They remind me of camouflage mimics—stonefish and "living rock" succulents. They are not cheery like piñons and junipers. Like old people they remain dignified—not lofty like sequoias but godlike nonetheless. Meditative rather than Olympian. Their best background music: occasional single piano notes.

A storm approached from the west, darkening the sky over the Schell Creek Range. The world was perfectly still, gray-blue. I heard the air riffling the primary feathers of two circling ravens. It was the only sound.

Rocky Mountain bighorn frequent this part of the mountain. Just knowing they still live here changes your perceptions. I once spent a summer studying bighorn sheep on Pikes Peak in Colorado. After many days of staring hard through binoculars, the slopes came alive even without sheep; in looking so intently for them, every middle-sized block of tan granite began to look like a bighorn. When I closed my eyes at night I saw sheep.

I saw no bighorn sheep on The Table, but

I could sense them. This sense has to do with a feeling of completeness. A mountain range without wolves, bears, mountain lions, or bighorn has an emptiness. It is a museum commemorating what used to be. Like Pompeii, you can wander around in it, imagine it fully alive, but it lacks suspense.

Mountain lions and bighorn still live in the Snake Range. Here you sit before a stage just after the curtain rises for the next act but before the players enter. Life poised to act, suspense, magic.

This same feeling of wholeness is the reason one need not visit a wilderness to value it. Its existence changes your reality, your awareness of options. Always you know you can retreat to such a place, a possibility that opens up the frontiers of consciousness.

I turned and hiked through knee-deep snow, leaving The Table for Hendrys Creek. I left behind two ravens, bristlecone pines, winter stillness. And unseen, but satisfying, the possibility of bighorn sheep.

Alpine Deserts
Great Basin Tundra

14

The alpine tundra is a land of contrast and incredible intensity, where the sky is the size of forever and the flowers the size of a millisecond. . . . The clarity of light confuses one's sense of scale. Faraway mountains are so sharp in outline that they seem much closer. . . . the great wash of light illuminating the alpine tundra gives one a sense of encompassing comprehension verging on euphoria. . . .

. . . in the White Mountains . . . the sun bursts on the morning slopes . . . as an "avalanche." . . . The whole landscape shimmers in a blinding liquid heat. It is impossible to tell if the flight of a small white butterfly is truly hesitant or if it is merely the distortion caused by heat radiating above the soil.

—Ann Zwinger,
Land Above the Trees, 1972

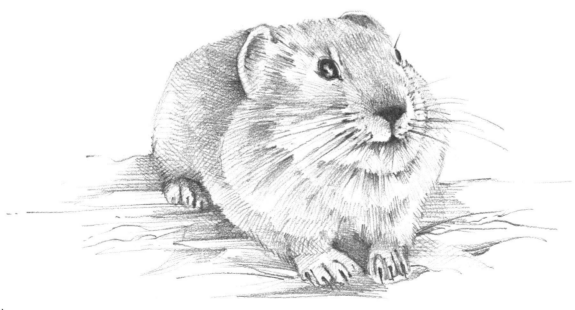

Pika

Above tree line lies tundra. Or does it? In lower ranges of the Great Basin, the top of the piñon-juniper woodland can mark upper tree line (as the lower woodland boundary marks lower tree line). Mountain summits may be treeless but not alpine: balds of mountain brush.

The Toiyabe Range rises high enough to have an alpine zone but remains too dry for tundra, covered by "alpine deserts" of scattered alpine grasses and a few drabas and buckwheats. Alpine grasslands top other ranges, such as Oregon's Steens Mountain (just 9,670 feet high but cold and wet), with meadows of grass, lupine, buckwheat, locoweed, and paintbrush giving way to what might pass for tundra only at the extreme summit.

Of all Great Basin ranges, the northern Ruby Mountains have the best-developed tundra. High and wet, with sheltering cirques carved from moisture-holding granite, only the Deep Creek Range on the Utah line musters alpine environments to compare with them. The rolling and expansive uplands of the White Mountains, highest range in the Great Basin, are so dry that they support only one-fourth the number of alpine plant species living on the Rubies.

Whatever variations in plants and animals may exist at such summits, they all share remarkable light. This flood of solar energy blasting the mountaintops has impressed not only Ann Zwinger. John Muir christened the Sierra Nevada the "Range of Light," but the high desert mountains just to the east as much deserve his title. Perhaps, though, Muir correctly placed his epithet: big enough to merit cordilleran status, in many ways the Sierra is really the ultimate Basin range.

Defining the beginning of the Great Basin alpine world is tricky. Alpine tundra usually means the zone of low-growing plants above tree line. But with indistinct subalpine forest on Great Basin ranges, tree line does not suffice to mark the boundary. The limits to upward growth of trees—a complicated interplay between cold, snowpack, and wind-blasted dryness—do not affect the downward extent of alpine plants in precisely the same way.

Tree line itself is fuzzy: in Utah's Deep Creek Range, trees survive at elevations some one hundred to two hundred feet higher on granite than on quartzite. Nearly at the top of Ibapah Peak, the highest Deep Creek summit, a last tenacious Engelmann spruce, rooted in a crack, shades a mat of moss campion on a patch of weathered fragments of granite. Trees almost always grow higher in elevation on nearby ridges than the lowest meadows of alpine plants, higher on the south side than the north side of ranges. On dolomite in the White Mountains, bristlecones and lobes of alpine plants interlock in a band spanning a thousand feet of elevation. Which marks the beginning of the alpine world, the uppermost tree or the lowermost alpine sedge or wildflower?

In his analysis of Great Basin alpine plant geography, Dwight Billings used nine thousand feet as the extreme lower limit for the alpine zone—a liberal estimate that allows for more and larger alpine islands than some would map. Others have proclaimed the official alpine beginning at the upper limit of shrubby sagebrush, both big sage and dwarf sage, at whatever elevation they cease to dominate. Either way, these alpine islands remain the most isolated of Great Basin communities and in their vegetation vary more from range to range than any other.

Even alpine tundra on the "mainland" cordilleras differs dramatically from the Sierra to the Rockies. Many arctic plants live in Rocky Mountain tundra, freshened, moistened, and cooled by summer thundershowers. With nearly continuous high-elevation connections northward, arctic plants could move south into the Rockies in colder late Wisconsinan times when tundra descended to about six thousand feet. Rocky Mountain alpine plants strongly dominate Great Basin tundra as far west as the Ruby Mountains.

Sierra Nevada alpine tundra, however, has fewer species and far fewer arctic species. The new Cascade volcanoes to the north have not provided much of a pathway for arctic plants

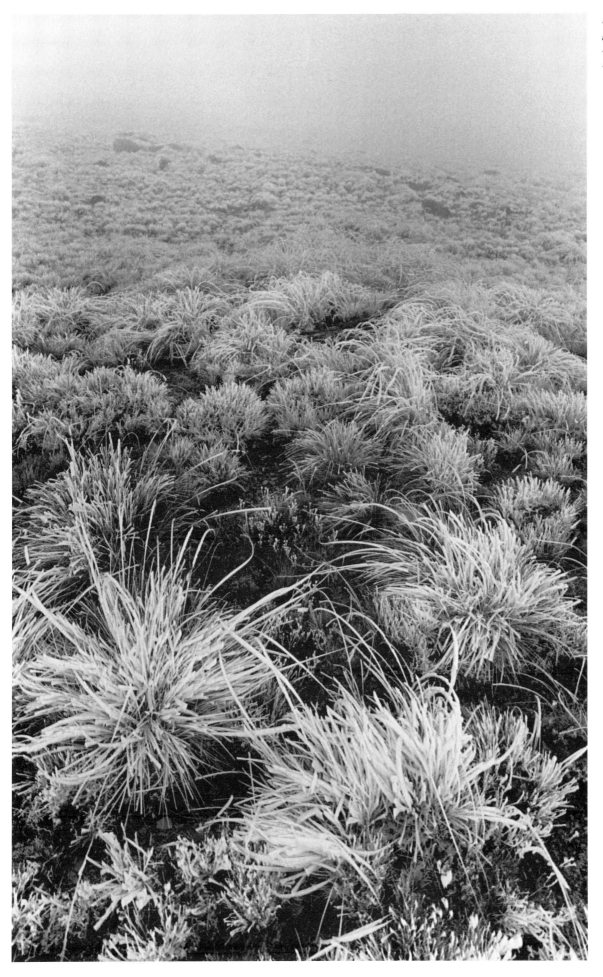

Frost-rimed alpine grassland at the summit of Steens Mountain.

*A last Engelmann
spruce seedling at
tree line on
Ibapah Peak,
Deep Creek
Range, Utah.*

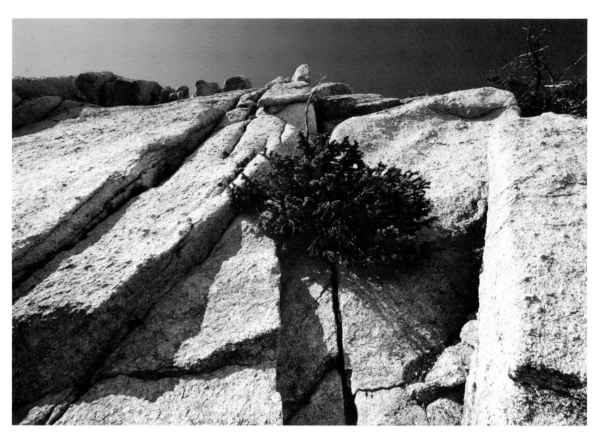

to reach southward. With dry warm summers complicating the demands of cold snowy winters, Sierra Nevada alpine plants must adapt to conditions extreme even for tundra. Many of them evolved from desert plants, moving up the hillside as the range rose. They grow in open, rocky places rather than in lush meadows. They have emigrated eastward into the Great Basin with little success.

The wind controls the pattern of tundra communities. Where winter gales blast slopes snow-free, they suffer extreme cold in winter and aridity in summer but with the longest growing season possible at this elevation. Wind-drifted snowbanks protect plants in winter, but as snowbeds linger in summer they make for growing seasons so cold and short (though well-watered) that only sedges and rushes reproducing from underground stems rather than seeds can survive at their edges.

Alpine plants have adapted to every combination between these two extremes. All deal with cold; even in the desertlike White Mountains the average daily alpine air temperature stays below freezing for at least eight months every year.

In the Rocky Mountains, alpine tundra communities range from sparse cushion plants on dry rocky slopes ("fellfields" so thinly vegetated they maintain no resident animals but insects), to dense turf, to rings of deep green sedges and herbs surrounding snowbanks and lining streams and marshes. In the Sierra, turf is rare; rocky communities dominate.

Similar alpine plants dwell in the most extensive and best-studied Great Basin tundra, in the Ruby Mountains. Lush meadows of Holm's Rocky Mountain sedge surround ponds, just as in the Colorado or Montana Rockies, and as nowhere else in the Great Basin except for the Carson Range. Above about ninety-seven hundred feet, sagebrush gives way to shrubby cinquefoil and streamside willows. Black-root (elk) sedge and arctic willow form real, honest-to-god alpine turf on the gently sloping north-facing cirque slopes. On slightly drier benches, Ross's avens reaches as much as 75 percent cover. Gravelly soils adjacent are mosaics of dwarf blueberry and blue fescue.

The Rubies feel less like desert mountains than any other Great Basin range.

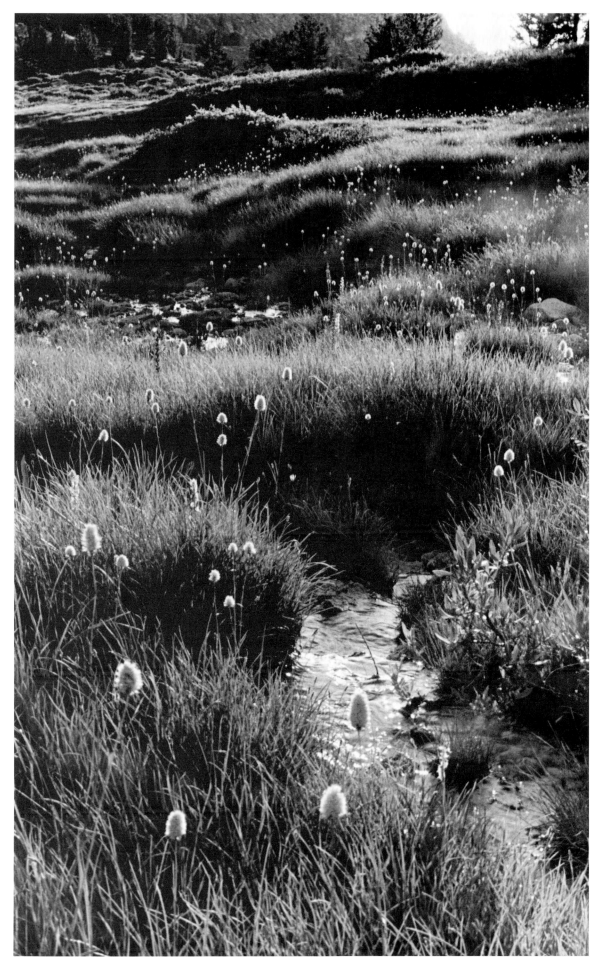

*Bistort meadow
below Favre Lake
in the Rubies—
the lushest and
wettest alpine
tundra in the
Great Basin.*

Even the names sound lush: Lamoille Canyon in the Ruby Mountains. No sun-baked desert names here: a local pioneer named the canyon for his home back in Lamoille County, Vermont.

These mountains could never be the Hungry Range or the Hot Creek Range, the Dead Camels or the Calicos. The Rubies are an undesertlike jewel as glossy as the local garnets that give them their name. Their highest ridges rise to 11,387 feet at the rocky fortress of Ruby Dome. They shelter some thirty alpine lakes and pull down almost fifty inches of precipitation yearly—five times as much as the low surrounding valleys.

The Rubies require superlatives. They are the wettest mountains in the Great Basin, even wetter than the higher Snake and Deep Creek ranges or the White Mountains. The most heavily glaciated mountains in Nevada, they have the most elaborately developed alpine tundra in the Basin.

For all their luxuriance, their ice-scoured headwalls, their sweeping U-shaped canyons, they remain friendly and accessible. I find it easy to be tender about the Rubies; they are not overwhelming or stark. They are ravishing.

I walked the Ruby Crest Trail in summer, past the still circles of the Dollar Lakes and more alpine Lamoille Lake, up and over Liberty Pass. On the pass, in boulderfields and in ledges high on the turreted and glaciated cliffs, mosses, clubmosses, and ferns pioneer. Where they gather a bit of soil around their roots they give way to woolly-sunflowers, rosy pussy-toes, tiny buckwheats, drabas, and parsleys; pink stone crop, Parry's primrose, fernleaf candytuft, and saxifrage.

On the far side of the divide, Liberty Lake sits just under the pass. Except for isolated Echo Lake, it is the largest and deepest of the Ruby Mountain lakes. Liberty fills the cirque from rim to rim, and the pass hangs over it in such a way that I looked right down on it like a soaring hawk. If I leaped, I could land in its chilled center with a great shocking splash.

A state game warden on horseback stopped me to see if I had a fishing license, mistaking from a distance the tripod over my shoulder for a fishing pole. He told me that the road up Lamoille Canyon was not paved until about 1970. Before that, access was tougher, visitors fewer, and the Rubies a paradise you could have to yourself. Today, you meet many other hikers, and campfire scars ring every lake. Erosion mars the gentle sweeping switchbacks of the Ruby Crest Trail where hikers and horses have cut across them, seeking shortcuts.

I passed Liberty Lake and switchbacked down to make camp in a whitebark pine grove on a grassy ledge above Favre Lake. Below, sun dappled the lake; feeding brook trout pricked the surface with delicate circles that broke across the longitudinal waves whipped up by the breeze. An abrupt slope beyond led through whitebark and willow to Castle Lake, just hidden from view but visible from the pass—a small high pool backed up against the headwall of Lake Peak, perched on a glacial shelf little larger than the lake.

The mosaic of plant communities was as complicated here as anywhere on the mountain. Just beyond the whitebark pine grove shading my tent, sagebrush covered an open knoll. A few feet away ran a creek bounded by a soggy, boggy meadow, filled with bog orchid and swamp laurel, along with onion, American bistort, columbine, whimsical pink bull elephant's-head, monkshood, California false-hellebore, and a forest of sedges. A lupine, silken with fine hairs, filled spaces between the shrubs. In the flat, mucky area along the creek at the lake outlet grew more bog plants, along with willow and cinquefoil on the slightly drier rises. Slender-sepal marsh-marigold, snowbed buttercup, and mountain-sorrel fringed a late-lying snowbed across the lake.

Meadow voles, shrews, and mice have been captured here, in what must be vole paradise, mouse heaven, a small-scale jungle for feeding, hiding, and scurrying. Pocket gophers work the meadow soil. But to the hiker such mammals are invisible. This basin feels more a place for birds and plants and insects, for the least curious naturalist cannot miss the clouds of mosquitoes.

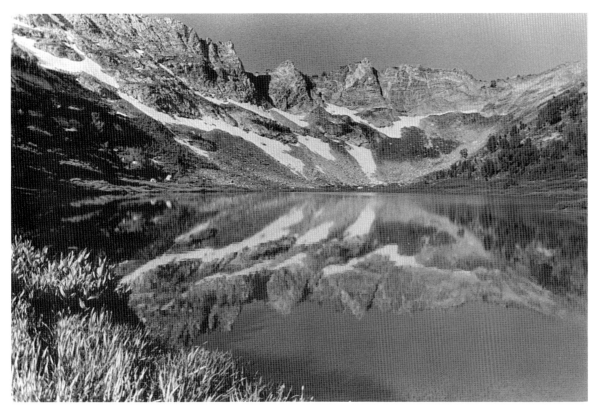

The Rubies catch as much snow as the Rockies. Intense glaciation in the Rubies made them a poor place for remnant stands of conifers to survive the Pleistocene but a great place for alpine plants. And, like the Rockies and the Sierra, unglaciated remnant uplands at the summit of the range support the most expansive tundra turf of all. The granite and metamorphic rocks of the northern Rubies keep water near the surface. Thus, glaciated cirque floors, which in other Great Basin ranges drain rapidly, here support wet tundra meadows.

Next day I tramped south. The basin below the next pass was lush. Ponds remained where the thirsty sedges had gobbled up what once was another lake. Gradual drying since the glacial lakes formed dooms many to meadows; while ponds remain, their boggy edges provide homey green tangles for moisture-loving plants and small mammals and deer. On the trail through these meadows I saw more hoof prints than boot prints.

Beyond a divide lay a last lake—North Furlong—with meadows dense with clumps of cinquefoil and willow, many of the latter with nesting White-crowned Sparrows. Sparrows flit at the periphery of your vision from

sagebrush right up to the tundra. In desert valleys it is Black-throated and Sage Sparrows. In marshes the flight of a Song Sparrow. In conifers the solitary chirp and flashing white outer tail feathers of juncos. And here in the willows the little seed-eaters with the bold black-and-white stripes on their crowns.

Beyond, ten miles of dry crestline reach south toward Overland Lake, named for the Overland Trail, which passed around the south end of the range. Though waterless, this rolling ridge offers a gentle old erosional surface with Ruby Mountain alpine tundra at its best. Here I walked through meadows of Ross's avens and carpet phlox and moss campion that could have passed muster in the Colorado Rockies. Rare in cirques, these plants dominate on the broad dry slopes of Wines Peak at 10,300 to 10,800 feet.

Here, too, I watched a dead grasshopper being devoured by ants and a variety of flies. Scavengers always find their food; decomposers stay busy even at the roof of the Basin world.

Flies are crucial as pollinators above tree line, for bees do not fly when the temperature drops below fifty degrees Fahrenheit. Simple flat flowers without fragrance such as Ross's avens and buttercups are designed for pollination by flies. Grasses rely on wind pollination, producing huge amounts of pollen. Beetles pollinate as well, but in an almost accidental way that could not be further from the elegant specificity of bee flowers. Take bull elephant's-head.

This little alpine flower, common in wet areas in the Rubies, has a long curved "trunk" surrounded by petals and lobes remarkably like the massive head and ears of an elephant in miniature. When a bumblebee lights on a spike of bull elephant's-head and probes a blossom in search of nectar, the trunk (enclosing the style) brushes the exact spot between its abdomen and thorax where the bee carries pollen from other flowers.

Though the Rubies receive an exceptional amount of snow and summer thundershowers, the Jarbidge Mountains and Snake and Schell Creek ranges also receive moisture adequate to support tundra. All the latter have alpine plants, but they grow in limited areas, mostly at subalpine seeps. The crucial difference, according to botanist Lloyd Loope, is rock and soil.

In the northern Rubies, impervious granite and metamorphic rock floor the cirques; drainage is poor, and the thin soils remain wet through most of the summer. Boulderfields do not cover the cirque floors. The Deep Creek Range has similar conditions over a smaller area.

But the limestones common in Great Basin ranges to the south suck water down toward the water table nearly as fast as it reaches the surface. Blocky debris clogs cirques in the southern Rubies and in the Snake and Schell Creek ranges, making for rapid runoff. In the Jarbidge cirques, rhyolite boulders pile several feet deep, preventing soil development and trapping moisture deep within their jumbled barrens.

Of the high, wet, cold, glaciated eastern Great Basin ranges not too far from the Rockies to be difficult to colonize, only the northern Rubies and neighboring East Humboldt Range, and, to a lesser extent, the Deep Creek Range, have rock capable of trapping moisture over extensive areas usable by alpine tundra plants. Their flora is mostly Rocky Mountain: a distinctive Great Basin alpine flora has not developed and Sierran species do not reach this far eastward. With an alpine area less than 5 percent that of the Sierra, the Rubies have about the same number of arctic species.

All told, some 189 Ruby Mountain plant species qualify as alpine, barely less than the tally for Montana's Beartooth Mountains (194). The Deep Creek Range has some 80 alpine species, the Toiyabe Range and White Mountains only 48 each.

Alpine species typical of the Sierra barely make it across the Owens Valley to the White Mountains. On this lofty range, plants at low elevations share much with the Sonoran and Mojave deserts; at mid-elevations the flora is typically Great Basin. At high elevations the plant list contains many Sierran and northwestern species. East of the Whites, however, Sierran alpine species drop out abruptly, tallying 51 percent of the White Mountain flora but only 17 percent of Wassuk Range alpine plants just fifty-five miles away.

Soil matters here. On dolomite above tree line in the Whites, plants cover less than 10 percent of the ground. White Mountain wild buckwheat and Coville's phlox dominate. On granite, in contrast, fellfield plants may cover all exposed soil. Here subalpine wild buckwheat, Sierra draba, and Mono clover combine with grasses and sedges in ragged stands. Rock piles offer a bit of extra protection from the wind, but on the summit pyramid itself, shifting rubble and virtually no soil limit plants to a very few tough customers. The only approximate alpine turf lines seeps and meltwater channels.

The drier continuum of moisture here offsets the distribution of plants. In dry years, in Ann Zwinger's words, "a snow accumulation area in the White Mountains, after the mucky late-covered areas of the Rockies, looks more like a fellfield." The same species of grasses grow in White Mountain alpine fields and in the range's

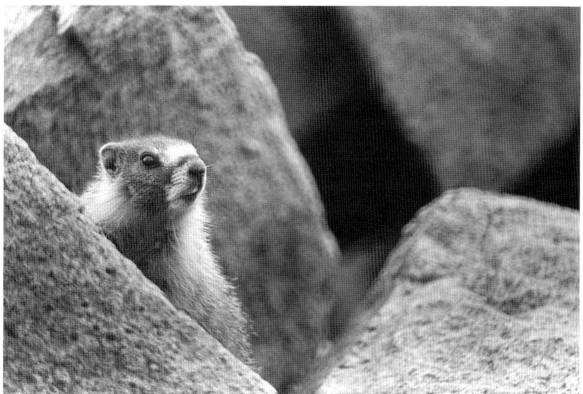

piñon-juniper woodland (bottle-brush grass and prairie junegrass, for example), though each is physiologically tuned to its environment. Alpine meadow-rue—common in the Rockies in moist, snow-free meadows—grows in the Whites in snowbed communities. Snowbed buttercups grow in the same communities but only in wet years.

Few animals live above tree line. Coyotes and bighorn sheep wander through, pikas and marmots scamper across alpine rockslides, pocket gophers, golden-mantled ground squirrels, and deer mice dwell in the alpine meadows. But none reach their maximum abundance here. Rosy Finches breed above tree line, and along with Water Pipits favor alpine haunts more than any other birds. They feed on riches of insects, harvesting them from pools and streams and the sun-scalloped surface of snowbanks.

Bighorn sheep once lived in the Rubies, but none have been seen since 1921. In their place the Nevada Department of Fish and Game has introduced mountain goats. These great, white alpine grazers, though historically not native mammals in Nevada, seem right at home; it says much for the alpine feeling of the Rubies

that they do. They have gradually increased in numbers and in 1982 numbered about forty individuals, frequenting the highest rocky ridges of the Rubies from Verdi Lake to Wines Peak, west to Ruby Dome.

High in the White Mountains near Barcroft Laboratory a marmot whistled; the piercing note demanded attention. I looked up to pick out the furry rodent perched on a boulder, a bit of gold mixed in with its deep brown fur, just as it disappeared toward a burrow with a second sharp-noted whistle. The entire display of warning and escape probably had nothing to do with me, for the marmot's call swept my eye upward to a Golden Eagle soaring close along the ridge line. Most eagles in flight can carry no more than four pounds, but that makes young marmots fair game.

Pikas live in these rockslides as well. They rarely venture more than thirty feet from their maze of talus-sheltered escape routes, and then only to gather grasses for their winter haypile. Their chirp of warning is just as public as the marmot's, but more burry. It takes hard, long searching for motion in the boulders to track down the source of the call. By the time I spot them they are ready to stop whistling

Meadows at the head of Lamoille Canyon separate mountain-mahogany and aspen below from subalpine forest and alpine tundra above.

194
___

The Basin Ranges

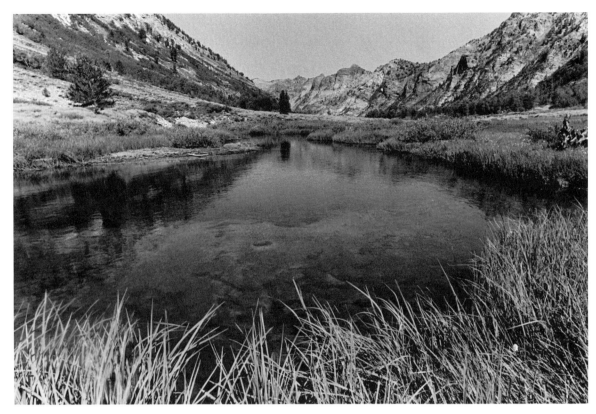

warnings and disappear into their rock shelters for good.

Pikas live in such rockslides from eleven-thousand-foot tundra in ranges like the White Mountains, Toquima Range, and Rubies to as low as fifty-seven hundred feet in juniper woodland in the northwestern corner of Nevada. Unique subspecies have evolved in the Rubies and in the cluster of central Nevada ranges from the Desatoya Mountains to the Monitor Range. Well-insulated against alpine cold, they do not live in low, hot valleys. Within climatic limits, rocky scree and talus define their occurrence as surely as cliff escape cover defines the range of bighorn sheep.

At the ghost town of Bodie, California, pikas have colonized old mine tailings, islands of boulders in a sea of sagebrush. Natural rock outcrops dot the plateau leading westward toward the Sierra, forming the likely path used by pikas to reach these islands of usable habitat at eighty-seven hundred feet. Here pikas live on the frontier of their climatic tolerance in an archipelago of rock piles. Large tailings support permanent pika populations and small ones turn over quickly, with cyclic local extinctions and recolonizations.

Surprisingly, some alpine plants and animals find immigration easier than forest animals absolutely requiring trees. The pikas at Bodie, for example, prove that a mammal can reach far outside its primary range given the right habitat—in this case, talus for dens combined with cool enough summers. Even the geographically distinct pikas of isolated Great Basin mountains seem closely related. In the Pleistocene they may have ranged nearly continuously across the Basin's mountains.

Many alpine plants grow in the subalpine zone or even lower. A dispersal path at sixty-four hundred feet connects the Wassuk Range, for example, with the Sweetwater Mountains thirty miles to the west—and very close to the Sierra. Given the elevation tolerances of Wassuk Range alpine plants, 36 percent could move freely between the two ranges today. With some two thousand feet of depression of vegetation zones during glaciation, 74 percent of the Wassuk plants could have emigrated from the Sweetwaters. And with a three-thousand-foot depression (still reasonable in light of paleoecologists' estimates), all but four species could have reached the range overland.

Most alpine species in the Ruby Mountains

also occur below tree line, some as much as three thousand feet below the alpine zone. Lloyd Loope says, "Migration of such species from Rocky Mountain source areas may have been easy at full-glacial." Those few alpine plants restricted to the highest elevations frequently have wide distributions. Some may reach new mountaintops via Rosy Finches. Such random, occasional transport by birds or by the wind may have dispersed most alpine plants to their rocky aeries.

Unique endemic alpine plants dwell on some ranges, frequently evolved from valley species specializing in high-elevation habitats or surviving as remnants of once-widespread plants. The Steens Mountain thistle nods beside the road in the alpine grassland, in mist losing its scale and looming like a strange prickly tree against the dark rock.

Nevada primrose grows only on the highest limestone ridges of the Grant and Snake ranges. Duran's alumroot lives only in the White and Sweetwater mountains and in the Wassuk Range. Unique buckwheats grow on the Snake Range, the Ruby/East Humboldts, and the White Mountains. Pairs of related species exist, high-elevation and low-elevation forms, probably once continuous, then separated by Pleistocene glaciation and subsequently differentiated.

But like all alpine plants, endemic or not, these are small and inconspicuous. Their distinctions do not leap out at you. Hardly anyone really looks at these flowers; they register as small splotches of vivid color, lumped together as "tiny alpine wildflowers." Even supposed naturalists such as me rarely take the time to key out plants. I prefer to identify by a few key characters lodged permanently in my brain, and it is easier for us nonspecialists to do so with shrubs and trees than with sedges and buckwheats.

But why not glory in the detail? Alpine plants have endless numbers of such fine

touches. Tiny rosettes of leaves adapted perfectly to the harsh climate. Blossoming cushions of life molded by wind currents an inch above ground. Long-lived plants a few inches high in a world of fleeting summers, difficult winters, and relentless, almighty sunlight.

I wait for moonrise, perched at my Ruby Mountain campsite above Favre Lake.

Well after sunset the glow of the moon lights the clouds from behind the ridge, just to the left of the castellated turrets carved on the skyline behind Castle Lake. It feels like fire beyond the moat, fields burning while we garrison the castle walls. The hot bright spot draws my eye just as a sunset—even more, since a competing trace of red still flares in the west, a ragged curtain of color pulled behind the horizon by the sun, the night flowing in behind it.

Avalanche tracks remain snow-filled on the face of the mountain above me; in near darkness they look like great swatches of white paint on a gray scene. One talus patch surrounded by snow forms a crescent—the mountain's smile. The hidden moon fires the opalescent clouds brighter, molten lead in their centers, quicksilver on their edges.

I hear the soft running of the brook cascading down from Liberty Lake behind me. A deeper roar comes from the lake below, Castle's outlet joining Favre's—perhaps deeper in sound only because it is more distant. And a barely noticed hum is the wind, the sound made in my ear canals as they respond to the whoosh of each gust. Like blowing across the top of a bottle.

The moon comes up, always brighter than I expect. After one blast of colorless light, clouds drift over it, right to left, the only clouds in the sky.

They drift on. The moon shines clearly. Its cold light draws the crest of the Rubies in bold, black silhouette.

V

Transition Forests
Beyond the Cordilleras

West of the Wasatch

15

He came down past the benches of the prehistoric lake to a plain of sage and stunted oak brush smelling of dust under a brazen sun. . . . the line of the Wasatch stretching south with perhaps a few patches of snow left still like outcrops of chalk just below the ridge, to the south the more desolate Oquirrhs canting westward toward the end of the lake, and then those bright, amazing waters with peaks rising from them and the sun striking a white fire from them and from the whiter sand.

. . . east is always the direction where you will see the Wasatch ridge and west the house of the sky where the sun sinks into the lake. The cottonwood leaves flutter always beyond the margins of awareness. . . . March starts the snows withdrawing up the peaks . . . sagebrush is a perfume and a stench, and at midnight there is a lighter line along the ridge where the sky begins.

—Bernard DeVoto,
The Year of Decision: 1846, 1942

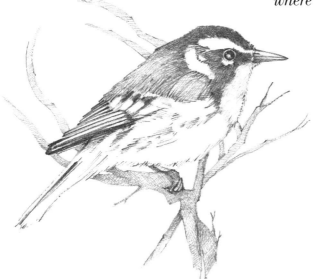

Grace's Warbler

When I was young, each year the *World Book Encyclopedia* came out with a set of transparent overlays in its yearbook that taught me some new piece of reality—the organ systems of "the visible man" or the physical and cultural resources of a distant continent. Layer by layer, the acetate films built on each other until the whole appeared from out of the parts, understood in a new way.

Understanding the distribution patterns of life in the Great Basin grows from a similar set of overlays. Each addition to the stack dictates rules to living things with the same sense of incontrovertibility as an encyclopedia.

Start with a topographic base map: the high Sierra and Wasatch on the west and east, the scatter of island ranges between. Relief shading indicates much better high-altitude connections from the Wasatch out to the central Basin ranges than from the Sierra, cut off by the Lahontan trough.

Over this lay a map of Pleistocene lakes for a sense of the toughest, saltiest lowland soils. A simplified geologic overlay shows the distinct difference between the overwhelmingly acidic, igneous rocks of the Sierra and the more diverse but largely basic rocks of the Great Basin and Rockies.

Next add two climatic overlays. One shows a broad line across the northern basin: behind this line to the north, frigid polar air hovers in winter. The second shades the area of summer rain, dark and important in the southeast, attenuated to the north and west until the northwestern section of the overlay is unshaded clear acetate—as clear as its summer skies.

Add a couple of decorative drawings in each corner, a ticking clock and a Clark's Nutcracker and Pinyon Jay, and the encyclopedia's promise comes true: in these overlays lie much of the story of Great Basin biogeography.

The Sierra casts its rain shadow eastward across these maps; it creates this desert. At the north edge, polar air intensifies, winters grow ever colder. Increasing elevation and latitude bring more snow; northward, the Great Basin Desert ends. Likewise, southward, with the sharp drop in elevation across south-central Nevada, cold-desert shadscale and sagebrush give way to hot deserts and creosote bush.

The clock symbolizes the remarkable recency of much of this desert; it marks off the alternating cycles of warming and cooling through the Pleistocene to the present. Shadscale flats of the Lahontan and Bonneville basins have appeared only in the last few thousand years where the Pleistocene lakes once filled the lowest valleys.

The clock began ticking at different moments for every range across the Basin. The Rockies are older than the Basin ranges, which in turn are older than the Sierra. Rocky Mountain plants thus had more time to emigrate into the Great Basin than Sierra Nevada plants. Sierran plants grow mostly in acidic soil, and this, too, has made it difficult for them to disperse eastward into the Basin.

Meanwhile, jays and nutcrackers flap across the map, caw-cawing. They pause here and there on mountain ranges. They leave behind sprouting groves of pines.

The Rockies cast their own rain shadow westward, blocking the Great Basin from Great Plains weather systems. Two additional shadows cast westward hint further at the influence of the Rockies: the high-elevation dispersal routes from Wasatch and High Plateau forest and the gradually diminishing summer rains. Along these overlapping patterns and pathways Rocky Mountain plants and animals spill over into the Great Basin.

The Wasatch and the Basin ranges just past it have a curious patchiness of vegetation unlike anything else in the Great Basin. Oak and maple make these mountains unique. Black coniferous greens, desert gray-greens, and bright deciduous greens form a lush mosaic, even more vivid in fall when oaks turn burnished gold and maples blaze red. John Muir saw this on the Oquirrh Mountains in spring:

> Gray, sagey plains circle around their bases, and up to a height of a thousand feet or more their sides are tinged with

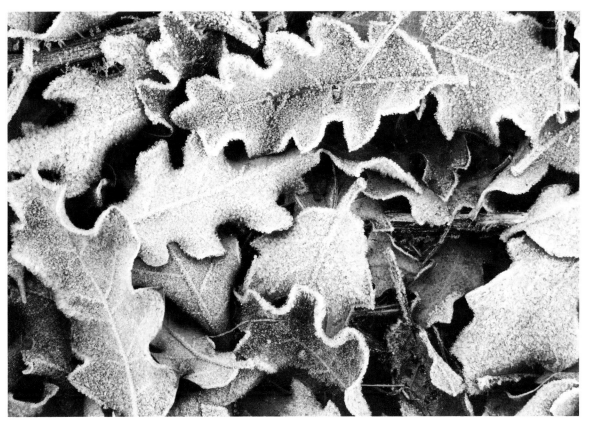

Frosted Gambel oak leaves; oak pioneered mountains on the eastern edge of the Great Basin in wetter times. It persists today as clones that reproduce vegetatively, but few seedlings survive.

purple . . . dwarf oak just coming into leaf. Higher you may detect faint tintings of green on a gray ground, from young grasses and sedges; then come the dark pine woods filling glacial hollows, and over all the smooth crown of snow.

Oak and maple brushlands of the Utah mountains merit their own title: Wasatch chaparral. Along the Wasatch front they form a zone that virtually replaces ponderosa pine forest and compresses piñon-juniper woodland.

In its favored elevational zone of five thousand to eight thousand feet, chaparral takes the place of ponderosa pines. To the north, the pines depend on May precipitation; to the south, the summer monsoons. In the chaparral belt neither rainy season provides enough moisture for ponderosa reproduction. Oak chaparral wins by default.

Fifteen inches of precipitation consistently limit oak survival. Near that limit, in places where piñon and juniper normally grow, chaparral prevails if autumn, winter, and spring are sufficiently wet. Oak dominates these chaparral communities, particularly on south-facing

slopes. Canyon maple grows in slightly wetter places, in ravines and on north-facing slopes. In rockier soils, and at its upper limits, oak gives way to mountain-mahogany–dominated brush akin to the mountain brushlands of the Basin ranges.

West of the Wasatch, out into the Basin, distribution of oak and maple is spotty. Both occur in the Canyon and Mineral mountains. Canyon maple reaches the Stansburys, but Gambel oak does not. An isolated oak stand in the Sheeprock Mountains lies twenty miles from the nearest Gambel oaks and is actively expanding on the range. Gambel oak reaches its northernmost limits at the south end of the Wellsville Mountains. It reaches into eastern Nevada from Utah's High Plateaus and Pine Valley Mountains.

The oak reproduces sexually by acorns and also sends up new shoots from its roots. Today, seedlings are rare in most oak stands, and ecologists gradually realized that, like aspen, these oak thickets grow in single clones— exceedingly old ones.

Since Gambel oak cannot reproduce from acorns in much of its northern range today, it must have established itself here in an entirely different climate. Oak chaparral survives only because of its ability to persist where neither oak nor pine can reproduce sexually. Several fascinating hints (largely untangled by Utah ecologists Earl Christensen and Walter Cottam) help prove this.

Gambel oak grows mostly to the south, where it interfingers with ponderosa pine forest; the patches of Wasatch chaparral at the edge of the Great Basin lie at its northwesternmost frontier—old clones no longer producing many seedlings. At upper elevations, thickets are continuous, established when oak invaded upward and northward as the Hypsithermal raised temperatures and probably brought summer rains farther north. Small clones invading downward into sagebrush benchlands have done so in the cooling climate since the Hypsithermal.

Another even more dramatic record of changing climate exists in Utah's oaks.

Today, shrub live oak—a species of southern desert mountains—reaches northward to Meadow Valley Wash below Caliente, Nevada, and the Pine Valley Mountains of southernmost Utah. But some 260 miles north, oaks in the Oquirrh Mountains show traits of this evergreen species: they clearly arose from the crossing of Gambel oak with shrub live oak. Hybrids here and south along the Wasatch at the eastern edge of old Lake Bonneville grow about five hundred to one thousand feet below the normal range of Gambel oak, in such ranges as the Canyon and Mineral mountains.

Intermediate between Gambel oak and shrub live oak, these hybrids evidently document the warm climate of some four thousand years ago, when shrub live oak could grow as far north as the Oquirrhs. However, some ecologists believe the crosses arose from ultra–long distance pollination rather than range extension of mature plants; these isolated stands also could be the work of acorn-dispersing Band-tailed Pigeons, jays, nutcrackers, or woodpeckers.

However they arrived, where the two oaks overlapped they hybridized (as they do today where they grow together). Later, the cooling climate eliminated the shrub live oaks. But

with increased cold tolerance inherited from their Gambel oak lineage, the hybrids survived in pockets of temperature inversion warmer than mountain slopes above and valleys below. Sexually sterile, they maintained themselves by root-suckering; today's relicts are enormous, isolated single clones.

Other experiments have pinned down Gambel oak's climatic needs for successful sexual reproduction. Cold stress increases northward as polar air makes spring freezes more and more likely. At the same time, summer drought deadly to seedlings increases to the north, farther and farther from moist gulf air and significant summer monsoons. At its northern limits, Gambel oak may simply get squeezed out as these two patterns converge.

Both chaparral plants resprout after fire, and the depressing cycle of overgrazing by livestock, invasion of exotic annual grasses, and recurring fire that prevails in sagebrush, grass, and juniper communities has not discouraged oak and maple. Reduced fire and grazing in this century likely have encouraged establishment of new clones at low elevations.

At higher elevations, western serviceberry and canyon maple—and, in some places, white fir—seem to be replacing oak. Even where oaks manage to produce seedlings, maples leaf and flower earlier; they better tolerate shade. At lower elevations, however, new oak clones have invaded downward into sagebrush. A changing climate continues to shift the pieces in the chaparral mosaic.

Anyone familiar with the forests of the central and southern Rockies will recognize this litany: ponderosa pine and Rocky Mountain juniper in the foothills; a little higher, white fir, Douglas-fir, and shrubby dwarf juniper; fire-adapted lodgepole pine; subalpine fir and Engelmann spruce to tree line; and five-needled pines (bristlecone, limber, and whitebark) on rocky ridges.

These bands of forest characterize the Utah Rockies (the Wasatch Range) and High Plateaus. But such trees reach into the Great Basin only tentatively. The highest ranges of the

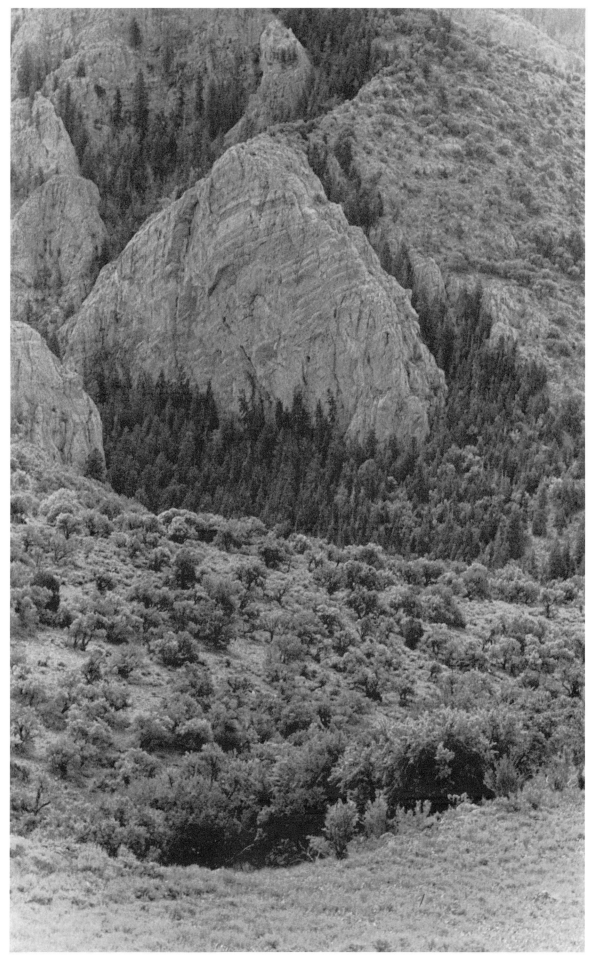

Ranges like the Schell Creek have complex assemblages of Great Basin- and Wasatch-style forests. Here, on the Success Loop Drive, tumbles of fir grow at the base of cliffs that funnel extra moisture to them. Below is a drier forest of mountain-mahogany.

eastern Basin have up to eight of these eleven species. Many ranges farther west have only limber or bristlecone pine and perhaps a mountain juniper. Some ranges have no conifers above woodland piñon and Utah juniper.

Most of the Basin mountain forests are attenuated pockets of Rocky Mountain forest. Whitebark pine is the most successful colonist from the Sierra-Cascades (though it too may have reached the Basin from the Rockies, from central Idaho or western Wyoming). Other magnificent Sierra conifers reach eastward into the Basin only at its westernmost edge, if at all. Some species grow in both the Rocky Mountains and Sierra (white fir, Douglas-fir, ponderosa pine, lodgepole pine), but in two populations distinctly different genetically—officially separate subspecies.

Like every other aspect of Great Basin biogeography, the key to these distributions lies in the history of the cycling glacial climate. But unlike some of the harder-to-document communities (tundra, for example), for conifers we have a finely detailed specimen collection made over the last twenty thousand years by wood rats.

By analyzing wood rat middens, Philip Wells has documented the changing forests of the Great Basin in remarkable detail. We have two hinge points: the modern distribution of forest trees; and the clearly understood full-glacial of ice-capped mountains above lake-filled basins, separated by monotonous forests of bristlecone and limber pine.

Most of the larger Basin ranges have retained the conifers they had at full-glacial: bristlecone, perhaps, and usually limber pine and the shrubby dwarf juniper. Western ranges like the Toiyabes have changed little, too isolated to have been colonized by additional species capable of surviving in the warming climate. Ranges farther east lie close enough to the cordillera for successful colonization by Rocky Mountain conifers.

Unlike birds, conifers cannot colonize freely across great spaces on their own. Instead, most of them rely on birds for help. Wells calculates the impossibly long times required for pines

and firs to disperse by wind and gravity alone and sums up the case for bird dispersal of seeds: "more inevitable than daring." Even the industrious nutcrackers, Pinyon Jays, and Band-tailed Pigeons usually follow the most obvious routes, and those routes lead out from the Rockies in two conspicuous prongs.

The northern prong follows a series of mountains straddling the Idaho border with Utah and Nevada, along the divide separating the Great Basin from the Snake River Plain. These stepping-stone mountains link the Bear River Range of southeast Idaho's Rockies with the western outpost of Rocky Mountain trees, the Jarbidge–Independence–Bull Run mountain group in northern Nevada. Considering their moderate elevation, these mountains are cold and wet. As a result, thoroughly subalpine trees have successfully moved west through these mountains.

Rocky Mountain lodgepole pine enters the Great Basin only along this route, in Idaho's South Hills reaching to within twelve miles of Nevada at Shoshone Creek, but not beyond. Subalpine fir extends all the way to the Independence Mountains; Douglas-fir and Engelmann spruce reach only half as far, to the Raft River and Albion mountains, stopping short of the South Hills.

In the Raft River Mountains, conifers do not form distinct zones of forest but grow in pockets nestled in the domed and rounded ridges. Here Douglas-fir grows at medium elevations, spruce and fir above, and limber pine on rocky ridges, all embedded in a matrix of black sagebrush.

In the Jarbidge Mountains, subalpine fir dominates a unique forest, growing from low river bottoms to high slopes. Its only coniferous companions are a few limber pine, whitebark pine at tree line, an occasional Rocky Mountain juniper, and dwarf juniper in the understory.

Pollen records give us finer detail. Lodgepole pine probably achieved continuous distribution across these ranges during full-glacial times. Subalpine fir also came west early. Spruce evidently never grew past its present

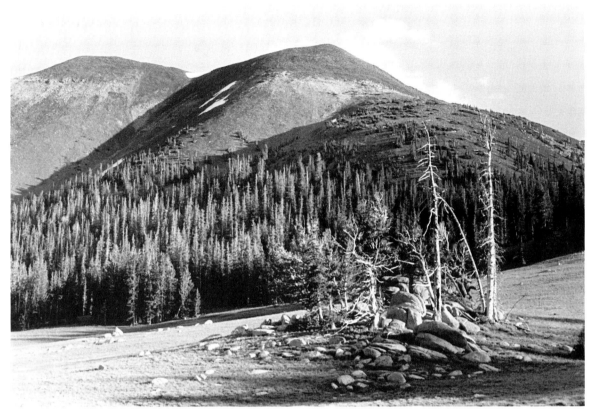

distribution, and Douglas-fir arrived late (absent 12,190 years ago in pollen records at Red Rock Pass, but present in tiny quantities by 10,190 years ago); lack of summer rains may limit its westward march. Southward, the pattern of summer rain becomes even more powerful in influencing where plants can survive.

More than any other Basin ranges, the Snake and Deep Creek ranges come closest to maintaining fully developed Rocky Mountain forest. Both island ranges support eight species of conifers above piñon-juniper woodland—the maximum for Great Basin mountains. Rising as they do from the sere Bonneville basin, the reasons for their diversity are not immediately obvious.

But if we go back to our overlays, two facts become clear. These ranges lie at the end of the second great high-elevation prong off the Rockies, and they also receive significant summer rains.

From the Wasatch in central Utah, the High Plateaus lead south to the Pine Valley Mountains in a high, green semicircle rimming the Bonneville basin. Middle-elevation country (today a broad continuous stand of piñon-juniper)

just northwest of the Pine Valley Mountains leads to the White Rock Range. Here two series of mountains lead north: in Utah, the Needle–Wah Wah–Confusion–House Range system and, in Nevada, the Wilson Creek and Snake ranges terminating back in Utah at the isolated and massive Deep Creek Range.

I came to the Snake Range from the east, from Milford, Utah, across valleys that had held arms of Lake Bonneville and over ranges that stood above it. The road I followed left the Bonneville basin as it crested the Wah Wah Mountains. With the Wah Wahs and the Snake Range begins the rhythmic chant of basin, range, basin, range that continues westward across Nevada to the Lahontan basin, another great sea of alluvium.

The contrast of the Snake Range with the surrounding sea of shadscale and saltbush makes these mountains even more imposing. The forest held high by the Snakes forms a discrete dark mantle over the range. Other than a few junipers and piñons that trickle down washes into the valley, the conifers remain abrupt in their ending, an island of trees.

I penetrated that island forest on Mount Moriah, along Hendrys Creek. Cottonwood and

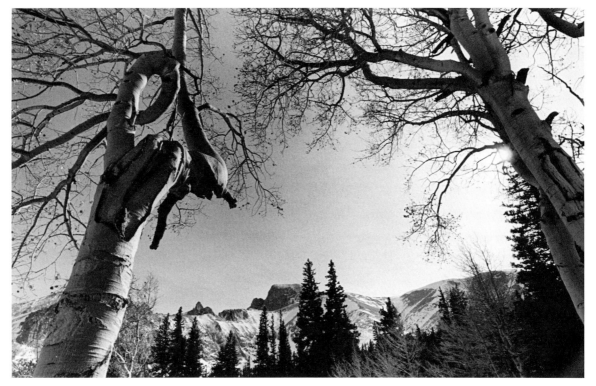

willow line the first mile or two of the stream above the valley. But with an elevation gain of a thousand feet, aspen takes over in dense stands, dense enough to make you feel you have entered the Rockies rather than a Great Basin range with a name as basinlike as Snake. All along, the understory is a tangle of choke-cherry, elderberry, gooseberry, Wood's (wild) rose. American dogwood branches hang over small cascades, sunlit, with bark as red as latigo leather.

In August the damp forest showed the results of rain in the growing season, of summer thundershowers; mushrooms bulged up from the earth, pushing aside leaves and pine needles with their surge of growth.

In October, growth had ceased for the winter. A single crimson rose hip caught the sun against a glen of aspen. These Hendrys Creek trees had yellowish bark, and the frosted leaf carpet was soft in hue. So the trailside had two colors: aspen cream with one bold stroke of rose-hip red.

I celebrated the coming of cold autumn nights with a campfire. As I went to sleep, whenever I opened my eyes and looked up through the door of my tent I looked past black silhouettes of sturdy, motionless trees aimed at the stars, the epitome of slow, dependable reality. When I closed my eyes and drifted off into a light sleep, a quick-changing haze of incoherent dreams took over. I opened and closed my eyes and felt the alternation of two worlds, reality neatly partitioned in halves.

Hours later I awoke. The tent opening framed three trees, set against eggshell-blue predawn sky with a cockling of white clouds. Closest were pine-green needles on whorled black branchlets of a ponderosa, a tree under which an Oriental philosopher might sit.

First sun on the top of the ponderosa switched on an inner light in the needles, burnished gold—natural Christmas bulbs at the ends of branches. A cloud blocked the sun and flicked them off. When full sun next hit them they were green.

To the left, spikes of a mountain-mahogany ended abruptly, looking like a transplanted bit of African thorn scrub or a freshly pruned winter ornamental from a royal garden. Finally, one aspen, with a few remaining gold brown leaves. As the first breeze shook it after sunrise, one-fourth of the leaves came tinkling down. Their slow whirling drift made it seem they did not yet feel like falling.

I broke camp and began climbing. High

above the creek I reached the ridge crest, where views began to open. First, Notch Peak out in the Bonneville basin, a mountain whose sheer face lacks only three hundred feet of matching Yosemite's El Capitan, with a powerful presence that keeps you always searching for it on the horizon and leaves you satisfied when you spot it. Far beyond, the Wasatch gleamed behind the Stansbury Mountains. North stood the Deep Creek Range, hulking over the white pan of the Great Salt Lake Desert. South, snow and spruce in the foreground, rose Wheeler Peak, rock-gray with lenticular storm clouds hovering over the summit, its great cirque contrary to any imagined desert.

These mountains are difficult, incomplete, fragmented. They suit the desert. They are islands. Mountain plants reach the Deep Creek Range by hopscotching from the Wasatch and High Plateaus around through the Snake Range. Up here I could almost feel the plants streaming northward.

Wood rat middens give us remarkably detailed information about the history of conifers in this east-central part of the Basin. In full-glacial times (20,000 to 12,500 years ago) only bristlecone pine, Engelmann spruce, and dwarf juniper grew on the Snake Range. Bristlecone (with dwarf juniper) dominated the forest from 5,400 feet to 8,800 feet. Spruce remained rare but grew as low as 6,200 feet (3,000 feet below its modern upland habitat). Even in the lower Utah ranges, the Wah Wah Mountains and Confusion Range, bristlecone grew from high ridges down to lower slopes until late-glacial time, when it shared dominance with limber pine.

In all his central Great Basin wood rat middens from the full-glacial, Wells has found not a trace of piñon, Utah juniper, mountain-mahogany, *Atriplex*, or prickly pear cactus. Only rare traces of black sagebrush turn up. Today's Great Basin woodland and desert plants—and most mountain conifers—grew to the south, in what is now the Mojave and Sonoran deserts. The modern North American deserts are no more than a few thousand years old.

As the glaciers waned, Great Basin forests began to change. Small ranges like the Confusions showed the most drastic fluctuations. Bristlecone died out there between 11,880 and 10,340 years ago, but at the latter date the summit still supported limber pine, Douglas-fir, and Rocky Mountain and dwarf juniper.

During the climatic vicissitudes of the Holocene, the Confusion Range went through what Wells aptly called "kaleidoscopic changes" in its forests. Subalpine conifers went from five species to two to five and back to two again. These two—Douglas-fir and Rocky Mountain juniper—survive today on the summit. Piñon and Utah juniper reached lower elevations sometime between 8,590 and 4,390 years ago.

The Snake Range, on the other hand, has seen a steady, gradual increase in numbers of conifers. Big enough to avoid local extinctions and to make an easy target for immigrants, the Snake Range also lies near the end of a nearly continuous spur of mountains that connects it to the Rockies.

At the southern rim of the Great Basin, along Meadow Valley Wash in the Clover-Delamar plateau, wood rat middens reveal the glacial refuge of other mountain conifers. At full-glacial, limber pine and Douglas-fir rather than spruce and bristlecone grew here between forty-four hundred and five thousand feet, along with the two mountain junipers. In late-glacial times, Douglas-fir increased at the expense of limber pine.

Soon after, Douglas-fir began to turn up in ranges to the north, the last conifer to move into the Great Basin while nearly continuous coniferous forest remained on the lower divides. Even then, Douglas-fir reached only the low Confusion Range at this time. By the time it reached the Snake Range, it had to leapfrog dry piñon-juniper woodlands.

Its companion, Rocky Mountain ponderosa pine, today is the veritable symbol of southwestern forests and remarkably widespread from the central Rockies southward. However, Rocky Mountain ponderosa evidently did not grow anywhere in the Rockies, Great Basin,

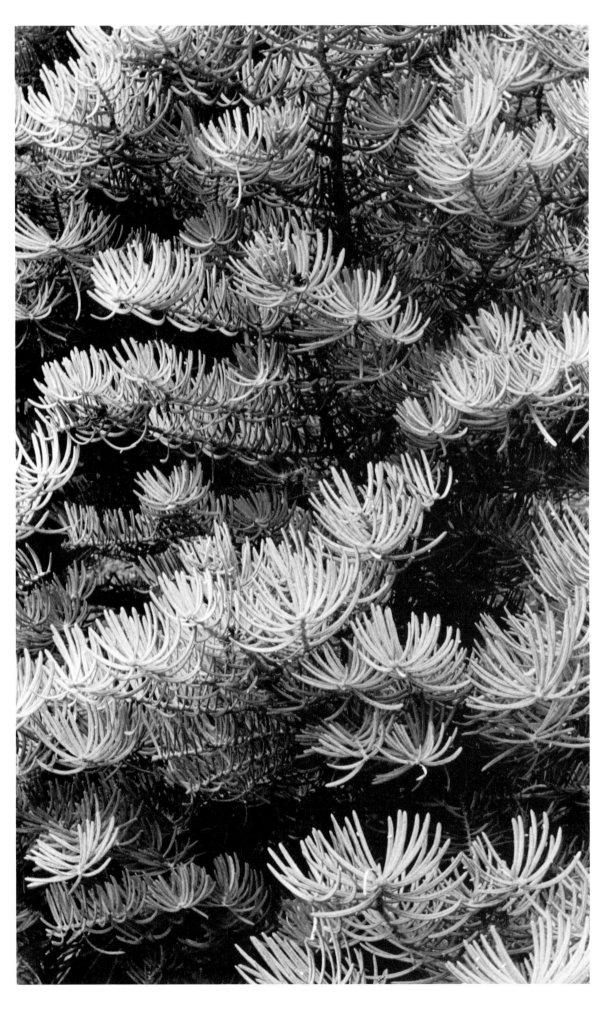

White fir, last Rocky Mountain conifer to move north into the Great Basin; Deep Creek Range, Utah.

or Mojave Desert at full-glacial. With subalpine forests to the north and piñon-juniper woodland to the south, ponderosas must have withdrawn still farther to the south, onto the southern high plains or in mountains near the Mexican border.

In the last eight thousand years, ponderosa has swept north through the Rockies as far as northern Utah; it reaches into the Great Basin to the Grant and Needle ranges, though only the Snake Range harbors much more than a few small stands.

White fir was the last Rocky Mountain conifer to move north, not appearing in the central Great Basin before the mid-Holocene (4,640 years ago in the Snake Range). Perhaps Douglas-fir, arriving first and competing for similar resources, made its establishment difficult. Nonetheless, white fir has reached more ranges than either ponderosa or Douglas-fir. It is the last holdout of the Rocky Mountain forest as you pass beyond abundant summer rains and easy emigration routes. White fir reaches the Rubies, the Pilot Range, and the White Pines, but not beyond to the Toiyabe, Toquima, and Monitor ranges.

Eastern Great Basin mountain forests thus gradually diminish from the full-blown Rocky Mountain versions of central Utah to the spartan, purely Basin forests of the Toiyabe Range and its neighbors. The 116th meridian makes a convenient marker for the westernmost penetration of Rocky Mountain trees. We can now account for these facts.

The glacial-relict subalpine bristlecone and limber pine and Engelmann spruce remain on the high ranges where they grew in the Pleistocene (with minor recent extensions). Subalpine fir has a spottier distribution; it moved west in late-glacial times to the Jarbidge Mountains and Deep Creek Range but not to the Rubies or the Snake Range.

Finally, the lower-elevation montane forests of white fir, with more isolated stands of Douglas-fir and ponderosa pine, arrived in the Holocene, along with the piñon-juniper woodlands of the drying desert margin. On ranges like the Snakes, Schell Creeks, and Deep Creeks, the Rocky Mountain conifers characterize the upper north-facing slopes of the range, while only depauperate Basin forests survive on the drier lower and south-facing sides.

The driving forces behind these patterns seem threefold. Emigration routes determine the pathways that trees take; birds—particularly nutcrackers and Pinyon Jays—help move them along the paths; and increasing summer drought limits their survival westward. On the northern fringe of the Basin, beyond the summer rains, polar air and chance dispersal seem to account for conifer distribution.

The Rubies sit at the outermost limits of nearly every Rocky Mountain influence, a unique combination. They receive considerable precipitation, but mostly as snow, for they lie near the polar fronts and at the distant northern fringes of summer rains. Though they have great topographic diversity, like the lushly forested Deep Creek and Snake ranges, they underwent more intense glaciation that left little room for relict forests, and they had to start nearly from scratch. The Rubies lie a bit beyond the major westward dispersal routes but equidistant from both—within reach (from the Jarbidges to the north) of plants like whitebark pine and, from the south, colonizing white fir and Engelmann spruce.

Their size and location make the Rubies anomalous. Beyond lie the truly isolated Basin ranges, with their dry canyons, strange depauperate forests, and bald mountains.

What does all this mean for animals?

In few ranges do these Rocky Mountain conifers form a forest. Most often they grow in isolated pockets or ragged stands. Only the limestone mountains around Ely (the Snake, Deep Creek, and Schell Creek ranges) and to a lesser extent the high mountains just west of the Wasatch (such as the Stansburys and Oquirrhs) have dense woods.

Mammals restricted to such dense forest simply do not occur on Great Basin mountains. Missing are mammals typical of boreal forest in the Rockies: marten, Douglas squirrel, fly-

*A colonnade of
subalpine fir and
Engelmann spruce
in the Stansbury
Mountains.*

210

*Transition
Forests*

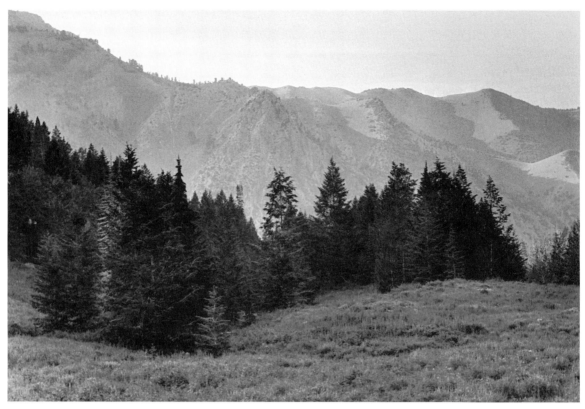

ing squirrel, boreal redback vole, and snow-shoe hare.

Some mammals and birds must have particular plants for food and nests. In the Rockies and the Southwest, ponderosa pine and Abert's squirrels, for instance, go together. But Abert's squirrels have not followed the scattered ponderosa stands westward into the Great Basin, likely because the trees arrived in leaps and bounds via bird dispersal, leaving gaps uncrossable by squirrels.

Grace's Warbler also prefers ponderosas to all other trees. This southwestern warbler has reached the Quinn Canyon Range but does not breed in the few ponderosas in the White Pine Range or in the extensive ponderosa stands in the Snake Range. All these breeding records fall after 1963: evidently the warbler has extended its range recently (or recent increases in bird observations mislead us). Since the tree's range extends beyond the bird's, some factor other than the simple existence of the ponderosa may fall off at these frontiers: pine arthropods that form the warbler's food supply or climatic barriers.

Birds have mobility; we assume they could colonize most any range if suitable habitat exists. With alpine and subalpine birds, their presence may be either relict or a product of fresh colonization. Among probable colonists from the Rocky Mountains, the Black-backed Woodpecker, Water Pipit, and Rosy Finch occur on different sets of ranges (the Rosy Finch as far as the Jarbidges and Rubies, the woodpecker in the Snake Range, the pipit west to the Deep Creek Range and four Nevada ranges). Their absence on neighboring ranges with similar habitat is perplexing, but what looks similar to us simply may not look that way to a woodpecker or pipit.

Animals typical of the Rocky Mountains reach into the Great Basin only as far as the Basin environment remains sufficiently like the Rockies to be survivable, and as far as they can physically immigrate. The same holds true for animals and plants reaching into the Great Basin from the north, south, and west. But Rocky Mountain creatures find the Basin closest to home. Their influence is strongest. Most of these mountains beyond the cordilleras feel more like the Rockies than the Sierra.

But not all of them.

The Forgotten Mountains

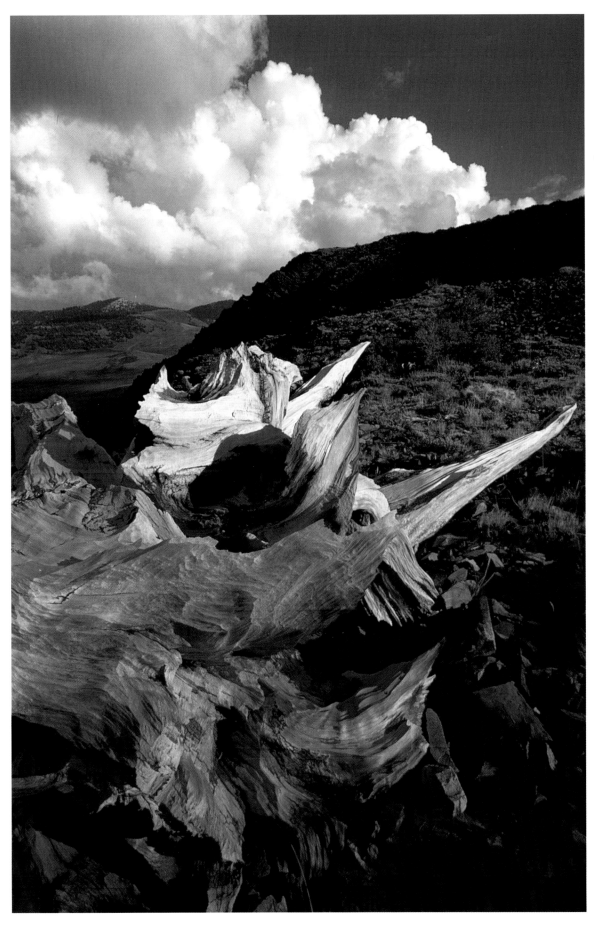

From dead bristlecones like these in the White Mountains come the crucial series of rings that extend the bristlecone tree-ring record back further than living trees can document—to 9,000 years.

The northernmost singleleaf piñons, in the City of Rocks below Cache Peak, Idaho.

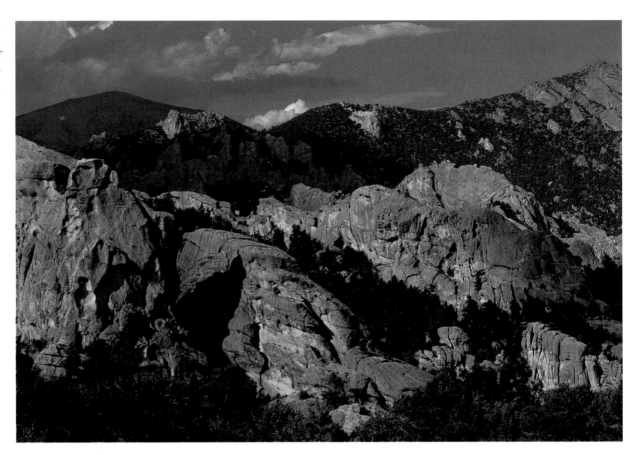

Great Basin bristlecone pines on Wheeler Peak, not far from where the oldest known living bristlecone was cut at 4,900 years plus.

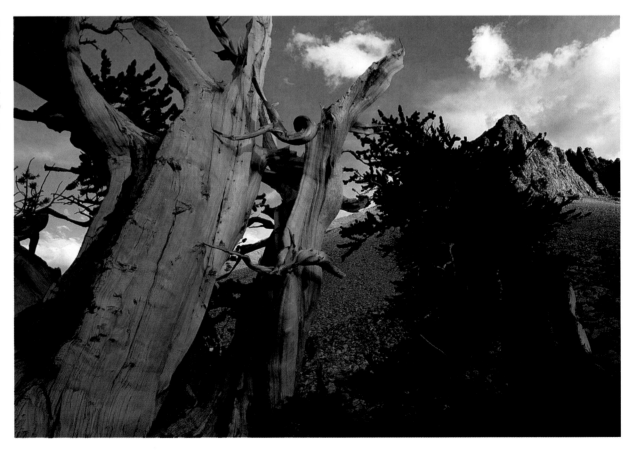

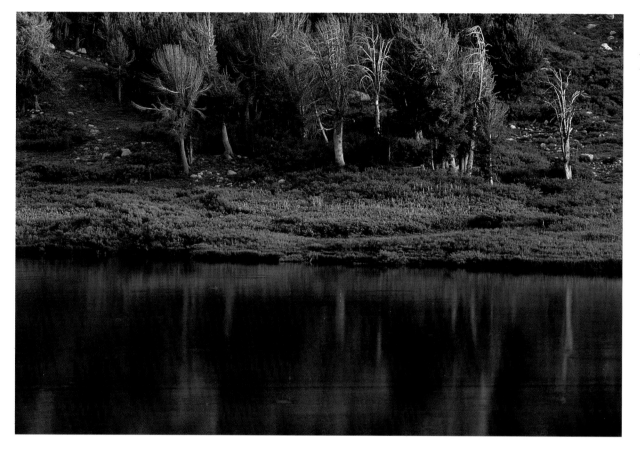

Whitebark pine at sunset, Favre Lake, Ruby Mountains.

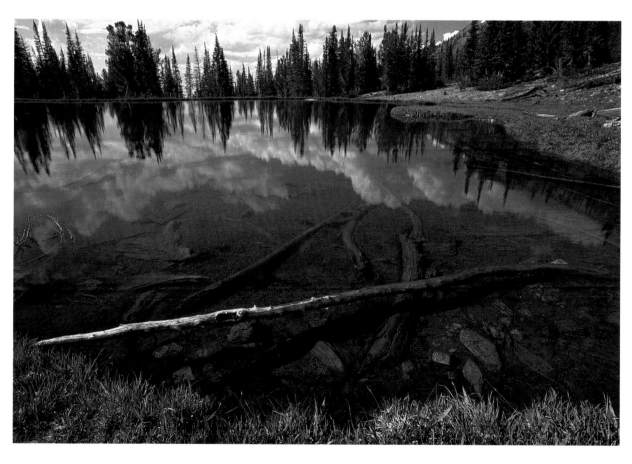

In Nevada's Jarbidge Mountains, subalpine fir dominates a unique forest, growing from river bottoms to ridgetops and slopes—as here at Jarbidge Lake.

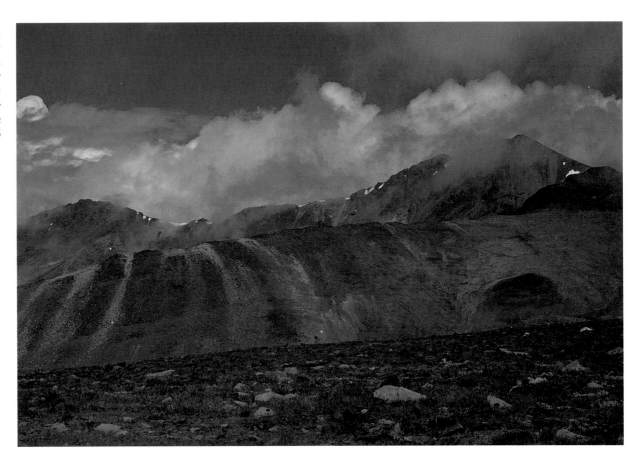

Highest mountain in the Great Basin, the barren rock and dry tundra meadows of White Mountain Peak rise to 14,246 feet.

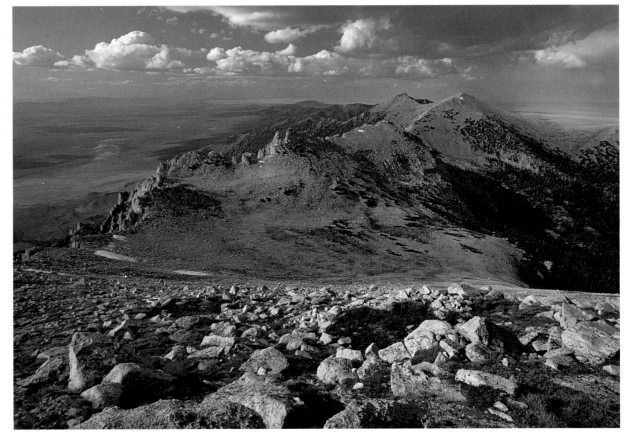

The view north from the 12,087-foot summit of Ibapah Peak in the Deep Creek Range soars past tundra meadows to plummet 7,000 feet down to the white salt flats of the Great Salt Lake Desert to the east.

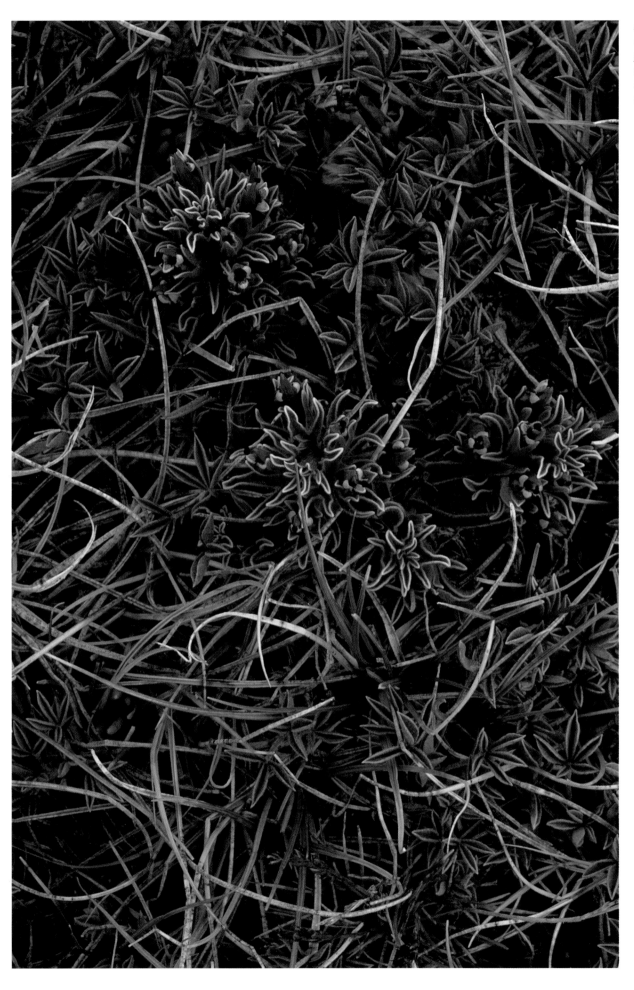

A tiny bouquet of alpine Indian paintbrush in tundra, White Mountains, California.

A mosaic of
sagebrush,
autumn aspen,
and blazing
crimson canyon
maple, Deep
Canyon,
Wellsville
Mountains.

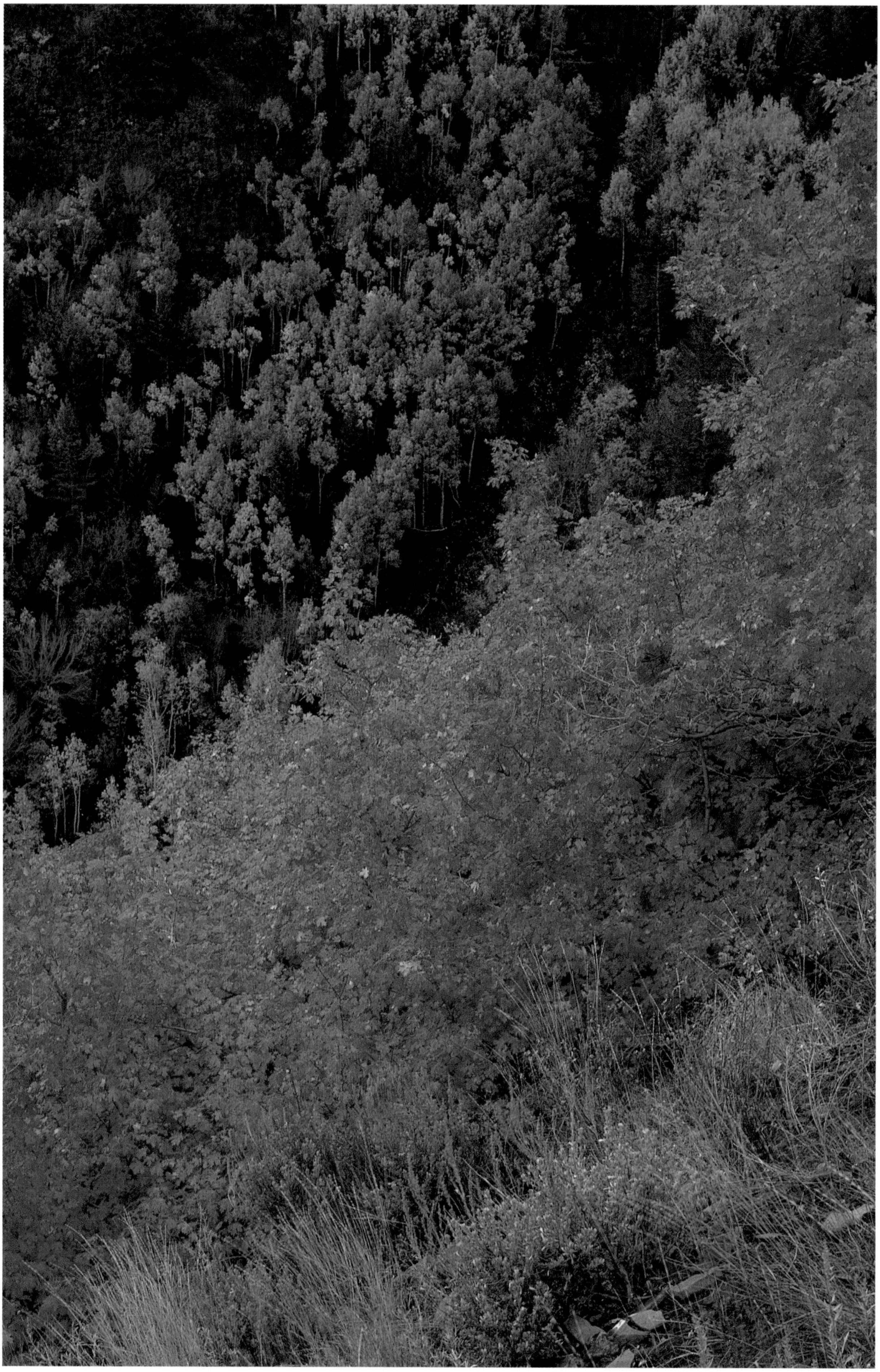

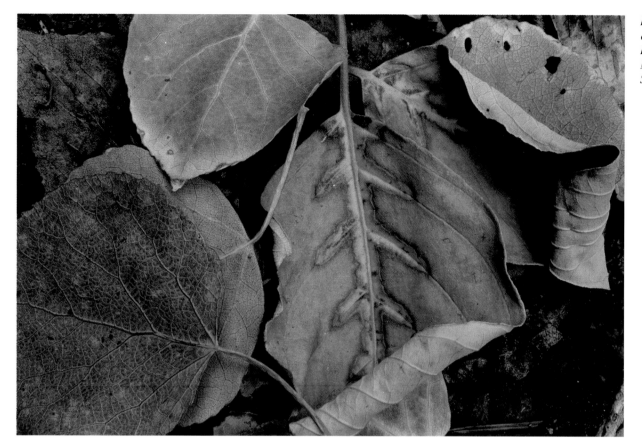

*Dogwood and
aspen leaves,
Hendrys Creek,
Mount Moriah,
Snake Range.*

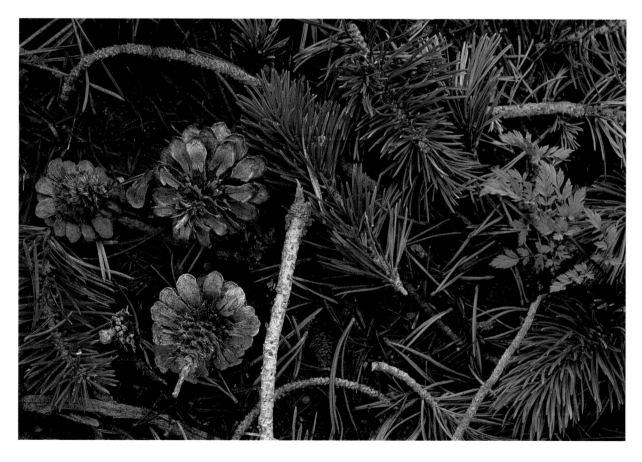

*Lodgepole pine
cones and duff on
the upper slopes
of Mount Rose,
Carson Range.*

Lake Tahoe from Mount Rose; condominiums aside, Tahoe still feels lush and heavenly, sumptuous and bold—unlike any other Great Basin lake.

East of the Sierra

16

The morning on the burntland came up quickly. The Sun shot over the far rolling hills and caught the night by surprise . . . the high wall of the Sierra mountains towering up green from the burntland. . . .

We climbed to the Sky. We climbed until the sun went down and set across the snow scarred mountains in a fierce rainbow. We climbed until there was nothing, nothing spreading out before us but the hide of a lake stretched blue and strained to its farthest shore beyond the grasp of the eye. . . . "You have journeyed long and arrived, you are home. You are home to the Big Water," he swept his arm in a wide circle around him, tracing the speared mountain peaks that slid into the Sky and sliced out of sight. . . . "Tahoe. You have returned to Tahoe. . . . You stand in a high place before all the power of the Mountain House. The high water rises higher before you. You have returned to Lake Tahoe."

—Thomas Sanchez,
Rabbit Boss, 1973

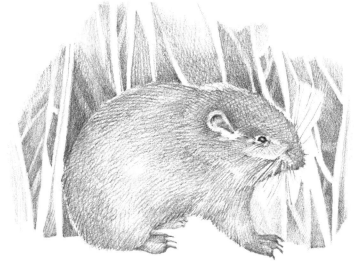

Mountain beaver

Most abrupt boundary of all, the Sierra and Cascades rise in a great green wall at the western edge of the Great Basin. They block the desert from Pacific moisture. They tower over it physically and psychologically.

The Sierran world differs dramatically from anything else in the Basin. Moving from the Stansburys to the Wasatch, from the Snake Range to the Aquarius Plateau, you simply go from a fragment of Rocky Mountain forest to the real thing. Traveling from the White Mountains to Kings Canyon or from Mono Lake to Yosemite, however, is to move between worlds, from the Desert of Light to the Range of Light. Suddenly a brand-new forest appears, two-hundred-foot-high California red firs and mountain hemlock, and within a few more miles the climax of the Sierra, the giant sequoias.

North of Susanville, California, the Cascades end nearly as suddenly at the edge of the Basin. Hart Mountain to Crater Lake means just as big a jump in ecology and spirit as any traverse of the Sierran wall.

Only at Lake Tahoe does Sierran forest slip over into the Great Basin. Tahoe, the largest mountain lake in North America, drains inland into the Truckee River. The Carson Range rims the eastern Tahoe basin, connecting with the main Sierra Nevada crest west of the lake.

In some ways today's commercial development has not affected the power of Lake Tahoe. It still feels lush and heavenly, sumptuous and bold—unlike any other Great Basin lake.

Such combinations of opposites fill the Carson Range, where you are never sure if you are in the Sierra or the Great Basin. Structurally, the Carson Range is a fault-block Basin range; it sends its waters into Great Basin rivers, the Truckee and Carson. But its granitic rocks and its forest are Sierran, the last holdout eastward of the real thing. Fittingly, the Carsons have a unique tree, Washoe pine, with an indecipherable ancestry to confuse botanists. Even the name of the range commemorates a man with a mixed reputation.

Kit Carson was one of the most stalwart and respected of mountain men. He guided John

Charles Frémont all over the West. Frémont said, "With me, Carson and truth are one," and made a hero of him. Yet Kit also could be ruthless. He destroyed the lifeway of the Navajos and is hated by many in the Southwest.

The Carson Range is complicated, it sums up the contrasts of the Great Basin. A Paiute woman once was offered the chance to spend a few days at Lake Tahoe. Her friend who extended the invitation as a special treat thought the desert Indian woman would find the woods around the lake a welcome respite from the brown land below. But the Paiute woman hated the lake. She said she felt hemmed in: "There was nothing to see."

Drive from Reno or Carson City toward Lake Tahoe and you climb over the Carson Range, transecting the Sierran forest zones. As you leave sagebrush in the Truckee Meadows or Carson Valley, first comes a mixed pine-fir forest at about five thousand to seventy-five hundred feet: ponderosa, Jeffrey, and sugar pines, along with white fir and a few incense-cedar. Fire-maintained chaparral fills many openings in this forest with shrubs and dense mats of greenleaf manzanita, bush chinquapin, and tobacco brush (snowbrush). But the expected woodland of piñon and juniper is missing from the Carson River north to Susanville, California; even then, northward only western juniper appears.

Above, on gentler slopes with deep soil, California red fir grows in magnificent, nearly pure stands, giving way at about eighty-three hundred feet to a mixed forest of smaller trees dominated by lodgepole pine and mountain hemlock, with scattered western white pine. Steep south-facing slopes may lack red fir, and on these drier places the mixed forest may grow as low as seventy-five hundred feet. Finally, from about ninety-three hundred feet to tree line above ten thousand feet, whitebark pine grows in its characteristic dwarfed and open stands.

Though four of these trees are familiar from deeper in the Basin (white fir and ponderosa, lodgepole, and whitebark pines), only white-

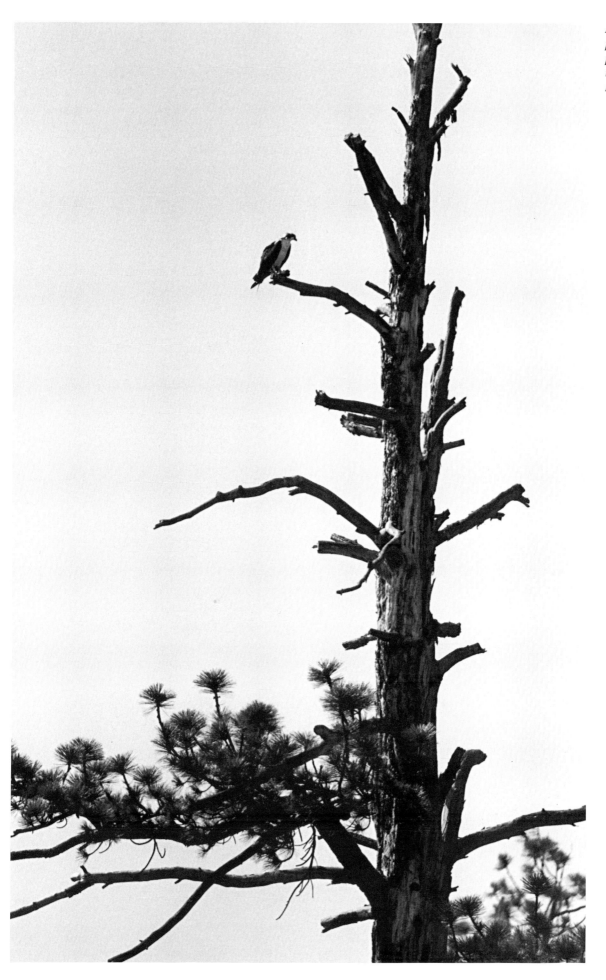

*A nesting Osprey
perched in a
ponderosa pine on
the shore of Eagle
Lake, California.*

bark pine is really the same tree here. The others are Sierran forms, subspecies distinct from their Rocky Mountain kin in appearance and in climatic tolerance. This is indeed a different forest, adapted to abundant winter moisture (commonly up to thirty feet of snow in one season) and extremely dry summers.

Fire controls the Sierran chaparral much more strongly than it does Wasatch chaparral. Timbering and repeated fires in the 1800s wiped out much of the original pine and fir forest and replaced it with chaparral. Fire continues to rejuvenate the shrubs in many places; elsewhere they succeed to second-growth forests in a century or so.

Greenleaf manzanita and tobacco brush both sprout vigorously from their roots after fire. They produce seeds in abundance that tolerate high temperatures, remain viable for long periods, and germinate only when heated. Dense rodent populations in chaparral (mostly deer mice and long-eared and yellow pine chipmunks) eat the majority of conifer seeds that find their way into the brush. Still, the shrubs enhance the soil and protect those conifer seedlings that get a start.

Around Lake Tahoe itself, Jeffrey pine dominates from about sixty-three hundred feet on the eastern shoreline up to eight thousand feet. Red fir joins it on wet sites. White fir, ponderosa pine, and incense-cedar scatter through this forest; sugar pine occurs sparsely. A few Douglas-fir grow on the eastern lakeshore. Lodgepole pine and western white pine usually grow no lower than seven thousand feet, mountain hemlock still higher.

Beginning tree watchers often have trouble distinguishing Jeffrey pine from ponderosa. Perhaps the most dependable difference is that ponderosa cones feel sharp and prickly compared to smoother Jeffrey cones with their incurved spines. Just as tricky is their ecological separation.

On the west slope of the Sierra, Jeffrey pine grows above ponderosa, the former clearly more tolerant of cold. On the east side, Jeffrey dominates to the south, where it handles drought more successfully than ponderosa.

But northeast of Tahoe, ponderosa seems to match Jeffrey pine's tolerance for cold. Along the Truckee River at the little town of Boca, one of the coldest spots in California, grow ponderosas, not Jeffreys, and here they seem adapted to extreme cold. These cold-tolerant ponderosas overlap the range of the closely related and extremely rare Washoe pine here. Since both Washoe pines and the local variety of ponderosa have extra-thick needles, the two may have hybridized.

Living below a mountain is satisfying. The mountain becomes a dominating presence in your life, a friend, and living or working where trees or buildings block its view is a constant frustration. Mount Rose has this presence. At 10,776 feet the high point of the northern Carson Range, it looks down on Reno with authority.

Weather swirls around it in idiosyncratic ways. The peak marks the passage of the seasons: snow gradually melts in summer as green takes over, modifying the pattern of remnant snowfields week by week. Then an autumn of browns and golds gives way to winter whites and blues.

In October, raindrops falling on the dried leaves of plants growing on south-facing hillsides make a sound like corn popping. In winter the mountain hemlocks along the Mount Rose Highway droop lower than usual with a flocking of snow. In spring, grass rears up and flowers bloom in waves behind the receding drifts.

One summer day I walked up the old road that forms the beginning of the Mount Rose trail. A Red-tailed Hawk lifted off a medium-sized lodgepole pine and let out the high, thin, mysterious cry of upset raptors. I stumped across a lush meadow at ninety-three hundred feet, my feet sinking deep into saturated mud along the stream. One bit of green at my feet, even brighter than the California false-hellebore, hopped out of my way into the creek. This was a Pacific treefrog, lime-green, with an elegant black eye-stripe—most distinctive character of the species. These frogs can vary

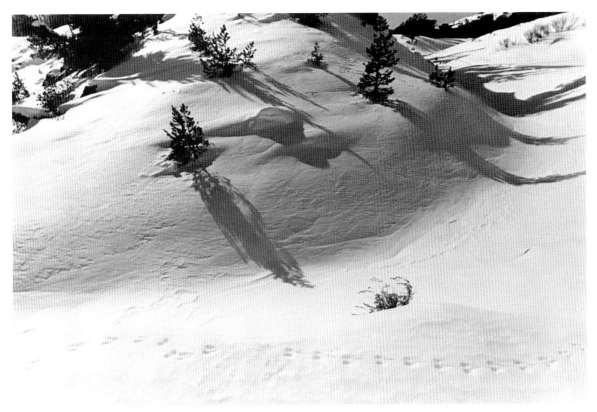

in color from dark brown to chameleon green
to match their surroundings, an individual
changing from the lightest to the darkest phase
it can muster in only eight to ten minutes. In
the bright subalpine sunlight of the summer
meadow, this frog stayed green.

It was not a lively season for the frog. It already had mated, a time when the males call
with a piercing "kreck-ek" generated with a
throat sac that expands to more than three
times the size of their head. No wonder a chorus
of Pacific treefrogs can "exclude most other
sounds," as herpetologist Robert Stebbins la-
conically puts it.

There is good reason for them to be noisy.
Like many frogs, Pacific treefrogs ensure mating within their species by singing notes distinctly different from other frogs. The double-
note of Pacific treefrogs allows them to find
their own species in the tumult of nighttime
mating choruses.

Now, in summer, the frog was relaxing after
its breeding season. All its energy went into
eating, snagging enough small insects to enter
fall hibernation healthy and plump and then to
wait in dark, unaware limbo for spring.

I came back to this meadow in winter and

snowshoed over the creek bed. Somewhere beneath the drift, in a miniature cave of frozen
earth, the frog must have been there still, its
feet tucked underneath it, waiting for spring
when rising temperatures would speed up its
metabolism once more.

We think of frogs as less-sophisticated animals than mammals. But Pacific treefrogs live
from sea level to above eleven thousand feet,
from hot deserts to tree line. They have pioneered islands off the California and Baja coast,
presumably floating out on accidental rafts of
vegetation. Naked, green, and noisy, with suc-
tion cups on their toes, they continue to live
successfully in all these places.

They do not live in isolation, however. On
the same day that I snowshoed above the hi-
bernating treefrog, I saw mammal tracks in
abundance. Voles and hares and mice had
scampered past in the snow, less seasonal if
not more sophisticated in metabolism than the
treefrog, for they can stay active throughout
the year with their constant internal climate-
control, warm-bloodedness.

Eastward beyond the Carson Range, Sierran
trees—and Sierran plants in general—barely

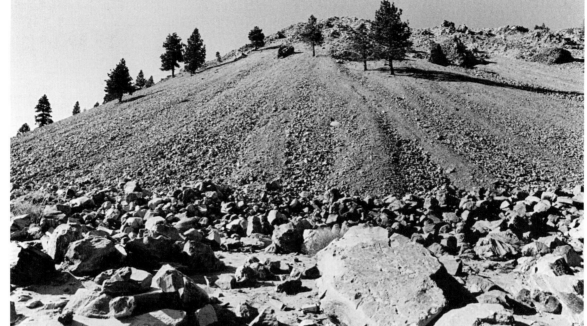

tumble over into the next line of ranges. Few Sierran trees can tolerate the enormous drop in moisture when they move east into the rain shadow. From Reno south to Bishop, spur ranges almost connect with the Sierra, but their trees give them away: these are Great Basin ranges.

The Pah Rah Range northeast of Reno has only ponderosa and Jeffrey pine. The Virginia Range, however, harbors white fir and lodgepole, whitebark, and western white pine in small numbers. Ponderosa and Jeffrey pine grow here, but only on volcanic rocks altered hydrothermally.

In another of his significant efforts to decipher Great Basin botany, Dwight Billings analyzed these Virginia Range conifer stands. Here the Sierran conifers grow in a matrix of piñon-juniper woodland, but only on phosphorus- and nitrogen-poor soil virtually uninhabitable by woodland trees and shrubs.

The common volcanic rock of the range is an andesite, much of it altered by hot water in mid-Tertiary time. These altered rocks weather to acidic clay poor in nutrients, and on these soils grow the Sierran pines. Billings believes the pines are relict from moister times, when

their forests covered much of the Virginia Range. Today they survive only where sagebrush and its allies cannot invade. The same story seems to account for these pines in the Pah Rah Range, where they also grow on hydrothermally altered rocks with some Sierran herbaceous plants—evident relicts from more continuous distributions. Nutcrackers and Pinyon Jays surely accomplish most new dispersal.

Such reduced competition seems to work to benefit other conifers, as well as a set of herbs not encountered again until the subalpine areas of the Carson Range. These soils weathered from altered rock mark the only place where sugar pine commonly grows on the east side of the Carson Range.

The next range south, the Pine Nut Mountains, comes close to connecting with the Sierra at Monitor Pass, and again western white pine makes it to the range. The Sweetwaters have extensive Sierran woods of white fir and lodgepole and Jeffrey pine, particularly on their south end, and a subalpine woodland of whitebark pine. Indeed, by one index of similarity, the range shares 90 and 93 percent, respectively, of its alpine and montane plants with the Sierra.

About thirty miles east of the Sweetwaters, past the Bodie Hills, lies the high Wassuk Range, the easternmost extension of Sierran granitic rock and fairly continuous high-elevation topography. Not surprisingly, the Wassuks harbor Jeffrey, western white, and probably whitebark pines, but these conifers grow no farther east. The Lahontan trough blocks them.

Jeffrey pines seem particularly good at pioneering beyond the Sierra. Along U.S. Highway 395 at Mono Craters, a dense stand of Jeffrey pine grows on pumice sands eastward to the Glass Mountains. The pine has managed this extension into piñon, juniper, and sagebrush country due east of the only significant gap in the Sierra crest between Lake Tahoe to south of Mount Whitney. Here storms push their way over the mountains to bring this area around Mammoth Lakes considerably more precipitation than elsewhere along the Sierra eastside.

Finally come the White Mountains, so close to the Sierra that the Palisade glaciers seem within reach on clear days, yet thoroughly isolated by the Owens Valley, thoroughly Great Basin. Lodgepole and ponderosa pines have pioneered in the White Mountains, but in only one canyon each. Jeffrey pine grows here on altered rocks. Fully one-third of the White Mountain plants are Great Basin/Rocky Mountain species. The lower altitudes have plants aligned with hot desert communities; Great Basin and Rocky Mountain plants dominate from mid-elevations to the subalpine; and a northwestern flora characterizes the highest elevations. Sierran species grow throughout but are most prevalent high on the north end of the range.

Beyond this first marshaling of ranges lies the low-elevation, hot, dry Lahontan trough. No Sierran conifer bridges this barrier. Beyond, forests of limber and bristlecone pine cloak the mountains for nearly two hundred miles before the western outliers of Rocky Mountain species begin to mingle with them.

In the northern Pacific mountain system, Cascade forests stop just as abruptly at the edge of the Great Basin. In Oregon, pine and fir forests of the Blue Mountains and Cascades fall away to sagebrush and an occasional western juniper. Sagebrush on lava covers sweeping plateaus between mountains, more like the Snake River Plain than central Nevada's regular succession of basin and range. In *Honey in the Horn,* H. L. Davis described this country: "There was little . . . to measure distance by except the time it took to traverse it."

Oregon's Basin ranges lie north of piñon and Utah juniper forests. Western juniper cloaks their foothills. The only other conifers reaching these isolated peaks are small groves of the Californian versions of white fir and ponderosa pine on Hart Mountain and grand fir in two canyons on Steens Mountain. These grand firs show traces of hybridization with white fir in the past, but the big trees are officially designated "grand"—their tiny stands deep, dank, and dark, one of the most majestic groves in the Great Basin.

Ponderosa pine also grows in a disjunct stand forty miles from Fort Rock, Oregon (and the nearest ponderosas). Here annual rainfall totals fewer than ten inches—half the average for ponderosa pine forest. Sandy soils that hold a little extra moisture allow this "lost forest" to survive, and also nourish some of the largest western junipers in the state.

Douglas-fir barely reaches past Susanville, California. At nearby Eagle Lake, in a high basin virtually in the shadow of Lassen Peak, Ospreys nest in ponderosas along the lakeshore. Here, too, California black oak extends eastward to the Great Basin.

Extreme northwestern Nevada (the East Warner Mountains and the adjacent Charles Sheldon Antelope Range) has a few additional outlying stands of white fir and ponderosa pine. But the Black Rock and Granite ranges and the Jackson Mountains rimming the Black Rock Desert have only junipers, no pines or firs. The Pine Forest Range has only whitebark pine, where it grows only on Sierran-style granitic rocks. The next range east, the Santa Rosas, supports only limber pine, a last western out-

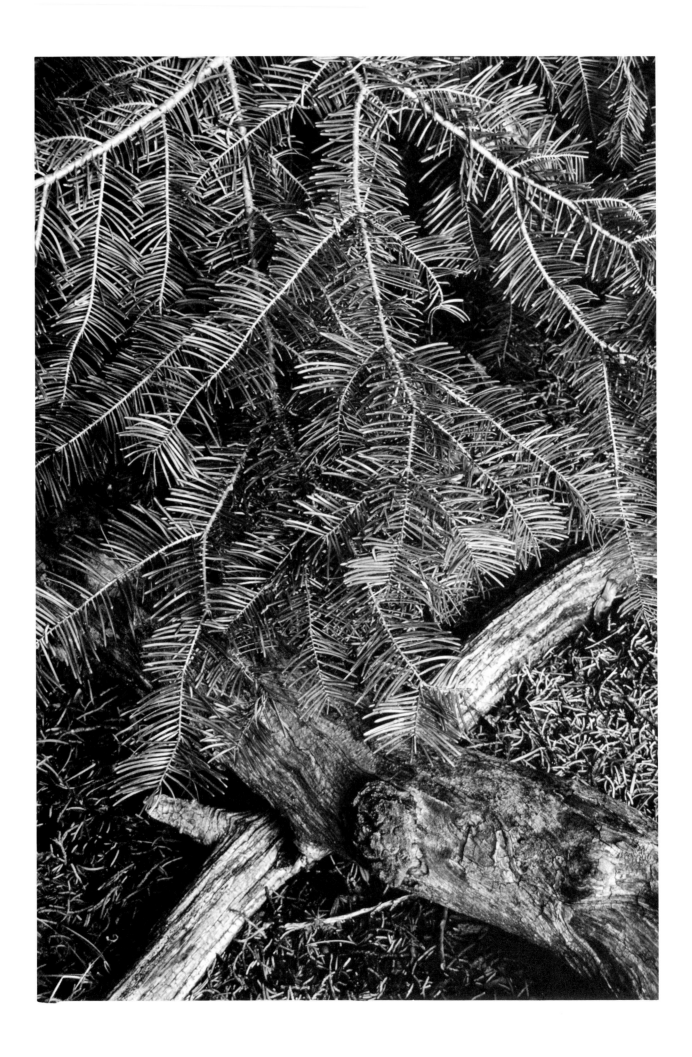

post of the Rocky Mountain conifers one hundred miles beyond their stronghold in the Independence and Jarbidge country.

Animals of deep Sierra woods match their distribution with the forest, not the trees. Ten kinds of mammals reach into the Great Basin only in the Carson Range and Tahoe area, not extending to the isolated disjuncts of pines and firs beyond. Black bear, marten, snowshoe hare, mountain beaver, northern flying squirrel, Trowbridge's shrew, mountain pocket gopher, and lodgepole, long-eared, and Townsend's chipmunk—all live eastward into the Basin only to the Carson Range. An additional twelve mammals ranging over other parts of Nevada have subspecies restricted (or nearly so) to this range. Douglas squirrels occur beyond the Carsons to the Pine Nut Mountains.

Some of these boreal mammals surely reached farther into the Basin in the Pleistocene. Continuous snow cover, if not forest, could have allowed passage across unforested valleys in winter for snowshoe hares and burrowing animals like montane voles.

The abrupt beginning of Great Basin climate at the foot of the Sierra profoundly affects the bird populations; the Lahontan trough obviously is not the primary barrier to high-flying bird colonists. About thirty distinctive California/Pacific/Sierra birds do not reach the Great Basin at all. In contrast, seven species characteristic of the Rockies range westward deep into the Basin. Many Rocky Mountain races range beyond the Lahontan trough to the Wassuk Range and the Sweetwater and White mountains. Other mountains along the transition (Carson Range, Pine Nut Mountains, Pine Grove Hills, and the Glass Mountains) have Sierran and widespread birds.

This climatic difference seems the most important demarcation line for both animals and plants. Rocky Mountain species have adapted to a harsh continental climate: cold, snowy winters and hot summers with afternoon thundershowers, but in no season the profligate abundance of moisture taken for granted close to the ocean. Animals and plants familiar with the Rockies find the Great Basin similar to home territory until the summer rains give out to the northwestward.

Sierra Nevada creatures, however, dramatically leave behind their home climate when they pass over the desert rim. Moisture suddenly becomes scarce. Trees shrink from two hundred feet to twenty feet. Lush understory gives way to sagebrush.

The epitome of lushness, Yosemite and the Range of Light, gives way to Mono Lake, Owens Valley, and the Land of Little Rain. In 1889, pioneer Great Basin geologist Israel Cook Russell described the transition: "One has the desolation and solitude of the Sahara, the other the rugged grandeur of the Pyrenees. Few journeys of equal length could present greater diversity in all the elements of scenery."

Perhaps more than anywhere, the Great Basin reveals its nature where it meets a landscape most dissimilar, as at the Sierra Nevada. Writer after writer waxes emotional looking east from the high peaks to the desert. The Carson Range, the first Basin range, straddles the transition in both topography and history.

The view from these mountains includes many worlds and suggestions of many times. The centuries of the Washoe, the People, who named Tahoe and lived closest to this land. The little lake off to the west called Donner, scene of tragic deeds that make one of the West's most harrowing stories.

At the south end of the Carson Range lies Jobs Peak, on whose summit a lightning bolt struck Clarence King in 1867; his "brain nerves were severely shocked," but he recovered to publish his version of the view from the peak, finish his survey of the fortieth parallel, and become first director of the U.S. Geological Survey. Across the valley southeastward lies the Virginia Range, mother of the Comstock Lode and generator of enough human energy to help forge a Mark Twain. On the summit of Mount Rose stand the ruins of an old stone weather station built by James E. Church in 1905 and prototype for the modern science of snow surveying.

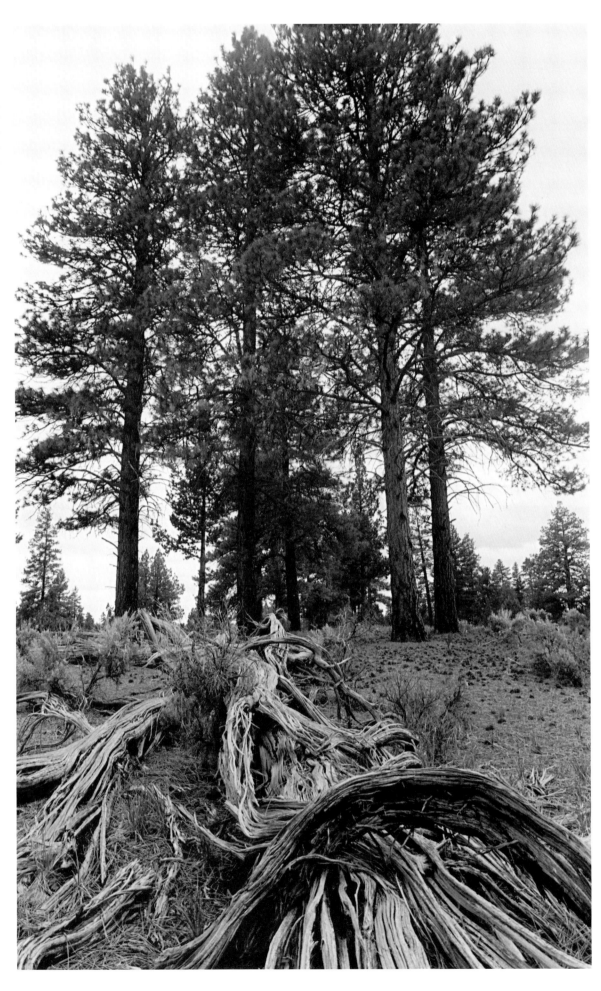

Forty miles from the nearest ponderosa pines, far out in Fort Rock basin, the ponderosas in Oregon's "lost forest" depend for survival on sandy soil that holds extra moisture.

Mount Rose hangs as talisman over every event in the life of Tim Hazard, central character in Walter Van Tilburg Clark's 1945 novel *The City of Trembling Leaves*. In Tim's day (and in Clark's Reno boyhood), to reach Lake Tahoe from Reno one walked over Mount Rose. The Mount Rose Highway did not exist. Tim went up to the mountain at crucial times in his life, yearning for its "purity."

Tim took his great love, Rachel Wells, to Mount Rose. He shared his meadows, his mountain, and his gods with her. "Until you are greatly moved by the beauty of mountain sadness and loneliness, and for a moment perceive time according to stars and wholly without mathematics . . . there is almost no use in coming."

From the summit:

> Far down in the basin in the west, lay Lake Tahoe, shrunken, and fitted neatly into all its bays and inlets in the wooded mountains. . . . But it was when they turned east that the world spread out under them, pale, painted, turbulent mountains, range after range toward the sky which curved beyond the shoulder of the world, all of them subdued by sun except the very last, a thin and broken edge of snow. In the north-east, through a distant pass, glittered an illusory sliver of Pyramid Lake. . . . It was the pale, burning and shadowed east that led the mind out.

The last time I stood on the summit of Mount Rose, smog lay over the Truckee Meadows too thickly to see Pyramid Lake. Tahoe was barely visible and no longer had the quiet and unblemished purity that moved Clark to call it an "unconscious saint." When the National Park Service sent out an investigator to evaluate Lake Tahoe's suitability as a national park in the twenties, he deemed it too developed to be suitable; today we lament a lake thoroughly casinoed and condominiumized.

Clark was right. The real Basin ranges—"pale, painted, turbulent mountains"—draw your eye eastward.

On Mount Rose, Tim Hazard said: "This . . . is what I've been after. . . . It was the suspension, without desire, without regret, with only the lucid, independent present, which was the gift of the mountain."

We share in this mountain's gift. We live in the present, with the desert.

In this desert lies an ocean of shrubs, several hundred mountain ranges, a few dozen ranches and towns, and considerably more dune grasshoppers, kangaroo rats, and Pinyon Jays. More than anything else, however, in this Great Basin lies a message about time.

I look out from Mount Rose to the eastern ranges, to the sharp raw blocks studding the smooth Basin, the lilting sequence of basin and range leading away toward Utah. I look into a haze, the present distilled from the past, the future discernible in the rawboned tans to some sufficiently visionary seer.

Dynamic plants and animals dominate the Great Basin's past. It has been a desert for only a few thousand years. Before that a lake covered much of this view, forest the rest. Still earlier this land was grassland, jungle, ocean.

A century ago, Israel Russell ended his classic work on Mono Lake with a prediction: "If the imperfect data now at hand may be trusted, it seems as if the last geologic change of climate had not yet culminated, and that increased humidity in the Great Basin might be expected in the future."

The future of this sagebrush ocean is bound to bring change. Time, climate, life, and history have "not yet culminated" here. They never will.

Appendix
Scientific Names of
Plants and Animals

PLANTS

alder
   thinleaf (mountain)   *Alnus tenuifolia*
alumroot
   Duran's   *Heuchera duranii*
Apache plume   *Fallugia paradoxa*
aspen
   quaking   *Populus tremuloides*
avens
   Ross's   *Geum rossii*
barberry
   creeping   *Berberis repens*
birch
   water (spring)   *Betula occidentalis*
bistort
   American   *Polygonum bistortoides*
bitterbrush
   antelope   *Purshia tridentata*
   desert (waxy)   *Purshia glandulosa*
blackbrush   *Coleogyne ramosissima*
blueberry
   dwarf   *Vaccinium caespitosum*
buckwheat
   subalpine wild   *Eriogonum ovalifolium*
       ssp. *vineum*
   White Mountain wild   *Erigonum gracilepes*
bud sagebrush   *Artemisia spinescens*
buffaloberry
   silver   *Shepherdia argentea*
bulrush
   three-square   *Scirpus americanus*
burreed   *Sparganium* sp.
buttercup
   snowbed   *Ranunculus eschscholtzii*
cactus
   cholla and prickly pear   *Opuntia* spp.
candytuft
   fernleaf   *Smelowskia calycina*
cattail
   broad leaf   *Typha latifolia*
chinquapin
   bush   *Castanopsis sempervirens*
chokecherry   *Prunus virginiana*
cinquefoil
   shrubby   *Potentilla fruticosa*

cliffrose   *Cowania mexicana* var. *stansburiana*
clover
   Mono   *Trifolium monoense*
columbine   *Aquilegia* sp.
cottonwood
   black   *Populus trichocarpa*
   Fremont   *Populus fremontii*
   narrowleaf   *Populus angustifolia*
creosote bush   *Larrea tridentata*
currant   *Ribes* spp.
deerbrush   *Ceanothus integerrimus*
desert blite   *Suaeda* sp.
desert thorn
   Cooper's   *Lycium cooperi*
dock
   sand   *Rumex hymenosepalus*
dogwood
   American (red-osier)   *Cornus sericea*
Douglas-fir   *Pseudotsuga menziesii*
draba
   Sierra   *Draba sierrae*
elderberry   *Sambucus* spp.
elephant's-head
   bull   *Pedicularis groenlandica*
ephedra
   green   *Ephedra viridis*
evening primrose   *Oenothera* spp.
false-hellebore (corn lily)
   California   *Veratrum californicum*
false-Solomon's-seal
   starry   *Smilacina stellata*
fern bush   *Chamaebatiaria millefolium*
filaree
   redstem   *Erodium cicutarium*
fir
   grand   *Abies grandis*
   California red   *Abies magnifica*
   subalpine   *Abies lasiocarpa*
   white   *Abies concolor*
four o'clock   *Mirabilis* sp.
glasswort
   Utah   *Sarcocornia utahensis*

goat's-beard
  meadow — *Tragopogon dubius*
gooseberry — *Ribes* spp.
grass
  alkali sacaton — *Sporobolus airoides*
  bluebunch wheatgrass — *Agropyron spicatum*
  blue grama — *Bouteloua gracilis*
  bottle-brush grass
    (squirreltail) — *Elymus elymoides (Sitanion hystrix)*
  cheat (downy brome) — *Bromus tectorum*
  common reed — *Phragmites australis*
  crested wheatgrass — *Agropyron cristatum*
  desert wheatgrass — *Agropyron desertorum*
  galleta — *Hilaria jamesii*
  Idaho fescue — *Festuca idahoensis*
  Indian ricegrass — *Oryzopsis hymenoides*
  medusahead — *Taeniatherum asperum*
  prairie junegrass — *Koeleria macrantha*
  Sandberg's bluegrass — *Poa secunda*
  sand dropseed — *Sporobolus cryptandrus*
  sewing needle-and-thread — *Stipa comata*
  Thurber's needlegrass — *Stipa thurberiana*
greasewood
  Bailey's (little) — *Sarcobatus baileyi*
  big — *Sarcobatus vermiculatus*
halogeton — *Halogeton glomeratus*
hedgemustard
  tall — *Sisymbrium altissimum*
hemlock
  mountain — *Tsuga mertensiana*
heron-bill
  redstem — *Erodium cicutarium*
hopsage
  spiny — *Grayia spinosa*
horned-pondweed — *Zannichellia palustris*
horsebrush
  littleleaf — *Tetradymia glabrata*
horsetail — *Equisetum* spp.
incense-cedar — *Calocedrus decurrens*
iodine bush — *Allenrolfea occidentalis*
Joshua tree — *Yucca brevifolia*
juniper
  dwarf — *Juniperus communis*
  Rocky Mountain — *Juniperus scopulorum*
  Utah — *Juniperus osteosperma*
  western — *Juniperus occidentalis*
    mountain — *Juniperus occidentalis* ssp. *australis*
king's crown — *Sedum rosea*
laurel
  swamp — *Kalmia polifolia*
lily, corn (see false-hellebore)
locoweed — *Astragulus* spp.
lupine — *Lupinus* spp.
mallow
  globemallow — *Sphaeralcea* sp.
manzanita
  greenleaf — *Arctostaphylos patula*

maple
  canyon — *Acer grandidentatum*
  Rocky Mountain (dwarf) — *Acer glabrum*
marsh-marigold
  slender-sepal — *Caltha leptosepala*
meadow-rue
  alpine — *Thalictrum alpinum*
molly
  green — *Kochia americana*
monkeyflower — *Mimulus* sp.
monkshood
  Columbia — *Aconitum columbianum*
Mormon tea — *Ephedra viridis*
moss campion — *Silene acaulis*
mountain-mahogany
  curlleaf — *Cercocarpus ledifolius*
  littleleaf — *Cercocarpus intricatus*
mountain-sorrel — *Oxyria digyna*
mustard
  pinnate tansy — *Descurainia pinnata*
ninebark — *Physocarpus* sp.
oak
  California black — *Quercus kelloggii*
  Gambel — *Quercus gambelii*
  shrub live — *Quercus turbinella*
onion — *Allium* sp.
orchid
  bog — *Habenaria dilatata*
paintbrush — *Castilleja* sp.
peach
  desert — *Prunus andersonii*
penstemon
  Palmer's — *Penstemon palmerii*
phlox
  carpet — *Phlox caespitosa* ssp. *pulvinata*
  Coville's — *Phlox covillei*
pine
  Great Basin bristlecone — *Pinus longaeva*
  Jeffrey — *Pinus jeffreyi*
  limber — *Pinus flexilis*
  lodgepole — *Pinus contorta*
  ponderosa — *Pinus ponderosa*
  sugar — *Pinus lambertiana*
  Washoe — *Pinus washoensis*
  western white — *Pinus monticola*
  whitebark — *Pinus albicaulis*
piñon
  Colorado — *Pinus edulis*
  singleleaf — *Pinus monophylla*
pondweed — *Potamogeton* sp.
poplar
  Lombardy — *Populus nigra* var. *italica*
prickly-phlox
  granite — *Leptodactylon pungens*
prickly-poppy
  white — *Argemone munita*
primrose
  Nevada — *Primula nevadensis*

Parry's — *Primula parryi*
pussy-toes
  rosy — *Antennaria rosea*
rabbitbrush
  green — *Chrysothamnus viscidiflorus*
rockmat
  tufted — *Petrophyllum caespitosum*
rose
  Wood's (wild) — *Rosa woodsii*
rush
  Baltic — *Juncus balticus*
Russian thistle — *Salsola* sp.
sagebrush
  big — *Artemisia tridentata*
    basin — *Artemisia tridentata* ssp. *tridentata*
    mountain — *Artemisia tridentata* ssp. *vaseyana*
    subalpine — *Artemisia tridentata* ssp. *spiciformis*
    Wyoming — *Artemisia tridentata* ssp. *wyomingensis*
  alkali — *Artemisia longiloba*
  dwarf — *Artemisia arbuscula*
    black — *Artemisia arbuscula* var. *nova*
  pygmy — *Artemisia pygmaea*
salsify — *Tragopogon dubius*
saltbush
  four-winged — *Atriplex canescens*
saltgrass — *Distichlis spicata* var. *stricta*
saltsage — *Atriplex tridentata*
  sickle — *Atriplex falcata*
saltwort
  red — *Salicornia rubra*
scurfpea
  lance-leaf — *Psoralea lanceolata*
seepweed — *Suaeda* sp.
sedge
  black-root (elk) — *Carex elynoides*
  Holm's Rocky Mountain — *Carex scopulorum*
serviceberry
  western — *Amelanchier alnifolia*
shadscale — *Atriplex confertifolia*
smokebush — *Psorothamnus polydenius*
snakeweed — *Gutierrezia sarothrae*
snowberry — *Symphoricarpos* spp.
snowbrush — *Ceanothus velutinus*
spikerush — *Eleocharis* sp.
spruce
  Engelmann — *Picea engelmannii*
stone crop
  pink — *Sedum rosea*
tamarisk — *Tamarix* spp.
thistle
  Steens Mountain — *Cirsium peckii*

tobacco brush — *Ceanothus velutinus*
water milfoil — *Myriophyllum* sp.
wildrye
  giant — *Elymus giganteus*
  Great Basin — *Elymus cinereus*
willow
  arctic — *Salix arctica*
winterfat — *Ceratoides lanata*
woolly-sunflower
  Mono — *Eriophyllum lanatum* var. *monoense*
wolfberry (Cooper's desert thorn) — *Lycium cooperi*
yucca
  Mojave — *Yucca schidigera*

INVERTEBRATES

ant
  harvester — *Pogonomyrmex* sp.
beetles
  tenebrionid — *Eleodes* sp.
brine flies
  Great Salt Lake — *Ephydra cinerea* & *E. hians*
  Mono — *Ephydra hians*
brine shrimp
  Great Salt Lake — *Artemia salina*
  Mono — *Artemia monica*
grasshoppers
  dune — *Trimerotropis arenacea* & *T. barnumi*
Mormon cricket — *Anabrus simplex*
sagebrush webworm — *Aroga websteri*
shrimp
  clam — Conchostraca
  fairy — Anostraca
  tadpole — Notostraca

FISH

bass
  white — *Morone chrysops*
carp
  common — *Cyprinus carpio*
chub
  Alvord — *Gila alvordensis*
  tui — *Gila bicolor*
dace
  desert — *Eremichthys acros*
  speckled — *Rhinichthys osculus*
springfish
  Railroad Valley — *Crenichthys nevadae*
sucker
  cui-ui — *Chasmistes cujus*
  Tahoe — *Catostomus tahoensis*
trout
  brook — *Salvelinus fontinalis*

brown	*Salmo trutta*	Snowy	*Egretta thula*
cutthroat		Finch	
Bonneville	*Salmo clarki utah*	Rosy	*Leucosticte arctoa*
Humboldt	*Salmo clarki henshawi*	Flicker	
Lahontan	*Salmo clarki henshawi*	Northern	*Colaptes auratus*
rainbow	*Salmo gairdneri*	Goose	
		Canada	*Branta canadensis*

AMPHIBIANS AND REPTILES

boa		Grebe	
rubber	*Charina bottae*	Clark's	*Aechmophorus clarkii*
lizard		Eared	*Podiceps nigricollis*
desert spiny	*Sceloporus magister*	Western	*Aechmophorus occidentalis*
leopard	*Crotaphytus wislizenii*	Grouse	
sagebrush	*Sceloporus graciosus*	Sage	*Centrocercus urophasianus*
side-blotched	*Uta stansburiana*		
western whiptail	*Cnemidophorus tigris*	Gull	
zebra-tailed	*Callisaurus draconoides*	California	*Larus californicus*
rattlesnake		Harrier	
Great Basin western	*Crotalus viridis lutosus*	Northern	*Circus cyaneus*
snake		Hawk	
gopher	*Pituophis melanoleucus*	Ferruginous	*Buteo regalis*
western ground	*Sonora semiannulata*	Red-tailed	*Buteo jamaicensis*
western patch-nosed	*Salvadora hexalepsis*	Heron	
treefrog		Great Blue	*Ardea herodias*
Pacific	*Hyla regilla*	Ibis	
		White-faced	*Plegadis chihi*
		Jay	
		Pinyon	*Gymnorhinus cyanocephalus*

BIRDS		Scrub	*Aphelocoma coerulescens*
		Steller's	*Cyanocitta stelleri*
Avocet		Junco	
American	*Recurvirostra americana*	Dark-eyed	*Junco hyemalis*
Blackbird		Kestrel	
Yellow-headed	*Xanthocephalus xanthocephalus*	American	*Falco sparverius*
		Killdeer	*Charadrius vociferus*
Bushtit	*Psaltriparus minimus*	Kingbird	
Canvasback	*Aythya valisineria*	Western	*Tyrannus verticalis*
Chat		Kinglet	
Yellow-breasted	*Icteria virens*	Golden-crowned	*Regulus satrapa*
Chickadee		Ruby-crowned	*Regulus calendula*
Mountain	*Parus gambeli*	Lark	
Chukar	*Alectoris chukar*	Horned	*Eremophila alpestris*
Coot		Nighthawk	
American	*Fulica americana*	Common	*Chordeiles minor*
Cormorant		Nutcracker	
Double-crested	*Phalacrocorax auritus*	Clark's	*Nucifraga columbiana*
Crane		Oriole	
Sandhill	*Grus canadensis*	Northern	*Icterus galbula*
Creeper		Scott's	*Icterus parisorum*
Brown	*Certhia americana*	Osprey	*Pandion haliaetus*
Cuckoo		Owl	
Yellow-billed	*Coccyzus americanus*	Burrowing	*Athene cunicularia*
Dove		Pelican	
Mourning	*Zenaida macroura*	American White	*Pelecanus erythrorhynchos*
Eagle			
Golden	*Aquila chrysaetos*	Phalarope	
Egret		Red-necked	*Phalaropus lobatus*
Great	*Casmerodius albus*	Wilson's	*Phalaropus tricolor*

Pigeon
  Band-tailed   *Columba fasciata*
Pintail
  Northern   *Anas acuta*
Pipit
  Water   *Anthus spinoletta*
Plover
  Snowy   *Charadrius*
                         alexandrinus

Raven
  Common   *Corvus corax*
Redhead   *Aythya americana*
Robin
  American   *Turdus migratorius*
Sapsucker
  Williamson's   *Sphyrapicus thyroideus*
  Yellow-bellied   *Sphyrapicus varius*
Shrike
  Loggerhead   *Lanius ludovicianus*
  Northern   *Lanius excubitor*
Solitaire
  Townsend's   *Myadestes townsendi*
Sparrow
  Black-throated   *Amphispiza bilineata*
  Brewer's   *Spizella breweri*
  Sage   *Amphispiza belli*
  Song   *Melospiza melodia*
  White-crowned   *Zonotrichia leucophrys*
Stilt
  Black-necked   *Himantopus mexicanus*
Swan
  Trumpeter   *Cygnus buccinator*
  Tundra   *Cygnus columbianus*
Tern
  Caspian   *Sterna caspia*
Thrasher
  Sage   *Oreoscoptes montanus*
Titmouse
  Plain   *Parus inornatus*
Towhee
  Green-tailed   *Pipilo chlorurus*
Vireo
  Gray   *Vireo vicinior*
Warbler
  Grace's   *Dendroica graciae*
  Yellow   *Dendroica petechia*
Woodpecker
  Black-backed   *Picoides arcticus*
Wren
  Marsh   *Cistothorus palustris*
  Rock   *Salpinctes obsoletus*

MAMMALS

badger   *Taxidea taxus*
bear
  black   *Ursus americanus*
  grizzly   *Ursus arctos*

beaver   *Castor canadensis*
bison   *Bison bison*
bobcat   *Lynx rufus*
chipmunk   (*Tamias* = *Eutamias*)
  cliff   *Tamias dorsalis*
  least   *Tamias minimus*
  lodgepole   *Tamias speciosus*
  long-eared   *Tamias*
                         quadrimaculatus
  Townsend's   *Tamias townsendii*
  Uinta   *Tamias umbrinus*
  yellow pine   *Tamias amoenus*
cougar   *Felis concolor*
coyote   *Canis latrans*
deer
  mule   *Odocoileus hemionus*
elk   *Cervus elaphus*
ermine (short-tailed weasel) *Mustela erminea*
fox
  kit   *Vulpes macrotis*
goat
  mountain   *Oreamnos americanus*
ground squirrel
  golden-mantled   *Spermophilus lateralis*
  white-tailed antelope *Ammospermophilus*
                         leucurus
hare
  snowshoe (varying hare
    or snowshoe rabbit) *Lepus americanus*
jackrabbit
  black-tailed   *Lepus californicus*
  white-tailed   *Lepus townsendii*
kangaroo mouse
  dark   *Microdipodops*
                         megacephalus
  pale   *Microdipodops pallidus*
kangaroo rat
  chisel-toothed   *Dipodomys microps*
  desert   *Dipodomys deserti*
  Merriam's   *Dipodomys merriami*
  Ord's   *Dipodomys ordii*
  Panamint   *Dipodomys*
                         panamintinus
marmot
  yellow-bellied   *Marmota flaviventris*
marten   *Martes americana*
mountain beaver   *Aplodontia rufa*
mountain lion   *Felis concolor*
mouse
  canyon   *Peromyscus crinitus*
  deer   *Peromyscus*
                         maniculatus
  northern grasshopper *Onychomys leucogaster*
  piñon   *Peromyscus truei*
  southern grasshopper *Onychomys torridus*
  western harvest   *Reithrodontomys*
                         megalotis
muskrat   *Ondatra zibethicus*
pack rat (wood rat)   *Neotoma* spp.
pika   *Ochotona princeps*

pocket gopher		Trowbridge's	*Sorex trowbridgii*
Botta's	*Thomomys bottae (Thomomys umbrinus)*	squirrel	
		Abert's	*Sciurus aberti*
		Douglas	*Tamiasciurus douglasii*
mountain	*Thomomys monticola*	northern flying	*Glaucomys sabrinus*
northern	*Thomomys talpoides*	red	*Tamiasciurus hudsonicus*
pocket mouse			
little	*Perognathus longimembris*	vole	
		boreal (southern) redback	*Clethrionomys gapperi*
long-tailed	*Perognathus formosus*	heather	*Phenacomys intermedius*
porcupine	*Erethizon dorsatum*		
pronghorn ("antelope")	*Antilocapra americana*	meadow	*Microtus pennsylvanicus*
rabbit		montane	*Microtus montanus*
desert cottontail	*Sylvilagus audubonii*	sagebrush	*Lagurus curtatus*
Nuttall's cottontail	*Sylvilagus nuttallii*	weasel	
pygmy	*Sylvilagus idahoensis*	long-tailed	*Mustela frenata*
snowshoe (snowshoe hare)	*Lepus americanus*	short-tailed (see ermine)	
		wood rat (pack rat)	
raccoon	*Procyon lotor*	bushy-tailed	*Neotoma cinerea*
sheep		desert	*Neotoma lepida*
bighorn (mountain)	*Ovis canadensis*	wolf	
shrew		gray	*Canis lupus*
Merriam's	*Sorex merriami*	wolverine	*Gulo gulo (Gulo luscus)*

228

———

Appendix

Notes

1. The Four Great Basins

The best introduction to the Great Basin as a physiographic division of the continent is Hunt (1974). McPhee (1980) makes Basin and Range geology into a great story. A National Park Service study (1981) offers a general overview of the national park proposals in the Snake Range.

The literature on the historic Great Basin is rich. See Bartlett and Goetzmann (1982) and Jackson (1975) for an introduction; Stegner (1942), Cline (1963), Stewart (1962), Holliday (1981), and Wheeler (1972) for more detail; Gilbert (1983) for Joe Walker; and DeVoto's magnificent *The Year of Decision: 1846* (1942) most of all. The Frémont quote comes from Nevins (1956). Hollon (1966) muses about the concept of the "Great American Desert." George (1977) discusses deserts with a global perspective.

The sequence of scientific papers defining the Great Basin Desert leads from Shreve (1942) through Jaeger (1957) to Holmgren (1972, who also divides the Basin in floristic sections) and MacMahon (1979).

2. The Making of a Desert

Great Basin weather patterns are summarized in Stevens (forthcoming). See Houghton, Sakamoto, and Gifford (1975) for Nevada, Jackson and Stevens (1981) for Utah Valley, and Ferguson and Ferguson (1978) for southeastern Oregon (the latter also contains a good review of desert adaptations). The Egyptian ecologist's quote comes from MacMahon (1979), the Shreve quote from his 1934 paper, the Twain quotes from *Roughing It* (1872), and the others from Eiseley (1978), Leopold (1949), and Dillard (1982).

I based the discussion of desert adaptations mostly on Whittaker (1975). For more technical detail, see papers in Goodall and Perry (1979). A good source for jackrabbit ecology is McAdoo and Young (1980).

3. Natural Communities

For reviews of community classification, see Dice (1952) and Whittaker (1975). See also Merriam (1898); MacMahon and Wieboldt (1978) for application of the Holdridge scheme to Utah; Gleason and Cronquist (1964) for floristic provinces; and Steele et al. (1979) for a review of the habitat-type concept and an almanac of southeast Idaho forest h.t.'s.

Billings (1952) discusses the effect of environment on plants. Holmgren (1972) gives the basic background for Great Basin communities. Brown and Gibson (1983) approach biogeography from the same wide-ranging perspective that I use here.

The Frémont quote is from Nevins (1956); other quotes are from Reveal (1979) and Billings (1951)— the latter the best summary of Great Basin life zones. Loope (1969) and Lewis (1971) provide details of Ruby Mountain plant communities.

4. Great Basin Paleobiogeography

Great Basin biogeography prior to the Pleistocene comes from Cronquist (1978), Daubenmire (1978), and Tidwell, Rushforth, and Simper (1972). See Hintze (1973) and Stokes (1986) as background for Utah geology, Stewart (1980) for Nevada, and Fiero (1986) for the Great Basin in general.

The three crucial references for the story of the Great Basin Pleistocene are Reveal (1979), Thompson and Mead (1982), and Wells (1983). Davis (1984) discusses seasonal differences in Hypsithermal maximum temperatures. See also Van Devender and Spaulding (1979) for the greater Southwest, and Thompson (1978) for further details on the Snake Range. Martin and Wright (1967) introduce the overkill hypothesis; Kurten and Anderson (1980) and Martin and Klein (1984) further discuss Pleistocene extinctions.

5. Mountains as Islands

The Cronquist quote comes from his paper in *Intermountain Biogeography: A Symposium* (Harper and Reveal, 1978), which includes the biggest concentration of papers examining the Great Basin in the light of island biogeographical theory (Billings for alpine plants; Harper, et al. for whole floras; Behle and Johnson for birds; and Brown for birds and mammals). See also earlier papers by Johnson (1975) and Brown (1971a) and the more recent Brown and Gibson (1983).

For the original papers on the equilibrium theory,

see MacArthur and Wilson (1963, 1967) and Mac-Arthur (1972). Brown (1978) and Brown and Gibson (1983) provide a good summary; Gilbert (1980) offers a tough critique.

See Grayson (1981) for Gatecliff Shelter records; Grayson (1977) for Fort Rock basin; Thompson and Mead (1982) for Smith Creek Cave (and good general discussion); Grayson (1982) for mammals; and Wells (1983) for the conifers of the east-central Basin and more general discussion.

6. Playas and Salt Deserts

For quotes, see Culmer (1909) and Schiel's description of the Great Salt Lake Desert in Bachmann and Wallace (1957). As always, for general orientation, see Holmgren (1972) and Reveal (1979). Branson, Miller, and McQueen (1967) evaluate the various schemes of classification of salt desert shrub communities. See also Skougard (1976). Mozingo (1987) discusses all Great Basin shrubs.

Wheeler (1978) summarizes the history and natural history of the Black Rock Desert. Holliday (1981) follows the overlanders across the desert. Stewart (1951) wrote a slightly fictionalized account of a writer living for a year at Black Rock Point.

Crawford (1981) summarizes playa invertebrate biology. Flowers (1934) and Flowers and Evans (1966) describe the Great Salt Lake Desert. Fautin (1946) and Vest (1962) expand Flowers's work in massive detail. Comparable detail for the Lahontan basin comes from Billings (1945, 1949).

7. Shadscale: The New Desert

Kearney et al. (1914) did pioneer work in Tooele Valley, quoted in my text. As in the playa chapter, see Fautin (1946), Vest (1962), and Billings (1945, 1949). Beatley's papers (1975, 1976) are the best source for shadscale country on the edge of the Mojave Desert in southern Nevada. See Bakker (1971) for a well-written nontechnical synthesis of California communities, including Great Basin Desert valleys.

Rogers (1982) documents vegetation change in the Bonneville basin with photographs. Foster (1965) summarizes Utah Great Basin plant communities. See Scott et al. (1983) for the latest thinking on cycles of Lake Bonneville.

For more detail on winterfat, see Workman and West (1967), Eckert (1954), and Tueller (1966). For budsage, see Wood (1966). My discussion of animal distribution patterns uses Armstrong (1977), Hall (1946), Reveal (1979), Pianka (1967), and Tanner (1978). Larrison and Johnson (1973) looked at rodents in Raft River Valley. Kenagy (1972, 1973) tells the chisel-toothed kangaroo rat story.

Stutz's work (1978, 1979; Stutz, Melby, and Livingston, 1975; Stutz, Pope, and Sanderson, 1979; and Stutz and Sanderson, 1979) traces the *Atriplex* story. Evans, Young, et al. tell the halogeton story. The quote from Frischknecht appears in his 1967 paper.

See Cottam (1947) for a classic analysis of the desertification of the Intermountain grasslands. Stewart, Cottam, and Hutchings (1940) document grazing impact. West (1979b) found better survival of grazed plants than traditionally expected; see also his 1982 summary of chenopod community dynamics. Evans and Young (1980) discuss invasion of barbwire Russian thistle.

Neil West's 1968 salt desert shrub bibliography lists nearly all important work up to that date.

8. Ocean of Sagebrush

Mark Twain (1872) vividly described the Carson Sink, the Great Salt Lake Desert, and other Basin landscapes, in addition to his famous sagebrush commentary. Holmgren (1972), Vale (1973, 1975), West (1983), Tueller (1975), and the Utah State University sagebrush symposium volume (1979) provide general reviews of the sagebrush community.

For deeper understanding of sagebrush taxonomy (including keys for field identification), see the series of papers by McArthur (McArthur, 1979, 1983; McArthur and Plummer, 1978; McArthur et al., 1979; McArthur, Pope, and Freeman, 1981); and by Winward (Winward and Tisdale, 1977; Winward, 1980, 1981).

Descriptions of specific sagebrush habitat types include Young, Evans, and Major (1977) for California; Franklin and Dyrness (1973) for Oregon; Zamora and Tueller (1973) for low sage communities in Nevada; Beatley (1976) for southern Nevada; and Hironaka and Fosberg (1981) for southern Idaho.

Christensen and Johnson (1964) and Hull and Hull (1974) document the amount of grass on sagebrush range prior to grazing. Rogers (1982) records historic changes in vegetation in a good summary text and remarkable paired photographs.

For summaries of sagebrush animal communities, see Fautin (1946) and West (1983), who cites several papers to which I refer and gives the details of the Curlew Valley jackrabbit research. See Hall (1946) for mammals and Ryser (1985) for birds. Yoakum (1980) summarizes considerable information on pronghorn; Klebenow (1972) does the same for Sage Grouse. Wiley (1973) describes Sage Grouse mating behavior. See Green and Flinders (1980) for the story of pygmy rabbits and sagebrush. Hatley and Mac-Mahon (1980) and Allred (1975) discuss spiders.

The DeVoto quote (1942) hints at the rich historical perspective and superb writing offered in his book. Piemeisel (1951) summarizes the early work on cheatgrass; Mack (1984) gives a recent overview. But the prolific Young and Evans tell the story of historic changes better than anyone (Evans and Young, 1970;

Young and Evans, 1970, 1978; Young, Evans, and Major, 1971; Young, Evans, and Kay, 1975; Young, Evans, and Tueller, 1976; Young, Eckert, and Evans, 1979). See also Young and Sparks (1985).

Leopold (1949) includes an essay on cheatgrass. Christensen (1970) summarizes Chukar biology. West et al. (1984) document decreases in grasses even when grazing ceases. West (1979a) examines future management choices. And Ferguson and Ferguson (1983) present a detailed and devastating documentation of the abuse of federal rangelands by the livestock industry.

9. The World of Dunes

In *Desert Notes* (1976) Barry Lopez speaks of the Great Basin—particularly playas and sere valleys like the Alvord and Black Rock deserts—with a unique voice, in short pieces that lie somewhere between essays and poetry. This quote comes from the piece "The Wind."

Billings (1945) describes Lahontan dunes, Vest (1962), Bonneville dunes. Bowers (1982, 1986) reviews dune plant ecology in the West. Stutz, Melby, and Livingston (1975) report on the unique Little Sahara four-winged saltbush.

Brown's papers on seed-eating desert rodents refer to most related important work (Brown, 1973, 1975; Brown and Lieberman, 1973; Brown, Reichman, and Davidson, 1979; Bowers and Brown, 1982). See Ghiselin (1970) for kangaroo mice and McAdoo et al. (1983) for the influence of heteromyids on ricegrass. Thompson (1982) gives details of his observations of color-coded heteromyids.

10. Great Basin Wetlands

Little work has been published on riparian forest; see Thomas et al. (1980); Tueller (1975); Minckley and Brown (1982); and Wells (1983) for the origin of "swamp cedar." Ned Johnson's work on riparian birds appears in the indispensable Intermountain biogeography symposium volume (Johnson, 1978). See Hunt (1974) for a discussion of arroyo cutting. Klebenow and Oakleaf (1981) reevaluate Ridgway's Truckee River data. Ridgway (1877) includes classic early descriptions of Great Basin birds and environments. Lesperance et al. (1978) and Walker (1981) tell the wildrye story.

Bolen (1964) has studied Great Basin marsh ecology in greatest detail, at Fish Springs. For Malheur, see Duebbert (1969), for Lahontan basin marshes, Billings (1945). Hubbs, Miller, and Hubbs (1974); Behnke and Zarn (1976); Smith (1978); and Sigler and Sigler (1987) summarize the biogeography of Great Basin fish.

Several lakes have merited books and monographs that include history and geology as well as ecology:

Utah Lake (Heckmann and Merritt, 1981); Pyramid Lake (Wheeler, 1974); Great Salt Lake (Morgan, 1947; Stokes, 1984); and Mono Lake (Gaines et al., 1981). See also the classic Russell monographs (1885, 1889). For additional detail on Great Salt Lake, see also Stansbury (1852), Woodbury (1936), Flowers and Evans (1966), Jackson (1975), and Ryser (1985). For Mono Lake, see Winkler (1977). Contact the Mono Lake Committee, P.O. Box 29, Lee Vining, California 93541 for the latest update on Mono Lake's problems and to volunteer your help.

11. The Piñon-Juniper Woodland

Ronald Lanner's 1981 book on the piñon contains a wealth of exceedingly well written information on the pine and its woodland, particularly on evolution, relationships with jays, and chaining controversies. He also wrote the introductory chapter on the Southwestern piñons and junipers in the very useful piñon-juniper symposium volume (Utah State University, 1975).

For specific areas, see Jackman and Long (1977) and Franklin and Dyrness (1973) for Oregon; Vasek and Thorne (1977) for California; Woodbury (1947) for Utah; St. Andre, Mooney, and Wright (1965) for the White Mountains; and Critchfield and Allenbaugh (1969) for northern Nevada.

West et al. (1978) and Tueller et al. (1979) summarize a major group effort to understand the climatic controls on woodland distribution. They build on work by Billings (1954a) and Beeson (1974).

Frischknecht (1975) summarizes p-j animal ecology. See also Johnson (1978) for birds; Hall (1946) for mammals; Young (1978) for Mormon crickets; and Van Dyke et al. (1984) for bighorn. Brown (1971b) tells the cliff and Uinta chipmunk story.

Blackburn and Tueller (1970), Rogers (1982), Young and Evans (1981), and Tausch, West, and Nabi (1981) give the evidence for piñon-juniper invasion and its relation to fire cycles. See Young and Budy (1979) for the history of nineteenth-century woodland use and West (1984) for the management implications of invasion.

12. Mountain Brush and Aspen Glens

Simpson (1876) is one of the basic sources for early descriptions of the Great Basin.

Billings and Mark (1957) address the causes of "bald" mountains in the central Great Basin. See Mooney (1973) for a description of the zone in the White Mountains and Tueller (1975) for Nevada.

Tueller and Monroe (1975) and Tueller (1979) analyze the interrelationship of mountain brush and mule deer. Brayton and Mooney (1966) discuss mountain-mahogany hybrids in the White Mountains. Bitterbrush and cliffrose ecology and evolution are covered well in the many papers in Tiedemann and Johnson (1983).

For details of aspen ecology, see the Utah State University symposium volume (DeByle, 1981). Lanner (1984) and Sibley (1984) also provide quick summaries of aspen ecology.

13. Great Basin Subalpine Forest

Basic distribution of subalpine trees comes from Holmgren (1972) and Critchfield and Allenbaugh (1969). Harper et al. (1978) also examine the causes of island distribution of conifers. Lanner (1984) outlines the stories of the three subalpine pines, emphasizing their relation to nutcrackers. Lewis (1971) and Loope (1969) discuss whitebark pine in the Ruby Mountains.

The bristlecone literature is rich. The Muir quotes come from "Nevada's Timber Belt," reprinted in *Steep Trails*. Schulman (1958) is the classic announcement of the antiquity of the trees. Lambert (1972) gives a good popular summary in a large-format book with David Muench photographs. Bailey (1970) announces the new taxonomy.

Ferguson (1968) and Fritts (1969) summarize the perspective of the dendrochronologists. Mooney and his associates have untangled much of the ecology of the tree in the White Mountains (see Mooney, 1973; Mooney, St. Andre, and Wright, 1962; Wright and Mooney, 1965). Beasley and Klemmedson (1980) studied bristlecone ecology in the Snake Range.

LaMarche documents the advance and retreat of bristlecones at tree line and inquires into the causes of longevity (LaMarche, 1969, 1973; LaMarche and Mooney, 1967, 1972). Thompson and Mead (1982) put Pleistocene bristlecone distribution in regional perspective.

14. Great Basin Tundra

Zwinger and Willard's book (1972) provides the best introduction to tundra ecology. See also Whitney (1979). The most intense research in Great Basin tundra is Loope's (1969) dissertation on the Rubies and other ranges of northeastern Nevada. Billings (1978) compares Great Basin tundra areas to each other and to the Rockies and Sierra.

For other specific ranges, see Bell and Johnson (1980) for the Wassuks; Linsdale, Howell, and Linsdale (1952) for the Toiyabes; McMillan (1948) for the Deep Creeks; and Mitchell, LaMarche, and Lloyd (1966) and Mooney (1973) for the White Mountains. Lewis (1971) complements Loope for the Rubies.

Borell and Ellis (1934) studied Ruby Mountain mammals. Mike Hess at the Nevada Department of Game and Fish in Reno talked to me about the mountain goat reintroduction. And Hart (1981) gives detailed hiking information for the Ruby Crest and many other Great Basin mountains.

Smith's papers (1974a, 1974b, 1980) tell the story of pikas at Bodie. Hall (1946) talks about Nevada pocket gophers. Reveal (1979) discusses speciation and endemic tundra plants.

15. West of the Wasatch

Papers by Cottam, Tucker, and Drobnick (1959) and Christensen (1949) are the foundation for biogeography of the oak/maple chaparral. Neilson and Wullstein (1983) further analyze the climatic controls on the community. See also Horton (1975), Kunzler (1980), and Rogers (1982). The John Muir quote comes from "Mormon Lilies" in *Steep Trails*.

Wells (1983) is the crucial reference for history of the eastern Great Basin forests. Harper et al. (1978) discuss the current patterns. For specific ranges, see McMillan (1948) for the Deep Creeks, Lewis (1973) for the Snakes, Preece (1950) for the Raft Rivers, Taye (1981) for the Stansburys, Billings (1954b) for Nevada, and Critchfield and Allenbaugh (1969) and Loope (1969) for northeastern Nevada.

Johnson (1978) and Behle (1978) discuss Rocky Mountain birds in the Basin. Brown (1971a) lists the missing mammals.

16. East of the Sierra

For detailed descriptions of Sierran forests, see Whitney (1979). Billings (1951) puts them in Great Basin perspective. Skau, Meeuwig, and Townsend (1970) summarize the ecology of Sierran chaparral. Haller (1961) discusses the interrelations of Jeffrey, Washoe, and ponderosa pine.

For distribution of Sierran trees beyond the Carsons, see Billings (1950, 1954b), Critchfield and Allenbaugh (1969), Mooney (1973), Lavin (1983), Lanner (1984), and Holmgren (1972).

Hall (1946) maps the limits of Sierran mammals. Johnson (1978) analyzes bird biogeography along the Sierra–Great Basin transition.

Schaffer (1975) gives details of the Mount Rose trail. Treefrog information comes from Stebbins (1954). The King lightning story appears in Bartlett (1962), the Church story in Houghton, Sakamoto, and Gifford (1975), the quote from Russell in his 1889 report. I highly recommend Clark's novel (1945).

Bibliography

Allred, Donald M. 1975. "Arachnids as Ecological Indicators." *Great Basin Naturalist* 35:405–6.

Armstrong, David M. 1977. "Distributional Patterns of Mammals in Utah." *Great Basin Naturalist* 37: 457–74.

Bachmann, Frederick W., and William Swilling Wallace, eds. and trans. 1957. *The Land Between: Dr. James Schiel's Account of the Gunnison-Beckwith Expedition into the West, 1853–1854.* Los Angeles: Westernlore Press.

Bailey, D. K. 1970. "Phytogeography and Taxonomy of *Pinus* Subsection *Balfourianae.*" *Annals of the Missouri Botanical Garden* 57:210–49.

Bakker, Elna S. 1971. *An Island Called California: An Ecological Introduction to Its Natural Communities.* Berkeley: University of California Press.

Barbour, Michael G., and Jack Major, eds. 1977. *Terrestrial Vegetation of California.* New York: Wiley Interscience.

Bartlett, Richard A. 1962. *Great Surveys of the American West.* Norman: University of Oklahoma Press.

Bartlett, Richard A., and William H. Goetzmann. 1982. *Exploring the American West, 1803–1879.* U.S. Department of the Interior. National Park Service Handbook 116. Washington, D.C.

Beasley, R. S., and J. O. Klemmedson. 1980. "Ecological Relationships of Bristlecone Pine." *American Midland Naturalist* 104:242–252.

Beatley, Janice C. 1975. "Climates and Vegetation Pattern across the Mojave/Great Basin Desert Transition of Southern Nevada." *American Midland Naturalist* 93:53–70.

———. 1976. *Vascular Plants of the Nevada Test Site and Central-Southern Nevada: Ecologic and Geographic Distributions.* U.S. Energy Research and Development Administration. Office of Technical Information. Technical Information Center.

Beeson, Dwight W. 1974. "The Distribution and Synecology of Great Basin Pinyon-Junipers." M.S. thesis, University of Nevada, Reno.

Behle, William H. 1978. "Avian Biogeography of the Great Basin and Intermountain Region." *Great Basin Naturalist Memoirs* 2:55–80.

Behnke, R. J., and Mark Zarn. 1976. *Biology and Management of Threatened and Endangered Western Trouts.* U.S. Department of Agriculture. Forest Service. Rocky Mountain Forest and Range Experiment Station, General Technical Report RM-28. Fort Collins, Colorado.

Bell, Katherine L., and Richard E. Johnson. 1980. "Alpine Flora of the Wassuk Range, Mineral County, Nevada." *Madroño* 27:25–35.

Billings, W. D. 1945. "The Plant Associations of the Carson Desert Region, Western Nevada." *Butler University Botanical Studies* 7:89–132. (Reprinted 1980 as Northern Nevada Native Plant Society Occasional Paper no. 4, Reno.)

———. 1949. "The Shadscale Vegetation Zone of Nevada and Eastern California in Relation to Climate and Soils." *American Midland Naturalist* 42: 87–109.

———. 1950. "Vegetation and Plant Growth as Affected by Chemically Altered Rocks in the Western Great Basin." *Ecology* 31:62–74.

———. 1951. "Vegetational Zonation in the Great Basin of Western North America." In *Les bases écologiques de la régénération de la végétation des zone arides.* International Union of Biological Science, International Colloquium, ser. B 9:101–22.

———. 1952. "The Environmental Complex in Relation to Plant Growth and Distribution." *Quarterly Review of Biology* 27:251–65.

———. 1954a. "Temperature Inversions in the Pinyon-Juniper Zone of a Nevada Mountain Range." *Butler University Botanical Studies* 12:112–17.

———. 1954b. *Nevada Trees.* University of Nevada, Agricultural Extension Service, Bulletin no. 94. Reno.

———. 1978. "Alpine Phytogeography across the Great Basin." *Great Basin Naturalist Memoirs* 2:105–17.

Billings, W. D., and A. F. Mark. 1957. "Factors Involved in the Persistence of Montane Treeless Balds." *Ecology* 38:140–42.

Blackburn, Wilbert H., and Paul T. Tueller. 1970. "Pinyon and Juniper Invasion in Black Sagebrush Communities in East-Central Nevada." *Ecology* 51:841–48.

Bolen, Eric G. 1964. "Plant Ecology of Spring-Fed Salt Marshes in Western Utah." *Ecology* 34: 143–66.

Borell, A. E., and R. Ellis. 1934. "Mammals of the Ruby Mountains Region of Northeastern Nevada." *Journal of Mammalogy* 15:12–44.

Bowers, Janice E. 1982. "Review: The Plant Ecology of Inland Dunes in Western North America." *Journal of Arid Environments* 5:199–220.

———. 1986. *Seasons of the Wind: A Naturalist's*

Look at the Plant Life of Southwestern Sand Dunes. Flagstaff: Northland Press.

Bowers, Michael A., and James H. Brown. 1982. "Body Size and Coexistence in Desert Rodents: Chance or Community Structure?" *Ecology* 63: 391–400.

Branson, F. A., R. F. Miller, and I. S. McQueen. 1967. "Geographic Distribution and Factors Affecting the Distribution of Salt Desert Shrubs in the United States." *Journal of Range Management* 20: 287–96.

Brayton, Robert, and H. A. Mooney. 1966. "Population Variability of *Cercocarpus* in the White Mountains of California As Related to Habitat." *Evolution* 20:383–91.

Brown, James H. 1971a. "Mammals on Mountaintops: Nonequilibrium Insular Biogeography." *American Naturalist* 105:467–78.

———. 1971b. "Mechanisms of Competitive Exclusion between Two Species of Chipmunks." *Ecology* 52:305–11.

———. 1973. "Species Diversity of Seed-Eating Desert Rodents in Sand Dune Habitats." *Ecology* 54:775–87.

———. 1975. "Geographical Ecology of Desert Rodents." In *Ecology and Evolution of Communities,* eds. Martin L. Cody and Jared M. Diamond, 315–41. Cambridge: Harvard University Press, Belknap Press.

———. 1978. "The Theory of Insular Biogeography and the Distribution of Boreal Birds and Mammals." *Great Basin Naturalist Memoirs* 2:209–27.

Brown, James H., and Arthur C. Gibson. 1983. *Biogeography.* St. Louis, Mo.: C. V. Mosby.

Brown, James H., and Gerald A. Lieberman. 1973. "Resource Utilization and Coexistence of Seed-Eating Desert Rodents in Sand Dune Habitats." *Ecology* 54:788–97.

Brown, James H., O. J. Reichman, and Diane W. Davidson. 1979. "Granivory in Desert Ecosystems." *Annual Review of Ecology and Systematics* 10:201–27.

Christensen, Earl. 1949. "The Ecology and Geographic Distribution of Oak Brush (*Quercus gambelii* Nutt.) in Utah." M.S. thesis, University of Utah, Salt Lake City.

Christensen, Earl, and Hyrum Johnson. 1964. "Presettlement Vegetaton and Vegetatonal Change in Three Valleys in Central Utah." Brigham Young University Science Bulletin, Biological Series, vol. 4, no. 4. Provo.

Christensen, Glen C. 1970. *The Chukar Partridge: Its Introduction, Life History, and Management.* Nevada Department of Wildlife Biological Bulletin no. 4. Reno.

Clark, Walter Van Tilburg. 1945. *The City of Trembling Leaves.* New York: Random House.

Cline, Gloria Griffen. 1963. *Exploring the Great Basin.* Norman: University of Oklahoma Press.

Cottam, Walter P. 1947. "Is Utah Sahara Bound?" *University of Utah Bulletin* 37:1–40.

Cottam, Walter P., John M. Tucker, and Rudy Drobnick. 1959. "Some Clues to Great Basin Postpluvial Climates Provided by Oak Distributions." *Ecology* 40:361–77.

Crawford, Clifford S. 1981. *Biology of Desert Invertebrates.* Berlin: Springer Verlag.

Critchfield, William B., and Gordon L. Allenbaugh. 1969. "The Distribution of Pinaceae in and near Northern Nevada." *Madroño* 19:12–26.

Cronquist, Arthur. 1978. "The Biota of the Intermountain Region in Geohistorical Context." *Great Basin Naturalist Memoirs* 2:3–15.

Culmer, H. L. A. 1909. "The Scenic Glories of Utah." *Western Monthly* 10 (August):35–41.

Daubenmire, Rexford. 1978. *Plant Geography, with Special Reference to North America.* New York: Academic Press.

Davis, H. L. 1935. *Honey in the Horn.* New York: Harper and Brothers.

Davis, Owen K. 1984. "Multiple Thermal Maxima during the Holocene." *Science* 225:617–19.

DeByle, Norbert V., ed. 1981. *Symposium Proceedings, Situation Management of Two Intermountain Species: Aspen and Coyotes.* Vol. 1, *Aspen.* Utah State University, College of Natural Resources. Logan.

DeVoto, Bernard. 1942. *The Year of Decision: 1846.* Boston: Houghton-Mifflin.

Dice, Lee R. 1952. *Natural Communities.* Ann Arbor: University of Michigan Press.

Dillard, Annie. 1982. *Teaching a Stone to Talk: Expeditions and Encounters.* New York: Harper and Row.

Duebbert, Harold F. 1969. *The Ecology of Malheur Lake and Management Implications.* U.S. Fish and Wildlife Service Refuge Leaflet no. 412.

Eckert, Richard E. 1954. "A Study of Competition between Whitesage and Halogeton in Nevada." *Journal of Range Management* 7:223–25.

Eiseley, Loren. 1957. *The Immense Journey.* New York: Random House.

———. 1978. *The Star Thrower.* New York: Times Books.

Evans, Raymond A., and James A. Young. 1970. "Plant Litter and Establishment of Alien Annual Weed Species in Rangeland Communities." *Weed Science* 18:697–703.

———. 1980. "Establishment of Barbwire Russian Thistle in Desert Environments." *Journal of Range Management* 33:169–73.

Evans, Raymond A., James A. Young, Richard E. Eckert, Jr., and Philip C. Martinelli. "Halogeton." Unpublished manuscript in preparation.

Fautin, Reed W. 1946. "Biotic Communities of the Northern Desert Shrub Biome in Western Utah." *Ecological Monographs* 16:251–310.

Ferguson, C. W. 1968. "Bristlecone Pine: Science and Esthetics." *Science* 159:839–46.

Ferguson, Denzel, and Nancy Ferguson. 1978. *Oregon's Great Basin Country.* Burns, Ore.: Gail Graphics.

———. 1983. *Sacred Cows at the Public Trough.* Bend, Ore.: Maverick Publications.

Fiero, William. 1986. *Geology of the Great Basin.* Reno: University of Nevada Press.

Flowers, Seville. 1934. "Vegetation of the Great Salt Lake Region." *Botanical Gazette* 95:353–418.

Flowers, Seville, and Frederick R. Evans. 1966. "The Flora and Fauna of the Great Salt Lake Region, Utah." In *Salinity and Aridity,* ed. Hugo Boyko, 367–93. The Hague: W. Junk.

Foster, Robert H. 1965. "Distribution of the Plant Communities of the Great Basin." M.S. thesis, Brigham Young University, Provo, Utah.

Franklin, Jerry F., and C. T. Dyrness. 1973. *Natural Vegetation of Oregon and Washington.* U.S. Department of Agriculture. Forest Service. Pacific Northwest Forest and Range Experiment Station, General Technical Report PNW-8. Portland, Oregon.

Frischknecht, Neil C. 1967. "How Far Will Halogeton Spread?" *Journal of Soil and Water Conservation* 22:135–39.

———. 1975. "Native Faunal Relationships within the Pinyon-Juniper Ecosystem." In *The Pinyon-Juniper Ecosystem: A Symposium,* 55–65. Utah State University, College of Natural Resources. Logan.

Fritts, Harold C. 1969. *Bristlecone Pine in the White Mountains of California.* Papers of the Laboratory of Tree-Ring Research no. 4. Tucson: University of Arizona Press.

Gaines, David, and the Mono Lake Committee. 1981. *Mono Lake Guidebook.* Lee Vining, Calif.: Kutsavi Books.

George, Uwe. 1977. *In the Deserts of This Earth.* New York: Harcourt Brace Jovanovich.

Ghiselin, Jon. 1970. "Edaphic Control of Habitat Selection by Kangaroo Mice (*Microdipodops*) in Three Nevadan Populations." *Oecologia* 4:248–61.

Gilbert, Bil. 1983. *Westering Man: The Life of Joseph Walker.* Norman: University of Oklahoma Press.

Gilbert, F. S. 1980. "The Equilibrium Theory of Island Biogeography: Fact or Fiction?" *Journal of Biogeography* 7:209–35.

Gleason, H. A., and A. Cronquist. 1964. *The Natural Geography of Plants.* New York: Columbia University Press.

Goodall, D. W., and R. A. Perry, eds. 1979. *Arid-land Ecosystems: Structure, Functioning and Management,* Vol. 1. International Biological Programme 16. Cambridge: Cambridge University Press.

Grayson, Donald K. 1977. "On the Holocene History of Some Northern Great Basin Lagomorphs." *Journal of Mammalogy* 58:505–13.

———. 1981. "A Mid-Holocene Record for the Heather Vole, *Phenacomys* Cf. *intermedius,* in the Central Great Basin and Its Biogeographic Significance." *Journal of Mammalogy* 62:115–21.

———. 1982. "Toward a History of Great Basin Mammals During the Past 15,000 Years." In *Man and the Environment in the Great Basin,* eds. David B. Madsen and James F. O'Connell, 82–101. Society for American Archaeology Papers 2.

Green, J. S., and J. T. Flinders. 1980. "Habitat and Dietary Relationship of the Pygmy Rabbit." *Journal of Range Management* 33:136–42.

Hall, E. Raymond. 1946. *Mammals of Nevada.* Berkeley: University of California Press.

Haller, J. R. 1961. "Some Recent Observations on Ponderosa, Jeffrey, and Washoe Pines in Northeastern California." *Madroño* 16:126–32.

Harper, K. T., D. Carl Freeman, W. Kent Ostler, and Lionel G. Klikoff. 1978. "The Flora of Great Basin Mountain Ranges: Diversity, Sources, and Dispersal Ecology." *Great Basin Naturalist Memoirs* 2: 81–103.

Harper, K. T., and James L. Reveal, eds. 1978. "Intermountain Biogeography: A Symposium." *Great Basin Naturalist Memoirs* 2.

Hart, John. 1981. *Hiking the Great Basin.* San Francisco: Sierra Club Books.

Hatley, Cynthia L., and James A. MacMahon. 1980. "Spider Community Organization: Seasonal Variation and the Role of Vegetation Architecture." *Environmental Entomology* 9:632–39.

Hazleton, Lesley. 1980. *Where Mountains Roar: A Personal Report from the Sinai and Negev Desert.* New York: Penguin Books.

Heckmann, Richard A., and Lavere B. Merritt, eds. 1981. "Utah Lake Monograph." *Great Basin Naturalist Memoirs* 5.

Hintze, Lehi F. 1973. *Geologic History of Utah.* Brigham Young University Geology Studies, vol. 20, pt. 3. Studies for Students no. 8. Provo.

Hironaka, M., and M. A. Fosberg. 1981. *Non-Forest Habitat Type Workshop II.* University of Idaho Agricultural Experiment Station, Moscow.

Holliday, J. S. 1981. *The World Rushed In: The California Gold Rush Experience.* New York: Simon and Schuster.

Hollon, W. Eugene. 1966. *The Great American Desert Then and Now.* Lincoln: University of Nebraska Press.

Holmgren, Noel H. 1972. "Plant Geography of the Intermountain Region." In *Intermountain Flora,* Vol. 1, by Arthur Cronquist, Arthur H. Holmgren, Noel H. Holmgren, and James L. Reveal, 77–161. New York: Hafner Publishing Company.

Horton, L. E., comp. 1975. *An Abstract Bibliography of Gambel Oak (Quercus Gambelii Nutt.).* U.S. Department of Agriculture. Forest Service. Intermountain Region, Ogden, Utah.

Houghton, John G., Clarence M. Sakamoto, and Richard O. Gifford. 1975. *Nevada's Weather and Climate.* University of Nevada, Nevada Bureau of

Mines and Geology Special Publication 2. Reno.

Hubbs, C. L., R. R. Miller, and L. C. Hubbs. 1974. "Hydrographic History and Relict Fishes of the North-Central Great Basin." *Memoirs California Academy of Science* 7:1–259.

Hull, A. C., Jr., and Mary Kay Hull. 1974. "Presettlement Vegetation of Cache Valley Utah and Idaho." *Journal of Range Management* 27:27–29.

Hunt, Charles B. 1974. *Natural Regions of the United States and Canada.* W. H. Freeman, San Francisco.

Jackman, E. R., and R. A. Long. 1977. *The Oregon Desert.* Caldwell, Idaho: Caxton Printers.

Jackson, Donald Dale. 1975. *Sagebrush Country.* New York: Time-Life Books.

Jackson, Richard H., and Dale J. Stevens. 1981. "Physical and Cultural Environment of Utah Lake and Adjacent Areas." *Great Basin Naturalist Memoirs* 5:3–23.

Jaeger, Edmund C. 1957. *The North American Deserts.* Stanford: Stanford University Press.

Johnson, Ned K. 1975. "Controls of Number of Bird Species on Montane Islands in the Great Basin." *Evolution* 29:545–67.

———. 1978. "Patterns of Avian Geography and Speciation in the Intermountain Region." *Great Basin Naturalist Memoirs* 2:137–59.

Kearney, T. H., L. J. Briggs, H. L. Shantz, J. W. McLane, and R. L. Piemeisel. 1914. "Indicator Significance of Vegetation in Tooele Valley, Utah." *Journal of Agricultural Research* 1:365–417.

Kenagy, G. J. 1972. "Saltbush Leaves: Excision of Hypersaline Tissue by a Kangaroo Rat." *Science* 178:1094–96.

———. 1973. "Daily and Seasonal Patterns of Activity and Energetics in a Heteromyid Rodent Community." *Ecology* 54:1201–19.

Klebenow, Donald A. 1972. "The Habitat Requirements of Sage Grouse and the Role of Fire in Management." In *Proceedings Annual Tall Timbers Fire Ecology Conference,* 305–15.

Klebenow, Donald A., and Robert J. Oakleaf. 1981. "Avifaunal Changes in Riparian Habitat along the Truckee River, Nevada." *Conference on California Riparian Systems,* University of California, Davis.

Kunzler, Lynn M. 1980. "The Biology and Management of Gambel Oak in Utah." M.S. thesis, Brigham Young University, Provo, Utah.

Kurten, Bjorn, and E. Anderson. 1980. *Pleistocene Mammals of North America.* New York: Columbia University Press.

LaMarche, Valmore C., Jr. 1969. "Environment in Relation to the Age of Bristlecone Pines." *Ecology* 50:53–59.

———. 1973. "Holocene Climatic Variations Inferred from Treeline Fluctuations in the White Mountains, California." *Quaternary Research* 3:632–60.

LaMarche, Valmore C., Jr., and H. A. Mooney. 1967. "Altithermal Timberline Advance in Western United States." *Nature* 213:980–82.

———. 1972. "Recent Climatic Change and Development of the Bristlecone Pine (*P. longaeva* Bailey) Krummholz Zone, Mt. Washington, Nevada." *Arctic and Alpine Research* 4:61–72.

Lambert, Darwin, and David Muench. 1972. *Timberline Ancients.* Portland, Ore.: Charles H. Belding.

Lanner, Ronald M. 1981. *The Piñon Pine: A Natural and Cultural History.* Reno: University of Nevada Press.

———. 1984. *Trees of the Great Basin: A Natural History.* Reno: University of Nevada Press.

Larrison, Earl J., and Donald R. Johnson. 1973. "Density Changes and Habitat Affinities of Rodents of Shadscale and Sagebrush Associations." *Great Basin Naturalist* 33:255–64.

Lavin, Matt. 1983. "Floristics of the Upper Walker River, California and Nevada." *Great Basin Naturalist* 43:93–130.

Least Heat Moon, William. 1982. *Blue Highways: A Journey into America.* Boston: Little, Brown and Company.

Leopold, Aldo. 1949. *A Sand County Almanac and Sketches Here and There.* London: Oxford University Press.

Lesperance, A. L., James A. Young, Richard E. Eckert, Jr., and Raymond A. Evans. 1978. "Great Basin Wildrye." *Rangeman's Journal* 5:125–27.

Lewis, Mont E. 1971. *Flora and Major Plant Communities of the Ruby–East Humboldt Mountains, with Special Emphasis on Lamoille Canyon.* U.S. Department of Agriculture. Forest Service. Humboldt National Forest, Region 4.

———. 1973. *Wheeler Peak Area: Species List.* U.S. Department of Agriculture Forest Service. Intermountain Region, Ogden, Utah.

Linsdale, M. A., J. T. Howell, and J. M. Linsdale. 1952. "Plants of the Toiyabe Mountains Area." *Wasmann Journal of Biology* 10:129–200.

Loope, Lloyd L. 1969. "Subalpine and Alpine Vegetation of Northeastern Nevada." Ph.D. dissertation, Duke University, Durham, North Carolina.

Lopez, Barry Holstun. 1976. *Desert Notes: Reflections in the Eye of a Raven.* Kansas City, Mo.: Andrews and McMeel.

McAdoo, J. Kent, Carol C. Evans, Bruce A. Roundy, James A. Young, and Raymond A. Evans. 1983. "Influence of Heteromyid Rodents on *Oryzopsis hymenoides* Germination." *Journal of Range Management* 36:61–64.

McAdoo, J. Kent, and James A. Young. 1980. "Jackrabbits." *Rangelands* 2 (4):135–38.

McArthur, E. Durant. 1979. "Sagebrush Systematics and Evolution." In *The Sagebrush Ecosystem: A Symposium,* 14–22. Utah State University, College of Natural Resources. Logan.

———. 1983. "Taxonomy, Origin, and Distribution of Big Sagebrush (*Artemisia tridentata*) and Allies (Subgenus *Tridentatae*)." In *Proceedings First Utah Shrub Ecology Workshop,* ed. K. L. Johnson, 3–13. Utah State University. Logan.

McArthur, E. Durant, A. Clyde Blauer, A. Perry

Plummer, and Richard Stevens. 1979. *Characteristics and Hybridization of Important Intermountain Shrubs. 3, Sunflower Family.* U.S. Department of Agriculture. Forest Service. Intermountain Forest and Range Experiment Station, Research Paper INT–220. Ogden, Utah.

McArthur, E. Durant, and A. Perry Plummer. 1978. "Biogeography and Management of Native Western Shrubs: A Case Study, Section *Tridentatae* of *Artemisia.*" *Great Basin Naturalist Memoirs* 2:229–43.

McArthur, E. Durant, C. Lorenzo Pope, and D. Carl Freeman. 1981. "Chromosomal Studies of Subgenus *Tridentatae* of *Artemisia:* Evidence for Autopolyploidy." *American Journal of Botany* 68: 589–605.

MacArthur, Robert H. 1972. *Geographical Ecology: Patterns in the Distribution of Species.* New York: Harper and Row.

MacArthur, Robert H., and Edward O. Wilson. 1963. "An Equilibrium Theory of Insular Zoogeography." *Evolution* 17:373–87.

———. 1967. *The Theory of Island Biogeography.* Princeton: Princeton University Press.

Mack, Richard N. 1984. "Invaders at Home on the Range." *Natural History* (February):40–46.

MacMahon, James A. 1979. "North American Deserts: Their Floral and Faunal Components." In *Arid-land Ecosystems: Structure, Functioning and Management,* Vol. 1, eds. R. A. Perry and D. W. Goodall, 21–81. International Biological Programme 16. Cambridge: Cambridge University Press.

MacMahon, James A., and Thomas F. Wieboldt. 1978. "Applying Biogeographic Principles to Resource Management: A Case Study Evaluating Holdridge's Life Zone Model." *Great Basin Naturalist Memoirs* 2:245–57.

McMillan, Calvin. 1948. "A Taxonomic and Ecological Study of the Flora of the Deep Creek Mountains of Central Western Utah." M.S. thesis, University of Utah, Salt Lake City.

McPhee, John. 1980. *Basin and Range.* New York: Farrar, Straus, Giroux.

Martin, Paul S., and Richard G. Klein, eds. 1984. *Quaternary Extinctions: A Prehistoric Revolution.* Tucson: University of Arizona Press.

Martin, Paul S., and H. E. Wright, eds. 1967. *Pleistocene Extinction, the Search for a Cause.* New Haven: Yale University Press.

Merriam, C. Hart. 1898. *Life-Zones and Crop-Zones of the United States.* U.S. Department of Agriculture. Division of Biological Survey, bulletin 10.

Minckley, W. L., and David E. Brown. 1982. "Southwestern Wetlands." In "Biotic Communities of the American Southwest—United States and Mexico," ed. David E. Brown. *Desert Plants* 4: 224–36.

Mitchell, R. S., V. C. LaMarche, Jr., and R. M. Lloyd. 1966. "Alpine Vegetation and Active Frost Features of Pellisier Flats, White Mountains, California." *American Midland Naturalist* 75:516–25.

Mooney, H. A. 1973. "Plant Communities and Vegetation." In *A Flora of the White Mountains, California and Nevada,* eds. Robert M. Lloyd and Richard S. Mitchell, 7–17. Berkeley: University of California Press.

Mooney, H. A., G. St. Andre, and R. D. Wright. 1962. "Alpine and Subalpine Vegetation Patterns in the White Mountains of California." *American Midland Naturalist* 68:257–73.

Morgan, Dale L. 1947. *The Great Salt Lake.* Albuquerque: University of New Mexico Press.

Mozingo, Hugh N. 1987. *Shrubs of the Great Basin: A Natural History.* Reno: University of Nevada Press.

Muir, John. 1877–78. "Mormon Lilies," "Nevada Forests," and "Nevada's Timber Belt." Reprinted in *Steep Trails,* 1918. Boston: Houghton-Mifflin.

National Park Service. 1981. *Study of Alternatives: Great Basin, Snake Range/Spring Valley Study Area, Nevada.* U.S. Department of the Interior. National Park Service. Denver Service Center.

Neilson, R. P., and L. H. Wullstein. 1983. "Biogeography of Two Southwest American Oaks in Relation to Atmospheric Dynamics." *Journal of Biogeography* 10:275–97.

Nevins, Allan, ed. 1956. *Narratives of Exploration and Adventure by John Charles Frémont.* New York: Longmans, Green.

Pianka, Eric R. 1967. "On Lizard Species Diversity: North American Flatland Deserts." *Ecology* 48:333–51.

Piemeisel, R. L. 1951. "Causes Affecting Change and Rate of Change in a Vegetation of Annuals in Idaho." *Ecology* 32:53–72.

Preece, S. J. 1950. "Floristic and Ecological Features of the Raft River Mountains of Northwestern Utah." M.S. thesis, University of Utah, Salt Lake City.

Reveal, James L. 1979. "Biogeography of the Intermountain Region: A Speculative Appraisal." *Mentzelia* 4:1–87.

Ridgway, Robert. 1877. "Ornithology." In *Ornithology and Paleontology,* Vol. 4, ed. Clarence King. 306–669. U.S. Geological Explorations of the Fortieth Parallel.

Rogers, Garry F. 1982. *Then and Now: A Photographic History of Vegetation Change in the Central Great Basin Desert.* Salt Lake City: University of Utah Press.

Russell, Israel C. 1885. *Present and Extinct Lakes of Nevada.* U.S. Geological Survey, Washington. (Reprinted 1976 as Camp Nevada Monograph number 4, Reno.)

———. 1889. *Quaternary History of the Mono Valley, California.* U.S. Geological Survey, Washington. (Reprinted 1984 by Artemesia Press, Lee Vining, California.)

Ryser, Fred. 1985. *Birds of the Great Basin: A Natural History.* Reno: University of Nevada Press.

St. Andre, G., H. A. Mooney, and R. D. Wright.

1965. "The Pinyon Woodland Zone in the White Mountains of California." *American Midland Naturalist* 73:225–39.

Saint-Exupery, Antoine de. 1940. *Wind, Sand and Stars*. New York: Reynal and Hitchcock.

Sanchez, Thomas. 1973. *Rabbit Boss*. New York: Alfred A. Knopf.

Schaffer, Jeffrey P. 1975. *The Tahoe Sierra: A Natural History Guide to 100 Hikes in the Northern Sierra*. Berkeley, Calif.: Wilderness Press.

Schulman, Edmund. 1958. "Bristlecone Pine, Oldest Known Living Thing." *National Geographic* 113: 355–72.

Scott, William E., William D. McCoy, Ralph R. Shroba, and Meyer Rubin. 1983. "Reinterpretation of the Exposed Record of the Last Two Cycles of Lake Bonneville, Western United States." *Quaternary Research* 20:261–85.

Shreve, Forrest. 1934. "The Problems of the Desert." *Scientific Monthly* 40:199–209.

———. 1942. "The Desert Vegetation of North America." *Botanical Review* 8:195–246.

Sibley, George. 1984. "The Splash and Play of *Populus tremuloides* Tie Together the Rockies." *High Country News*, April 2, 6–7.

Sigler, William F., and John W. Sigler. 1987. *Fishes of the Great Basin: A Natural History*. Reno: University of Nevada Press.

Simpson, Captain James H. 1876. *Report of Explorations across the Great Basin of the Territory of Utah for a Direct Wagon-Route from Camp Floyd to Genoa, in Carson Valley, in 1859*. U.S. Government Printing Office, Washington, D.C. (Reprinted 1983 by University of Nevada Press, Reno.)

Skau, Clarence M., R. O. Meeuwig, and T. W. Townsend. 1970. *Ecology of Eastside Sierra Chaparral: A Literature Review*. University of Nevada, Agricultural Experiment Station Report no. R-71. Reno.

Skougard, Michael G. 1976. "Vegetational Response to Three Environmental Gradients in a Salt Playa near Goshen, Utah County, Utah." M.S. thesis, Brigham Young University, Provo, Utah.

Smith, Andrew T. 1974a. "The Distribution and Dispersal of Pikas: Consequences of Insular Population Structure." *Ecology* 55:1112–19.

———. 1974b. "The Distribution and Dispersal of Pikas: Influences of Behavior and Climate." *Ecology* 55:1368–76.

———. 1980. "Temporal Changes in Insular Populations of the Pika (*Ochotona princeps*)." *Ecology* 61:8–13.

Smith, Gerald R. 1978. "Biogeography of Intermountain Fishes." *Great Basin Naturalist Memoirs* 2:17–42.

Stansbury, Howard. 1852. *Exploration and Survey of the Valley of the Great Salt Lake*. Philadelphia: Lippincott, Grambo.

Stebbins, Robert C. 1954. *Amphibians and Reptiles of Western North America*. New York: McGraw-Hill.

Steele, Robert, Stephen V. Cooper, David M. Ondov, and Robert D. Pfister. 1979. *Forest Habitat Types of Eastern Idaho–Western Wyoming*. U.S. Department of Agriculture. Forest Service. Intermountain Forest and Range Experiment Station, Draft Research Paper. Ogden, Utah.

Stegner, Wallace. 1942. *Mormon Country*. Lincoln: University of Nebraska Press.

Steinbeck, John. 1962. *Travels with Charley in Search of America*. New York: Viking Press.

Stevens, Larry. Forthcoming. *Rivers and Lakes of the Great Basin*. Reno: University of Nevada Press.

Stewart, George R. 1951. *Sheep Rock*. New York: Random House.

———. 1962. *The California Trail: An Epic with Many Heroes*. New York: McGraw-Hill.

Stewart, George, W. P. Cottam, and Selar S. Hutchings. 1940. "Influence of Unrestricted Grazing on Northern Salt Desert Plant Associations in Western Utah." *Journal of Agricultural Research* 60:289–316.

Stewart, John H. 1980. *Geology of Nevada*. University of Nevada, Nevada Bureau of Mines and Geology Special Publication 4. Reno.

Stokes, William Lee. 1984. *The Great Salt Lake*. Salt Lake City: Starstone Publishing.

———. 1986. *Geology of Utah*. University of Utah, Utah Museum of Natural History Occasional Paper no. 6, Salt Lake City.

Stutz, Howard C. 1978. "Explosive Evolution of Perennial *Atriplex* in Western America." *Great Basin Naturalist Memoirs* 2:161–68.

———. 1979. "The Meaning of 'Rare' and 'Endangered' in the Evolution of Western Shrubs." *Great Basin Naturalist Memoirs* 3:119–28.

Stutz, Howard C., J. M. Melby, and G. K. Livingston. 1975. "Evolutionary Studies of *Atriplex*: A Relict Gigas Population of *Atriplex canescens*." *American Journal of Botany* 62:236–45.

Stutz, Howard C., C. Lorenzo Pope, and Stewart C. Sanderson. 1979. "Evolutionary Studies of *Atriplex*: Adaptive Products from the Natural Hybrid, 6N *A. tridentata* × 4N *A. canescens*." *American Journal of Botany* 66:1181–93.

Stutz, Howard C., and Stewart C. Sanderson. 1979. "The Role of Polyploidy in the Evolution of *Atriplex canescens*." In *Arid Land Plant Resources*, eds. J. R. Goodin and David K. Northington. Texas Tech University, International Center for Arid and Semi-Arid Land Studies. Lubbock.

Tanner, Wilmer W. 1978. "Zoogeography of Reptiles and Amphibians in the Intermountain Region." *Great Basin Naturalist Memoirs* 2:43–53.

Tausch, Robin J., Neil E. West, and Ageli A. Nabi. 1981. "Tree Age and Dominance Patterns in Great Basin Pinyon-Juniper Woodlands." *Journal of Range Management* 34:259–64.

Taye, Alan C. 1981. "A Floristic and Phytogeographic Study of the Stansbury Mountains, Utah." M.S. thesis, Brigham Young University, Provo, Utah.

Bibliography

Thomas, Jack Ward, Chris Maser, and Jon E. Rodiek. 1980. *Wildlife Habitats in Managed Rangelands— The Great Basin of Southeastern Oregon: Riparian Zones.* U.S. Department of Agriculture Forest Service. Pacific Northwest Forest and Range Experiment Station, General Technical Report PNW-80. La Grande, Oregon.

Thompson, Robert S. 1978. "Late Pleistocene and Holocene Packrat Middens from Smith Creek Canyon, White Pine County, Nevada." In *The Archaeology of Smith Creek Canyon, Eastern Nevada*, eds. D. Touhy and E. L. Rendall 363–80. Nevada State Museum Anthropological Papers no. 17.

Thompson, Robert S., and J. I. Mead. 1982. "Late Quaternary Environments and Biogeography in the Great Basin." *Quaternary Research* 17:39–55.

Thompson, Steven D. 1982. "Microhabitat Utilization and Foraging Behavior of Bipedal and Quadrupedal Heteromyid Rodents." *Ecology* 63:1303–12.

Tidwell, William D., Samuel R. Rushforth, and Daniel Simper. 1972. "Evolution of Floras in the Intermountain Region." In *Intermountain Flora*, Vol. 1, by Arthur Cronquist, Arthur H. Holmgren, Noel H. Holmgren, and James L. Reveal, 19–39. New York: Hafner Publishing Company.

Tiedemann, Arthur R., and Kendall L. Johnson, comps. 1983. *Proceedings—Research and Management of Bitterbrush and Cliffrose in Western North America.* U.S. Department of Agriculture. Forest Service. Intermountain Forest and Range Experiment Station, General Technical Report INT-152. Ogden, Utah.

Tueller, Paul T. 1966. "The Management of White-sage (*Eurotia lanata*) in Nevada." In *Salt Desert Shrub Symposium*, 189–202. Bureau of Land Management. Cedar City, Utah.

———. 1975. "The Natural Vegetation of Nevada." *Mentzelia* 1:3–28.

———. 1979. *Food Habits and Nutrition of Mule Deer on Nevada Ranges.* University of Nevada, Agricultural Experiment Station Report no. R-128. Reno.

Tueller, Paul T., C. Dwight Beeson, Robin J. Tausch, Neil E. West, and Kenneth H. Rea. 1979. *Pinyon-Juniper Woodlands of the Great Basin: Distribution, Flora, Vegetal Cover.* U.S. Department of Agriculture. Forest Service. Intermountain Forest and Range Experiment Station, Research Paper INT-229. Ogden, Utah.

Tueller, Paul T., and Leslie A. Monroe. 1975. *Management Guidelines for Selected Deer Habitats in Nevada.* University of Nevada, Agricultural Experiment Station Report no. R-104, Reno.

Twain, Mark. 1872. *Roughing It.* New York: Penguin Books.

Utah State University. 1975. *The Pinyon-Juniper Ecosystem: A Symposium.* College of Natural Resources. Logan.

———. 1979. *The Sagebrush Ecosystem: A Symposium.* College of Natural Resources. Logan.

Vale, Thomas R. 1973. "The Sagebrush Landscape of the Intermountain West." Ph.D. dissertation, University of California, Berkeley.

———. 1975. "Presettlement Vegetation in Sagebrush/Grass Area of the Intermountain West." *Journal of Range Management* 28:32–36.

Van Devender, Thomas R., and W. Geoffrey Spaulding. 1979. "Development of Vegetation and Climate in the Southwestern United States." *Science* 204:701–10.

Van Dyke, Walter A., Alan Sands, Jim Yoakum, Allan Polenz, and James Blaisdell. 1984. *Wildlife Habitats in Managed Rangelands—The Great Basin of Southeastern Oregon: Bighorn Sheep.* U.S. Department of Agriculture. Forest Service. Pacific Northwest Forest and Range Experiment Station, General Technical Report. Portland, Oregon.

Vasek, Frank C., and Robert F. Thorne. 1977. "Transmontane Coniferous Vegetation." In *Terrestrial Vegetation of California*, eds. Michael G. Barbour and Jack Major, 797–832. New York: Wiley Interscience.

Vest, E. Dean. 1962. *Biotic Communities in the Great Salt Lake Desert.* University of Utah, Division of Biological Sciences, Institute of Environmental Biological Research, Ecology and Epizoology Series no. 73. Salt Lake City.

Walker, Gregory R. 1981. "Ecological Relationships of Great Basin Wildrye in the Strawberry Valley of Central Utah." M.S. thesis, Brigham Young University, Provo, Utah.

Wells, Philip V. 1983. "Paloebiogeography of Montane Islands in the Great Basin since the Last Glaciopluvial." *Ecological Monographs* 53:341–82.

West, Neil E. 1968. *Ecology and Management of Salt Desert Shrub Ranges: A Bibliography.* Utah State University, Utah Agricultural Experiment Station Mimeograph Series 505. Logan.

———. 1979a. "Basic Synecological Relationships of Sagebrush-Dominated Lands in the Great Basin and the Colorado Plateau." In *The Sagebrush Ecosystem: A Symposium*, 33–41. Utah State University, College of Natural Resources. Logan.

———. 1979b. "Survival Patterns of Major Perennials in Salt Desert Shrub Communities of Southwestern Utah." *Journal of Range Management* 32:442–45.

———. 1982. "Dynamics of Plant Communities Dominated by Chenopod Shrubs." *International Journal of Ecology and Environmental Sciences* 8:73–84.

———. 1983. Reviews of North American Temperate Deserts and Semi-Deserts. In *Temperate Deserts and Semi-Deserts*, ed. Neil E. West, 321–98. Amsterdam: Elsevier Scientific Publishing Company.

———. 1984. "Successional Patterns and Productivity Potentials of Pinyon-Juniper Ecosystems." In *Developing Strategies for Rangeland Management*, National Research Council/National Academy of Sciences, 1301–32. Boulder, Colo.: Westview Press.

West, Neil E., Frederick D. Provenza, Patricia S. Johnson, and M. Keith Owens. 1984. "Vegetation Change after 13 Years of Livestock Grazing Exclusion on Sagebrush Semidesert in West Central Utah." *Journal of Range Management* 37:262–64.

West, Neil E., Robin J. Tausch, Kenneth H. Rea, and Paul T. Tueller. 1978. "Phytogeographical Variation within Juniper-Pinyon Woodlands of the Great Basin." *Great Basin Naturalist Memoirs* 2: 119–36.

Wheeler, Sessions S. 1972. *The Nevada Desert.* Caldwell, Idaho: Caxton Printers.

———. 1974. *The Desert Lake: The Story of Nevada's Pyramid Lake.* Caldwell, Idaho: Caxton Printers.

———. 1978. *The Black Rock Desert.* Caldwell, Idaho: Caxton Printers.

Whitney, Stephen. 1979. *A Sierra Club Naturalist's Guide to the Sierra Nevada.* San Francisco: Sierra Club Books.

Whittaker, Robert H. 1975. *Communities and Ecosystems.* New York: Macmillan.

Wiley, R. H. 1973. "Territoriality and Non-random Mating in Sage Grouse, *Centrocercus urophasianus.*" *Animal Behaviour Monographs* 6:85–169.

Winkler, David W., ed. 1977. *An Ecological Study of Mono Lake, California.* University of California, Institute of Ecology Publication no. 12. Davis. (Reprinted 1979 by the Mono Lake Committee, Lee Vining, California.)

Winward, A. H. 1980. *Taxonomy and Ecology of Sagebrush in Oregon.* Oregon State University, Agricultural Experiment Station Bulletin 642. Corvallis.

———. 1981. "Using Sagebrush Ecology in Management of Wildlands." In *Proceedings First Utah Shrub Ecology Workshop,* ed. K. L. Johnson, 10–15. Utah State University, Logan.

Winward, A. H., and E. W. Tisdale. 1977. *Taxonomy of the Artemisia Tridentata Complex in Idaho.* University of Idaho, Forest, Wildlife, and Range Experiment Station Bulletin no. 19. Moscow.

Wolfe, Thomas. 1937. *A Western Journal.* Pittsburgh: University of Pittsburgh Press.

Wood, Benjamin W. 1966. "An Ecological Life History of Budsage in Western Utah." M.S. thesis, Brigham Young University, Provo, Utah.

Woodbury, Angus M. 1936. "Animal Relationships of Great Salt Lake." *Ecology* 17:1–8.

———. 1947. "Distribution of Pigmy Conifers in Utah and Northeastern Arizona." *Ecology* 28: 113–26.

Workman, J. P., and N. E. West. 1967. "Germination of *Eurotia lanata* in Relation to Various Levels of Salinity and Temperature." *Ecology* 48:659–61.

Wright, R. D., and H. A. Mooney. 1965. "Substrate-oriented Distribution of Bristlecone Pine in the White Mountains of California." *American Midland Naturalist* 73:257–84.

Yoakum, Jim. 1980. *Habitat Management Guides for the American Pronghorn Antelope.* U.S. Department of the Interior. Bureau of Land Management, Technical Note 347. Denver, Colorado.

Young, James A. 1978. "Mormon Crickets." *Rangeman's Journal* 5:193–96.

Young, James A., and Jerry D. Budy. 1979. "Historical Use of Nevada's Pinyon-Juniper Woodlands." *Journal of Forest History* 23:113–21.

Young, James A., Richard E. Eckert, Jr., and Raymond A. Evans. 1979. "Historical Perspectives Regarding the Sagebrush Ecosystem." In *The Sagebrush Ecosystem: A Symposium,* 1–13. Utah State University, College of Natural Resources. Logan.

Young, James A., and Raymond A. Evans. 1970. "Invasion of Medusahead into the Great Basin." *Weed Science* 18:89–97.

———. 1978. "Population Dynamics after Wildfires in Sagebrush Grasslands." *Journal of Range Management* 31:283–89.

———. 1981. "Demography and Fire History of a Western Juniper Stand." *Journal of Range Management* 34:501–6.

Young, James A., Raymond A. Evans, and Burgess L. Kay. 1975. "Dispersal and Germination Dynamics of Broadleaf Filaree, *Erodium botrys* (Cav.) Bertol." *Agronomy Journal* 67:54–57.

Young, James A., Raymond A. Evans, and Jack Major. 1971. "Alien Plants in the Great Basin." *Journal of Range Management* 24:194–201.

———. 1977. "Sagebrush Steppe." In *Terrestrial Vegetation of California,* eds. Michael G. Barbour and Jack Major, 763–96. New York: Wiley Interscience.

Young, James A., Raymond A. Evans, and Paul T. Tueller. 1976. "Great Basin Plant Communities— Pristine and Grazed." In *Holocene Environmental Change in the Great Basin,* eds. Robert Elston and Patricia Headrick, 187–215. Nevada Archaeological Survey Research Paper no. 6.

Young, James A., and B. Abbott Sparks. 1985. *Cattle in the Cold Desert.* Logan: Utah State University Press.

Zamora, B., and P. T. Tueller. 1973. "*Artemisia arbuscula, A. longiloba,* and *A. nova* Habitat Types in Northern Nevada." *Great Basin Naturalist* 33: 225–42.

Zwinger, Ann H., and Beatrice E. Willard. 1972. *Land above the Trees: A Guide to American Alpine Tundra.* New York: Harper and Row.

240

———

Bibliography

Index

Page numbers for maps are indicated by boldface, and photographs and drawings by italics. Photographs in the four color sections are indexed by section number in Roman numerals followed by page number within each section.

246

Index